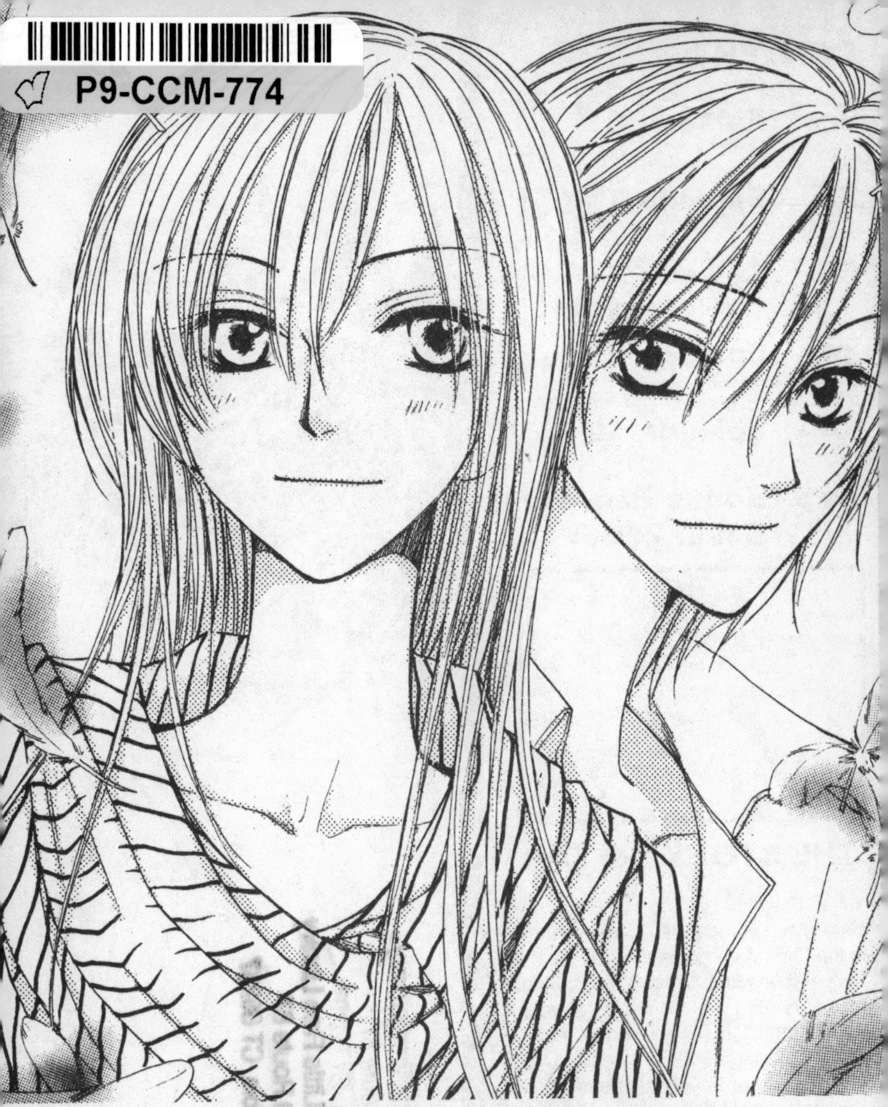

PENGUIN REVOLUTION

Volume 2

By Sakura Tsukuba

CONTENTS

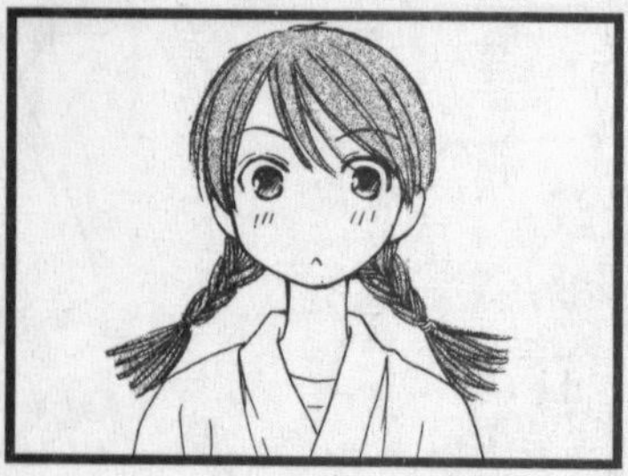

THE STORY SO FAR

Yukari Fujimaru has the power to literally see someone's potential talent in the form of wings on the person's back. At school, she sees these wings on a very attractive girl named "Ryoko." Except the girl is really a guy named Ryo Katsuragi. Ryo is in disguise under the direction of Shacho, his boss at the Peacock talent agency. After a series of events, Yukari gets herself named as Ryo's personal manager, but with the condition that she must pose as a man and be successful in keeping people fooled. In her new role, she now uses the name of Yutaka Fujimaru.

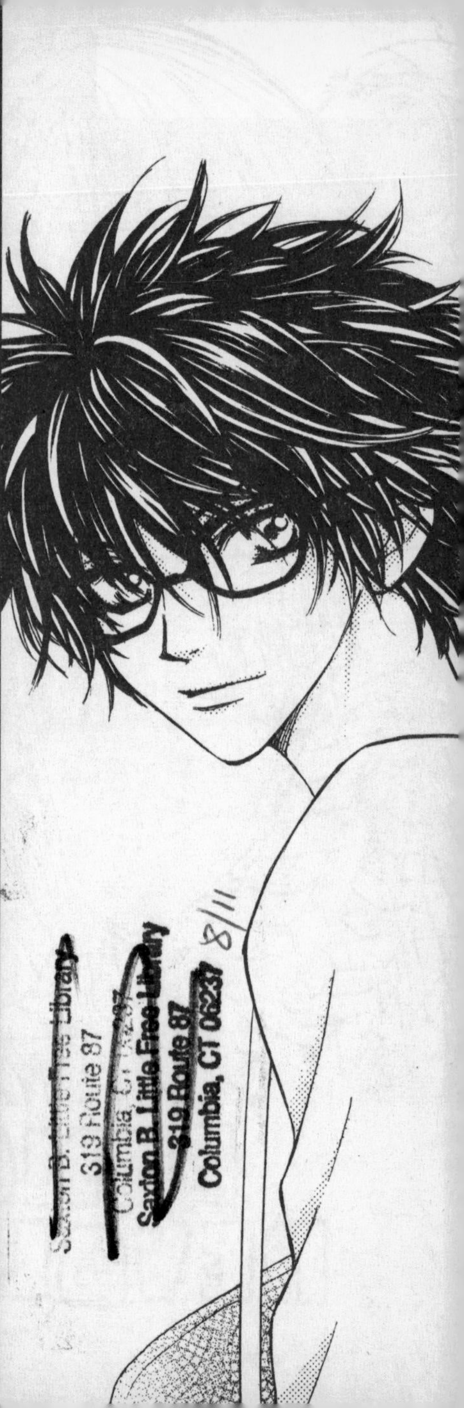

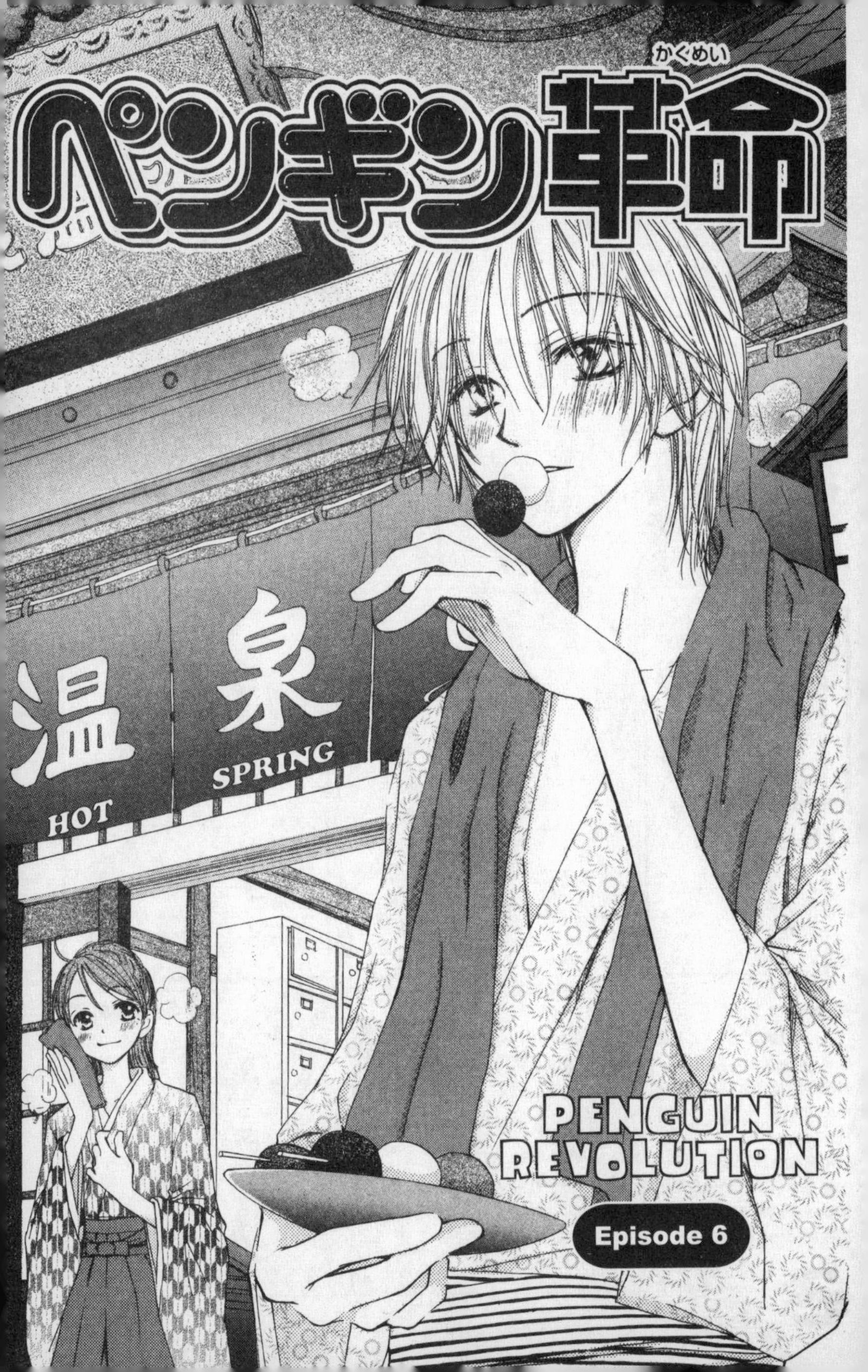

ペンギン革命（かくめい）
PENGUIN REVOLUTION
Episode 6
温泉
HOT SPRING

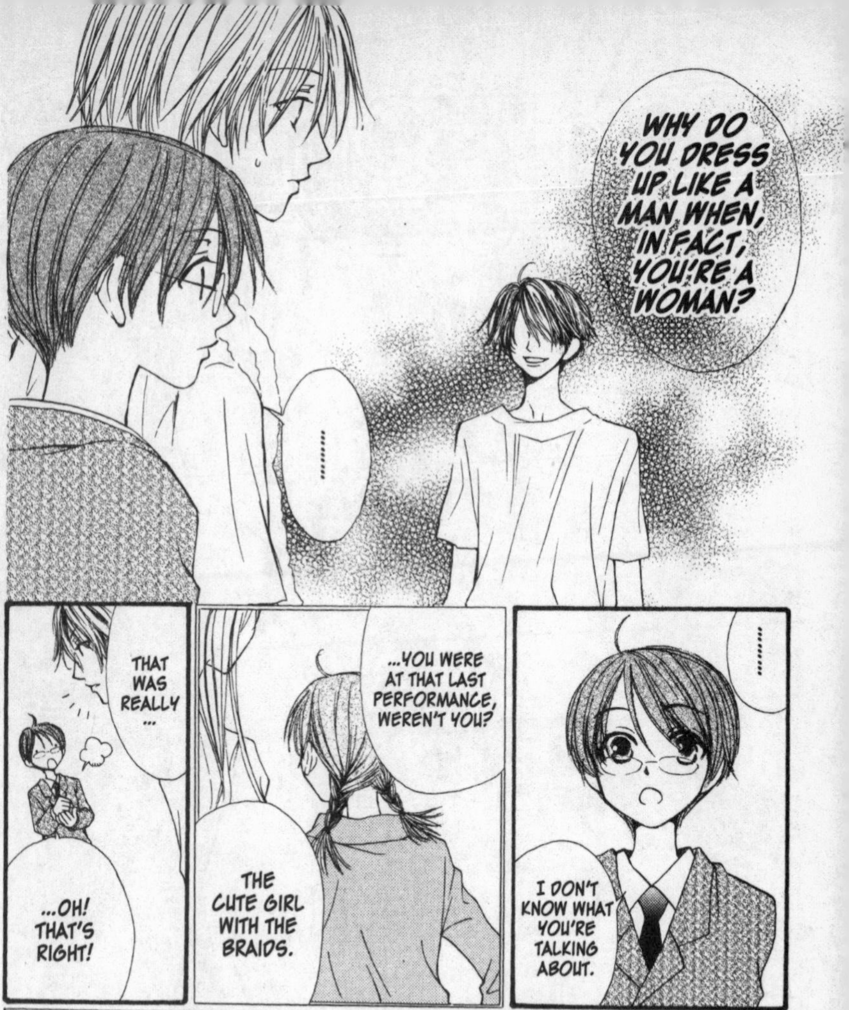
WHY DO YOU DRESS UP LIKE A MAN WHEN, IN FACT, YOU'RE A WOMAN?
......
......
I DON'T KNOW WHAT YOU'RE TALKING ABOUT.
...YOU WERE AT THAT LAST PERFORMANCE, WEREN'T YOU?
THE CUTE GIRL WITH THE BRAIDS.
THAT WAS REALLY ...
...OH! THAT'S RIGHT!

1/4 Sakura Mail

Hello! I'm Sakura Tsukuba. Thanks to you, we're here with Penguin Revolution volume two! Thank you for your support! Waaa!♥ Waaa!♥ This episode starts with Ryo and Yuka-chan in a pinch, and if you haven't already read volume one, it's a moment that'll leave you utterly clueless. Sorry.

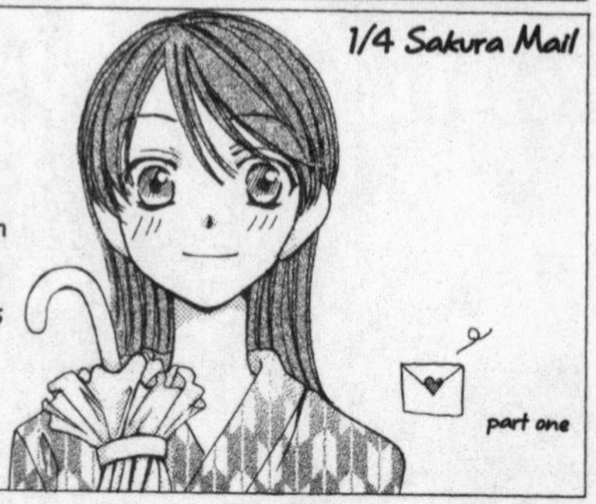
part one

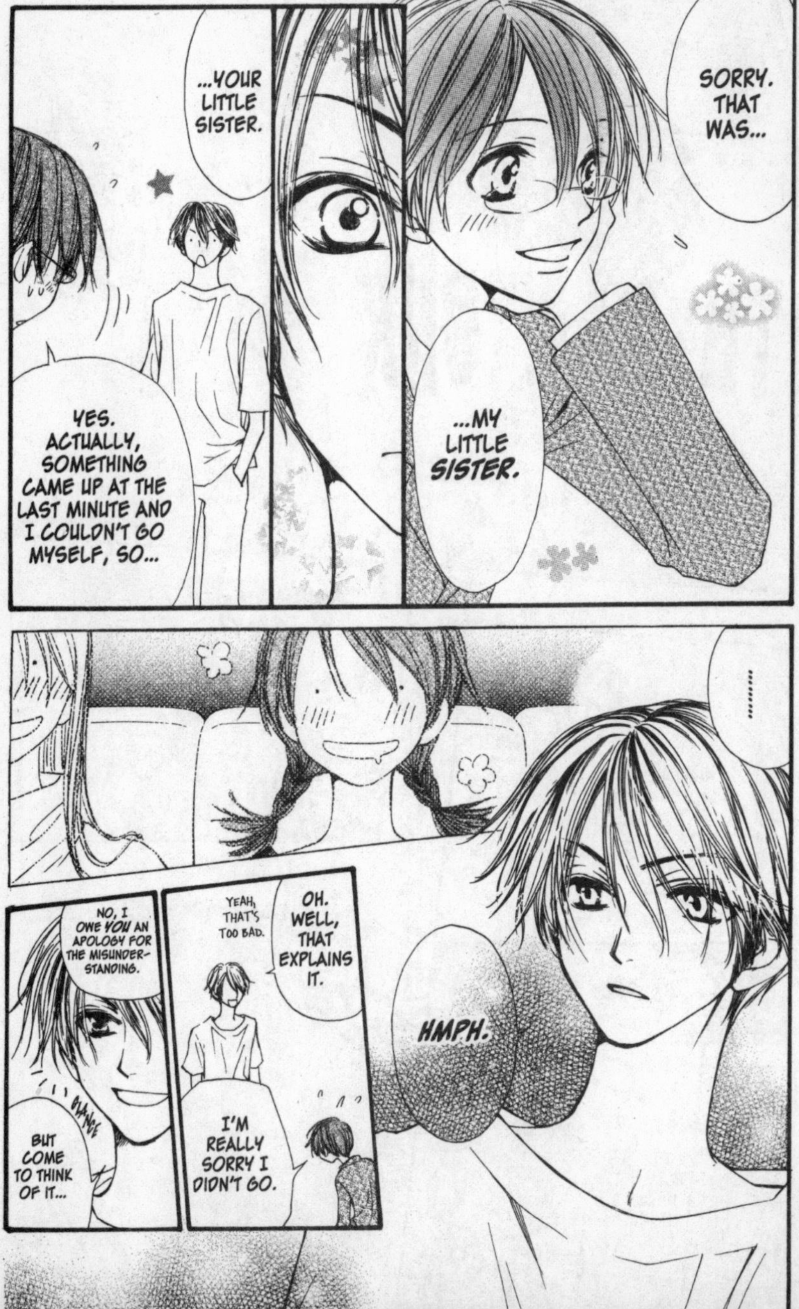
SORRY. THAT WAS...
...MY LITTLE SISTER.
...YOUR LITTLE SISTER.
YES. ACTUALLY, SOMETHING CAME UP AT THE LAST MINUTE AND I COULDN'T GO MYSELF, SO...
......
HMPH.
OH. WELL, THAT EXPLAINS IT.
YEAH, THAT'S TOO BAD.
I'M REALLY SORRY I DIDN'T GO.
NO, I OWE YOU AN APOLOGY FOR THE MISUNDERSTANDING.
GLANCE
BUT COME TO THINK OF IT...

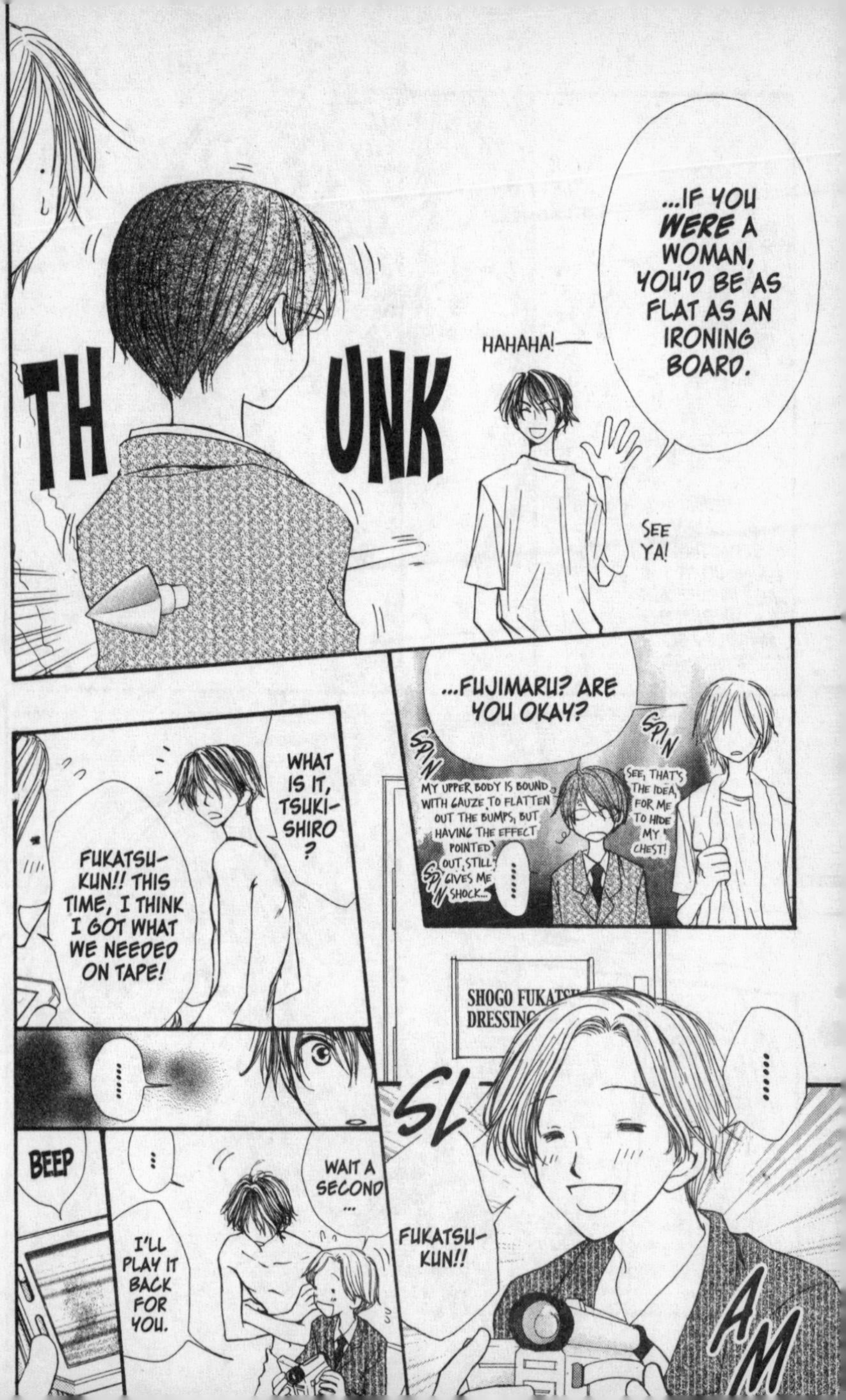
...IF YOU WERE A WOMAN, YOU'D BE AS FLAT AS AN IRONING BOARD.
HAHAHA!—
SEE YA!
THUNK
...FUJIMARU? ARE YOU OKAY?
SPIN
SEE, THAT'S THE IDEA, FOR ME TO HIDE MY CHEST!
MY UPPER BODY IS BOUND WITH GAUZE TO FLATTEN OUT THE BUMPS, BUT HAVING THE EFFECT POINTED OUT STILL GIVES ME SHOCK...
SPIN
SPIN
......
WHAT IS IT, TSUKISHIRO?
FUKATSU-KUN!! THIS TIME, I THINK I GOT WHAT WE NEEDED ON TAPE!
SHOGO FUKATSU DRESSING
......
SLAM
......
WAIT A SECOND ...
FUKATSU-KUN!!
...
I'LL PLAY IT BACK FOR YOU.
BEEP

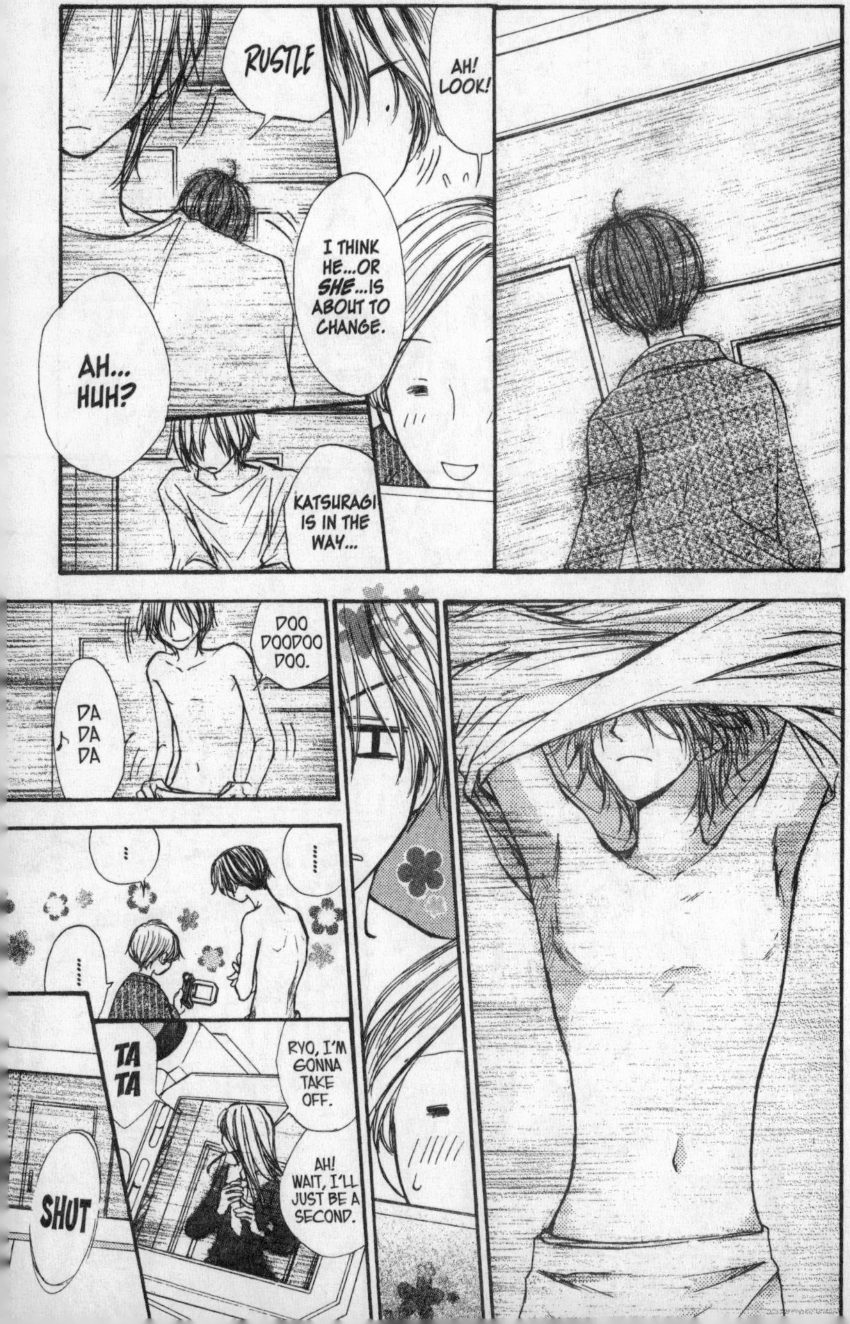
AH! LOOK!
RUSTLE
I THINK HE...OR SHE...IS ABOUT TO CHANGE.
AH... HUH?
KATSURAGI IS IN THE WAY...
DOO DOODOO DOO.
DA DA DA
......
...
......
RYO, I'M GONNA TAKE OFF.
TA TA
AH! WAIT, I'LL JUST BE A SECOND.
SHUT

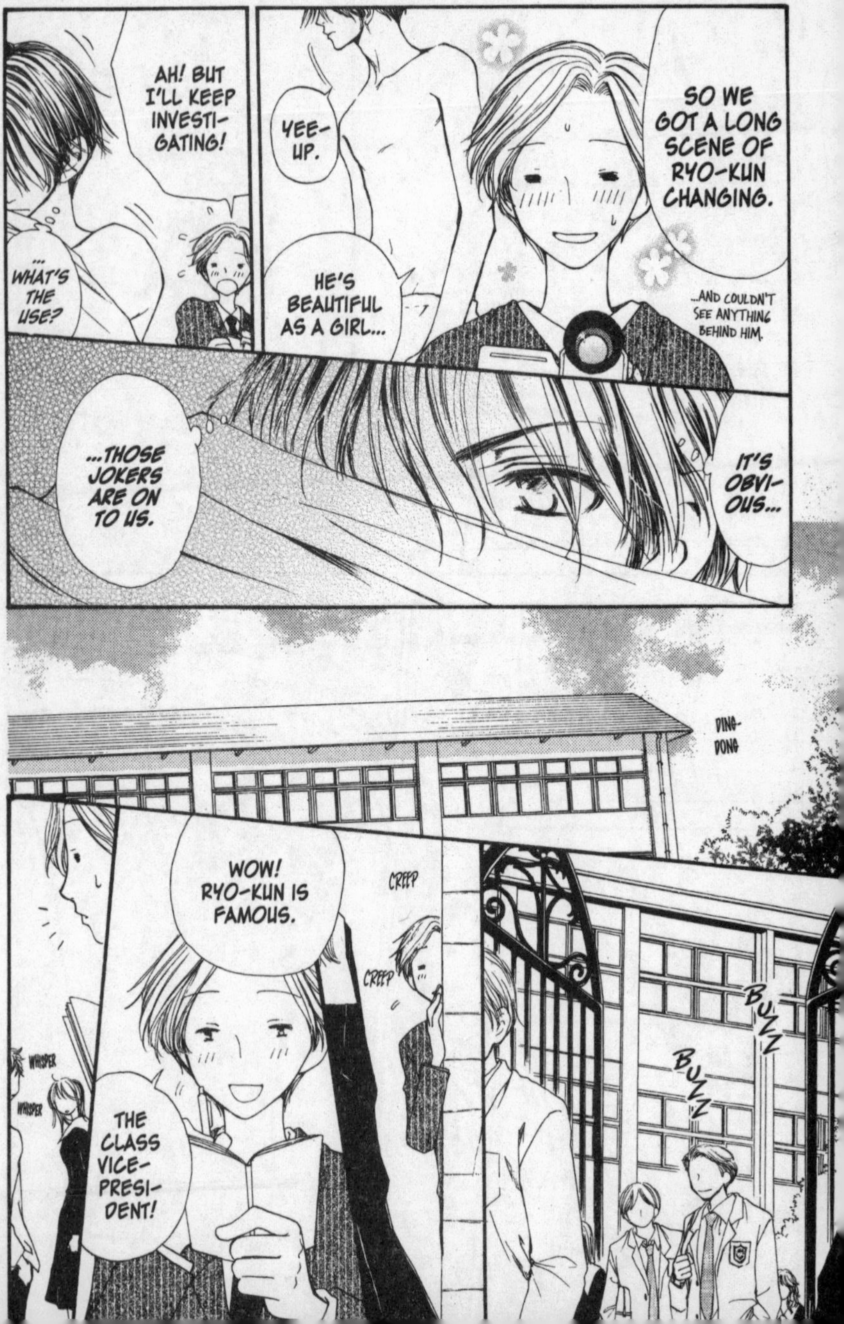
SO WE GOT A LONG SCENE OF RYO-KUN CHANGING.
YEE-UP.
HE'S BEAUTIFUL AS A GIRL...
...AND COULDN'T SEE ANYTHING BEHIND HIM.
AH! BUT I'LL KEEP INVESTI-GATING!
...WHAT'S THE USE?
IT'S OBVI-OUS...
...THOSE JOKERS ARE ON TO US.
DING-DONG
BUZZ
BUZZ
WOW! RYO-KUN IS FAMOUS.
CREEP
CREEP
THE CLASS VICE-PRESI-DENT!
WHISPER
WHISPER

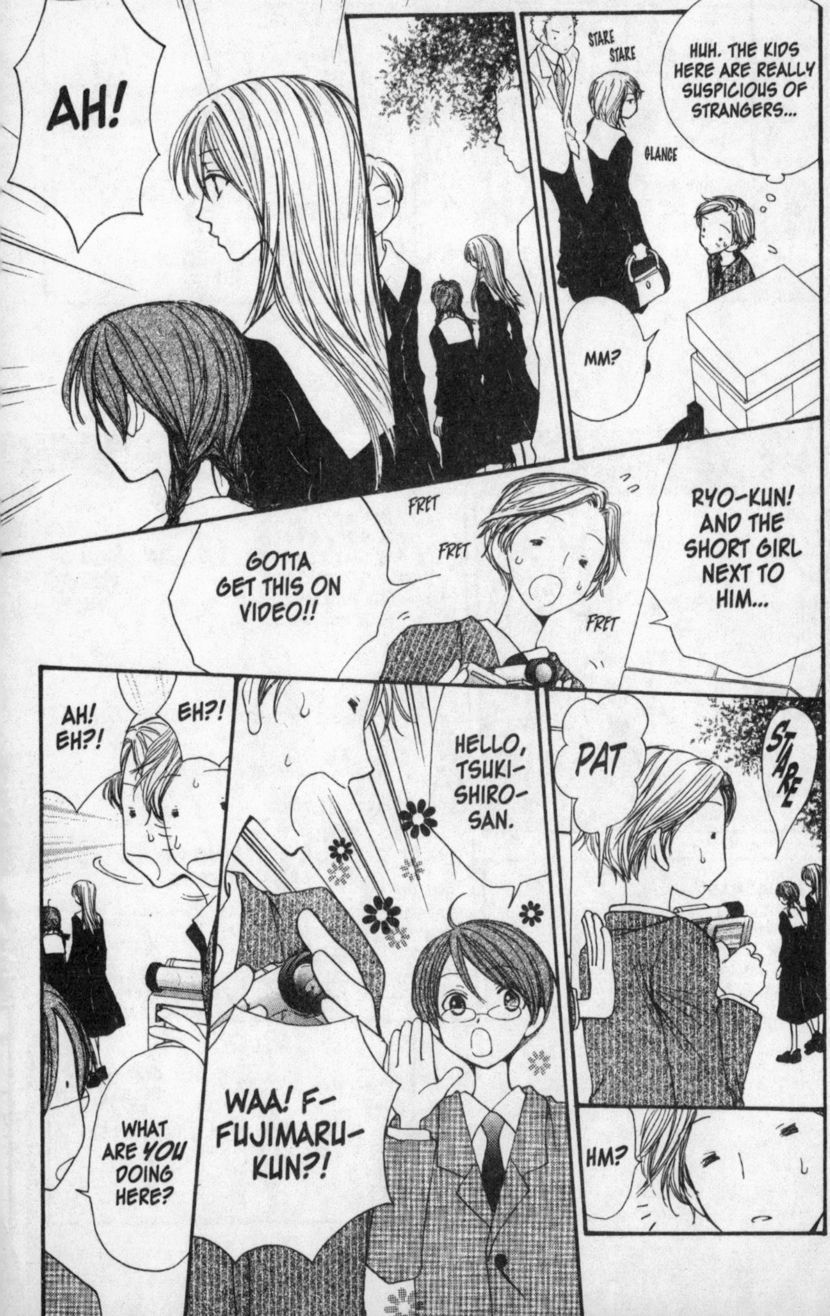
STARE
STARE
HUH. THE KIDS HERE ARE REALLY SUSPICIOUS OF STRANGERS...
GLANCE
MM?
AH!
RYO-KUN! AND THE SHORT GIRL NEXT TO HIM...
FRET
FRET
FRET
GOTTA GET THIS ON VIDEO!!
STARE
PAT
HM?
HELLO, TSUKISHIRO-SAN.
WAA! F-FUJIMARU-KUN?!
EH?!
AH! EH?!
WHAT ARE YOU DOING HERE?

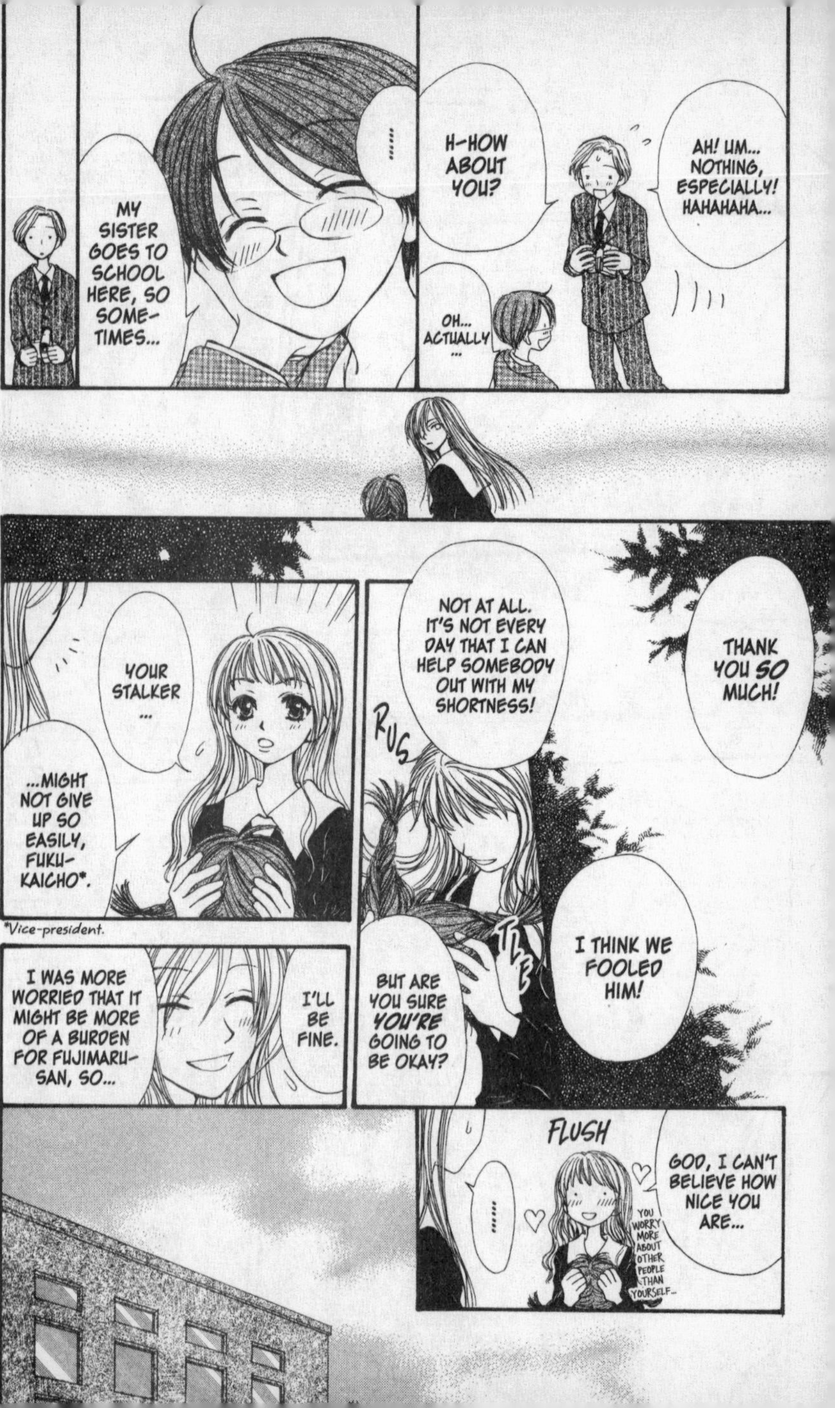
AH! UM... NOTHING, ESPECIALLY! HAHAHAHA...
H-HOW ABOUT YOU?
OH... ACTUALLY...
......
MY SISTER GOES TO SCHOOL HERE, SO SOME-TIMES...
THANK YOU SO MUCH!
NOT AT ALL. IT'S NOT EVERY DAY THAT I CAN HELP SOMEBODY OUT WITH MY SHORTNESS!
RUS
I THINK WE FOOLED HIM!
TLE
BUT ARE YOU SURE YOU'RE GOING TO BE OKAY?
YOUR STALKER...
...MIGHT NOT GIVE UP SO EASILY, FUKU-KAICHO*.
I'LL BE FINE.
I WAS MORE WORRIED THAT IT MIGHT BE MORE OF A BURDEN FOR FUJIMARU-SAN, SO...
GOD, I CAN'T BELIEVE HOW NICE YOU ARE...
FLUSH
YOU WORRY MORE ABOUT OTHER PEOPLE THAN YOURSELF...
......
*Vice-president.

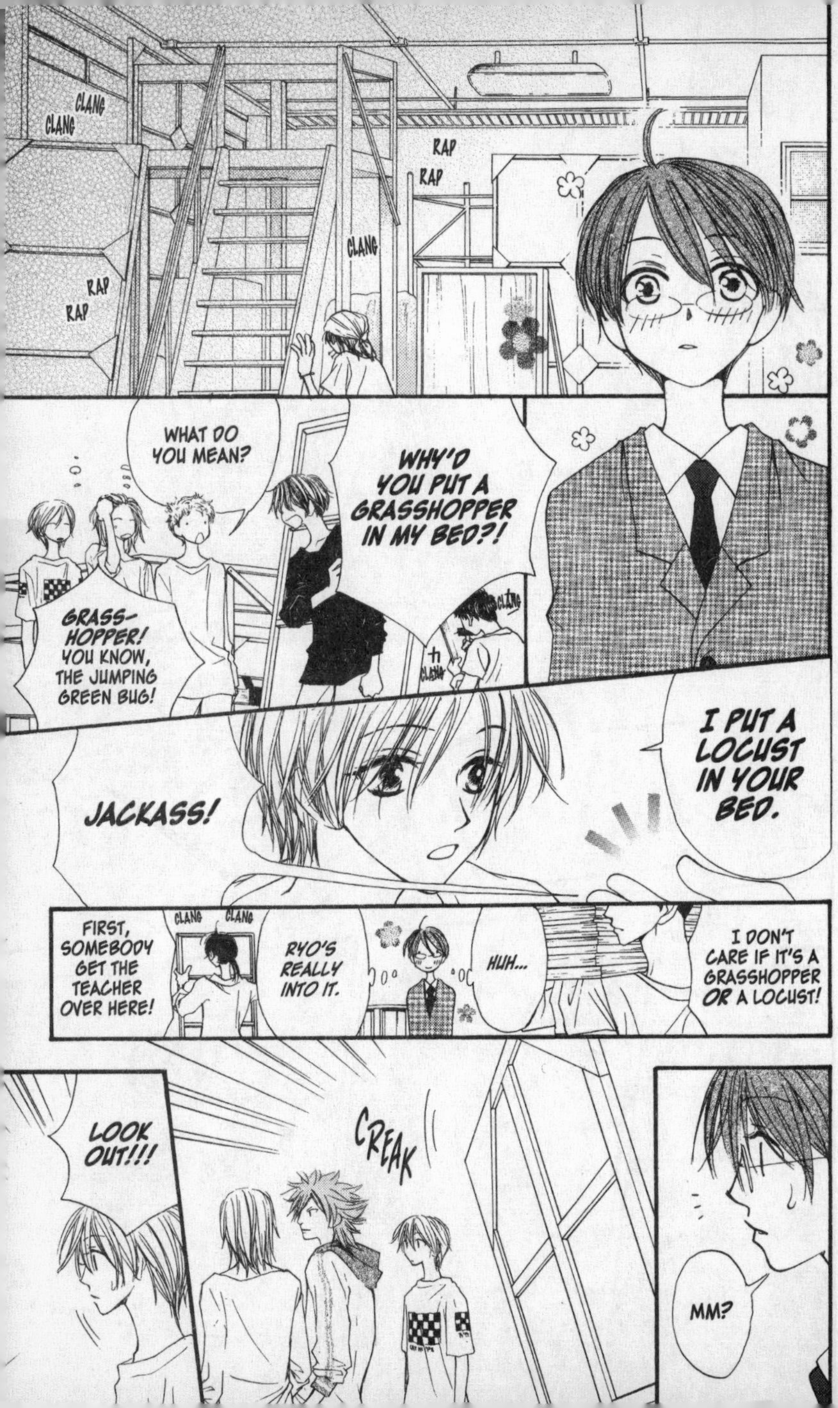
RAP
RAP
CLANG
CLANG
CLANG
RAP
RAP
WHY'D YOU PUT A GRASSHOPPER IN MY BED?!
WHAT DO YOU MEAN?
CLANG
CLANG
GRASS-HOPPER! YOU KNOW, THE JUMPING GREEN BUG!
I PUT A LOCUST IN YOUR BED.
JACKASS!
I DON'T CARE IF IT'S A GRASSHOPPER OR A LOCUST!
HUH...
RYO'S REALLY INTO IT.
CLANG
CLANG
FIRST, SOMEBODY GET THE TEACHER OVER HERE!
MM?
CREAK
LOOK OUT!!!

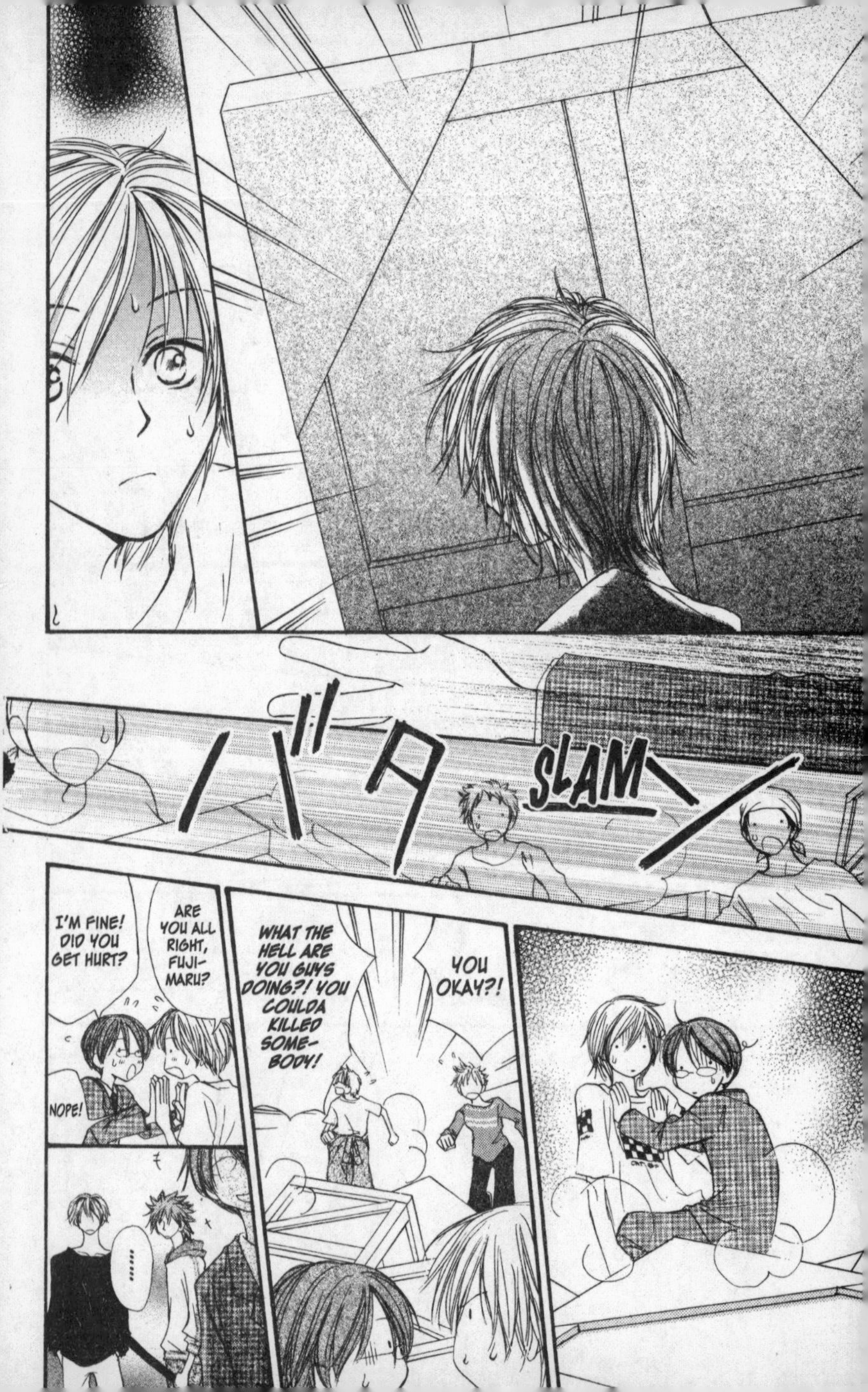
バタ
SLAM
YOU OKAY?!
WHAT THE HELL ARE YOU GUYS DOING?! YOU COULDA KILLED SOME-BODY!
ARE YOU ALL RIGHT, FUJI-MARU?
I'M FINE! DID YOU GET HURT?
NOPE!
......

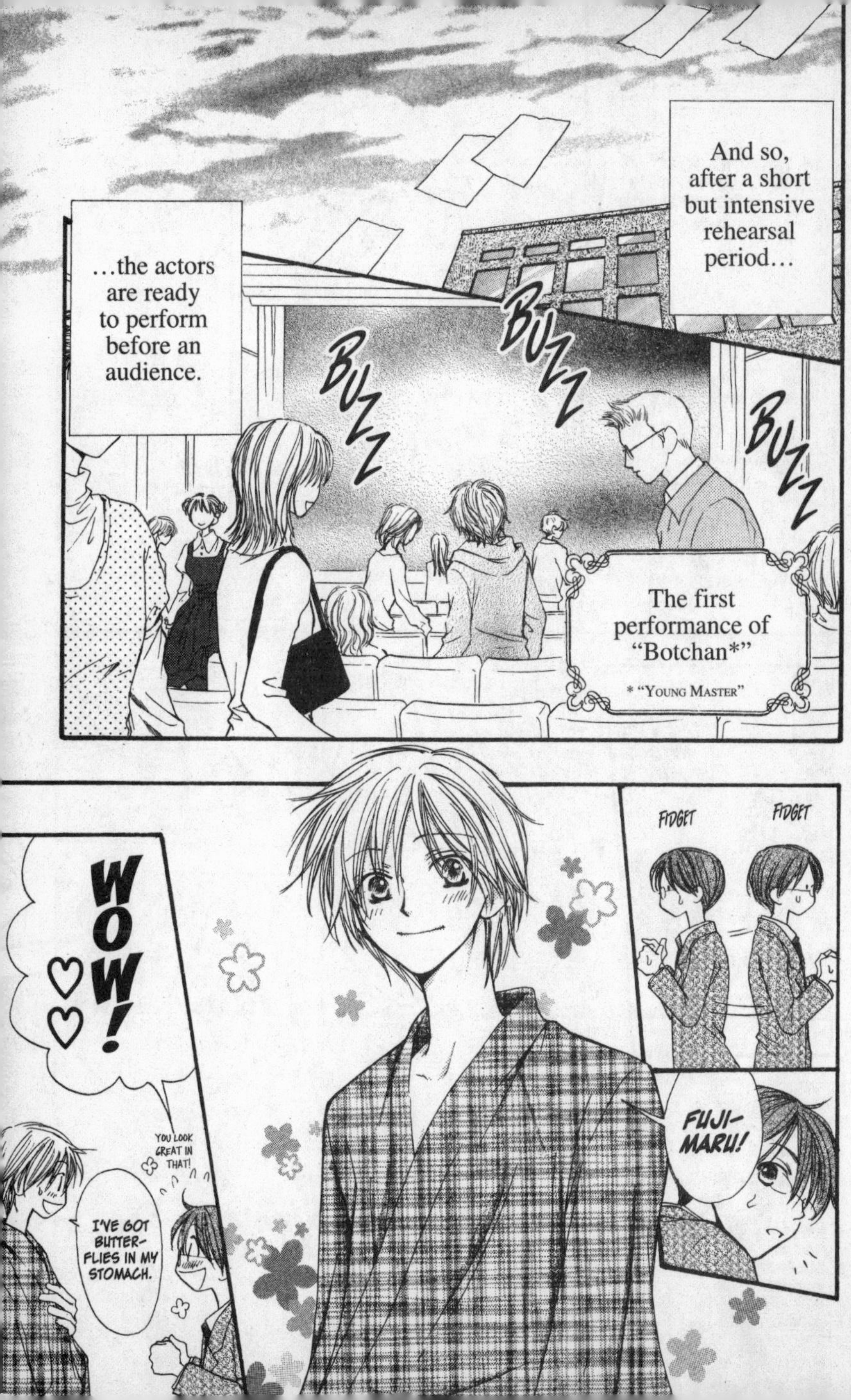
And so, after a short but intensive rehearsal period…
…the actors are ready to perform before an audience.
BUZZ
BUZZ
BUZZ
The first performance of "Botchan*"
* "Young Master"
FIDGET
FIDGET
FUJI-MARU!
WOW! ♡♡
YOU LOOK GREAT IN THAT!
I'VE GOT BUTTER-FLIES IN MY STOMACH.

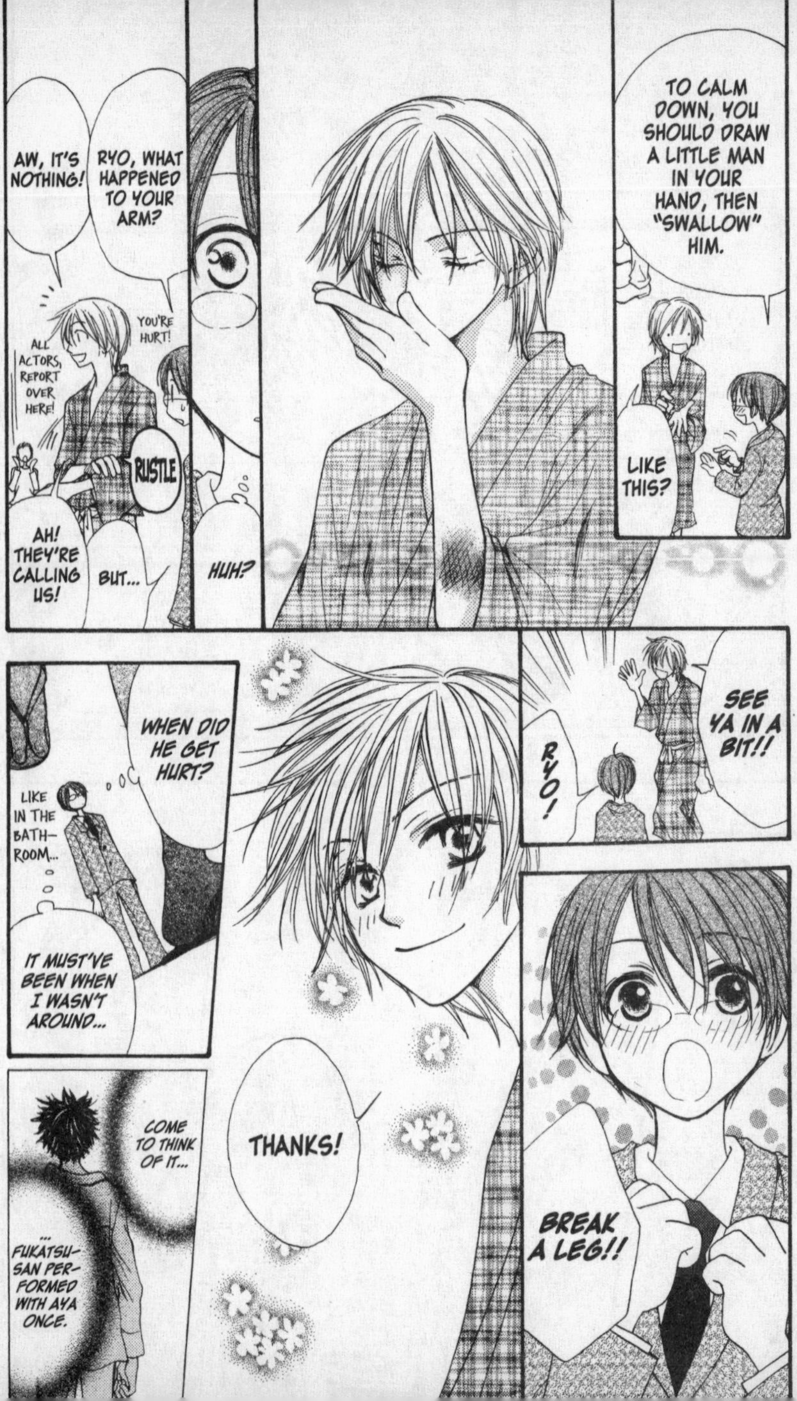
TO CALM DOWN, YOU SHOULD DRAW A LITTLE MAN IN YOUR HAND, THEN "SWALLOW" HIM.
LIKE THIS?
HUH?
RYO, WHAT HAPPENED TO YOUR ARM?
AW, IT'S NOTHING!
YOU'RE HURT!
ALL ACTORS, REPORT OVER HERE!
RUSTLE
BUT...
AH! THEY'RE CALLING US!
SEE YA IN A BIT!!
RYO!
BREAK A LEG!!
THANKS!
WHEN DID HE GET HURT?
LIKE IN THE BATH-ROOM...
IT MUST'VE BEEN WHEN I WASN'T AROUND...
COME TO THINK OF IT...
...FUKATSU-SAN PER-FORMED WITH AYA ONCE.

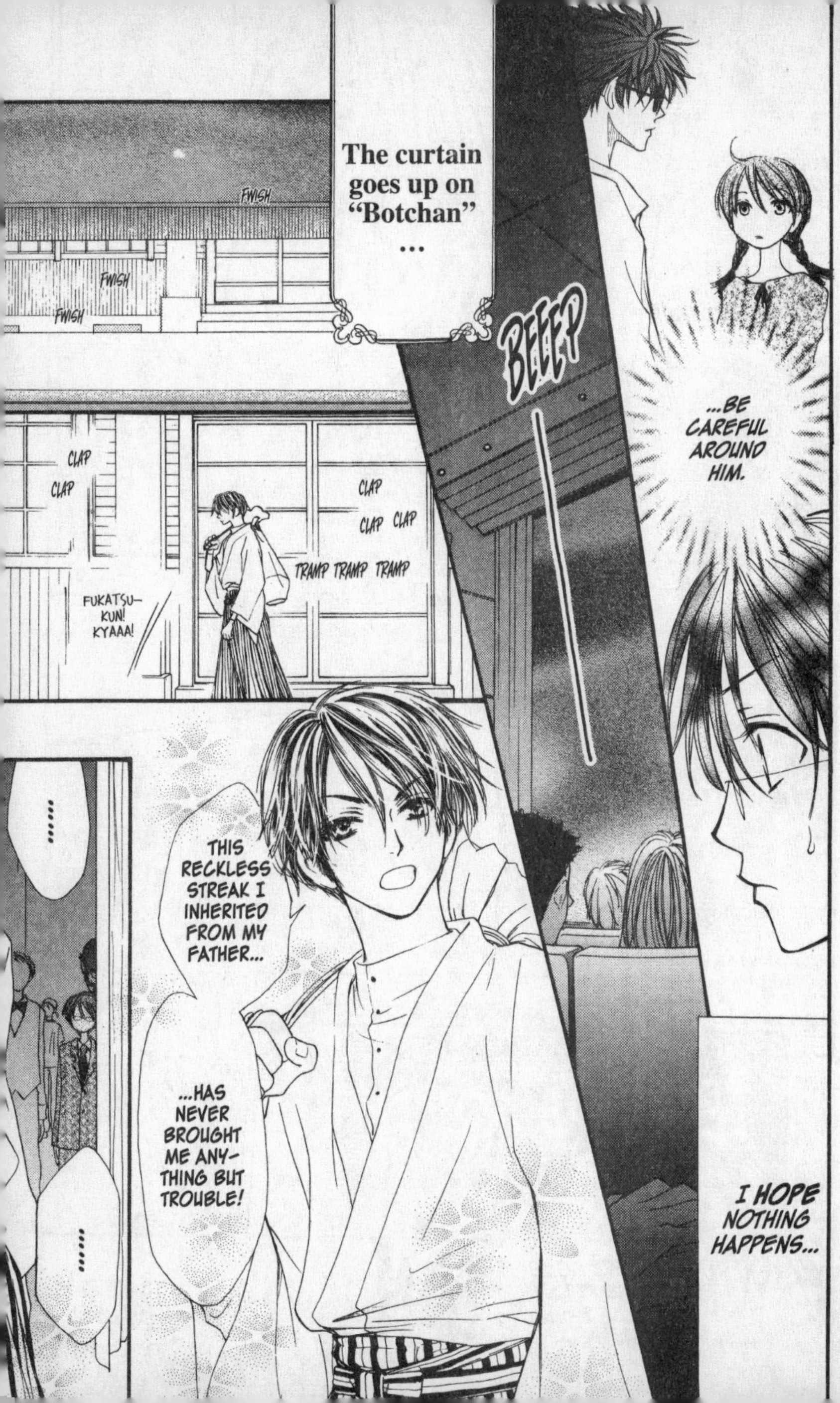
...BE CAREFUL AROUND HIM.
I HOPE NOTHING HAPPENS...
BEEEP
The curtain goes up on "Botchan" ...
FWISH
FWISH
FWISH
CLAP CLAP
CLAP CLAP CLAP
TRAMP TRAMP TRAMP
FUKATSU-KUN! KYAAA!
THIS RECKLESS STREAK I INHERITED FROM MY FATHER...
...HAS NEVER BROUGHT ME ANY-THING BUT TROUBLE!
......
......

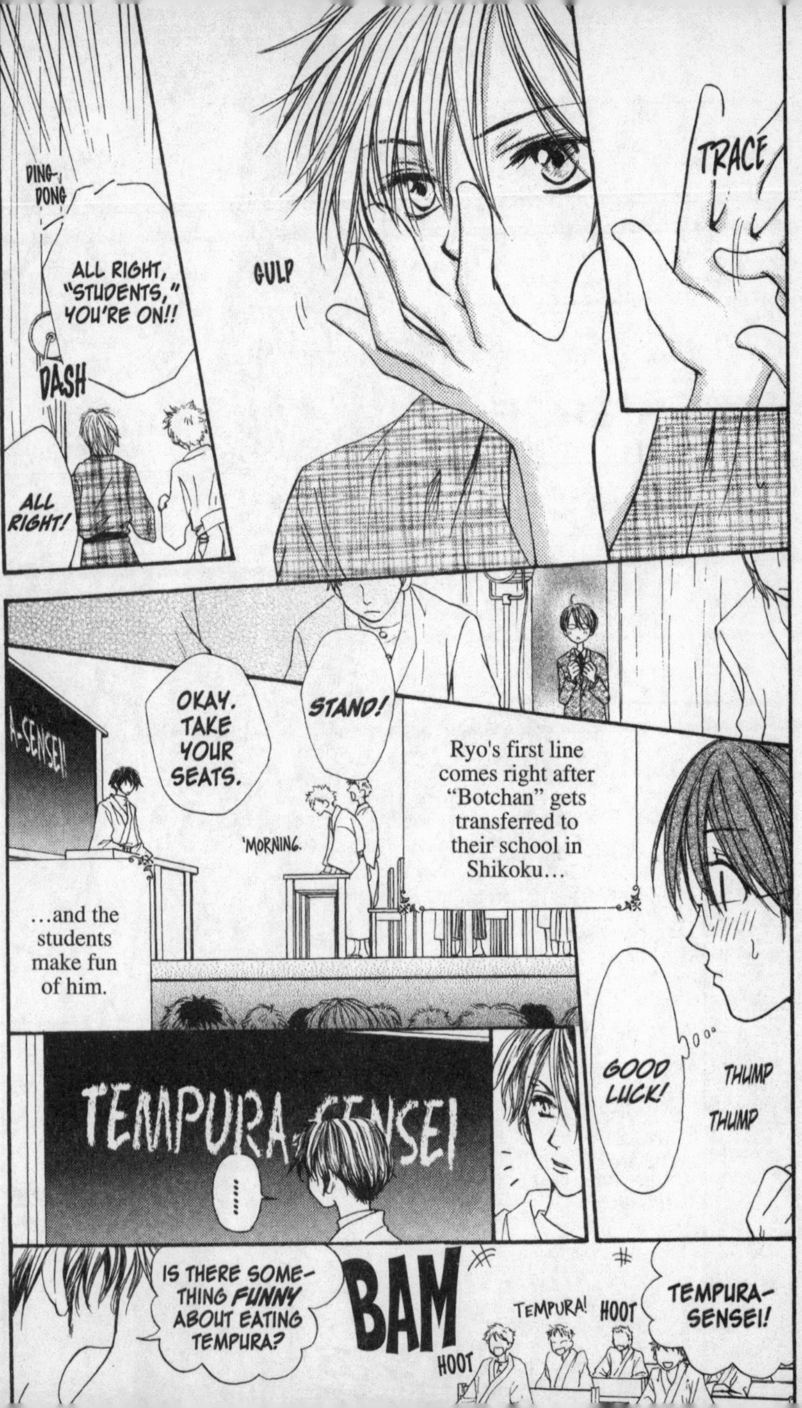
TRACE
GULP
DING-DONG
ALL RIGHT, "STUDENTS," YOU'RE ON!!
DASH
ALL RIGHT!
Ryo's first line comes right after "Botchan" gets transferred to their school in Shikoku…
STAND!
OKAY. TAKE YOUR SEATS.
'MORNING.
…and the students make fun of him.
GOOD LUCK!
THUMP
THUMP
TEMPURA-SENSEI
……
TEMPURA-SENSEI!
HOOT
TEMPURA!
HOOT
BAM
IS THERE SOMETHING FUNNY ABOUT EATING TEMPURA?

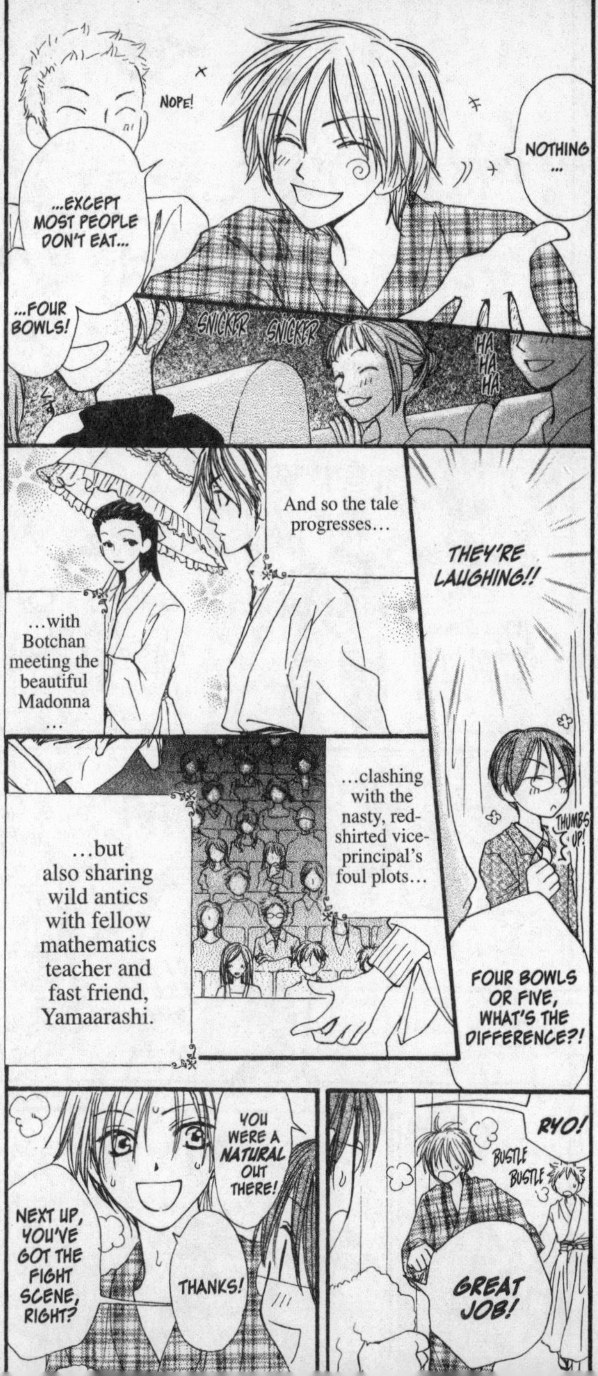
NOTHING ...
NOPE!
...EXCEPT MOST PEOPLE DON'T EAT...
HA HA HA
SNICKER
SNICKER
...FOUR BOWLS!
THEY'RE LAUGHING!!
THUMBS UP!
FOUR BOWLS OR FIVE, WHAT'S THE DIFFERENCE?!
And so the tale progresses…
…with Botchan meeting the beautiful Madonna …
…clashing with the nasty, red-shirted vice-principal's foul plots…
…but also sharing wild antics with fellow mathematics teacher and fast friend, Yamaarashi.
RYO!
BUSTLE BUSTLE
GREAT JOB!
YOU WERE A NATURAL OUT THERE!
NEXT UP, YOU'VE GOT THE FIGHT SCENE, RIGHT?
THANKS!

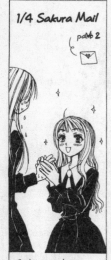

1/4 Sakura Mail

part 2

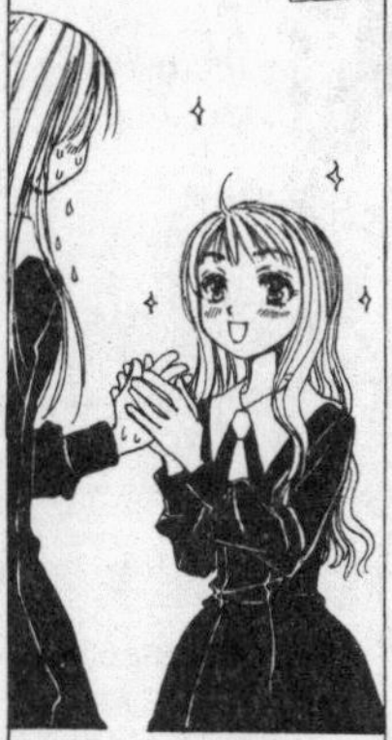

So here we have Ryo's first stage performance. I love the kimonos...or, more accurately, I love Botchan's Meiji Taisho era outfit. I had a lot of fun drawing it... Because of the influence of "Botchan," I've been wanting to go to a hot spring for a while now. And here at work, I've taken to using the phrases of the period in my speech, like "zona moshi" to end a sentence. Those are words that students actually used at the time. So peppering my speech with those outdated expressions is fun for me, too.

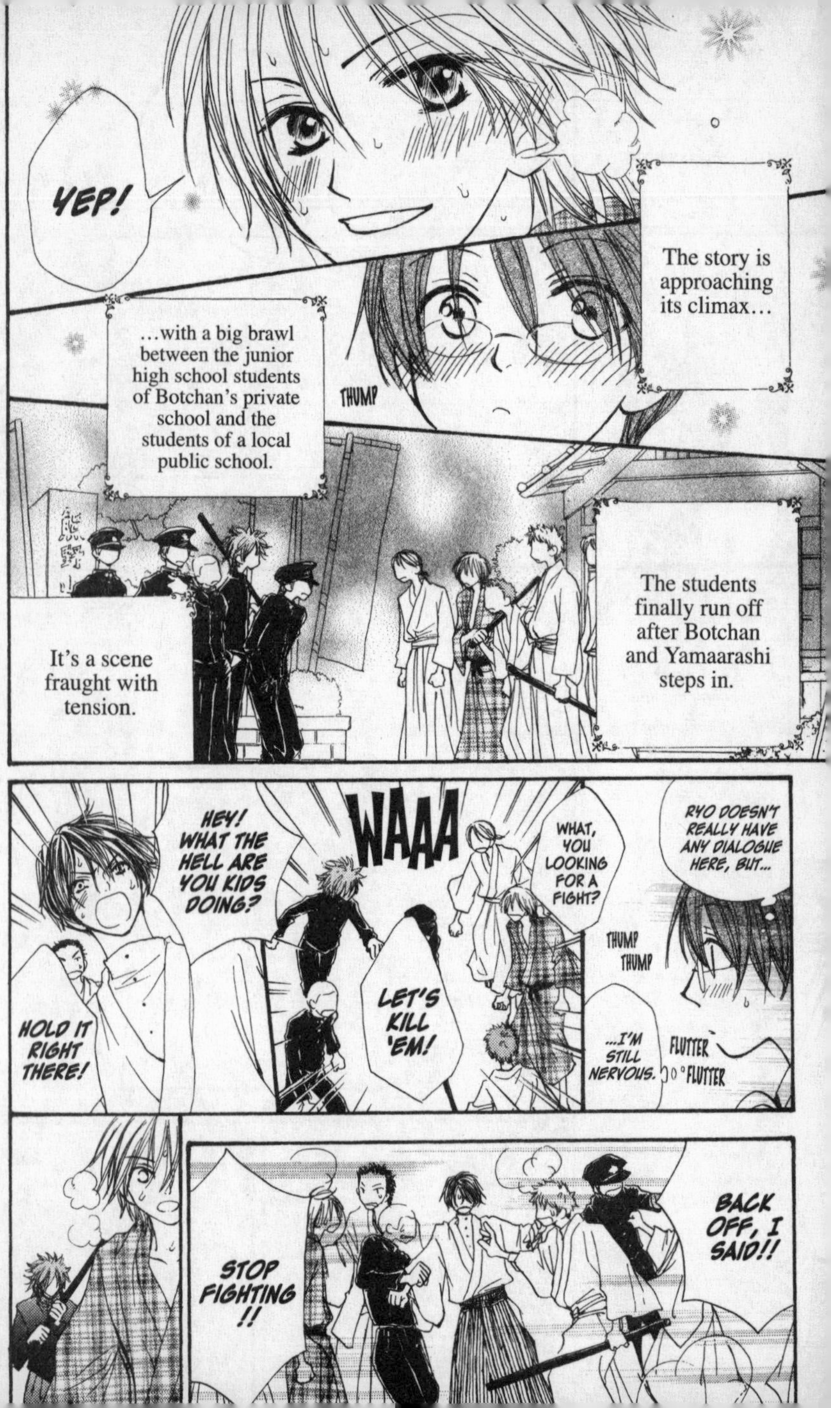
YEP!
The story is approaching its climax…
THUMP
…with a big brawl between the junior high school students of Botchan's private school and the students of a local public school.
The students finally run off after Botchan and Yamaarashi steps in.
It's a scene fraught with tension.
RYO DOESN'T REALLY HAVE ANY DIALOGUE HERE, BUT...
THUMP THUMP
...I'M STILL NERVOUS.
FLUTTER FLUTTER
WHAT, YOU LOOKING FOR A FIGHT?
WAAA
LET'S KILL 'EM!
HEY! WHAT THE HELL ARE YOU KIDS DOING?
HOLD IT RIGHT THERE!
BACK OFF, I SAID!!
STOP FIGHTING!!

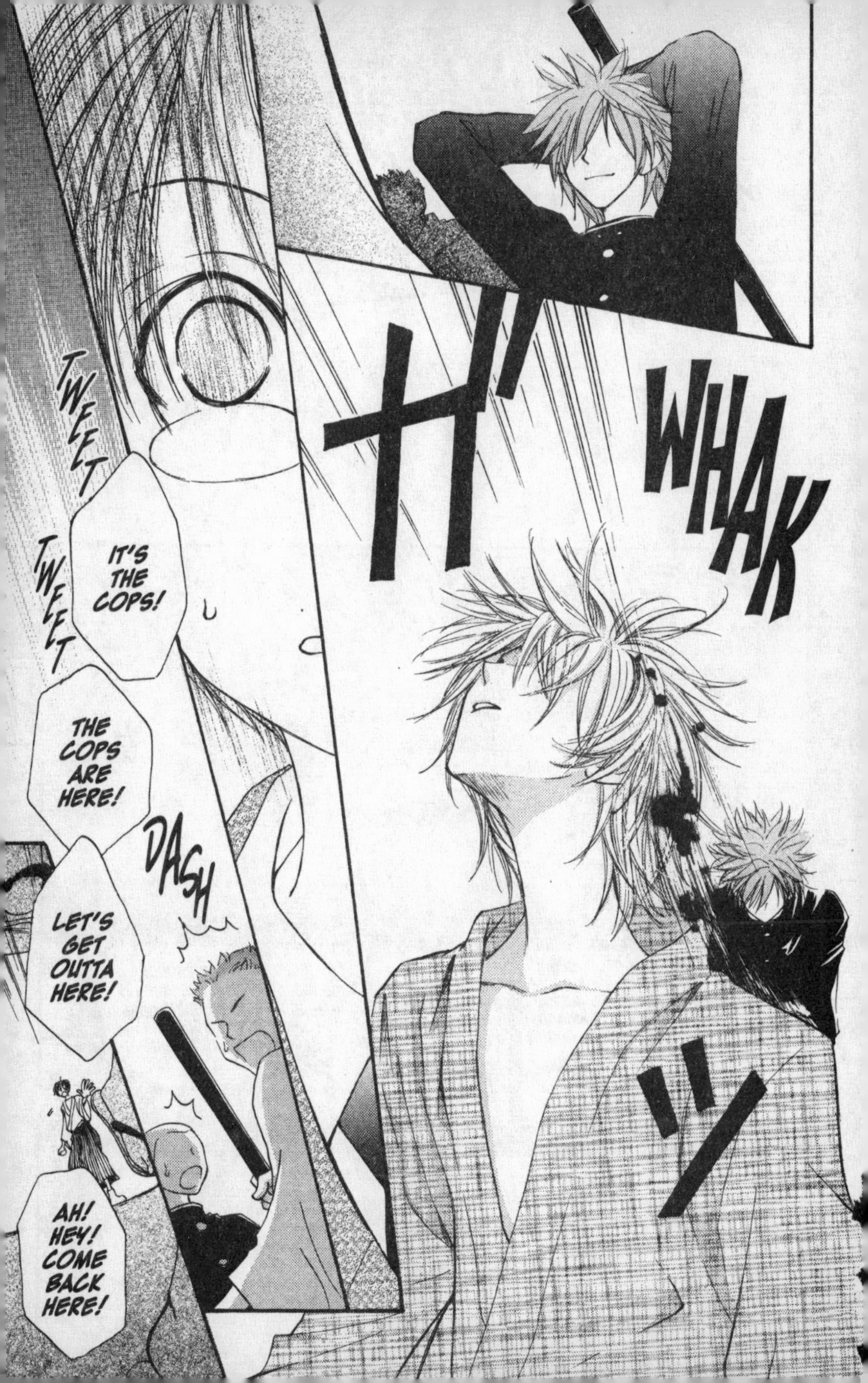
WHAK
TWEET
TWEET
IT'S THE COPS!
THE COPS ARE HERE!
DASH
LET'S GET OUTTA HERE!
AH! HEY! COME BACK HERE!

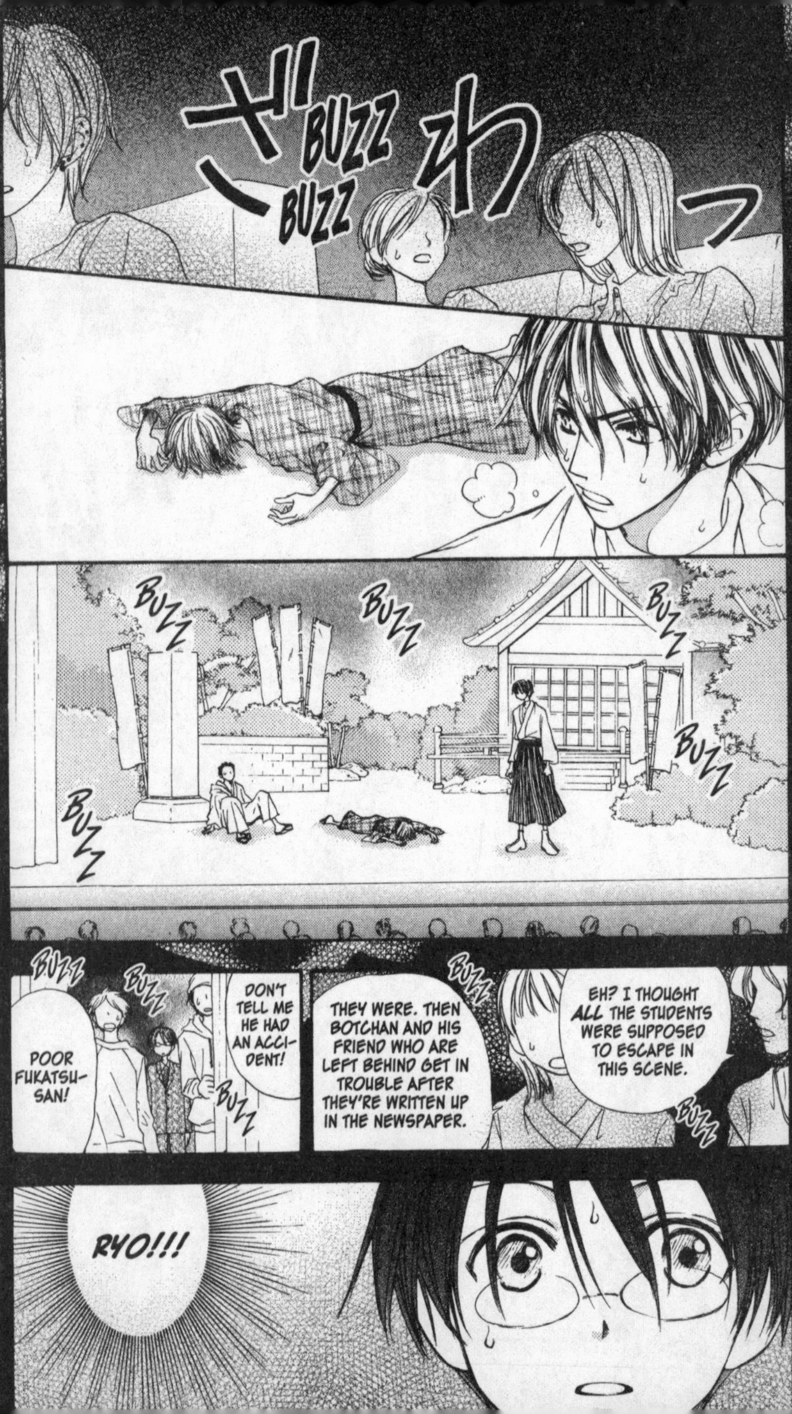
ざわっ
BUZZ BUZZ
BUZZ
BUZZ
BUZZ
BUZZ
BUZZ
BUZZ
EH? I THOUGHT ALL THE STUDENTS WERE SUPPOSED TO ESCAPE IN THIS SCENE.
BUZZ
THEY WERE. THEN BOTCHAN AND HIS FRIEND WHO ARE LEFT BEHIND GET IN TROUBLE AFTER THEY'RE WRITTEN UP IN THE NEWSPAPER.
BUZZ
BUZZ
DON'T TELL ME HE HAD AN ACCI-DENT!
BUZZ
POOR FUKATSU-SAN!
BUZZ
RYO!!!

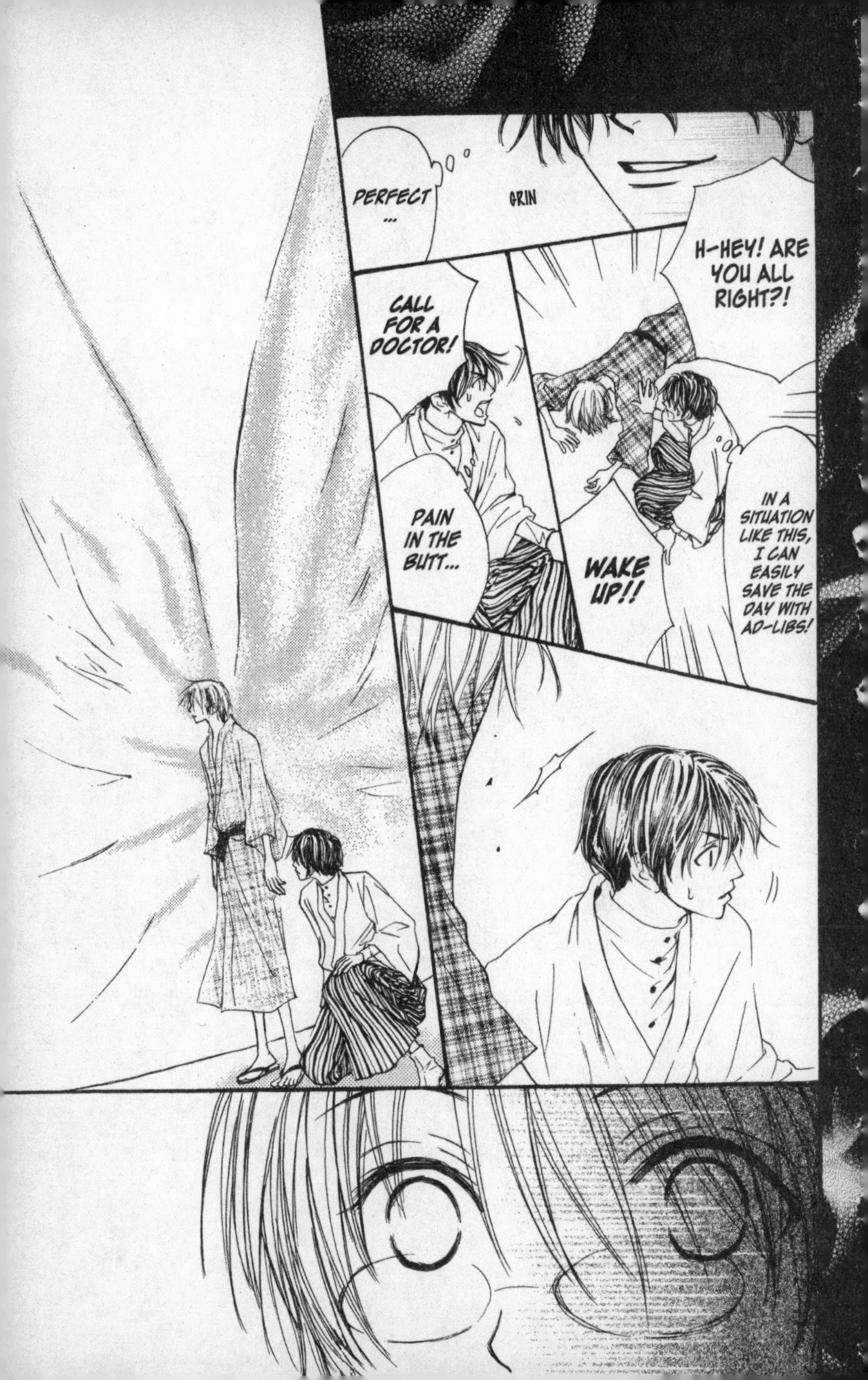
PERFECT ...
GRIN
H-HEY! ARE YOU ALL RIGHT?!
IN A SITUATION LIKE THIS, I CAN EASILY SAVE THE DAY WITH AD-LIBS!
WAKE UP!!
CALL FOR A DOCTOR!
PAIN IN THE BUTT...

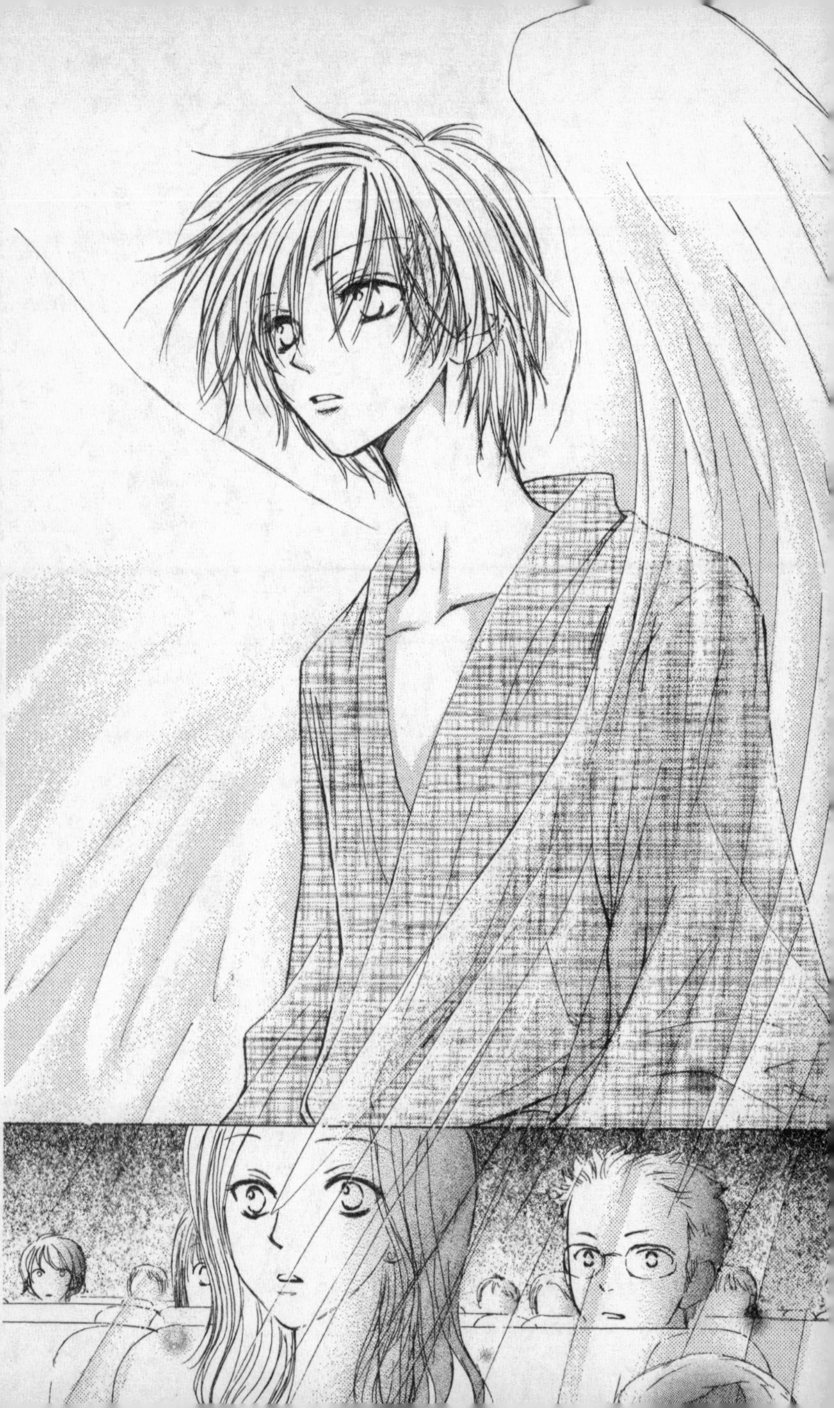

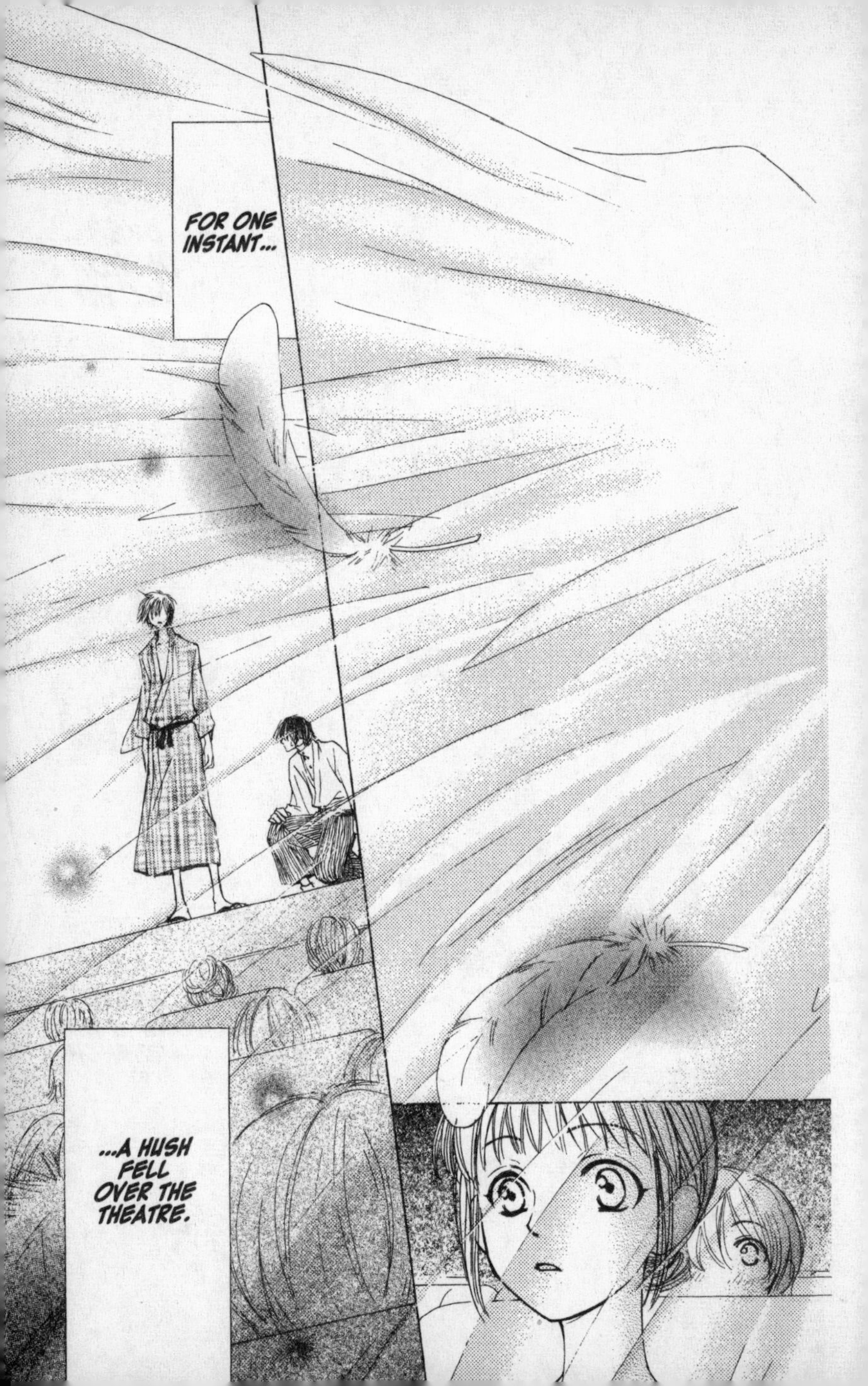
FOR ONE INSTANT...
...A HUSH FELL OVER THE THEATRE.

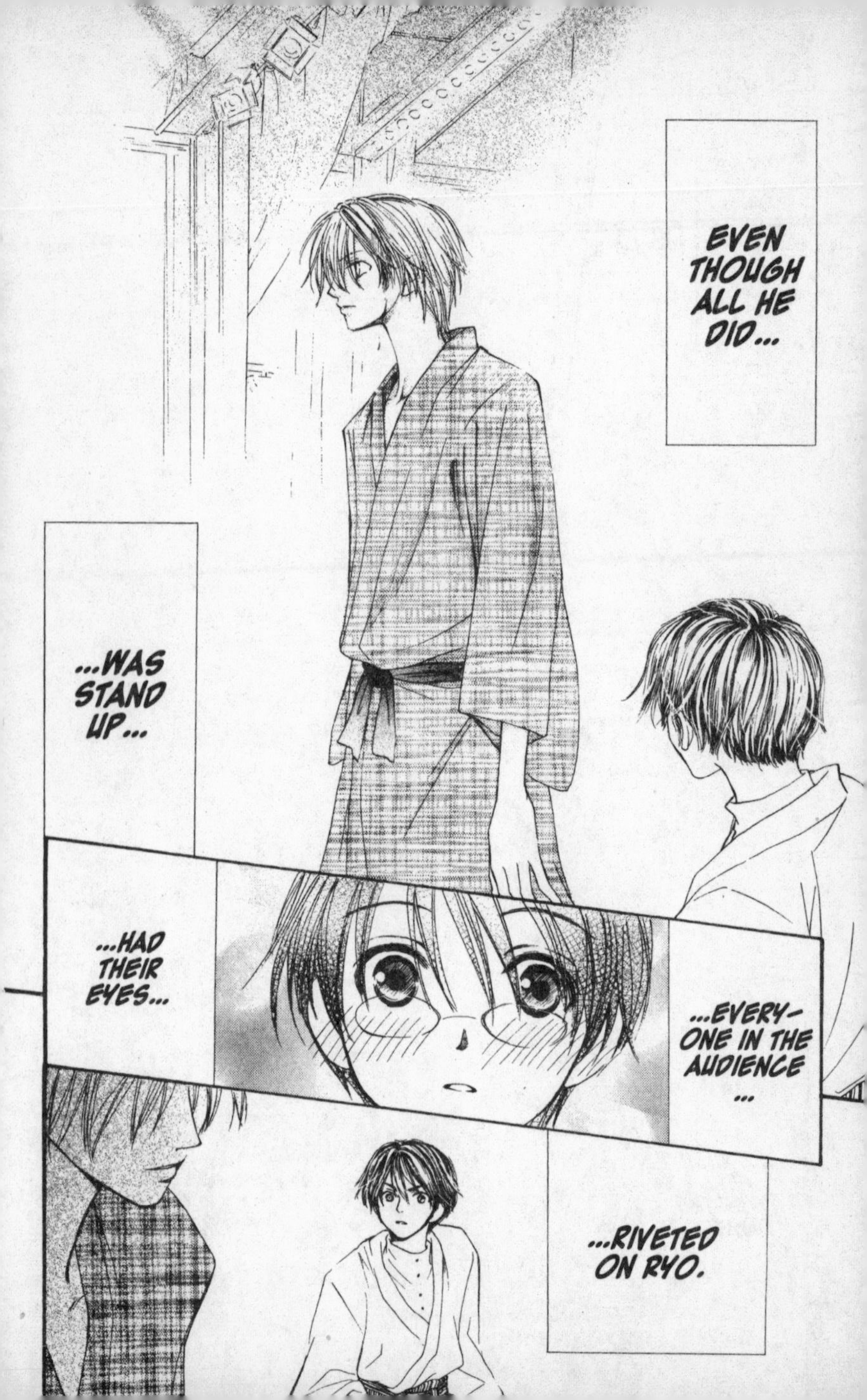
EVEN THOUGH ALL HE DID...
...WAS STAND UP...
...EVERY-ONE IN THE AUDIENCE ...
...HAD THEIR EYES...
...RIVETED ON RYO.

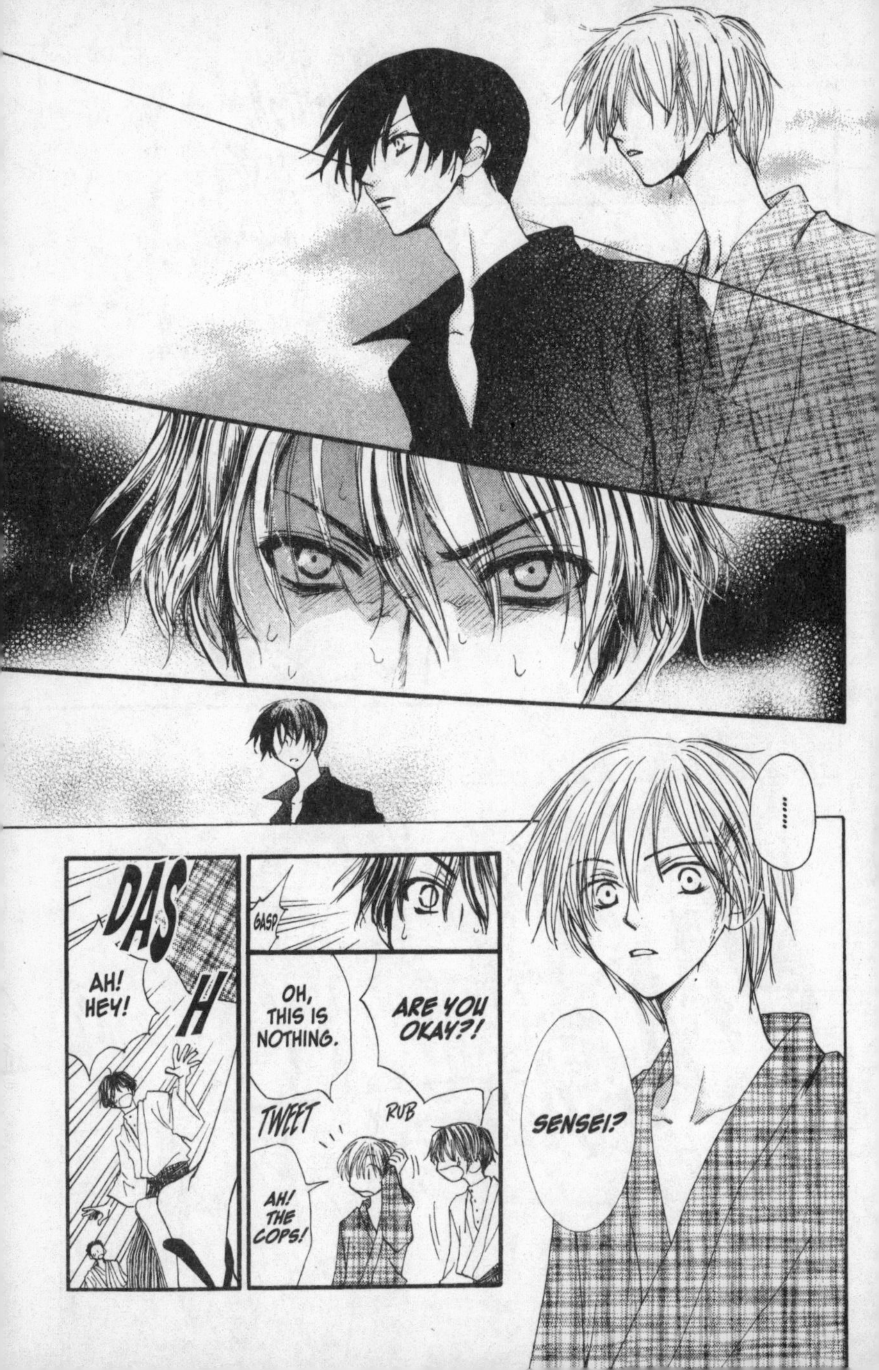
......
SENSEI?
GASP
ARE YOU OKAY?!
OH, THIS IS NOTHING.
RUB
TWEET
AH! THE COPS!
DASH
AH! HEY!

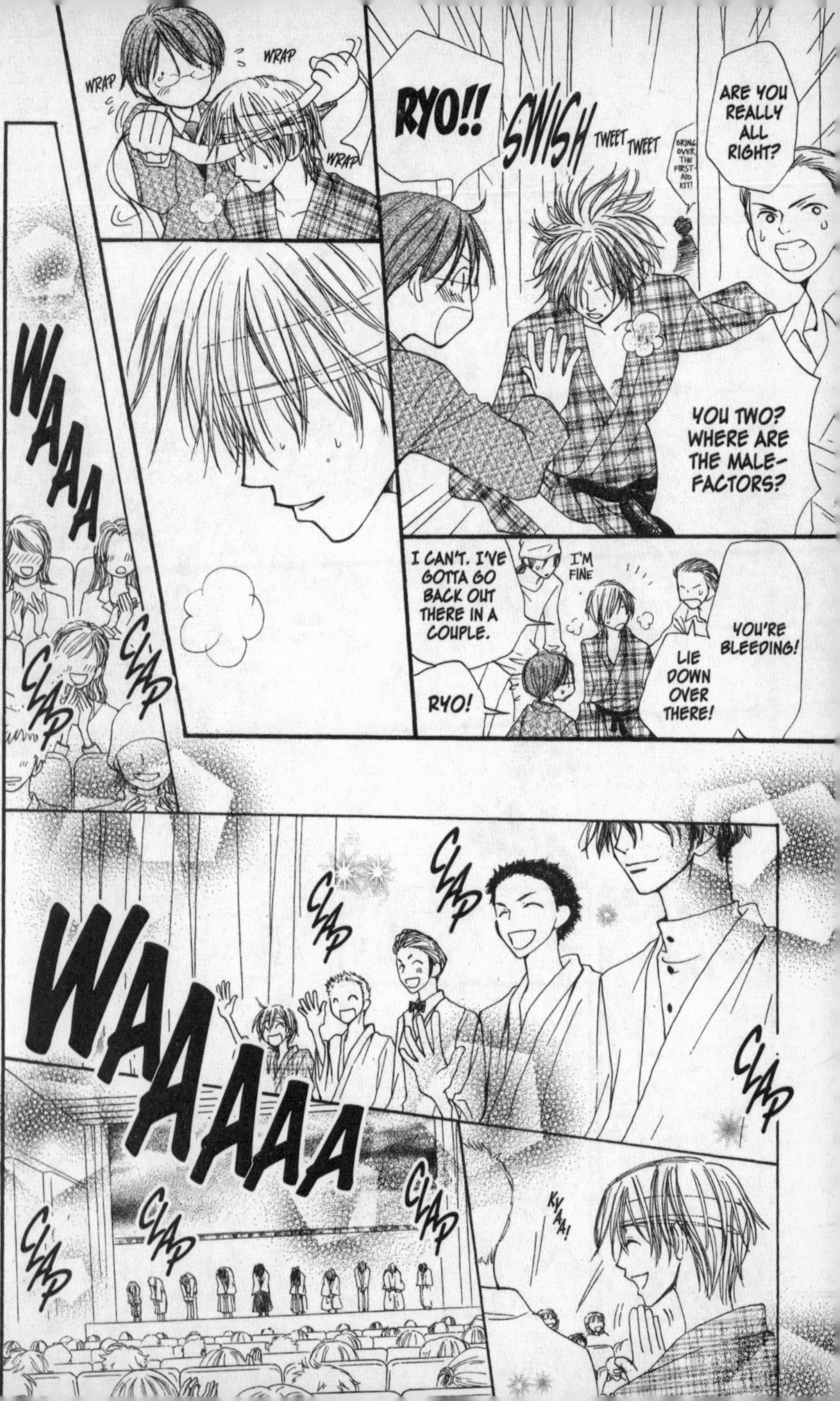
ARE YOU REALLY ALL RIGHT?
BRING OVER THE FIRST-AID KIT!
TWEET TWEET
SWISH
RYO!!
YOU TWO? WHERE ARE THE MALE-FACTORS?
WRAP
WRAP
WRAP
YOU'RE BLEEDING!
LIE DOWN OVER THERE!
I'M FINE
I CAN'T. I'VE GOTTA GO BACK OUT THERE IN A COUPLE.
RYO!
WAAAA
CLAP
CLAP
CLAP
CLAP
CLAP
WAAAAAAA
CLAP
KYAA!
CLAP
CLAP
CLAP

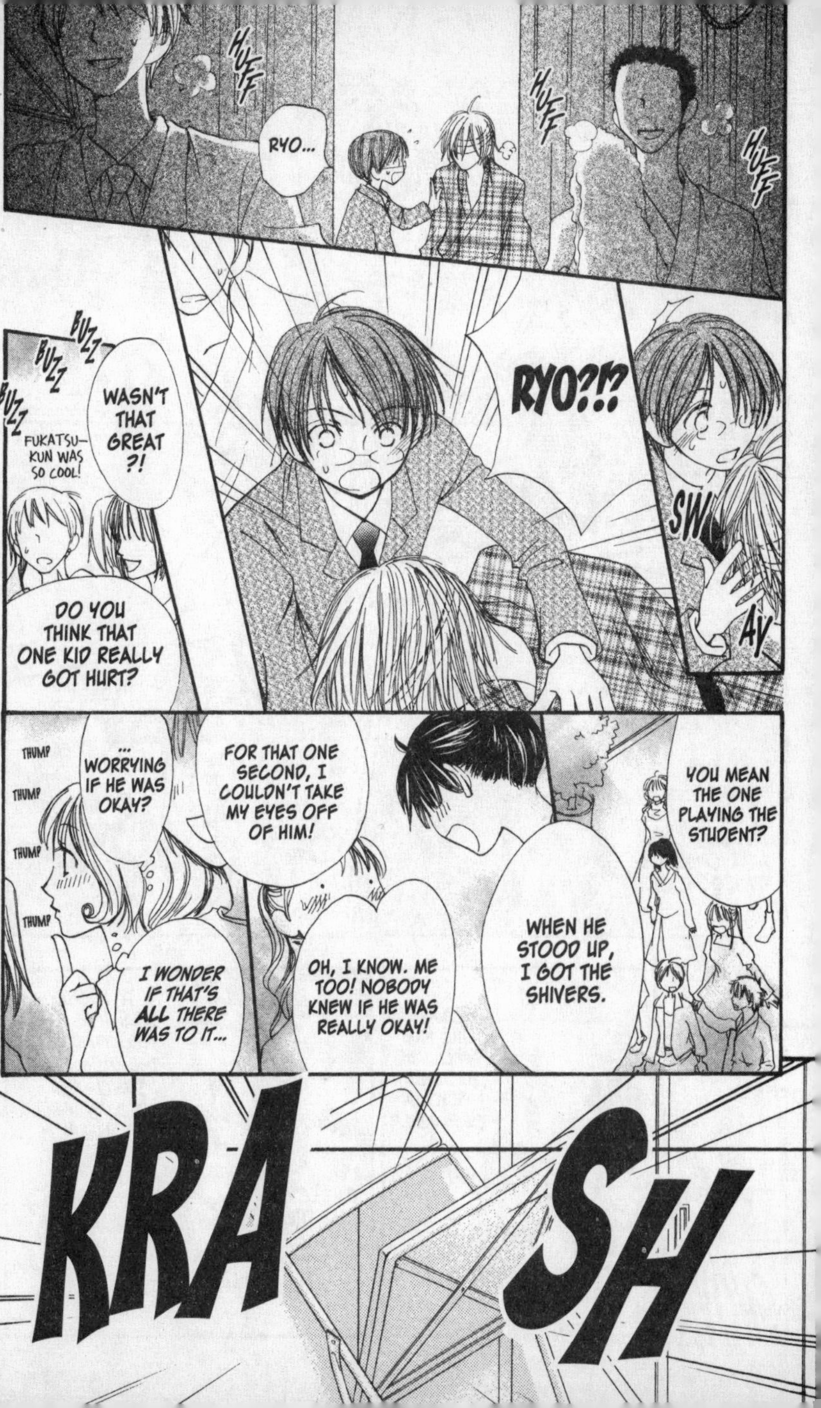
HUFF
HUFF
RYO...
HUFF
RYO?!?
SW
AY
BUZZ BUZZ BUZZ
WASN'T THAT GREAT?!
FUKATSU-KUN WAS SO COOL!
DO YOU THINK THAT ONE KID REALLY GOT HURT?
YOU MEAN THE ONE PLAYING THE STUDENT?
WHEN HE STOOD UP, I GOT THE SHIVERS.
FOR THAT ONE SECOND, I COULDN'T TAKE MY EYES OFF OF HIM!
OH, I KNOW. ME TOO! NOBODY KNEW IF HE WAS REALLY OKAY!
... WORRYING IF HE WAS OKAY?
I WONDER IF THAT'S ALL THERE WAS TO IT...
THUMP
THUMP
THUMP
THUMP
KRA
SH

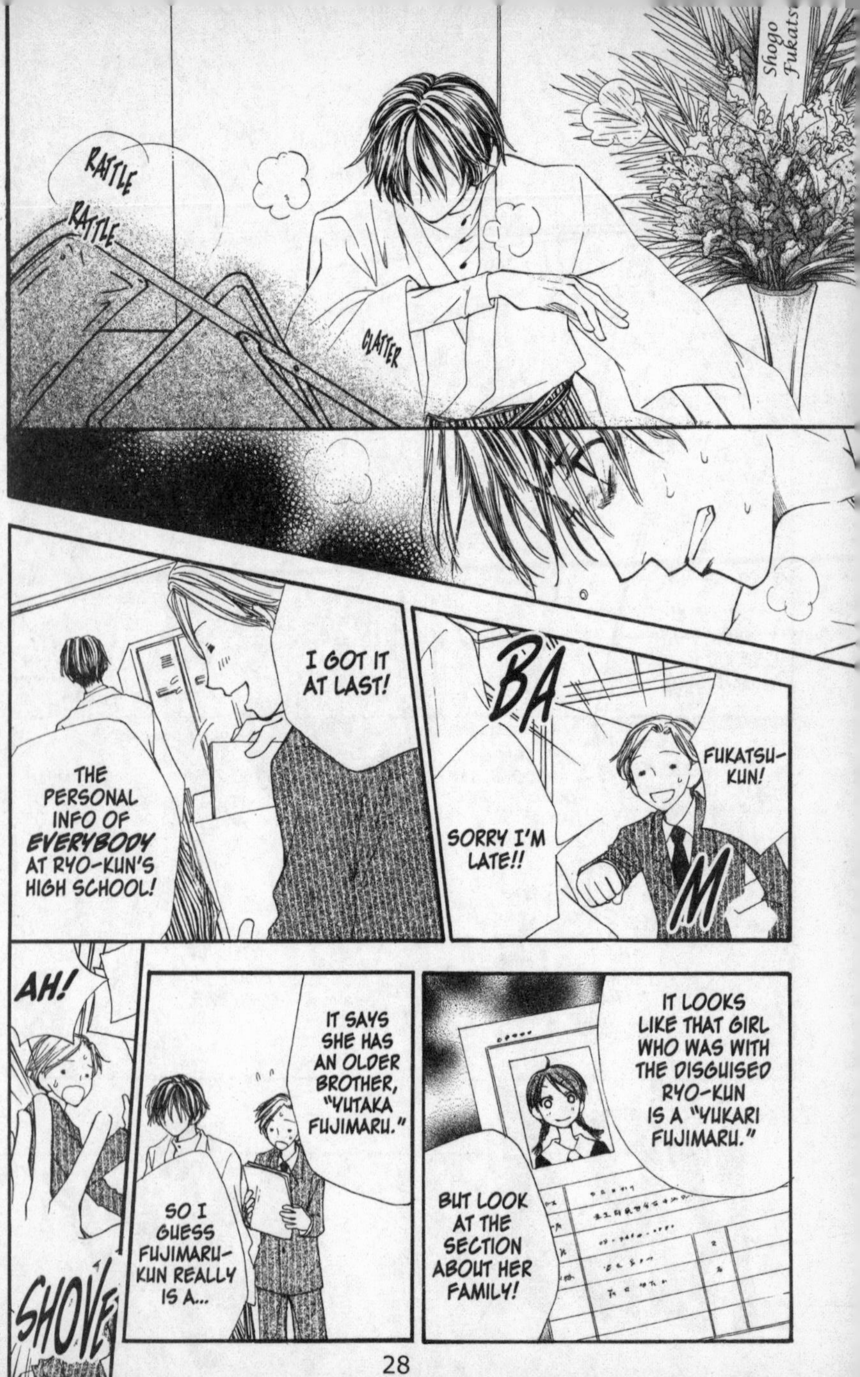
Shogo Fukats
RATTLE RATTLE
CLATTER
BAM
FUKATSU-KUN!
SORRY I'M LATE!!
I GOT IT AT LAST!
THE PERSONAL INFO OF *EVERYBODY* AT RYO-KUN'S HIGH SCHOOL!
IT LOOKS LIKE THAT GIRL WHO WAS WITH THE DISGUISED RYO-KUN IS A "YUKARI FUJIMARU."
BUT LOOK AT THE SECTION ABOUT HER FAMILY!
IT SAYS SHE HAS AN OLDER BROTHER, "YUTAKA FUJIMARU."
SO I GUESS FUJIMARU-KUN REALLY IS A...
AH!
SHOVE

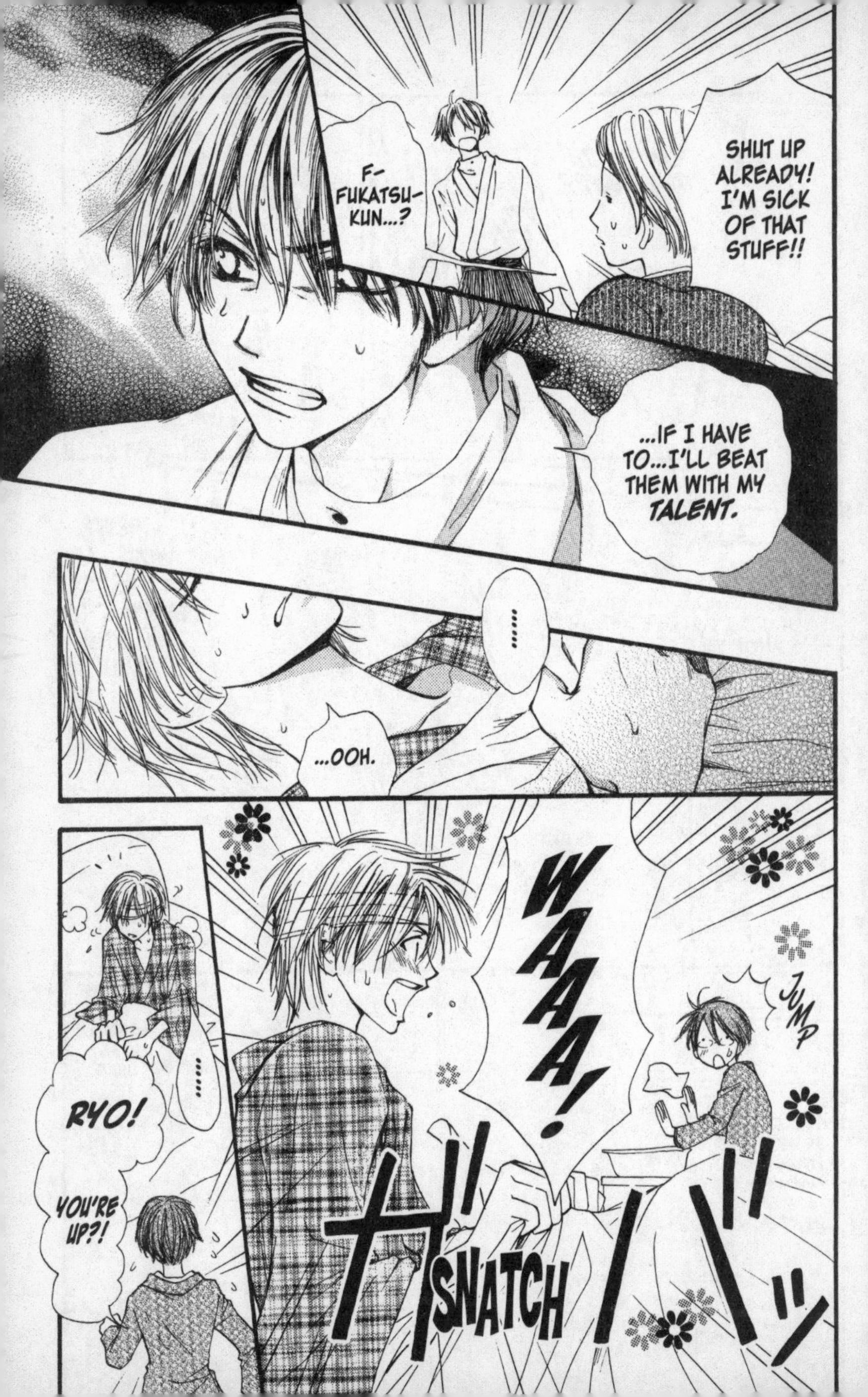
SHUT UP ALREADY! I'M SICK OF THAT STUFF!!
F-FUKATSU-KUN...?
...IF I HAVE TO...I'LL BEAT THEM WITH MY *TALENT.*
......
...OOH.
JUMP
WAAAA!
SNATCH
......
RYO!
YOU'RE UP?!

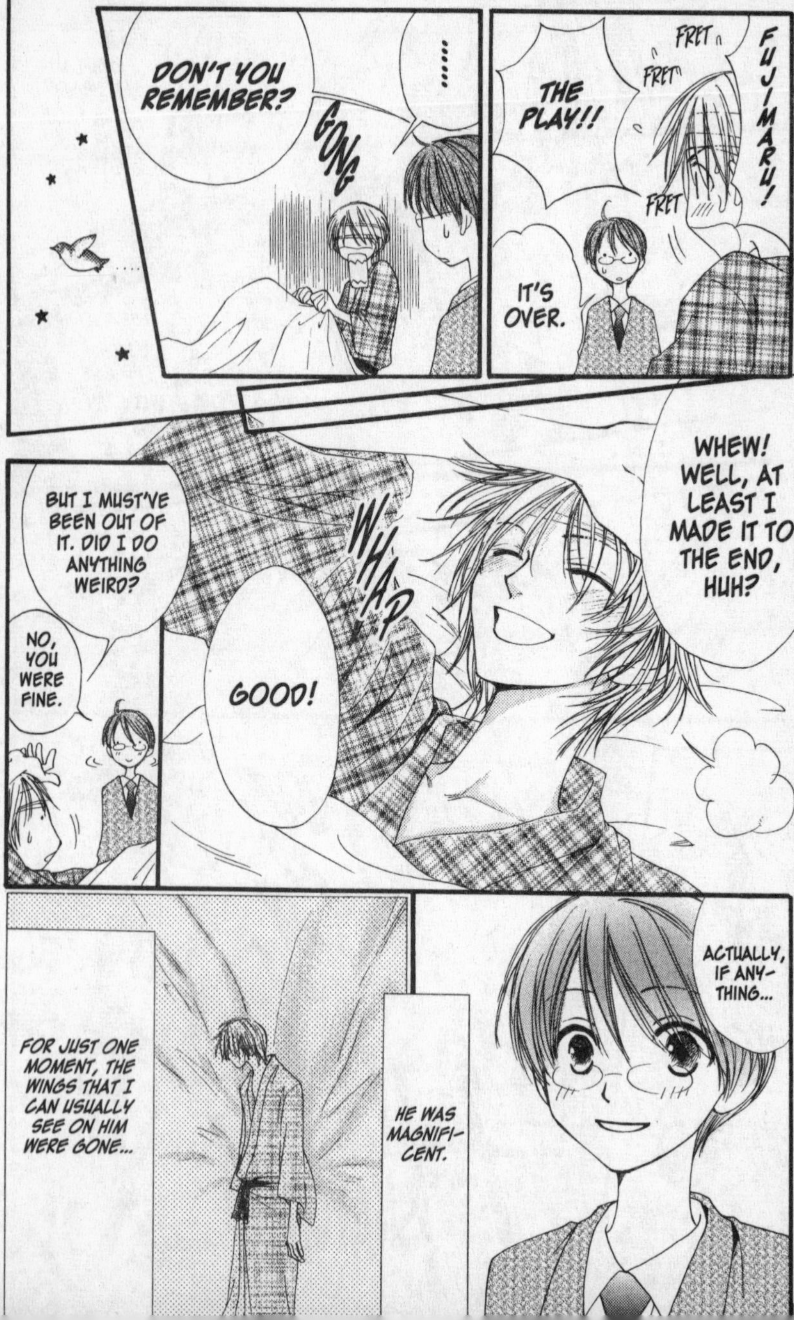
FUJIMARU!
FRET
FRET
FRET
THE PLAY!!
IT'S OVER.
......
GONG
DON'T YOU REMEMBER?
WHEW! WELL, AT LEAST I MADE IT TO THE END, HUH?
WHAP
GOOD!
BUT I MUST'VE BEEN OUT OF IT. DID I DO ANYTHING WEIRD?
NO, YOU WERE FINE.
ACTUALLY, IF ANY-THING...
HE WAS MAGNIFI-CENT.
FOR JUST ONE MOMENT, THE WINGS THAT I CAN USUALLY SEE ON HIM WERE GONE...

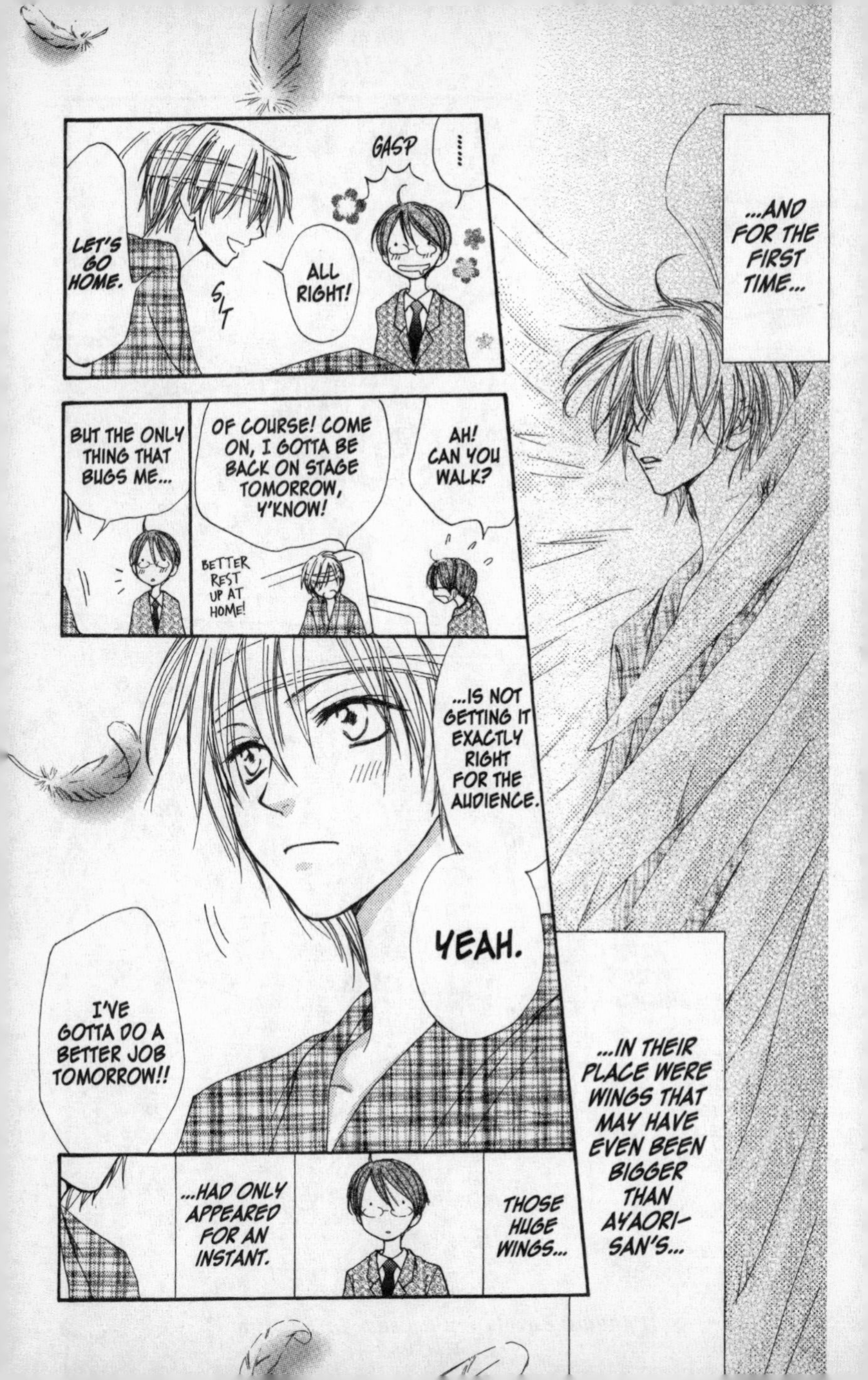
...AND FOR THE FIRST TIME...
...IN THEIR PLACE WERE WINGS THAT MAY HAVE EVEN BEEN BIGGER THAN AYAORI-SAN'S...
GASP
......
ALL RIGHT!
LET'S GO HOME.
S/T
AH! CAN YOU WALK?
OF COURSE! COME ON, I GOTTA BE BACK ON STAGE TOMORROW, Y'KNOW!
BETTER REST UP AT HOME!
BUT THE ONLY THING THAT BUGS ME...
...IS NOT GETTING IT EXACTLY RIGHT FOR THE AUDIENCE.
YEAH.
I'VE GOTTA DO A BETTER JOB TOMORROW!!
THOSE HUGE WINGS...
...HAD ONLY APPEARED FOR AN INSTANT.

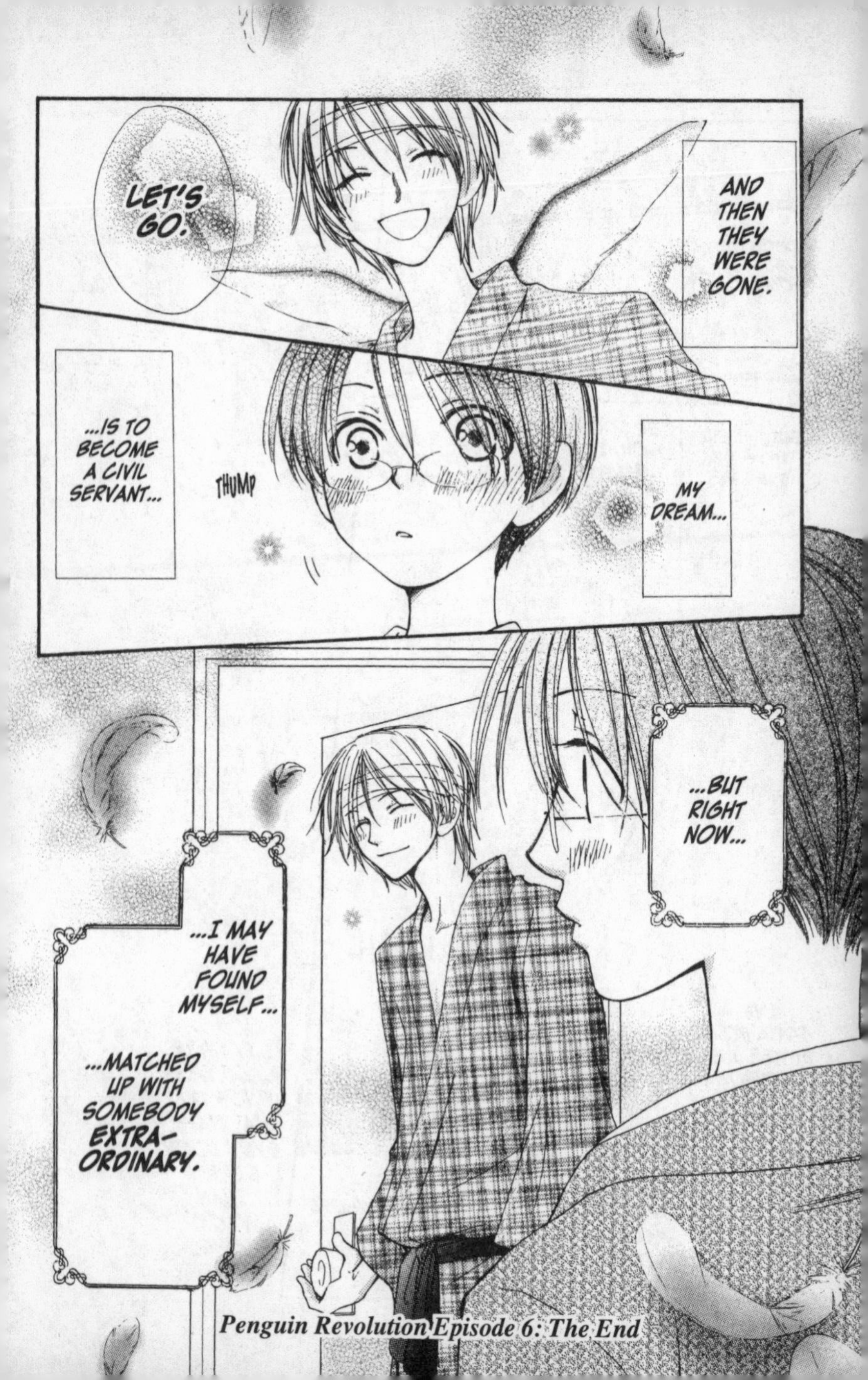
AND THEN THEY WERE GONE.
LET'S GO.
MY DREAM...
THUMP
...IS TO BECOME A CIVIL SERVANT...
...BUT RIGHT NOW...
...I MAY HAVE FOUND MYSELF...
...MATCHED UP WITH SOMEBODY EXTRA-ORDINARY.

Penguin Revolution Episode 6: The End

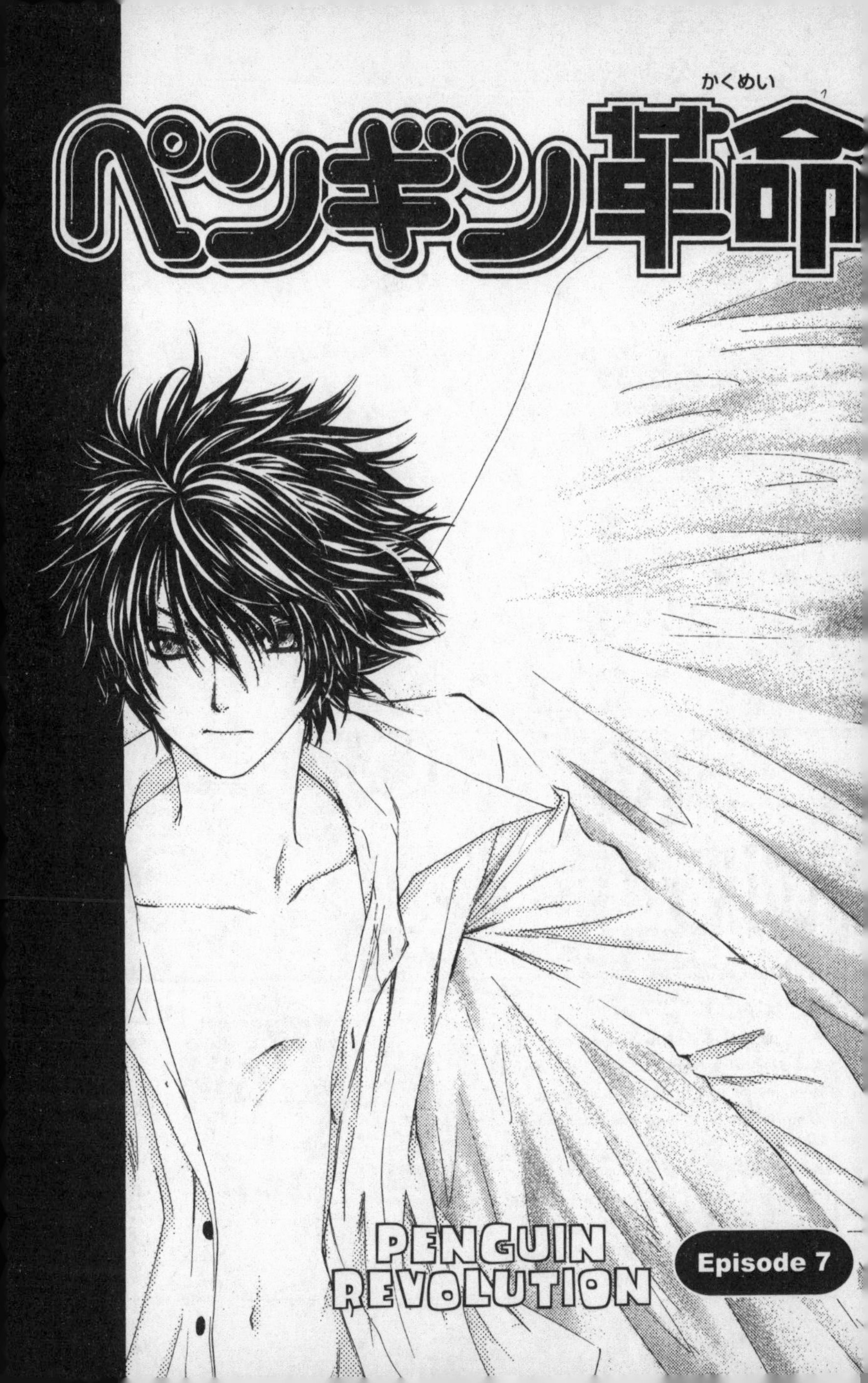
かくめい
ペンギン革命
PENGUIN REVOLUTION
Episode 7

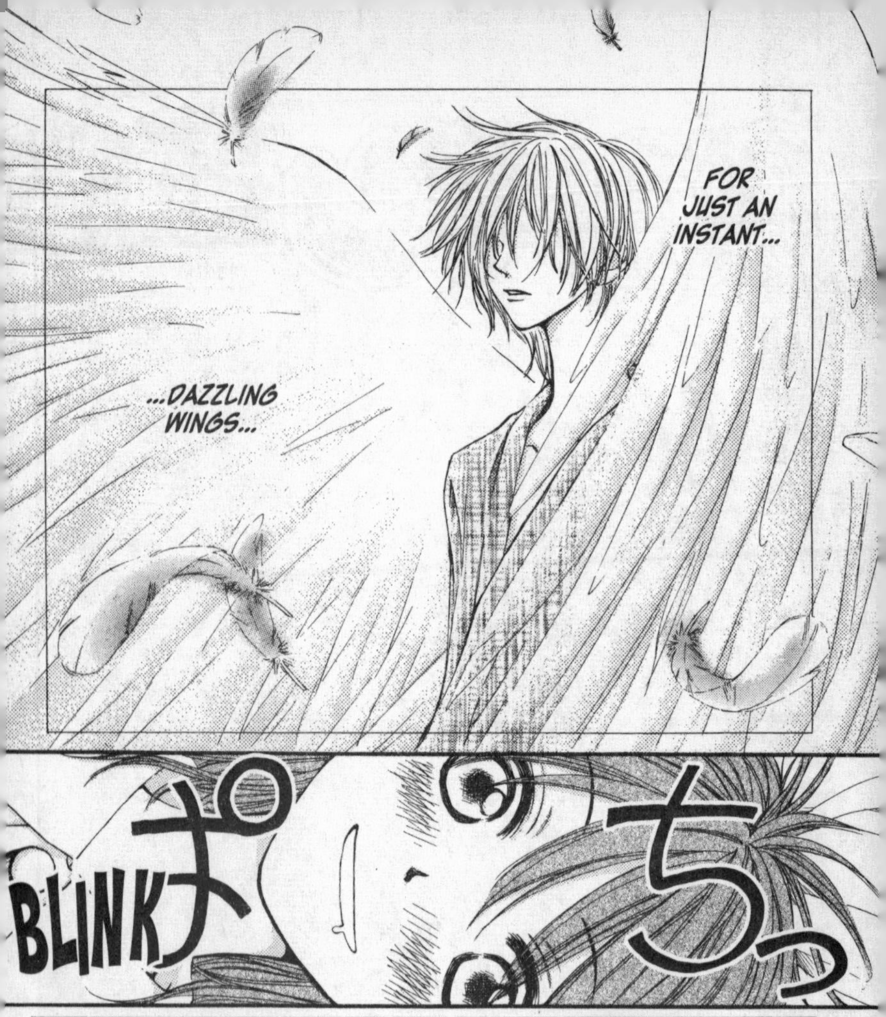

FOR JUST AN INSTANT...
...DAZZLING WINGS...
ぱちっ
BLINK

1/4 Sakura Mail

The spotlight is on Aya this episode. Ryo and Yuka-chan have been hogging the storyline thus far, so I thought I'd give them a chance to cool down. This is the most I've ever drawn Aya within one episode, so I gave it my all...which is good, because his hair takes a looong time to draw... And I discovered that drawing his "cool" hairstyle is harder than drawing him with wild and wooly hair!

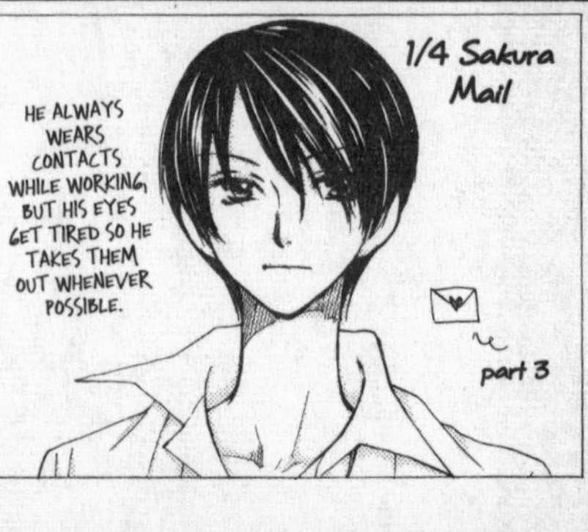

HE ALWAYS WEARS CONTACTS WHILE WORKING, BUT HIS EYES GET TIRED SO HE TAKES THEM OUT WHENEVER POSSIBLE.

part 3

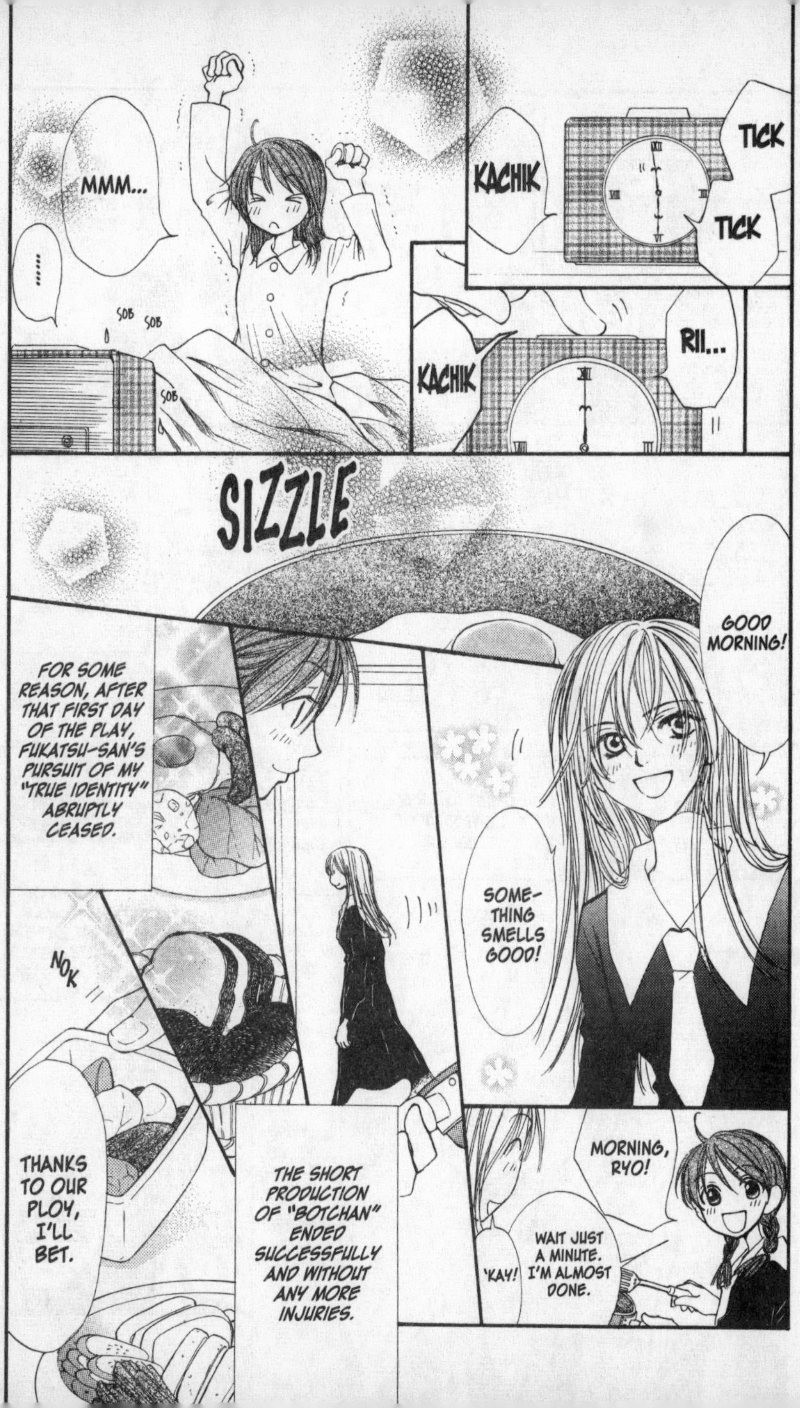
TICK
KACHIK
TICK
RII...
KACHIK
MMM...
......
SOB SOB
SOB
SIZZLE
GOOD MORNING!
SOME-THING SMELLS GOOD!
FOR SOME REASON, AFTER THAT FIRST DAY OF THE PLAY, FUKATSU-SAN'S PURSUIT OF MY "TRUE IDENTITY" ABRUPTLY CEASED.
NOK
MORNING, RYO!
WAIT JUST A MINUTE. I'M ALMOST DONE.
'KAY!
THE SHORT PRODUCTION OF "BOTCHAN" ENDED SUCCESSFULLY AND WITHOUT ANY MORE INJURIES.
THANKS TO OUR PLOY, I'LL BET.

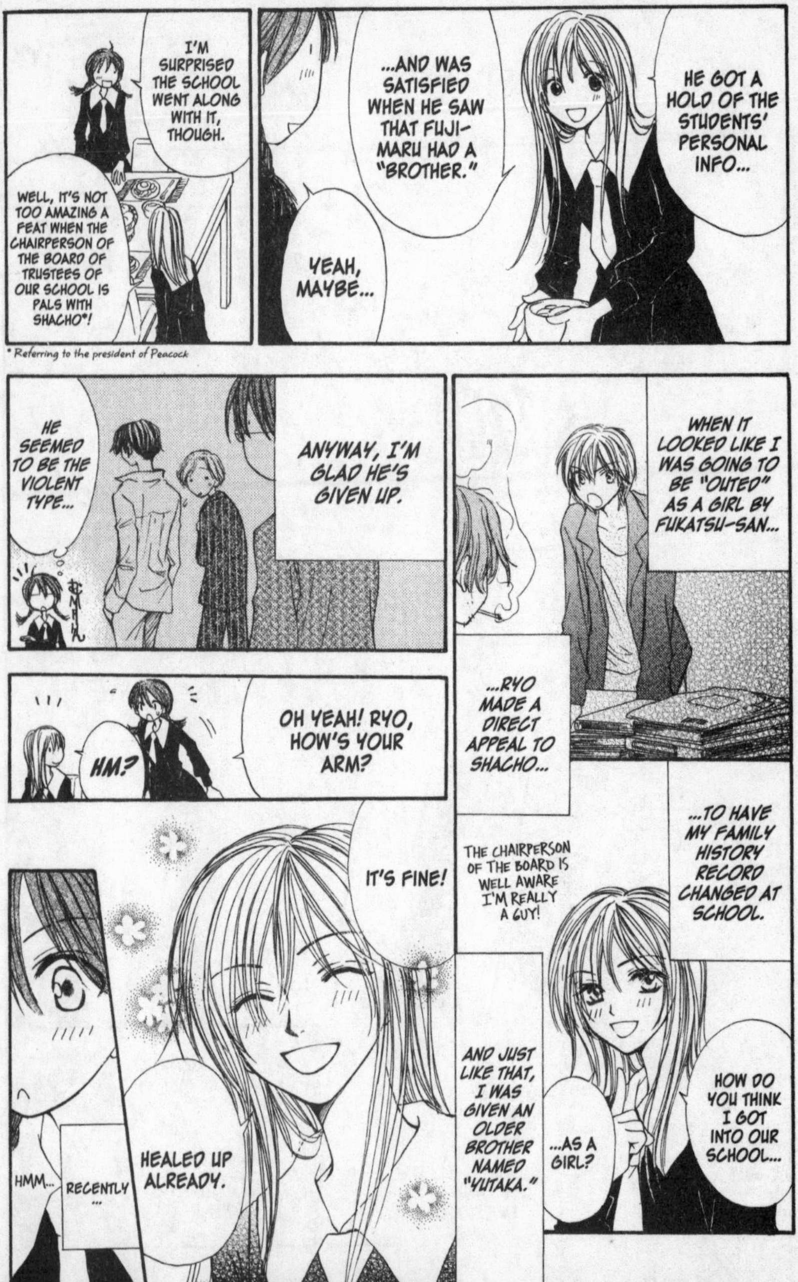
HE GOT A HOLD OF THE STUDENTS' PERSONAL INFO...
...AND WAS SATISFIED WHEN HE SAW THAT FUJIMARU HAD A "BROTHER."
YEAH, MAYBE...
I'M SURPRISED THE SCHOOL WENT ALONG WITH IT, THOUGH.
WELL, IT'S NOT TOO AMAZING A FEAT WHEN THE CHAIRPERSON OF THE BOARD OF TRUSTEES OF OUR SCHOOL IS PALS WITH SHACHO*!
WHEN IT LOOKED LIKE I WAS GOING TO BE "OUTED" AS A GIRL BY FUKATSU-SAN...
...RYO MADE A DIRECT APPEAL TO SHACHO...
...TO HAVE MY FAMILY HISTORY RECORD CHANGED AT SCHOOL.
THE CHAIRPERSON OF THE BOARD IS WELL AWARE I'M REALLY A GUY!
HOW DO YOU THINK I GOT INTO OUR SCHOOL...
...AS A GIRL?
AND JUST LIKE THAT, I WAS GIVEN AN OLDER BROTHER NAMED "YUTAKA."
ANYWAY, I'M GLAD HE'S GIVEN UP.
HE SEEMED TO BE THE VIOLENT TYPE...
OH YEAH! RYO, HOW'S YOUR ARM?
HM?
IT'S FINE!
HEALED UP ALREADY.
RECENTLY...
HMM...

* Referring to the president of Peacock

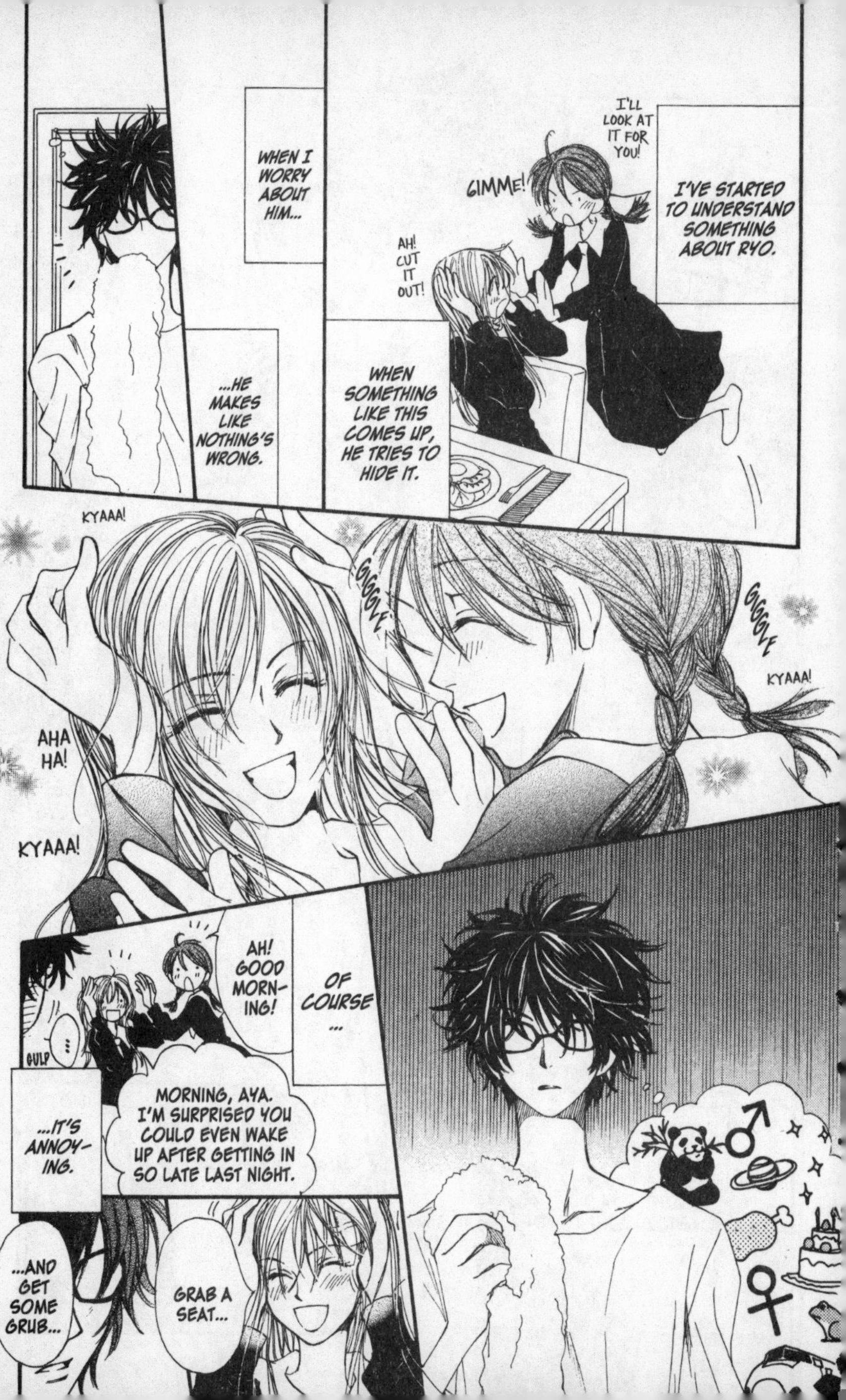
I'VE STARTED TO UNDERSTAND SOMETHING ABOUT RYO.
I'LL LOOK AT IT FOR YOU!
GIMME!
AH! CUT IT OUT!
WHEN SOMETHING LIKE THIS COMES UP, HE TRIES TO HIDE IT.
WHEN I WORRY ABOUT HIM...
...HE MAKES LIKE NOTHING'S WRONG.
GIGGLE
KYAAA!
GIGGLE
KYAAA!
AHA HA!
KYAAA!
OF COURSE...
AH! GOOD MORN-ING!
...
GULP
MORNING, AYA. I'M SURPRISED YOU COULD EVEN WAKE UP AFTER GETTING IN SO LATE LAST NIGHT.
...IT'S ANNOY-ING.
GRAB A SEAT...
...AND GET SOME GRUB...

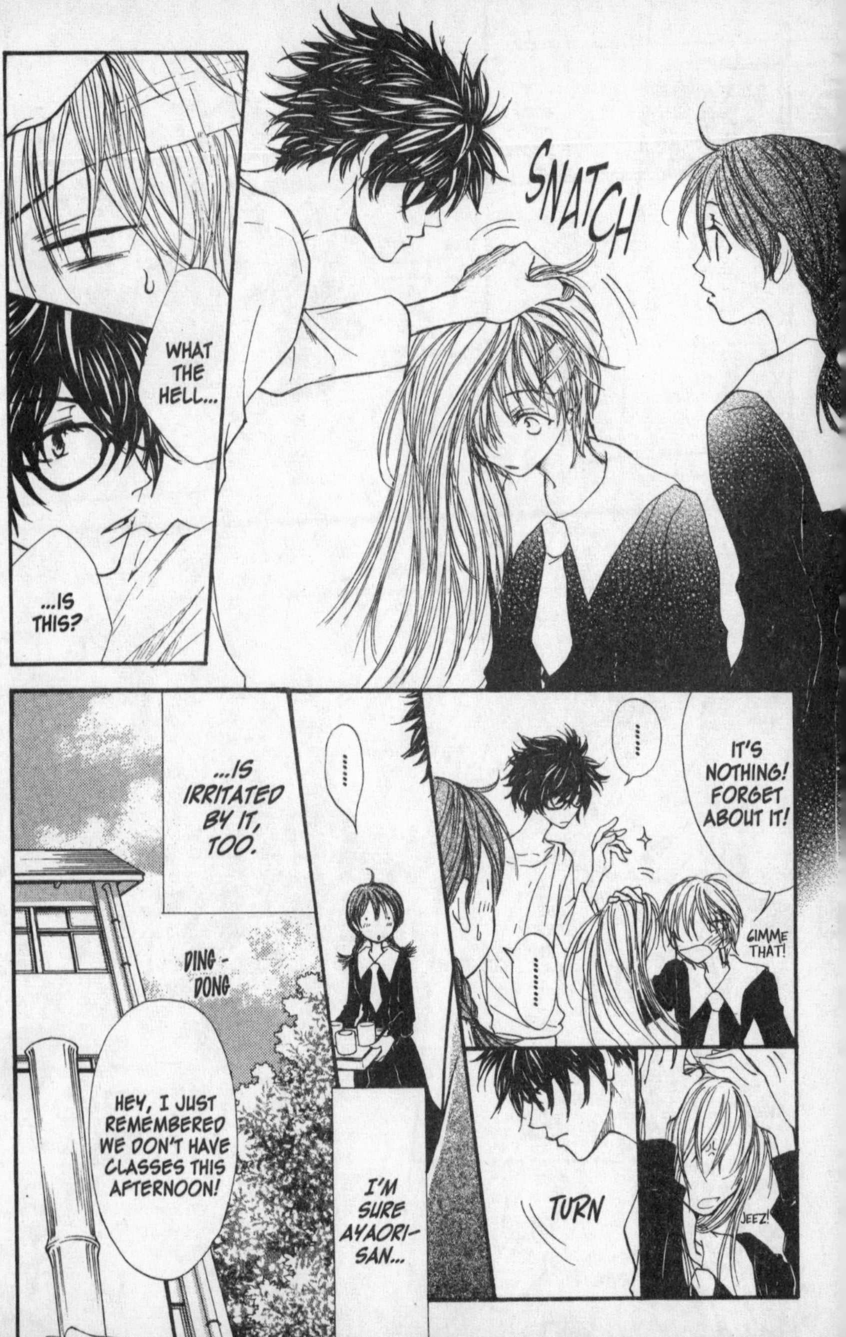
SNATCH
WHAT THE HELL...
...IS THIS?
IT'S NOTHING! FORGET ABOUT IT!
......
......
GIMME THAT!
JEEZ!
TURN
......
I'M SURE AYAORI-SAN...
...IS IRRITATED BY IT, TOO.
DING-DONG
HEY, I JUST REMEMBERED WE DON'T HAVE CLASSES THIS AFTERNOON!

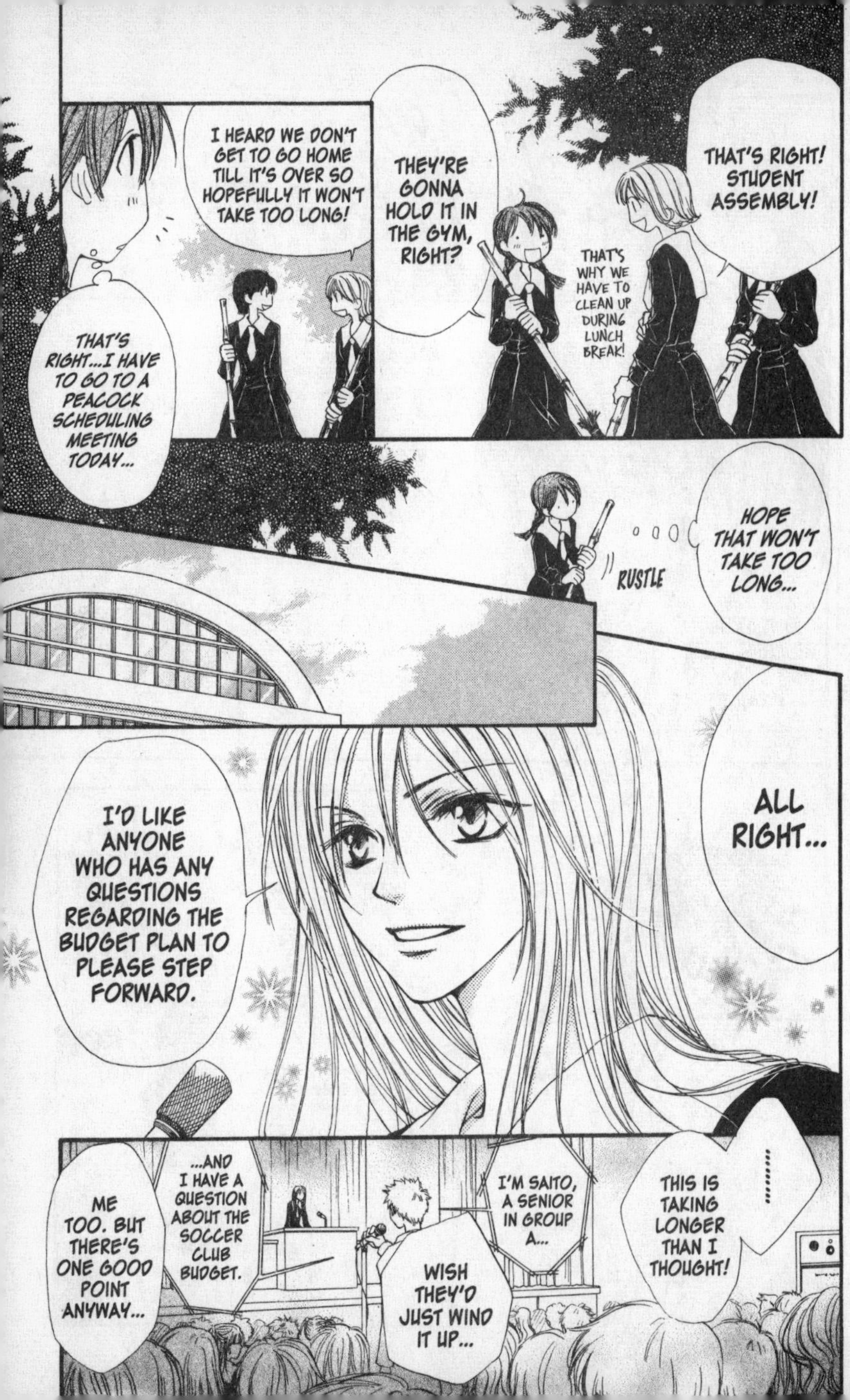
THAT'S RIGHT! STUDENT ASSEMBLY!
THAT'S WHY WE HAVE TO CLEAN UP DURING LUNCH BREAK!
THEY'RE GONNA HOLD IT IN THE GYM, RIGHT?
I HEARD WE DON'T GET TO GO HOME TILL IT'S OVER SO HOPEFULLY IT WON'T TAKE TOO LONG!
THAT'S RIGHT...I HAVE TO GO TO A PEACOCK SCHEDULING MEETING TODAY...
HOPE THAT WON'T TAKE TOO LONG...
RUSTLE
ALL RIGHT...
I'D LIKE ANYONE WHO HAS ANY QUESTIONS REGARDING THE BUDGET PLAN TO PLEASE STEP FORWARD.
......
THIS IS TAKING LONGER THAN I THOUGHT!
I'M SAITO, A SENIOR IN GROUP A...
WISH THEY'D JUST WIND IT UP...
...AND I HAVE A QUESTION ABOUT THE SOCCER CLUB BUDGET.
ME TOO. BUT THERE'S ONE GOOD POINT ANYWAY...

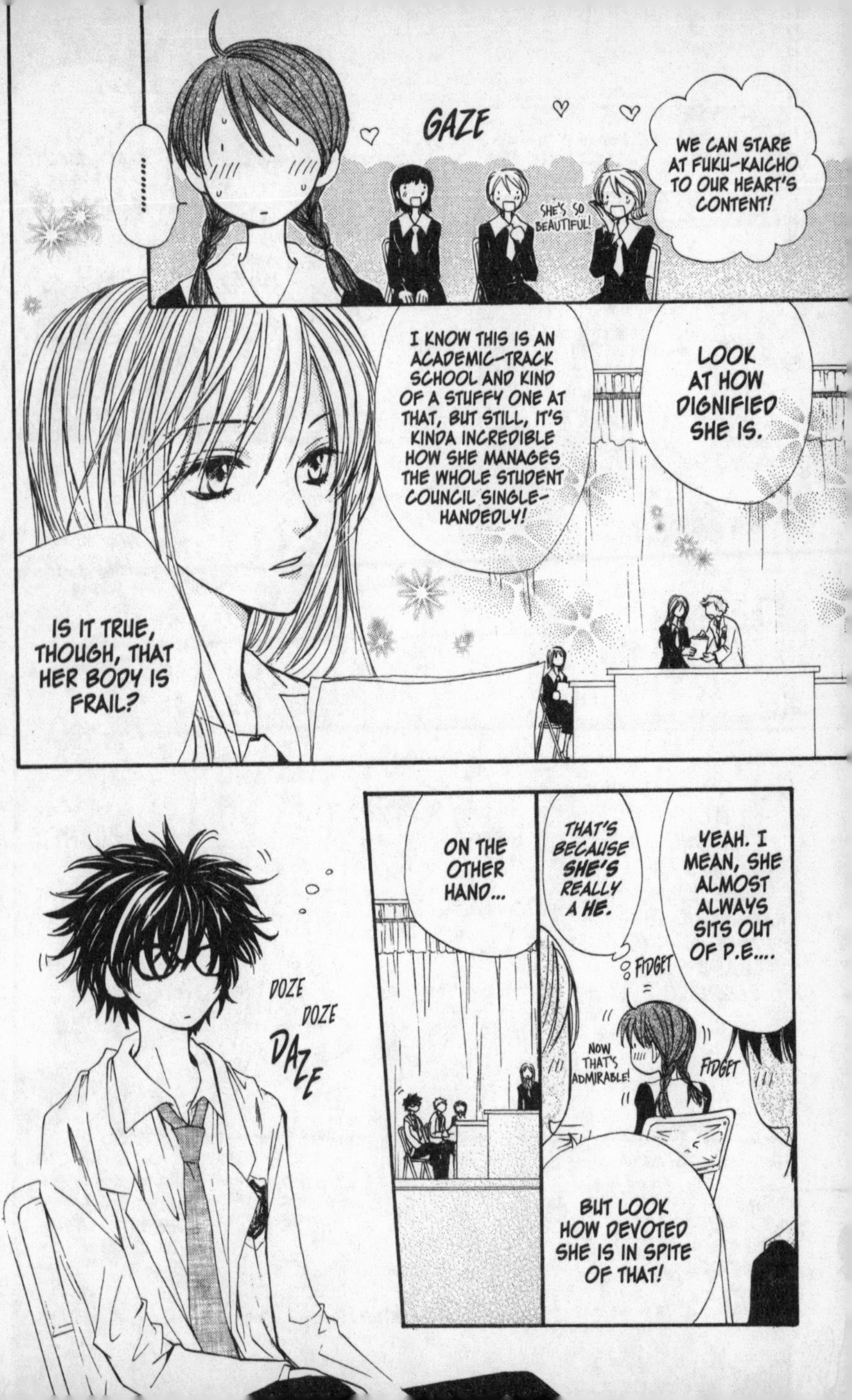
WE CAN STARE AT FUKU-KAICHO TO OUR HEART'S CONTENT!
SHE'S SO BEAUTIFUL!
GAZE
......
LOOK AT HOW DIGNIFIED SHE IS.
I KNOW THIS IS AN ACADEMIC-TRACK SCHOOL AND KIND OF A STUFFY ONE AT THAT, BUT STILL, IT'S KINDA INCREDIBLE HOW SHE MANAGES THE WHOLE STUDENT COUNCIL SINGLE-HANDEDLY!
IS IT TRUE, THOUGH, THAT HER BODY IS FRAIL?
YEAH. I MEAN, SHE ALMOST ALWAYS SITS OUT OF P.E....
THAT'S BECAUSE SHE'S REALLY A HE.
FIDGET
FIDGET
NOW THAT'S ADMIRABLE!
BUT LOOK HOW DEVOTED SHE IS IN SPITE OF THAT!
ON THE OTHER HAND...
DOZE
DOZE
DAZE

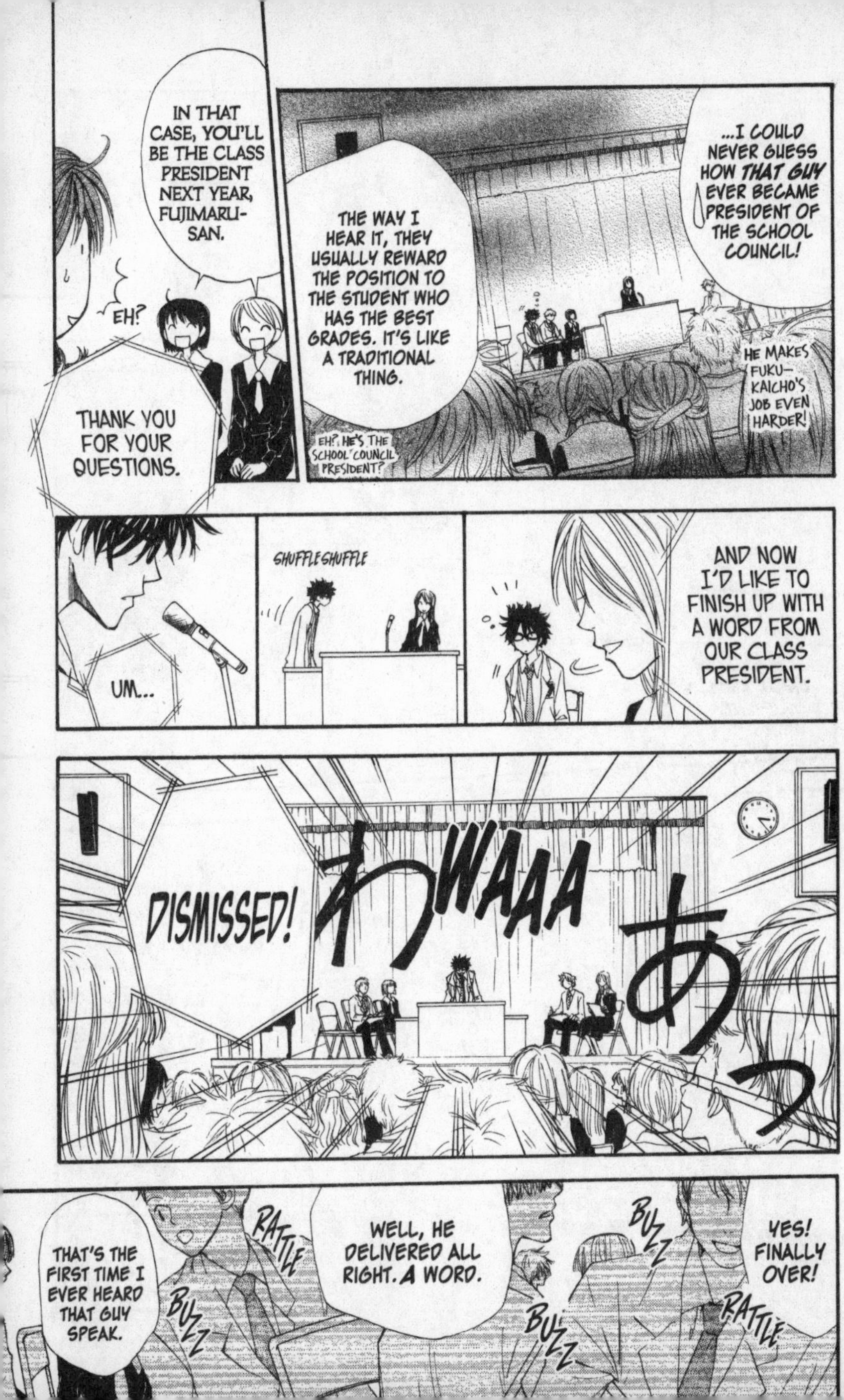
...I COULD NEVER GUESS HOW THAT GUY EVER BECAME PRESIDENT OF THE SCHOOL COUNCIL!
HE MAKES FUKU-KAICHO'S JOB EVEN HARDER!
THE WAY I HEAR IT, THEY USUALLY REWARD THE POSITION TO THE STUDENT WHO HAS THE BEST GRADES. IT'S LIKE A TRADITIONAL THING.
EH?, HE'S THE SCHOOL COUNCIL PRESIDENT?
IN THAT CASE, YOU'LL BE THE CLASS PRESIDENT NEXT YEAR, FUJIMARU-SAN.
EH?
THANK YOU FOR YOUR QUESTIONS.
AND NOW I'D LIKE TO FINISH UP WITH A WORD FROM OUR CLASS PRESIDENT.
SHUFFLESHUFFLE
UM...
あっ
わWAAA
DISMISSED!
YES! FINALLY OVER!
RATTLE
BUZZ
BUZZ
WELL, HE DELIVERED ALL RIGHT. A WORD.
RATTLE
BUZZ
THAT'S THE FIRST TIME I EVER HEARD THAT GUY SPEAK.

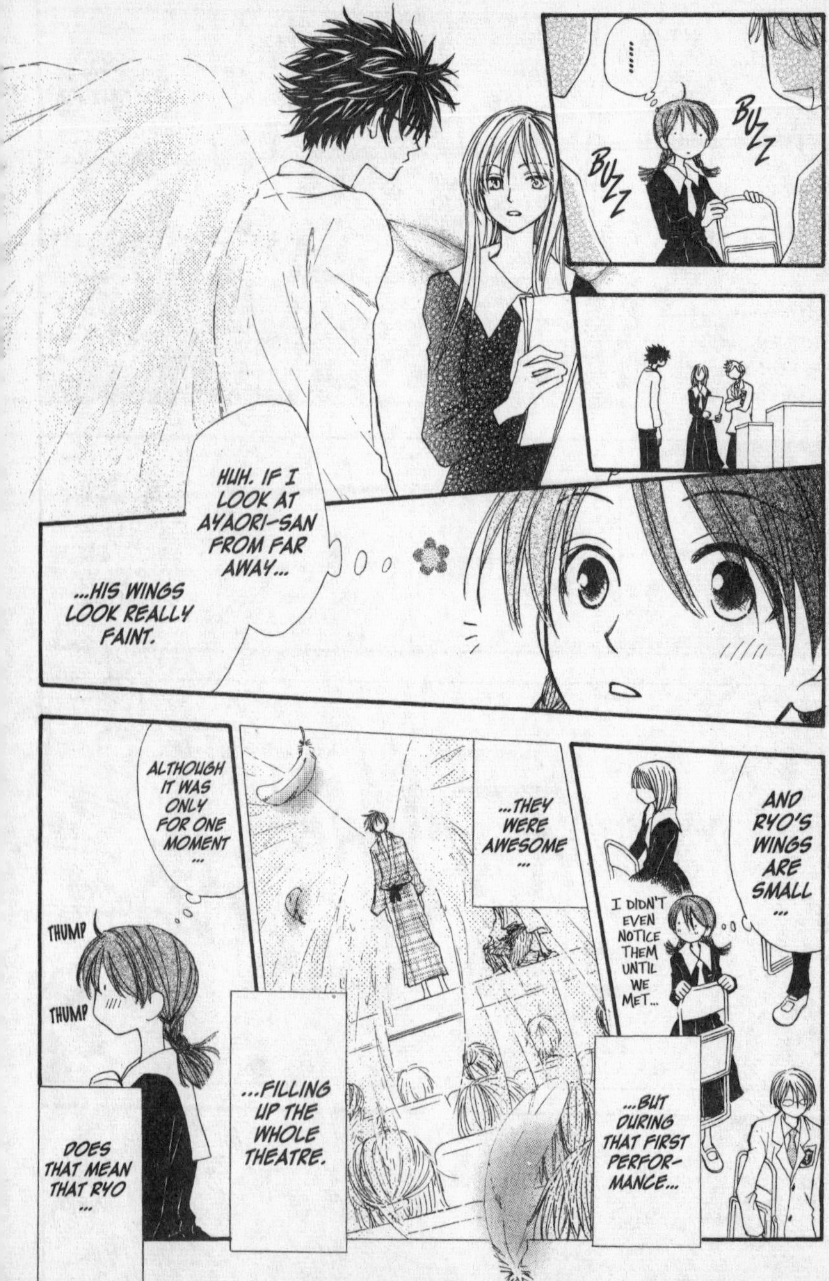
......
BUZZ
BUZZ
HUH. IF I LOOK AT AYAORI-SAN FROM FAR AWAY...
...HIS WINGS LOOK REALLY FAINT.
AND RYO'S WINGS ARE SMALL...
I DIDN'T EVEN NOTICE THEM UNTIL WE MET...
...BUT DURING THAT FIRST PERFORMANCE...
...THEY WERE AWESOME...
...FILLING UP THE WHOLE THEATRE.
ALTHOUGH IT WAS ONLY FOR ONE MOMENT...
THUMP
THUMP
DOES THAT MEAN THAT RYO...

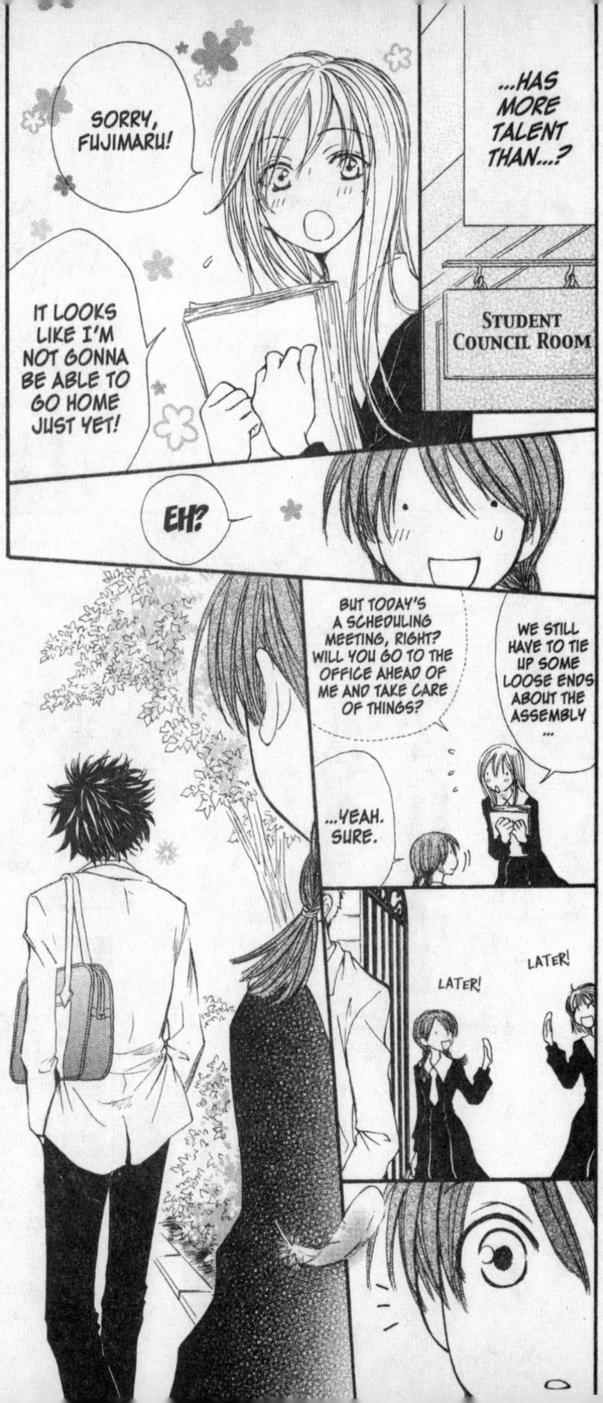
...HAS MORE TALENT THAN...?
STUDENT COUNCIL ROOM
SORRY, FUJIMARU!
IT LOOKS LIKE I'M NOT GONNA BE ABLE TO GO HOME JUST YET!
EH?
WE STILL HAVE TO TIE UP SOME LOOSE ENDS ABOUT THE ASSEMBLY ...
BUT TODAY'S A SCHEDULING MEETING, RIGHT? WILL YOU GO TO THE OFFICE AHEAD OF ME AND TAKE CARE OF THINGS?
...YEAH. SURE.
LATER!
LATER!

1/4 Sakura Mail

part 4

I like Aya's disheveled hair with its lathered-on look, but with the neat style. I always have to apply a sheen to make it look good! That's my intention, anyway, but it usually doesn't work out the way I imagined.
I respect mangakas who can make glossy hair look beautiful... If a lot of characters with slicked-up hair appear on the same page together, they all stand out...Anyway, I'm going to introduce a lot of characters with lustrous hair, which will make drawing school scenes a lot more fun.
Another thing I have fun drawing are Adélie penguins, for their beautiful black and white design.

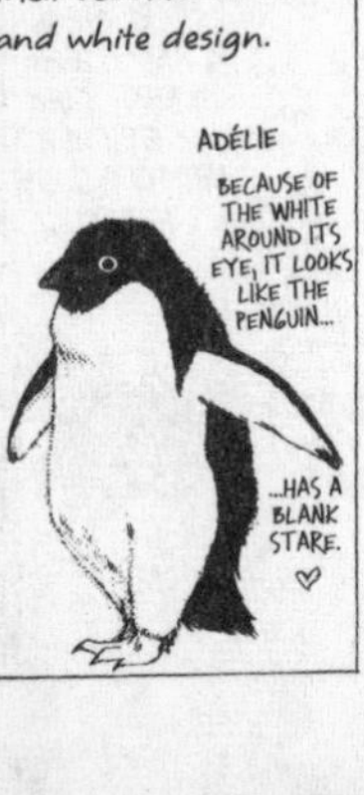
ADÉLIE
BECAUSE OF THE WHITE AROUND ITS EYE, IT LOOKS LIKE THE PENGUIN...
...HAS A BLANK STARE.
♡

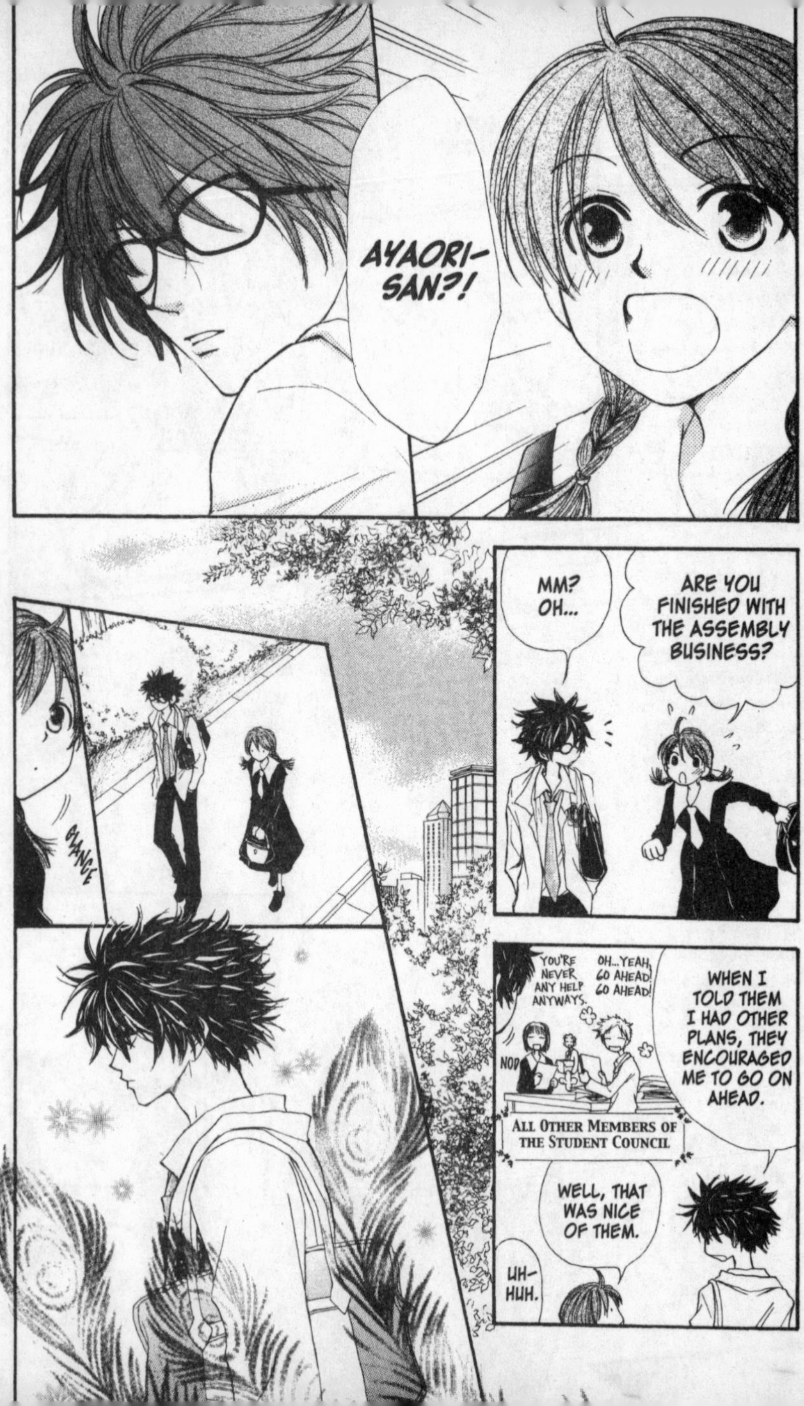
AYAORI-SAN?!
ARE YOU FINISHED WITH THE ASSEMBLY BUSINESS?
MM? OH...
WHEN I TOLD THEM I HAD OTHER PLANS, THEY ENCOURAGED ME TO GO ON AHEAD.
OH...YEAH, GO AHEAD! GO AHEAD!
YOU'RE NEVER ANY HELP ANYWAYS.
NOD
ALL OTHER MEMBERS OF THE STUDENT COUNCIL
WELL, THAT WAS NICE OF THEM.
UH-HUH.
GLANCE

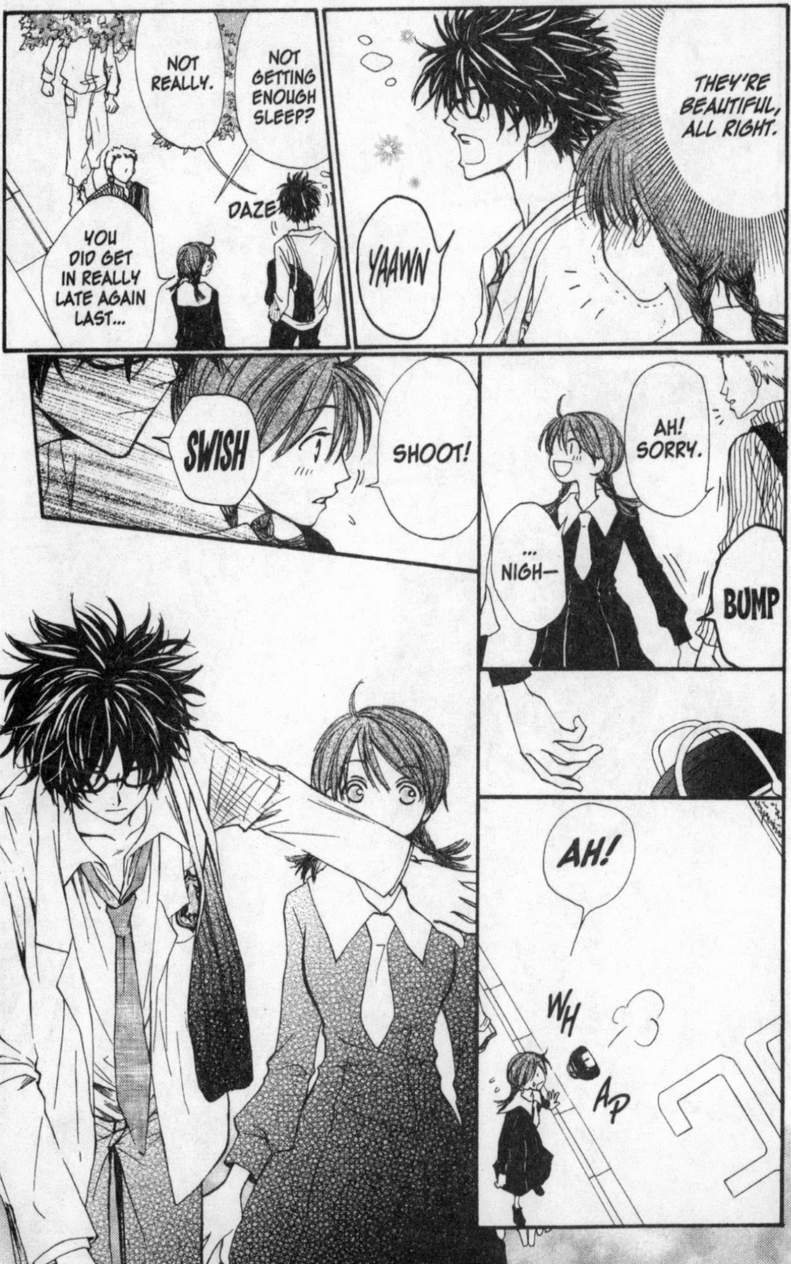
THEY'RE BEAUTIFUL, ALL RIGHT.
YAAWN
NOT GETTING ENOUGH SLEEP?
NOT REALLY.
DAZE
YOU DID GET IN REALLY LATE AGAIN LAST...
AH! SORRY.
BUMP
... NIGH—
AH!
WH
AP
SHOOT!
SWISH

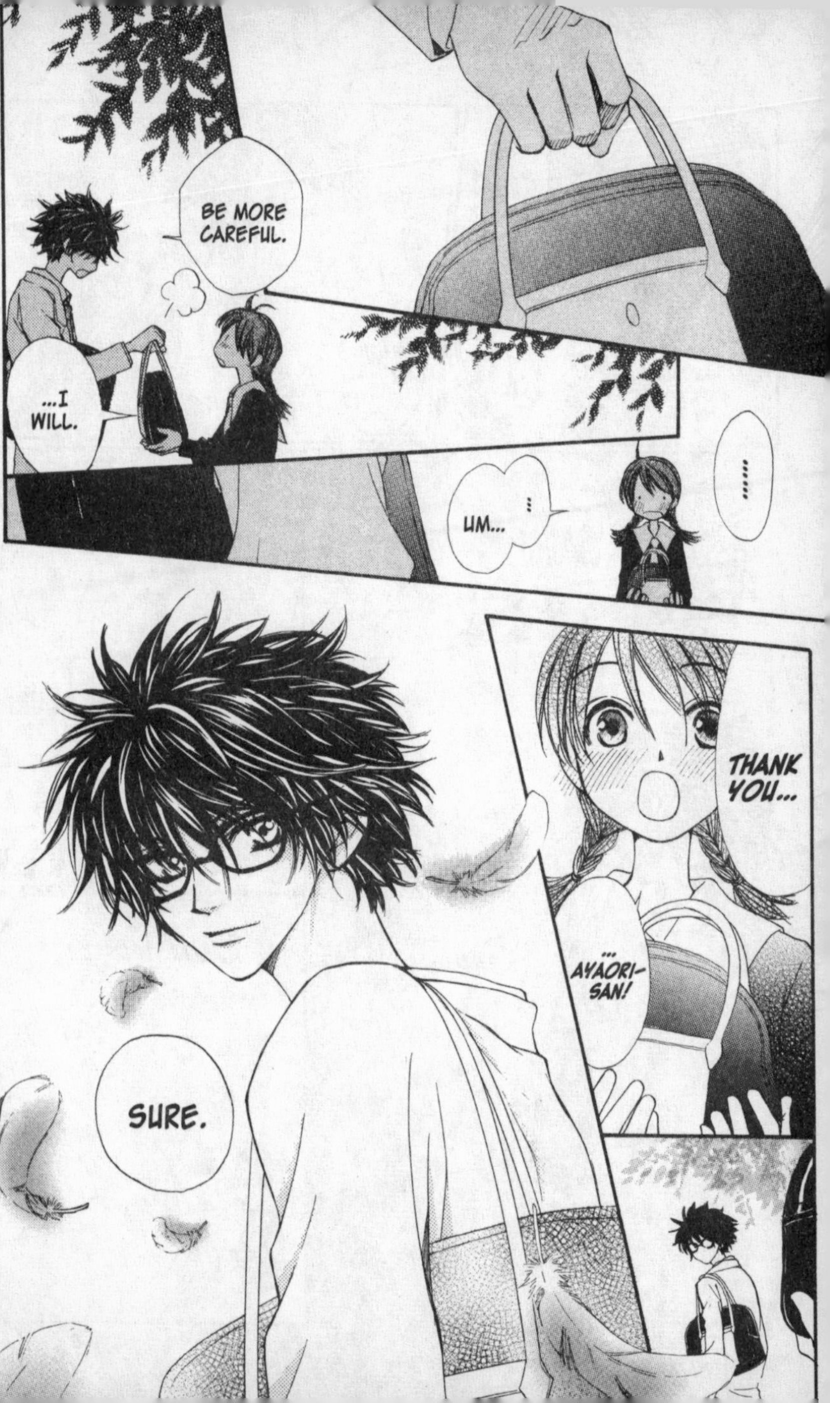

BE MORE CAREFUL.
...I WILL.
......
UM...
THANK YOU...
...AYAORI-SAN!
SURE.

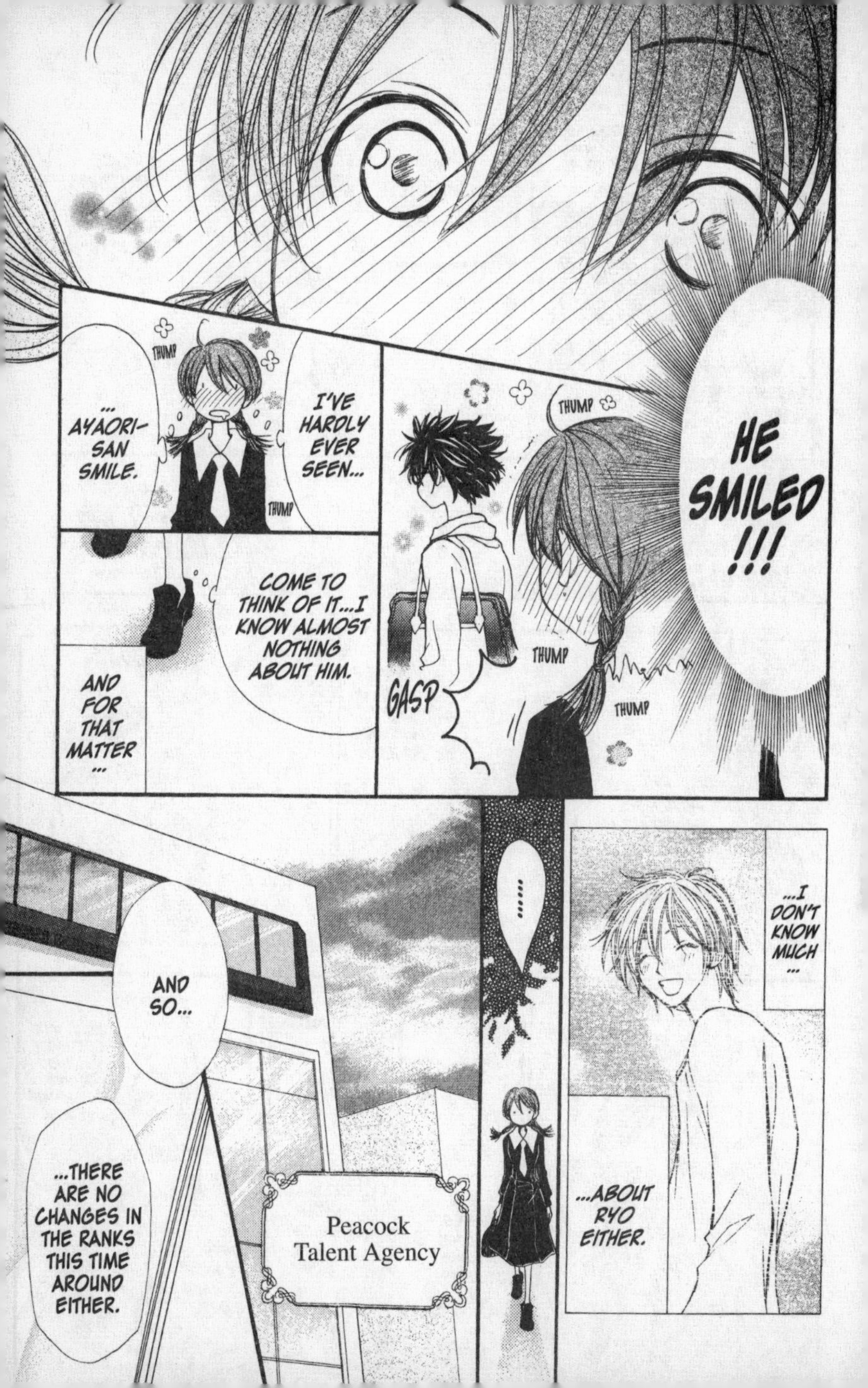
HE SMILED!!!
THUMP
GASP
THUMP
THUMP
I'VE HARDLY EVER SEEN...
...AYAORI-SAN SMILE.
THUMP
THUMP
COME TO THINK OF IT...I KNOW ALMOST NOTHING ABOUT HIM.
AND FOR THAT MATTER...
...I DON'T KNOW MUCH...
...ABOUT RYO EITHER.
......
AND SO...
Peacock Talent Agency
...THERE ARE NO CHANGES IN THE RANKS THIS TIME AROUND EITHER.

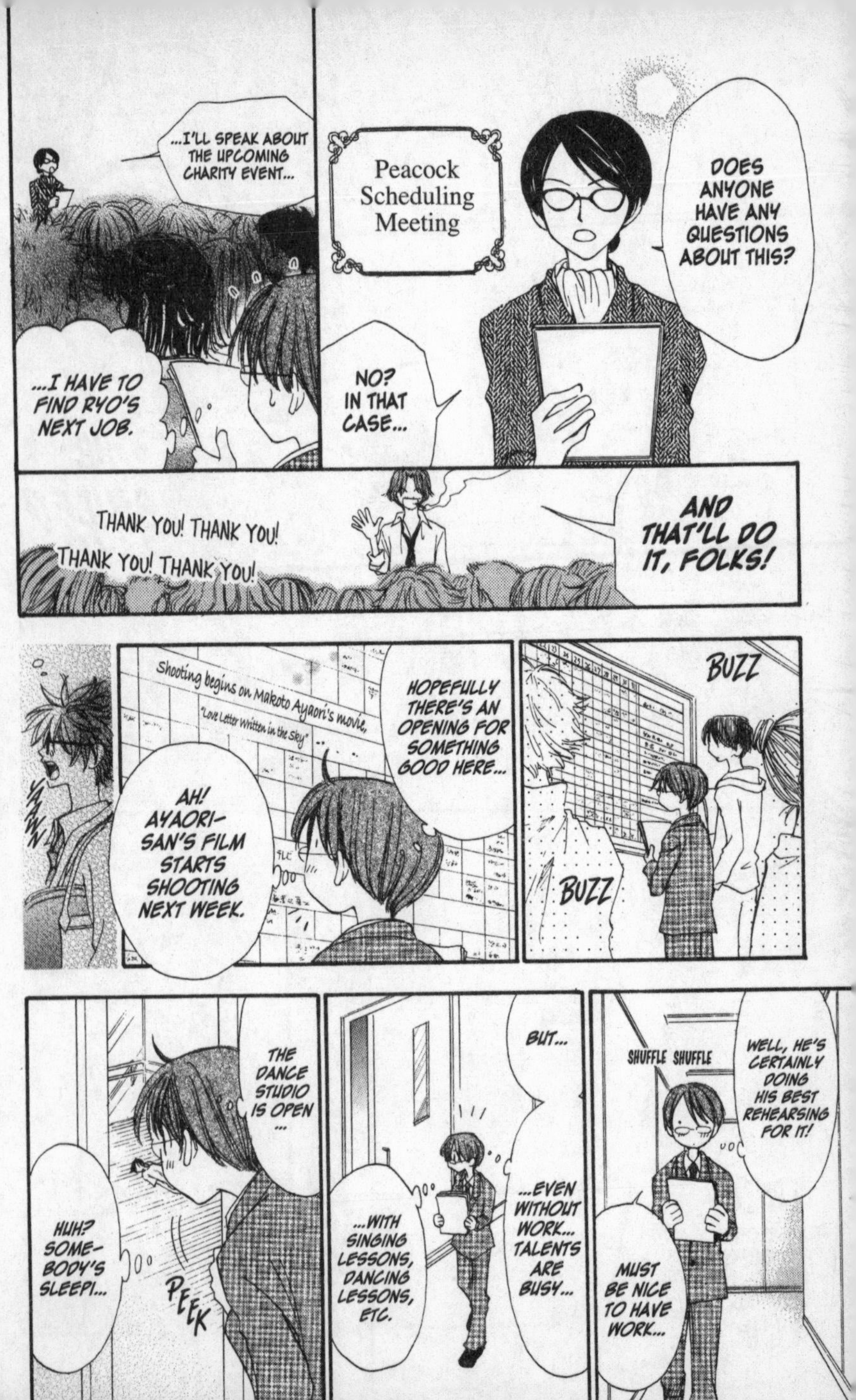
Peacock Scheduling Meeting
DOES ANYONE HAVE ANY QUESTIONS ABOUT THIS?
NO? IN THAT CASE...
...I'LL SPEAK ABOUT THE UPCOMING CHARITY EVENT...
...I HAVE TO FIND RYO'S NEXT JOB.
AND THAT'LL DO IT, FOLKS!
THANK YOU! THANK YOU!
THANK YOU! THANK YOU!
BUZZ
BUZZ
HOPEFULLY THERE'S AN OPENING FOR SOMETHING GOOD HERE...
Shooting begins on Makoto Ayaori's movie,
"Love Letter Written in the Sky"
AH! AYAORI-SAN'S FILM STARTS SHOOTING NEXT WEEK.
YAWN
WELL, HE'S CERTAINLY DOING HIS BEST REHEARSING FOR IT!
SHUFFLE SHUFFLE
MUST BE NICE TO HAVE WORK...
BUT...
...EVEN WITHOUT WORK... TALENTS ARE BUSY...
...WITH SINGING LESSONS, DANCING LESSONS, ETC.
THE DANCE STUDIO IS OPEN...
HUH? SOME-BODY'S SLEEPI...
PEEK

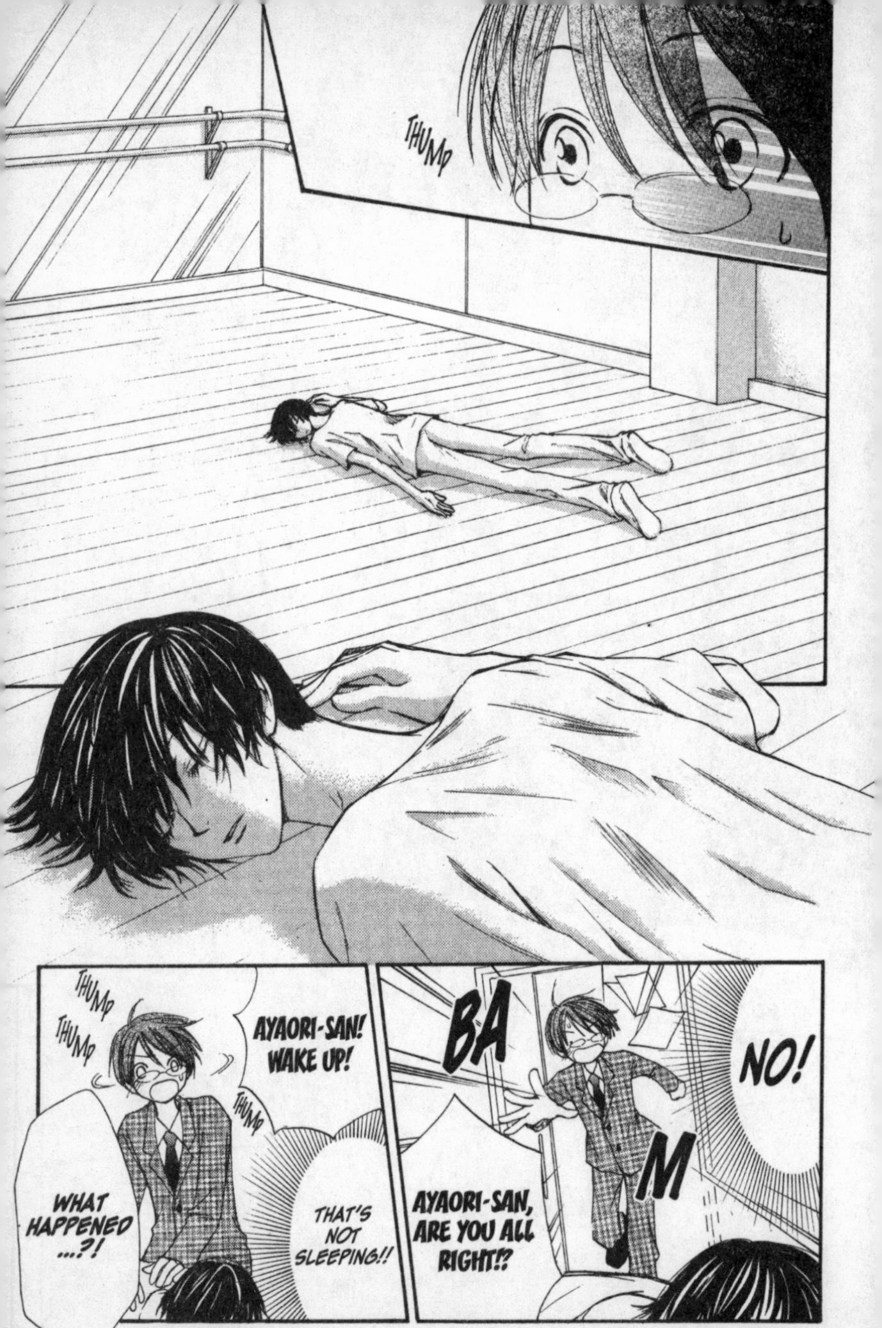
THUMP
NO!
BA
M
AYAORI-SAN, ARE YOU ALL RIGHT!?
AYAORI-SAN! WAKE UP!
THUMP
THUMP
THUMP
THAT'S NOT SLEEPING!!
WHAT HAPPENED ...?!

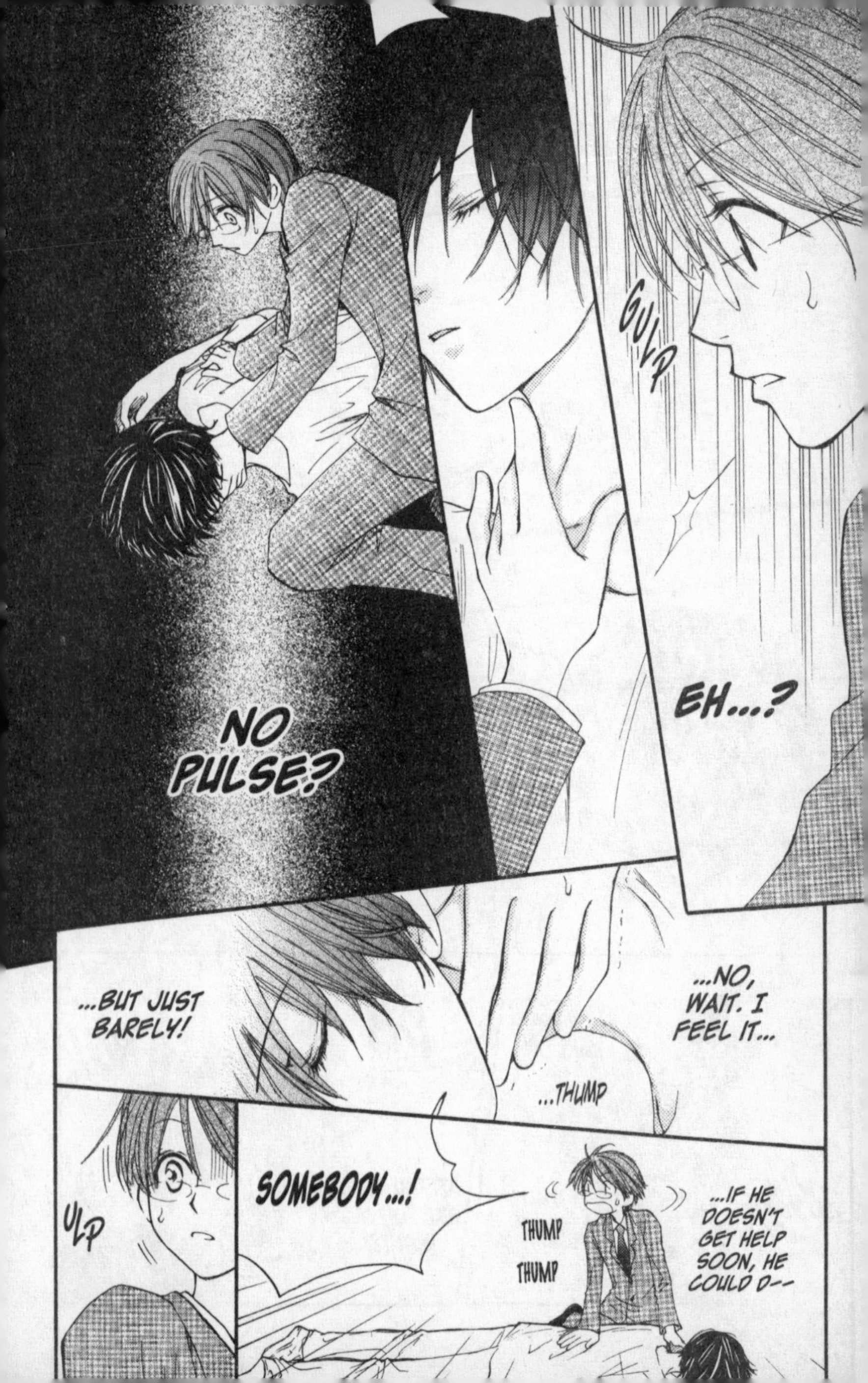
GULP
EH...?
NO PULSE?
...NO, WAIT. I FEEL IT...
...THUMP
...BUT JUST BARELY!
...IF HE DOESN'T GET HELP SOON, HE COULD D--
THUMP
THUMP
SOMEBODY...!
ULP

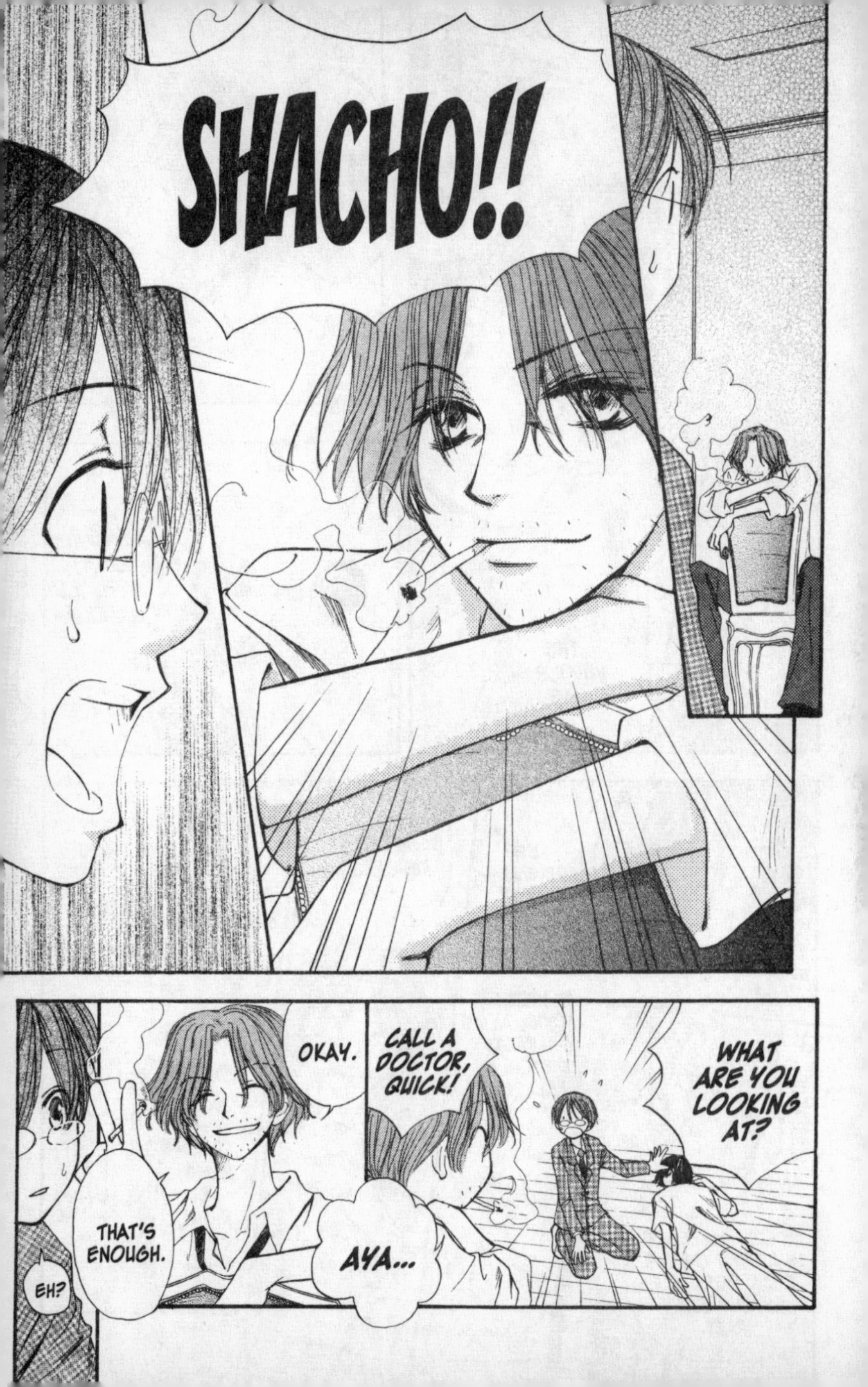
SHACHO!!
WHAT ARE YOU LOOKING AT?
CALL A DOCTOR, QUICK!
AYA...
OKAY.
THAT'S ENOUGH.
EH?

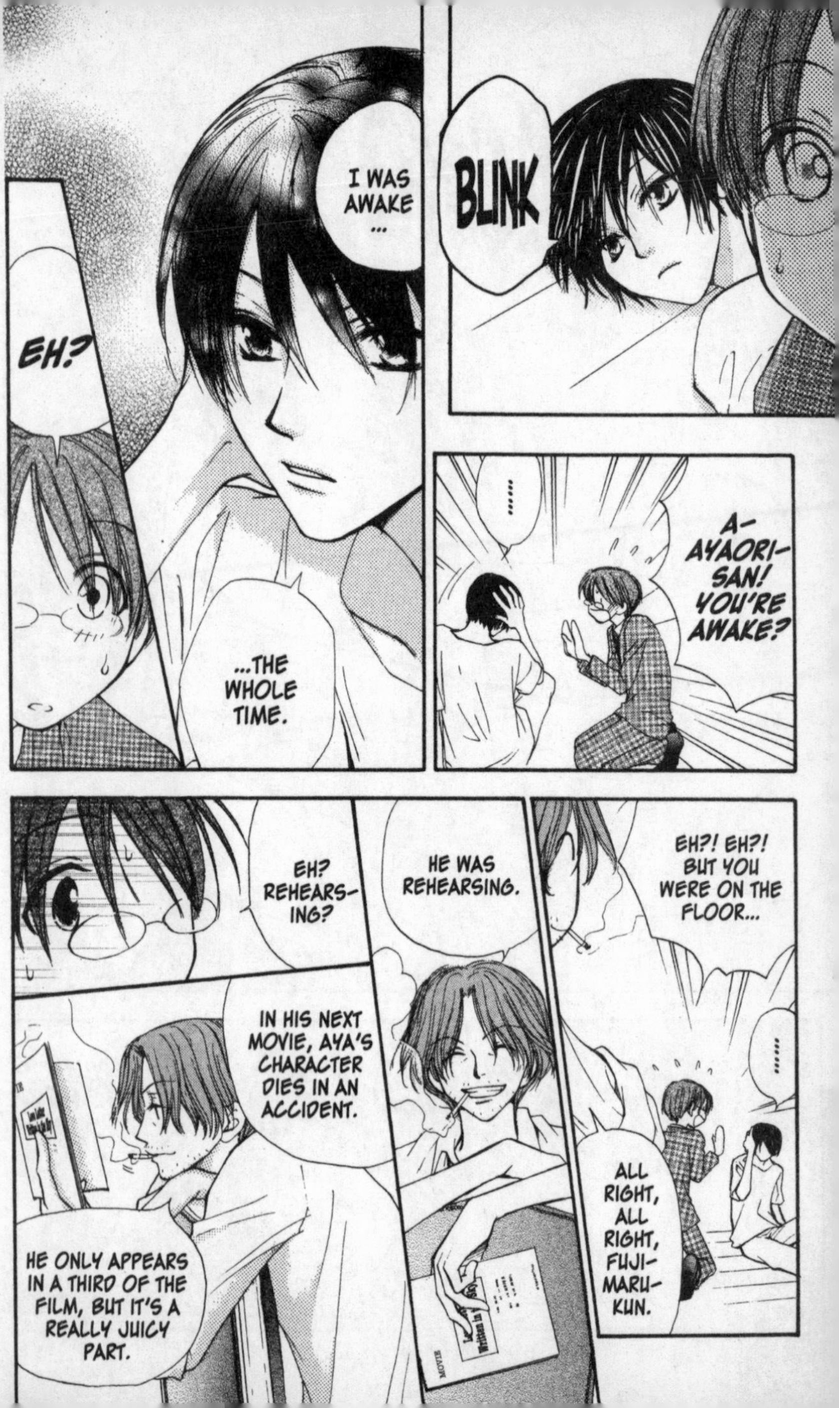
BLINK
A-AYAORI-SAN! YOU'RE AWAKE?
.....
I WAS AWAKE ...
EH?
...THE WHOLE TIME.
EH?! EH?! BUT YOU WERE ON THE FLOOR...
.....
ALL RIGHT, ALL RIGHT, FUJI-MARU-KUN.
HE WAS REHEARSING.
EH? REHEARS-ING?
IN HIS NEXT MOVIE, AYA'S CHARACTER DIES IN AN ACCIDENT.
HE ONLY APPEARS IN A THIRD OF THE FILM, BUT IT'S A REALLY JUICY PART.

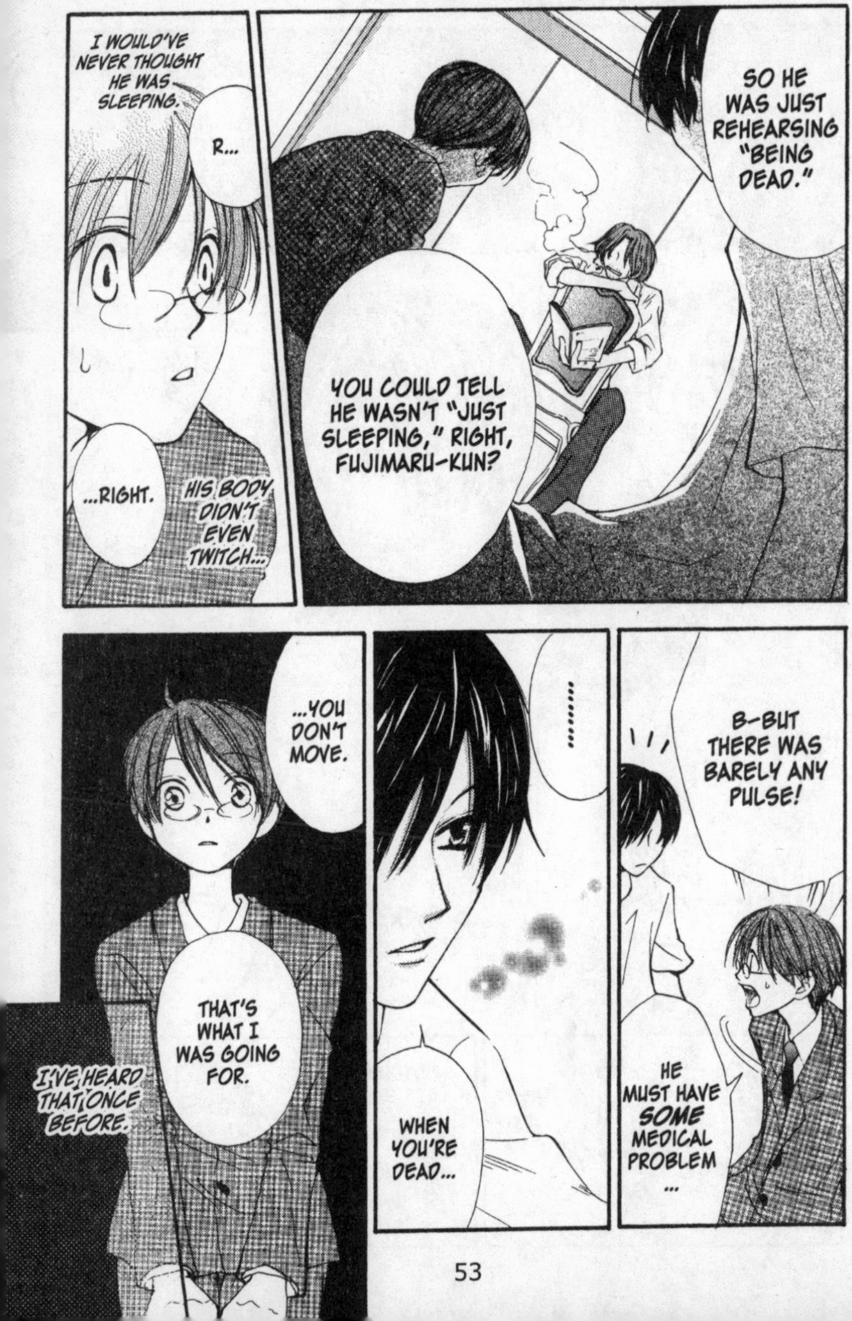
SO HE WAS JUST REHEARSING "BEING DEAD."
YOU COULD TELL HE WASN'T "JUST SLEEPING," RIGHT, FUJIMARU-KUN?
I WOULD'VE NEVER THOUGHT HE WAS SLEEPING.
R...
...RIGHT.
HIS BODY DIDN'T EVEN TWITCH...
B-BUT THERE WAS BARELY ANY PULSE!
HE MUST HAVE *SOME* MEDICAL PROBLEM ...
......
WHEN YOU'RE DEAD...
...YOU DON'T MOVE.
THAT'S WHAT I WAS GOING FOR.
I'VE HEARD THAT ONCE BEFORE.

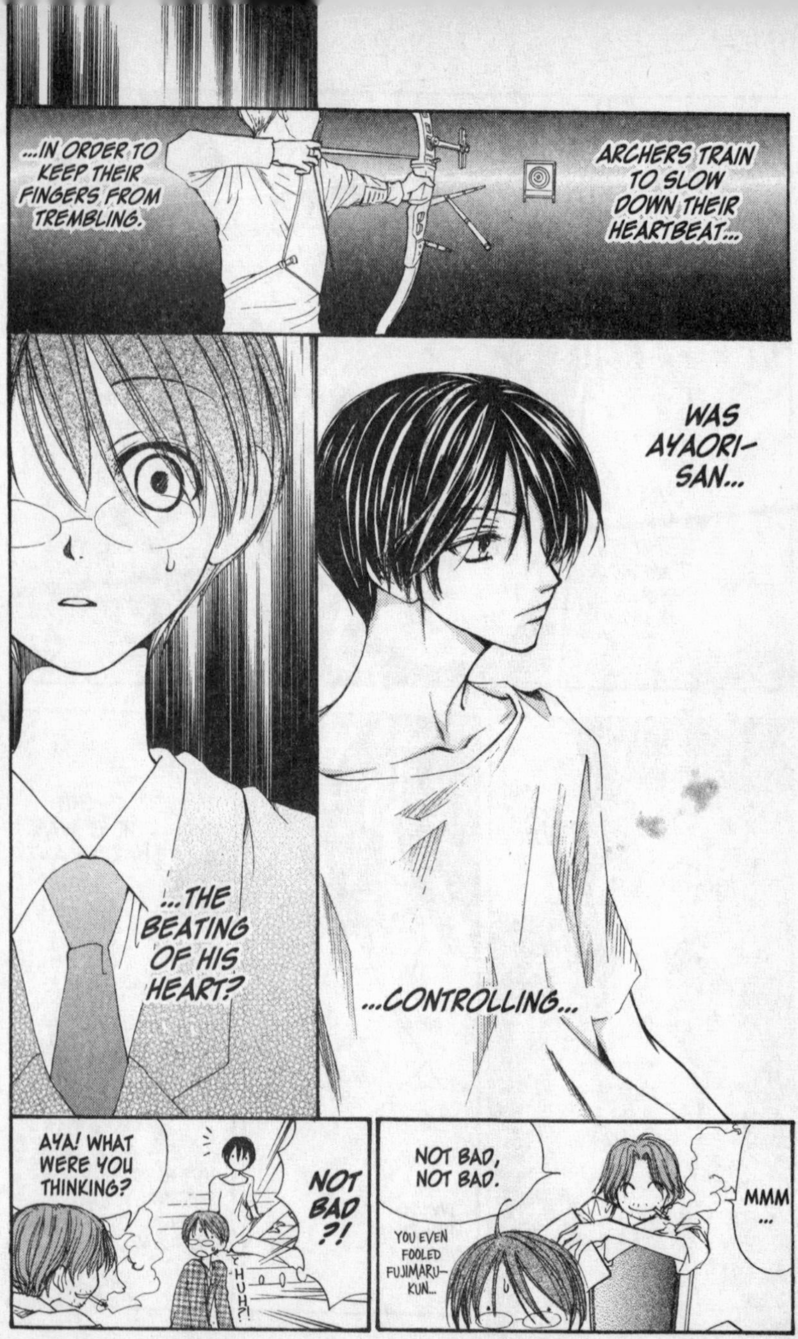
ARCHERS TRAIN TO SLOW DOWN THEIR HEARTBEAT...
...IN ORDER TO KEEP THEIR FINGERS FROM TREMBLING.
WAS AYAORI-SAN...
...CONTROLLING...
...THE BEATING OF HIS HEART?
MMM...
NOT BAD, NOT BAD.
YOU EVEN FOOLED FUJIMARU-KUN...
NOT BAD ?!
AYA! WHAT WERE YOU THINKING?
HUH?!

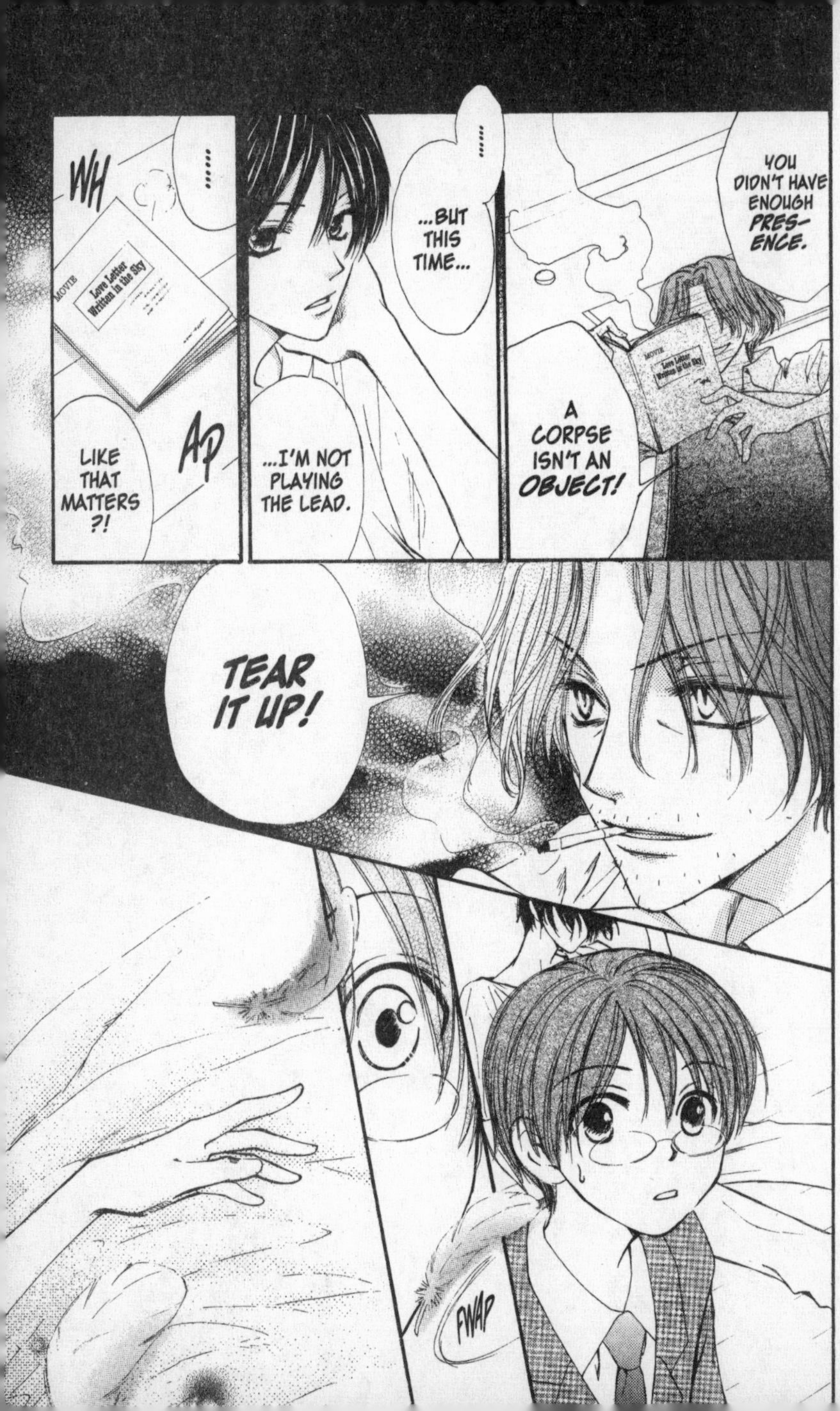

YOU DIDN'T HAVE ENOUGH PRESENCE.
A CORPSE ISN'T AN OBJECT!
MOVIE
Love Letter Written in the Sky
......
...BUT THIS TIME...
...I'M NOT PLAYING THE LEAD.
......
WH
MOVIE
Love Letter Written in the Sky
LIKE THAT MATTERS?!
AP
TEAR IT UP!
FWAP

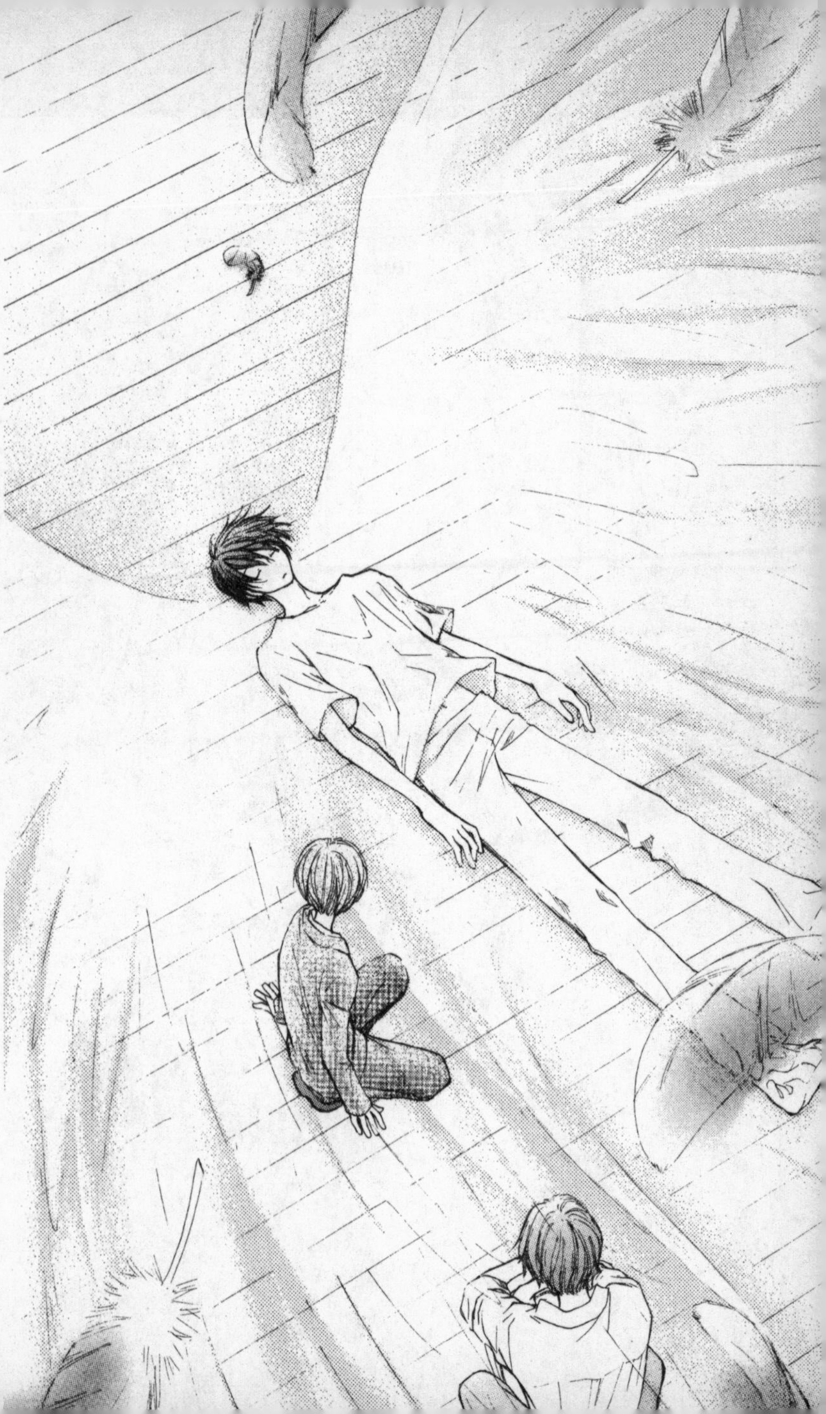

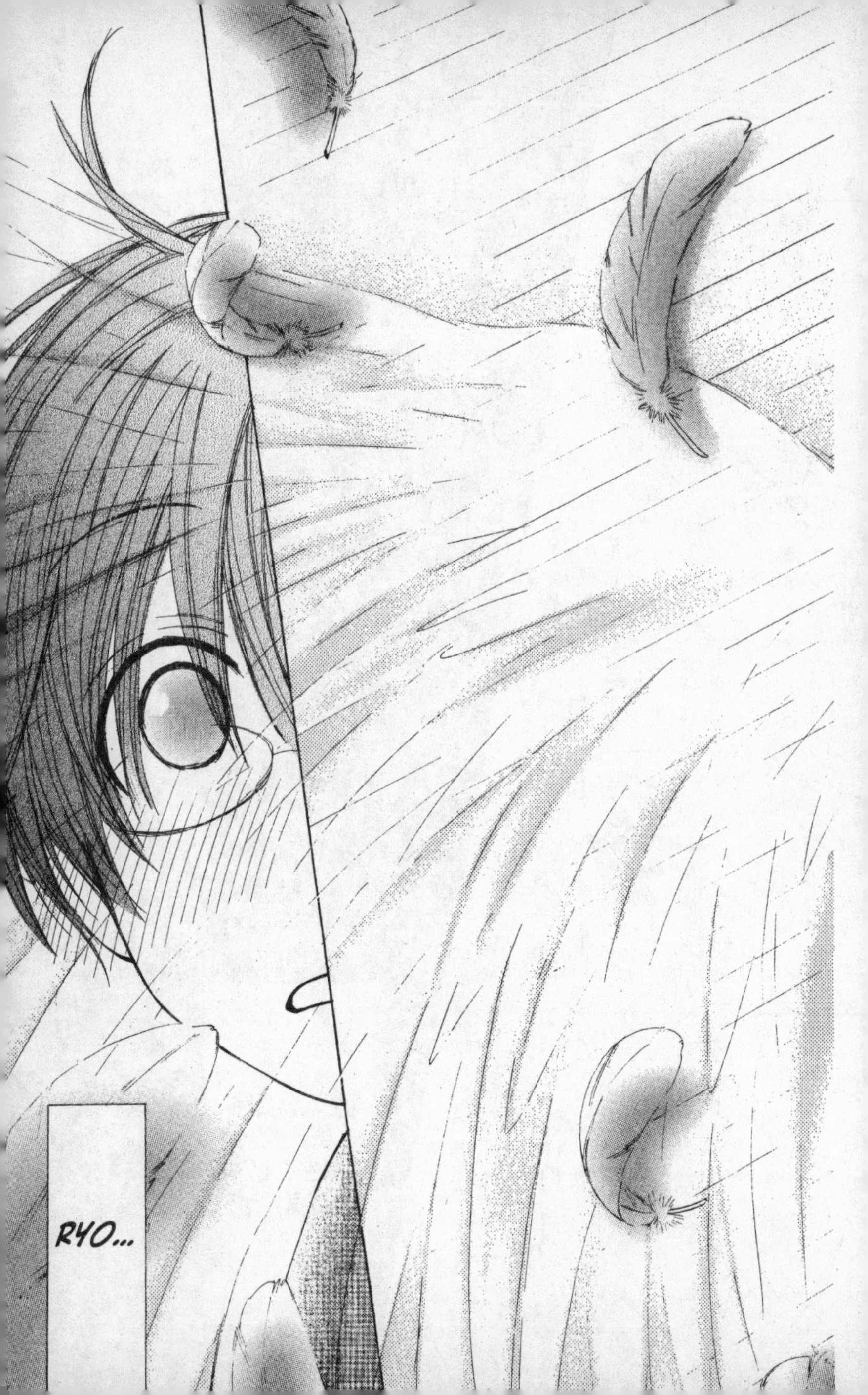
RYO...

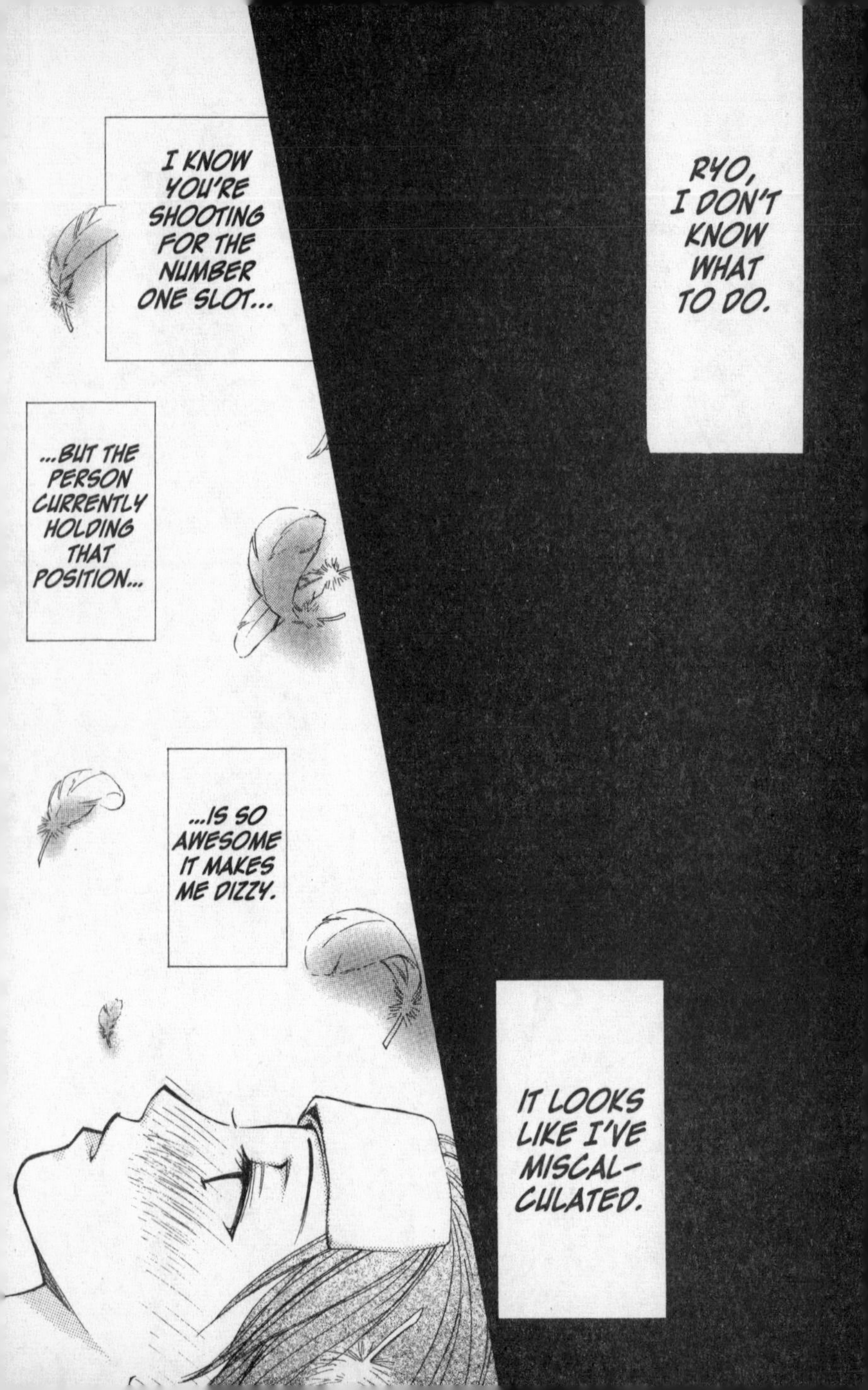
RYO, I DON'T KNOW WHAT TO DO.
I KNOW YOU'RE SHOOTING FOR THE NUMBER ONE SLOT...
...BUT THE PERSON CURRENTLY HOLDING THAT POSITION...
...IS SO AWESOME IT MAKES ME DIZZY.
IT LOOKS LIKE I'VE MISCAL-CULATED.

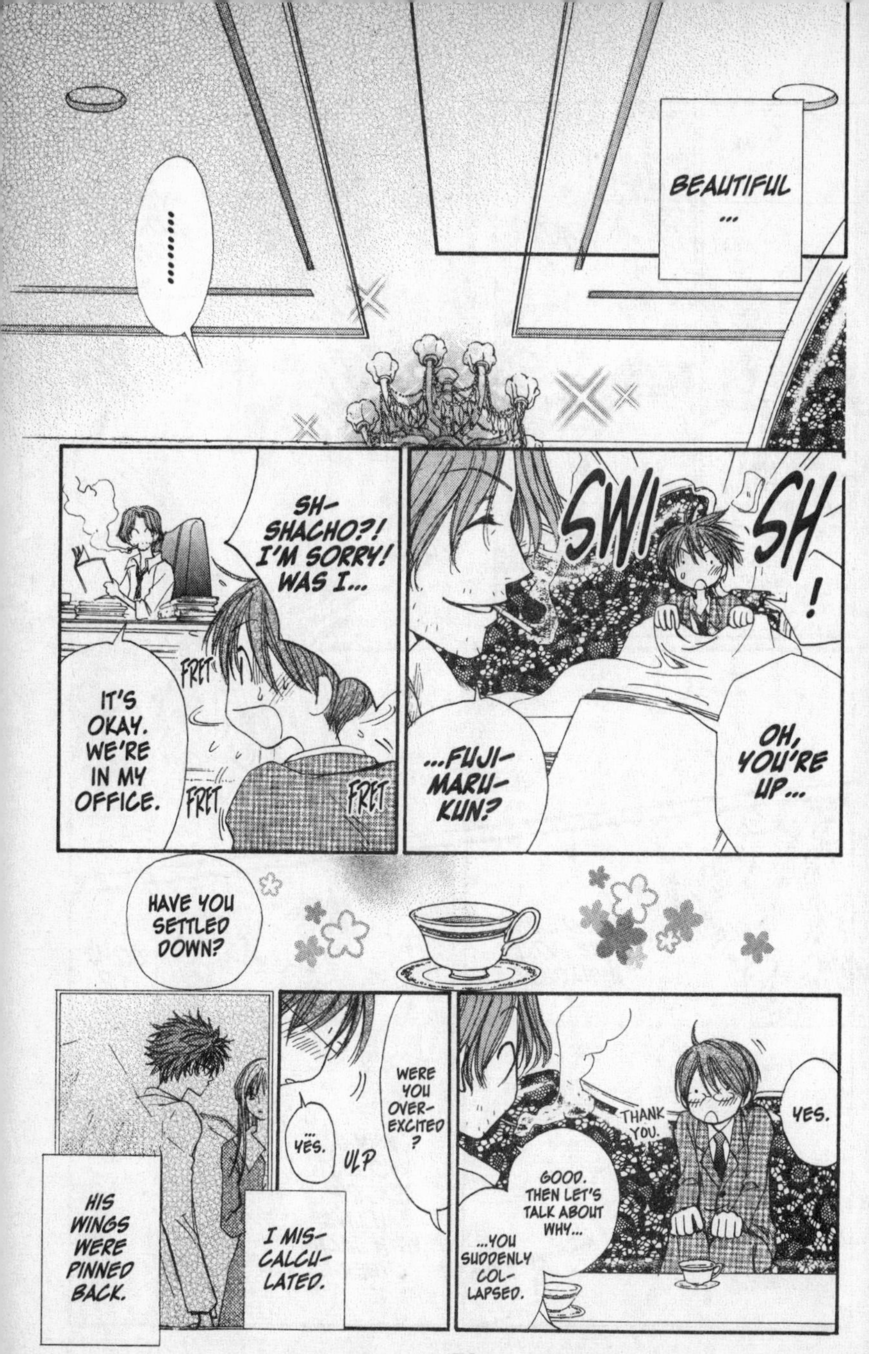
BEAUTIFUL ...
......
SWISH !
OH, YOU'RE UP...
...FUJI-MARU-KUN?
SH-SHACHO?! I'M SORRY! WAS I...
FRET
FRET
FRET
IT'S OKAY. WE'RE IN MY OFFICE.
HAVE YOU SETTLED DOWN?
YES.
THANK YOU.
GOOD. THEN LET'S TALK ABOUT WHY...
...YOU SUDDENLY COL-LAPSED.
WERE YOU OVER-EXCITED?
... YES.
ULP
I MIS-CALCU-LATED.
HIS WINGS WERE PINNED BACK.

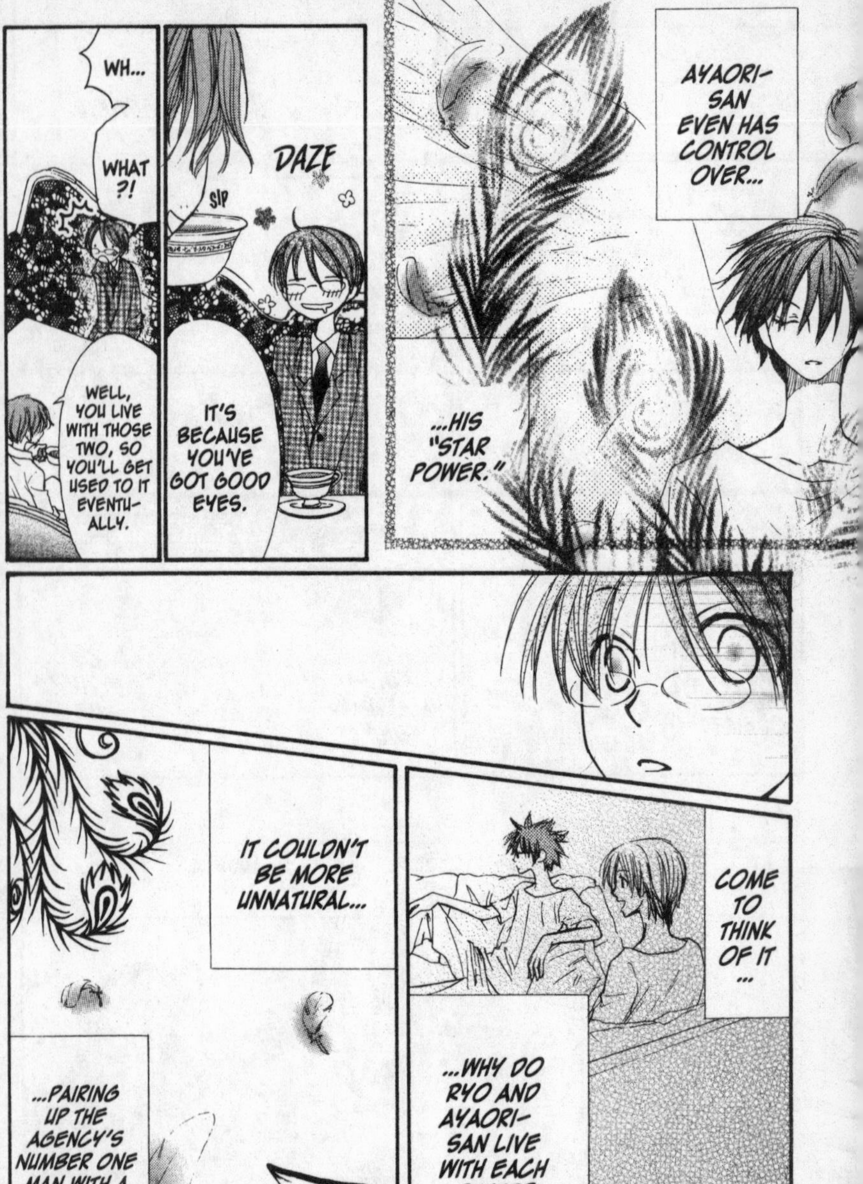
AYAORI-SAN EVEN HAS CONTROL OVER...
...HIS "STAR POWER."
DAZE
SIP
IT'S BECAUSE YOU'VE GOT GOOD EYES.
WH...
WHAT ?!
WELL, YOU LIVE WITH THOSE TWO, SO YOU'LL GET USED TO IT EVENTU-ALLY.
COME TO THINK OF IT ...
...WHY DO RYO AND AYAORI-SAN LIVE WITH EACH OTHER?
IT COULDN'T BE MORE UNNATURAL...
...PAIRING UP THE AGENCY'S NUMBER ONE MAN WITH A "PENGUIN."

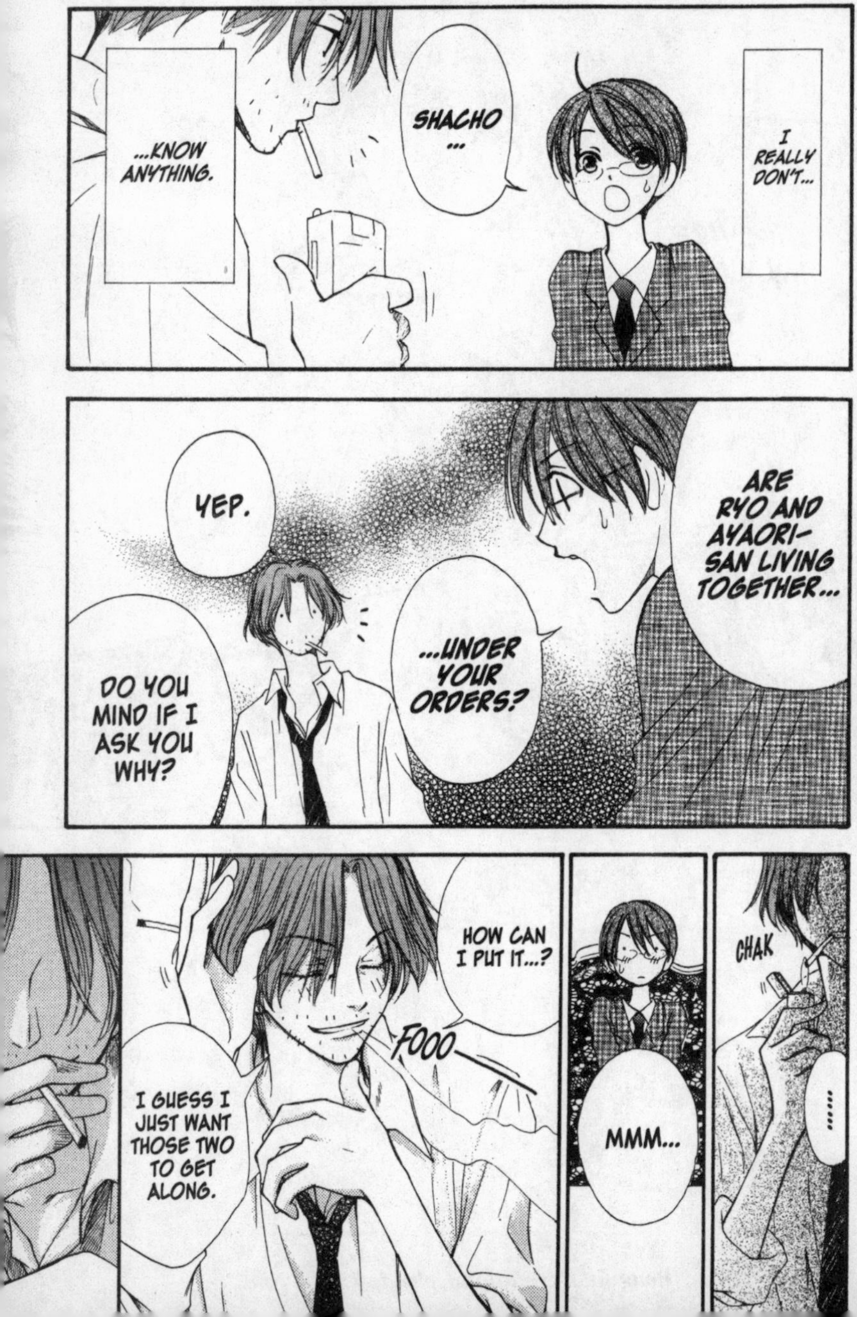
I REALLY DON'T...
SHACHO ...
...KNOW ANYTHING.
ARE RYO AND AYAORI-SAN LIVING TOGETHER...
...UNDER YOUR ORDERS?
YEP.
DO YOU MIND IF I ASK YOU WHY?
CHAK
......
MMM...
HOW CAN I PUT IT...?
FOOO
I GUESS I JUST WANT THOSE TWO TO GET ALONG.

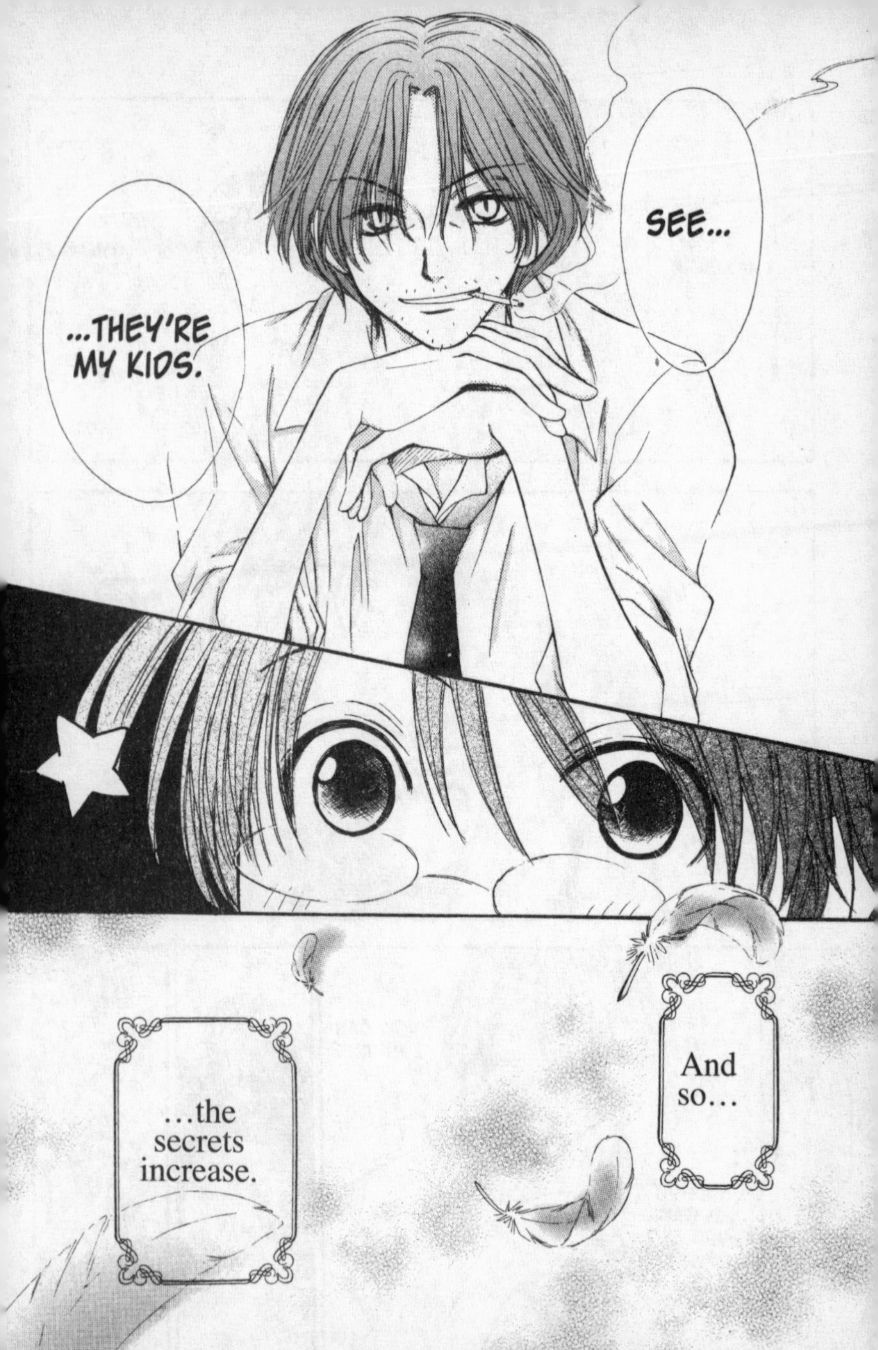
SEE...
...THEY'RE MY KIDS.
And so…
…the secrets increase.

Penguin Revolution Episode 7: The End

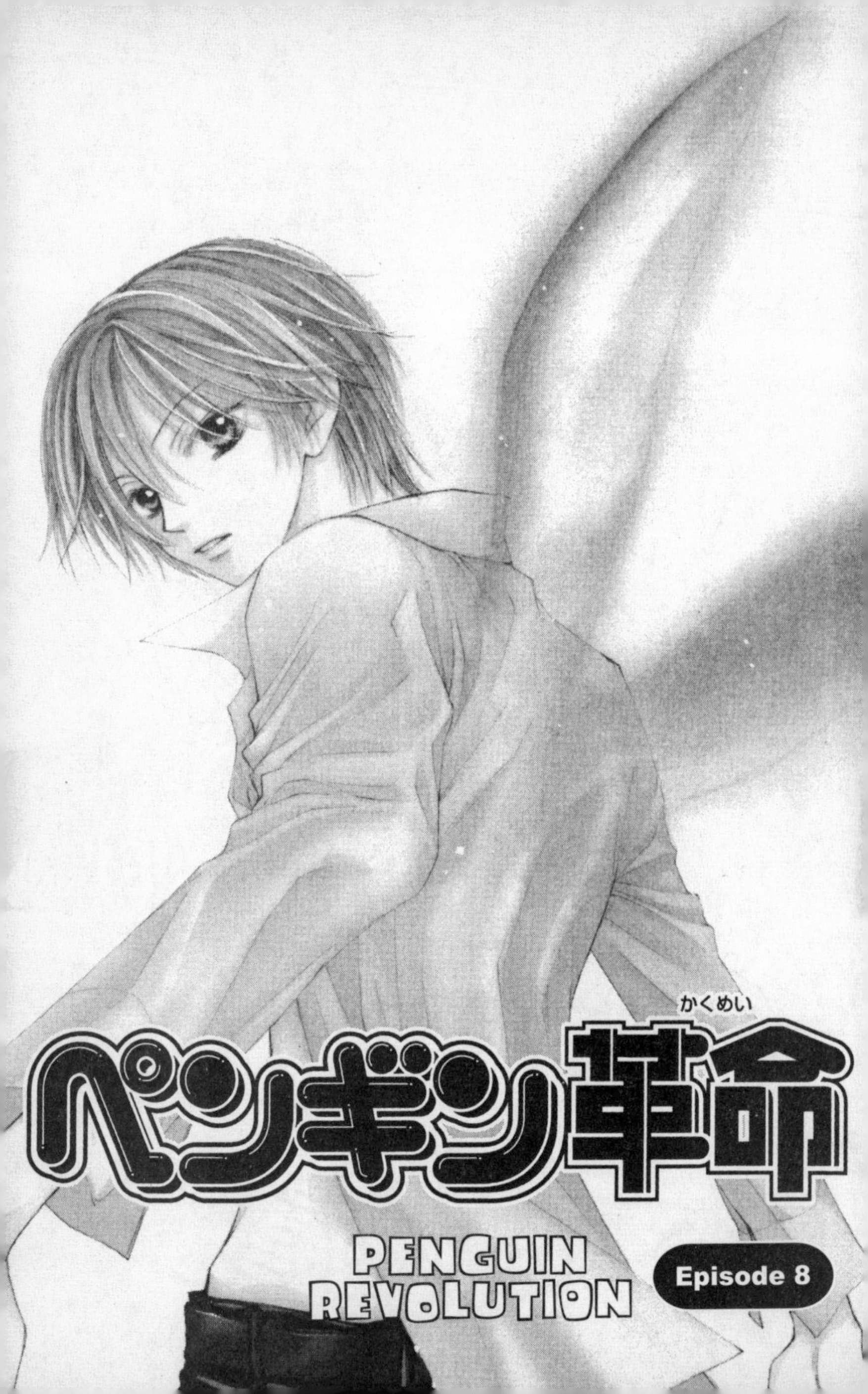
かくめい
ペンギン革命
PENGUIN
REVOLUTION
Episode 8

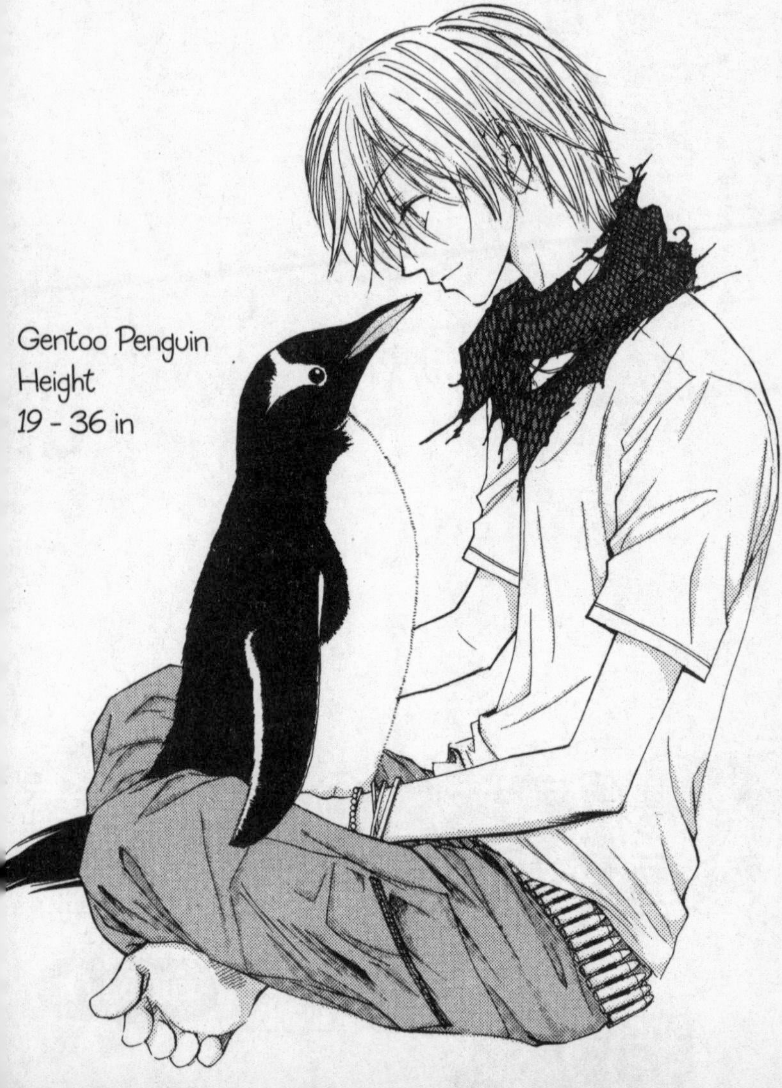
Ryo Katsuragi
Height
5 ft 9 in
Gentoo Penguin
Height
19 - 36 in

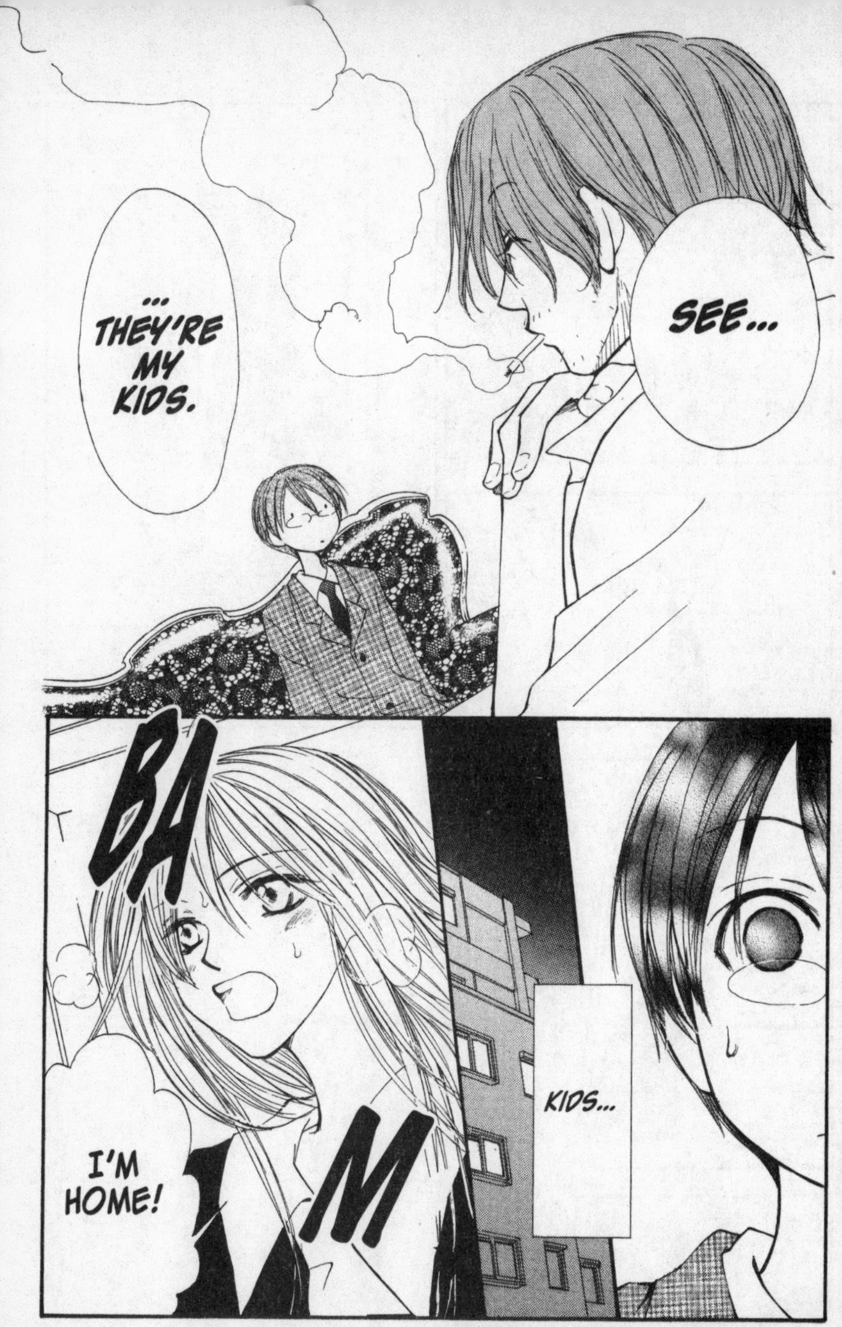
SEE...
...THEY'RE MY KIDS.
KIDS...
BAM
I'M HOME!

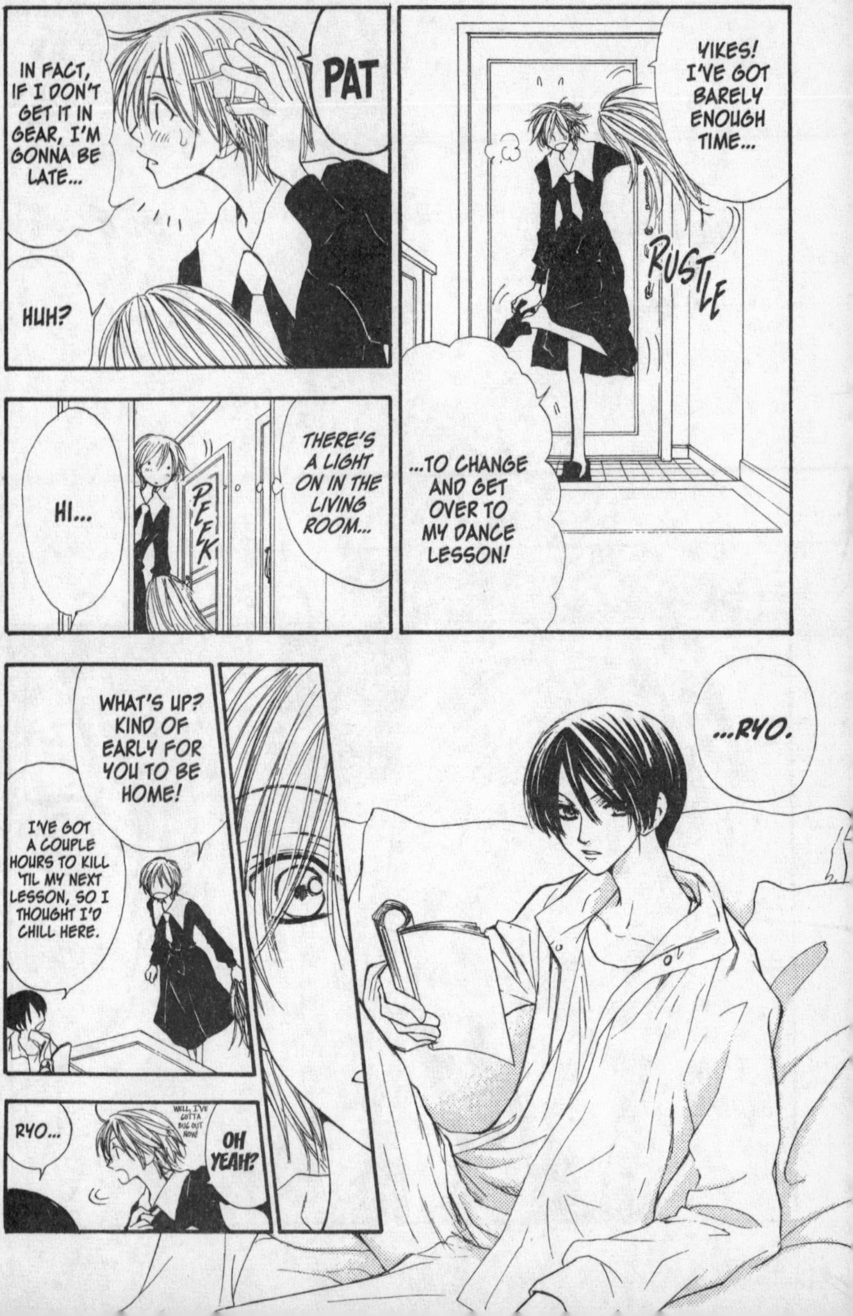

YIKES! I'VE GOT BARELY ENOUGH TIME...
RUSTLE
...TO CHANGE AND GET OVER TO MY DANCE LESSON!
PAT
IN FACT, IF I DON'T GET IT IN GEAR, I'M GONNA BE LATE...
HUH?
THERE'S A LIGHT ON IN THE LIVING ROOM...
PEEK
HI...
...RYO.
WHAT'S UP? KIND OF EARLY FOR YOU TO BE HOME!
I'VE GOT A COUPLE HOURS TO KILL 'TIL MY NEXT LESSON, SO I THOUGHT I'D CHILL HERE.
OH YEAH?
WELL, I'VE GOTTA BUG OUT NOW!
RYO...

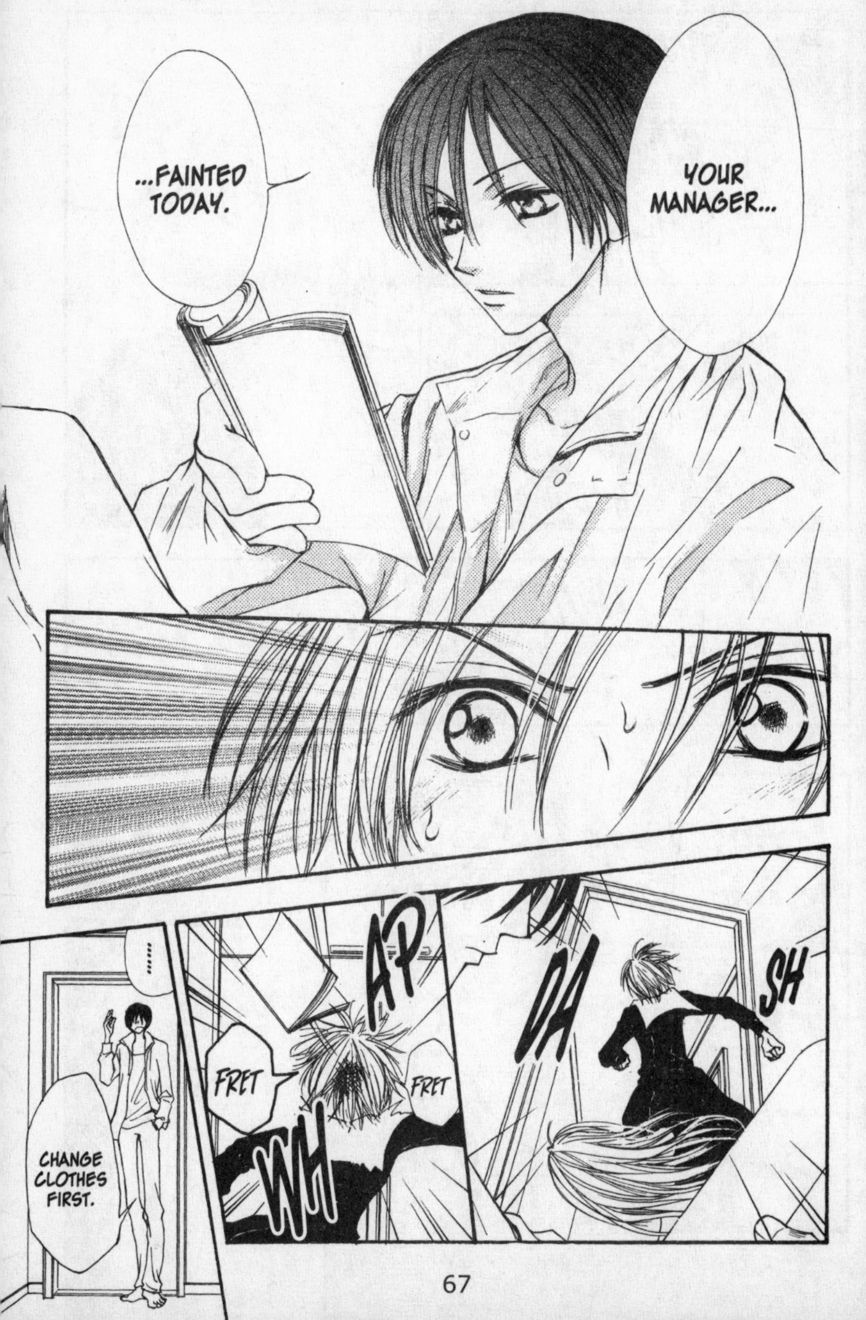
YOUR MANAGER...
...FAINTED TODAY.
SH
DA
AP
FRET
FRET
WH
......
CHANGE CLOTHES FIRST.

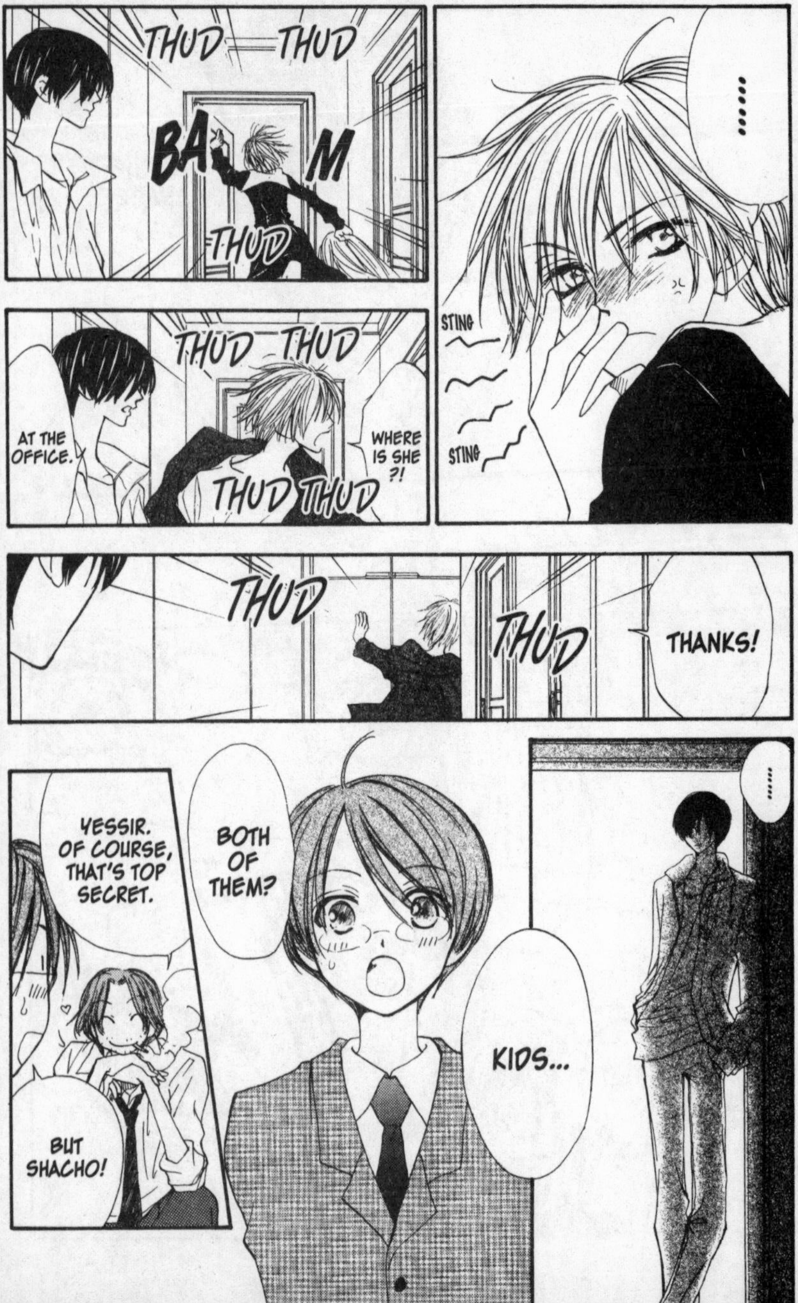
......
STING
STING
THUD THUD
BAM
THUD
WHERE IS SHE ?!
THUD THUD
AT THE OFFICE.
THUD THUD
THANKS!
THUD
THUD
......
BOTH OF THEM?
KIDS...
YESSIR. OF COURSE, THAT'S TOP SECRET.
BUT SHACHO!

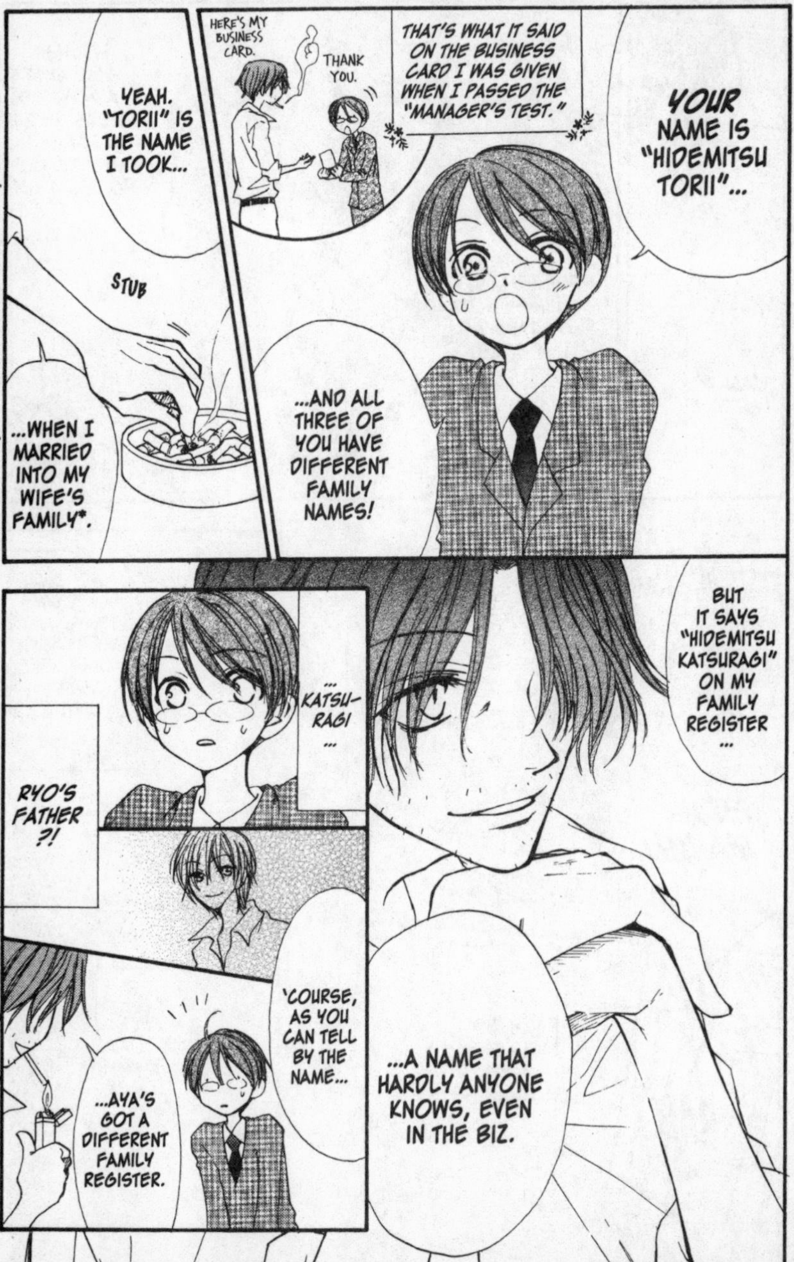
YOUR NAME IS "HIDEMITSU TORII"...
THAT'S WHAT IT SAID ON THE BUSINESS CARD I WAS GIVEN WHEN I PASSED THE "MANAGER'S TEST."
HERE'S MY BUSINESS CARD.
THANK YOU.
...AND ALL THREE OF YOU HAVE DIFFERENT FAMILY NAMES!
YEAH. "TORII" IS THE NAME I TOOK...
STUB
...WHEN I MARRIED INTO MY WIFE'S FAMILY*.
BUT IT SAYS "HIDEMITSU KATSURAGI" ON MY FAMILY REGISTER...
...A NAME THAT HARDLY ANYONE KNOWS, EVEN IN THE BIZ.
...KATSURAGI...
RYO'S FATHER?!
'COURSE, AS YOU CAN TELL BY THE NAME...
...AYA'S GOT A DIFFERENT FAMILY REGISTER.

*referring to the now uncommon practice in which a husband takes on his wife's family name in order to ensure that the family line lives on.

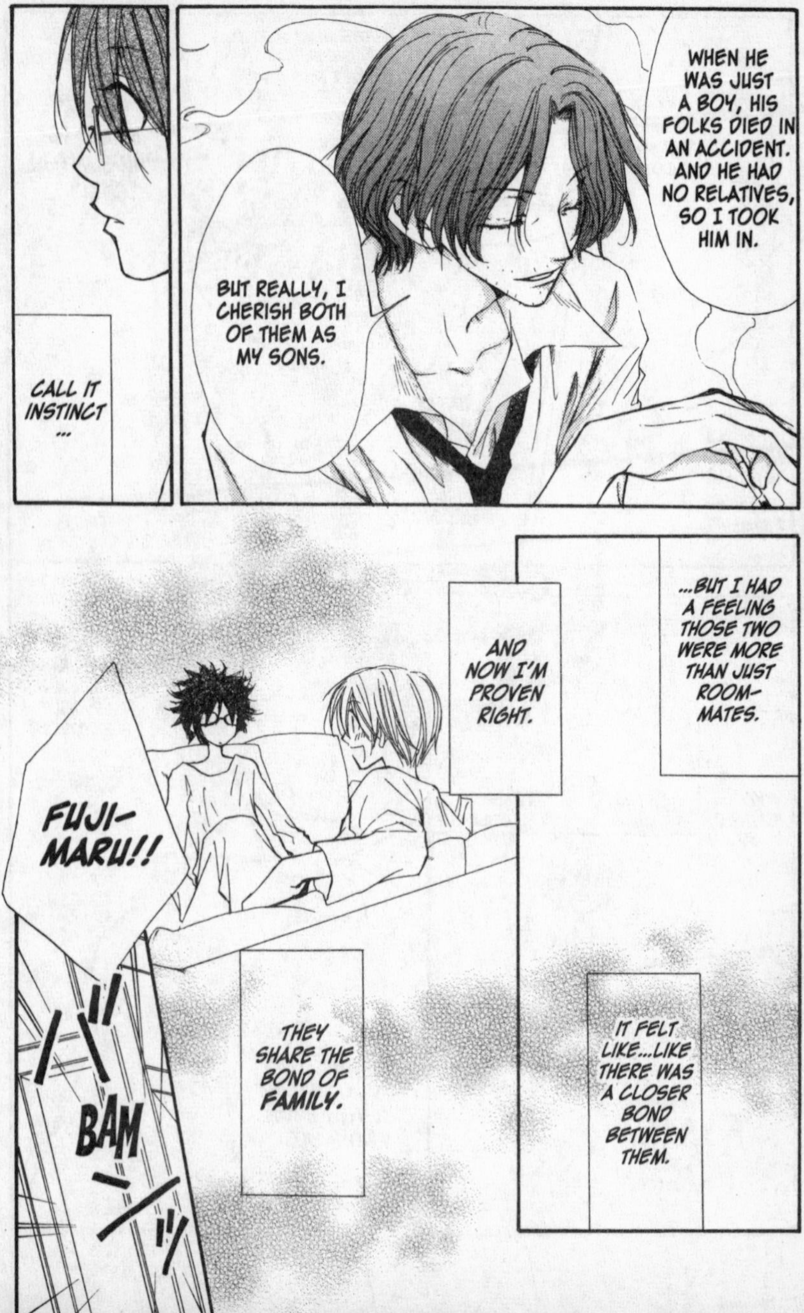
WHEN HE WAS JUST A BOY, HIS FOLKS DIED IN AN ACCIDENT. AND HE HAD NO RELATIVES, SO I TOOK HIM IN.
BUT REALLY, I CHERISH BOTH OF THEM AS MY SONS.
CALL IT INSTINCT ...
...BUT I HAD A FEELING THOSE TWO WERE MORE THAN JUST ROOM-MATES.
IT FELT LIKE...LIKE THERE WAS A CLOSER BOND BETWEEN THEM.
AND NOW I'M PROVEN RIGHT.
THEY SHARE THE BOND OF FAMILY.
FUJI-MARU!!
BAM

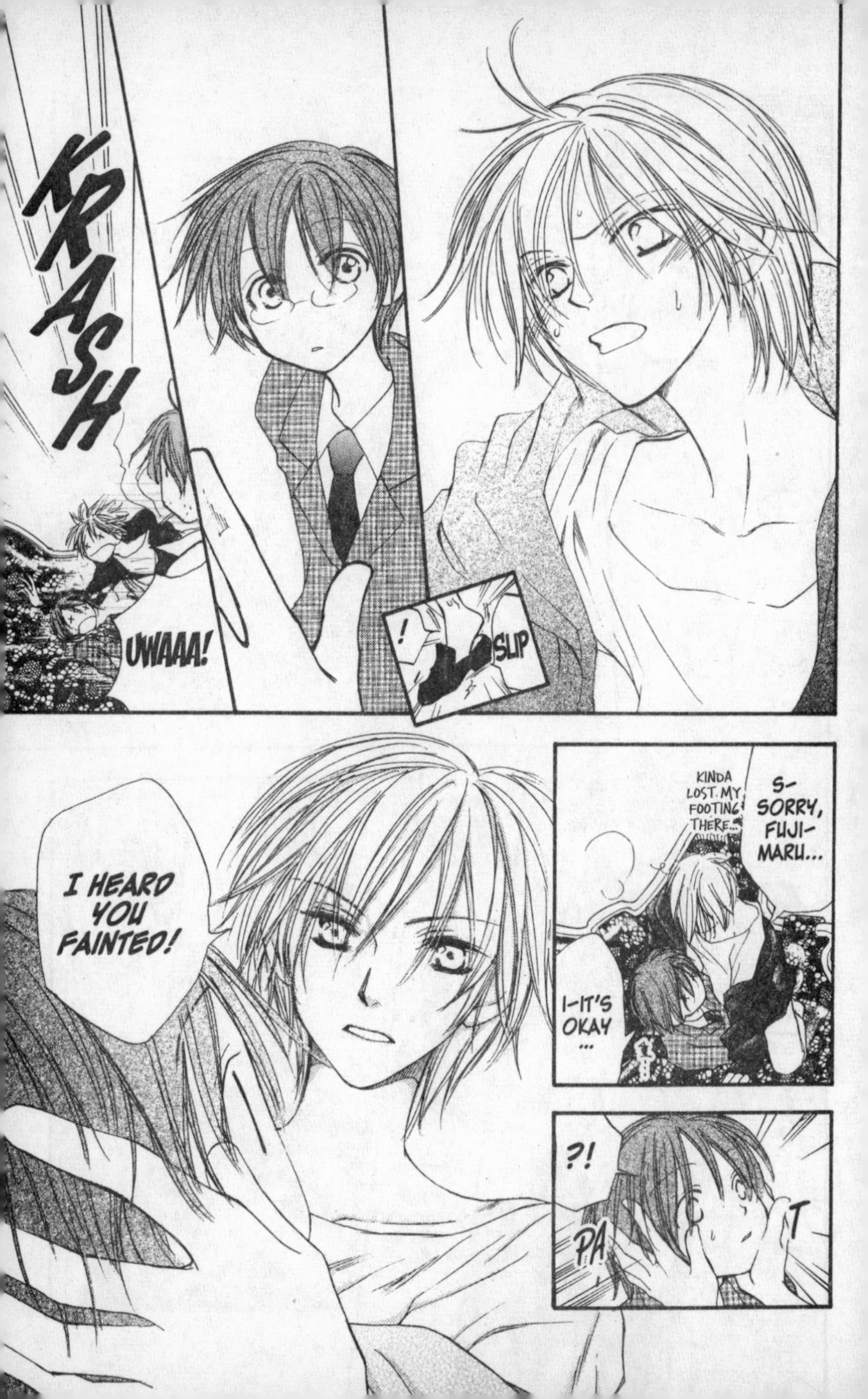
!
SLIP
KRASH
UWAAA!
S-SORRY, FUJI-MARU...
KINDA LOST MY FOOTING THERE...
I-IT'S OKAY ...
?!
PAT
I HEARD YOU FAINTED!

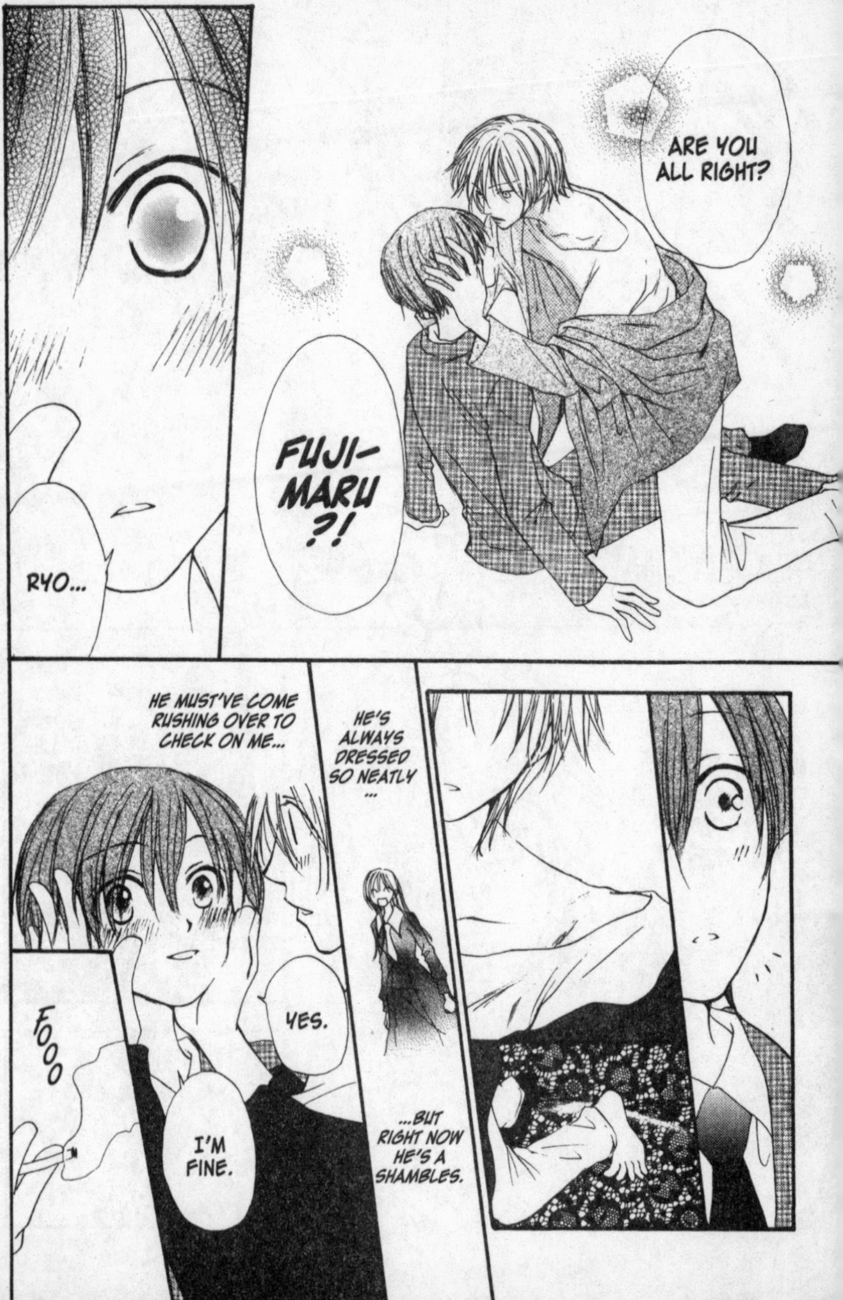
ARE YOU ALL RIGHT?
FUJI-MARU?!
RYO...
HE'S ALWAYS DRESSED SO NEATLY ...
...BUT RIGHT NOW HE'S A SHAMBLES.
HE MUST'VE COME RUSHING OVER TO CHECK ON ME...
YES.
I'M FINE.
FOOOO

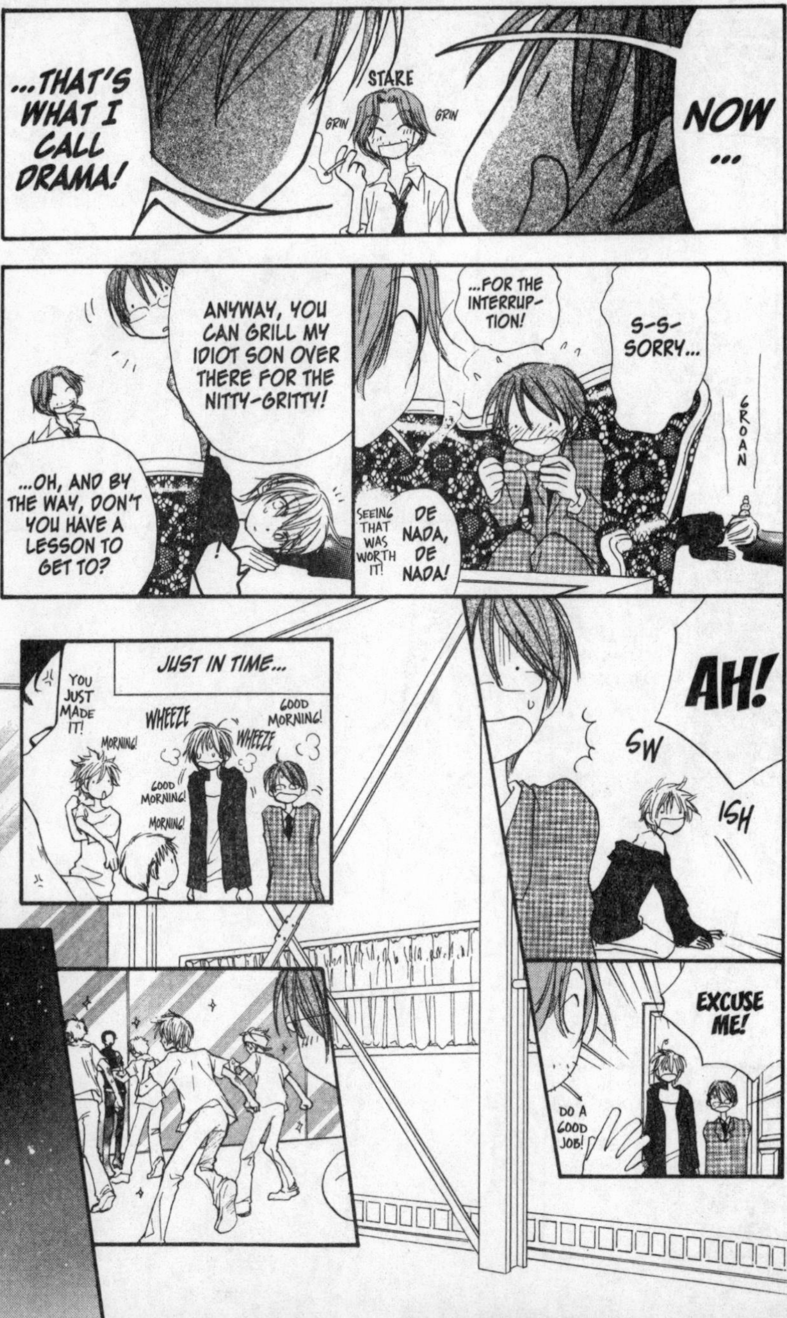
NOW ...
STARE
GRIN
GRIN
...THAT'S WHAT I CALL DRAMA!
S-S-SORRY...
...FOR THE INTERRUPTION!
GROAN
DE NADA, DE NADA!
SEEING THAT WAS WORTH IT!
ANYWAY, YOU CAN GRILL MY IDIOT SON OVER THERE FOR THE NITTY-GRITTY!
...OH, AND BY THE WAY, DON'T YOU HAVE A LESSON TO GET TO?
AH!
SW
ISH
EXCUSE ME!
DO A GOOD JOB!
JUST IN TIME...
GOOD MORNING!
WHEEZE
WHEEZE
YOU JUST MADE IT!
MORNING!
GOOD MORNING!
MORNING!

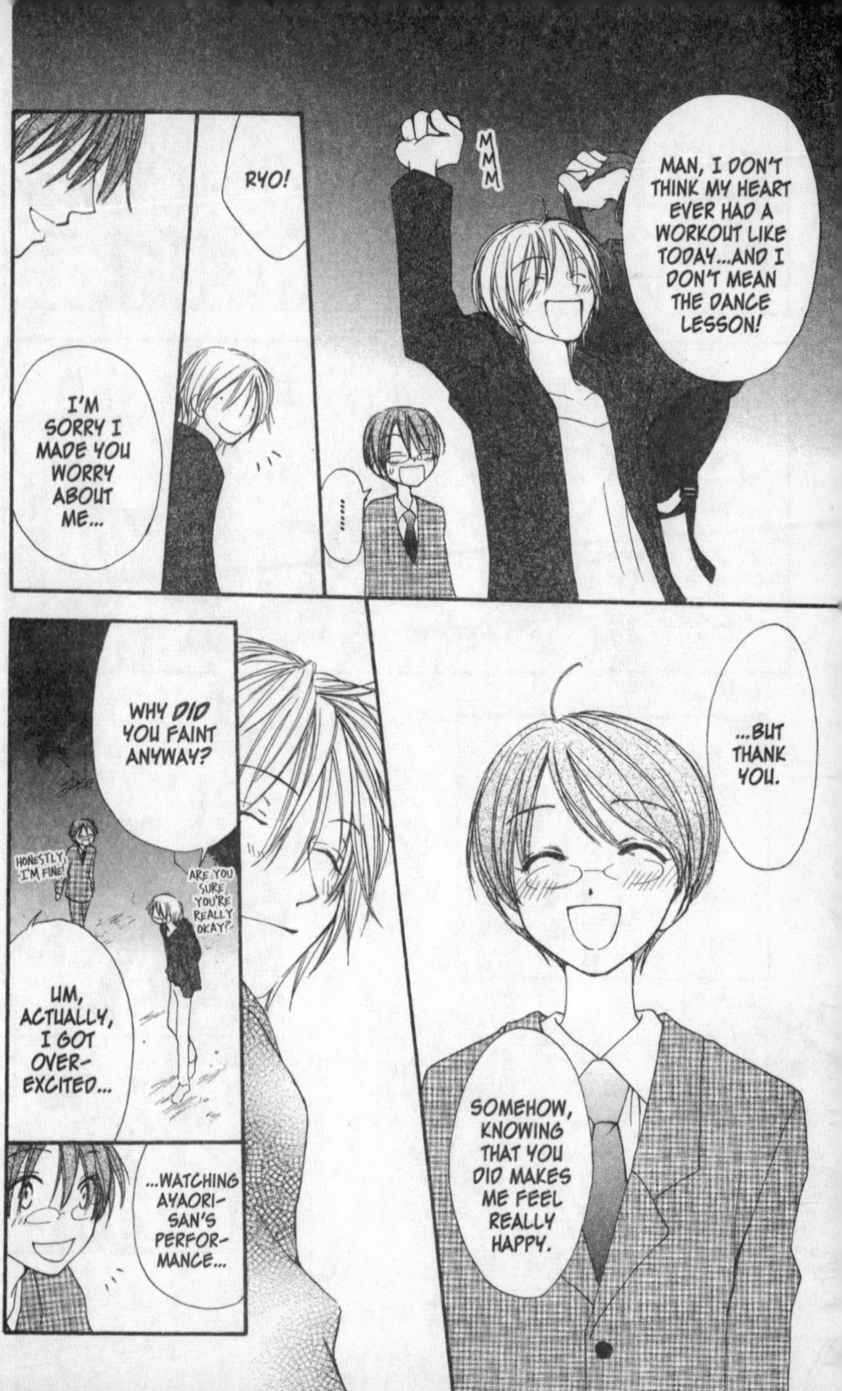
MMM
MAN, I DON'T THINK MY HEART EVER HAD A WORKOUT LIKE TODAY...AND I DON'T MEAN THE DANCE LESSON!
......
RYO!
I'M SORRY I MADE YOU WORRY ABOUT ME...
...BUT THANK YOU.
SOMEHOW, KNOWING THAT YOU DID MAKES ME FEEL REALLY HAPPY.
WHY DID YOU FAINT ANYWAY?
ARE YOU SURE YOU'RE REALLY OKAY?
HONESTLY, I'M FINE!
UM, ACTUALLY, I GOT OVER-EXCITED...
...WATCHING AYAORI-SAN'S PERFORMANCE...

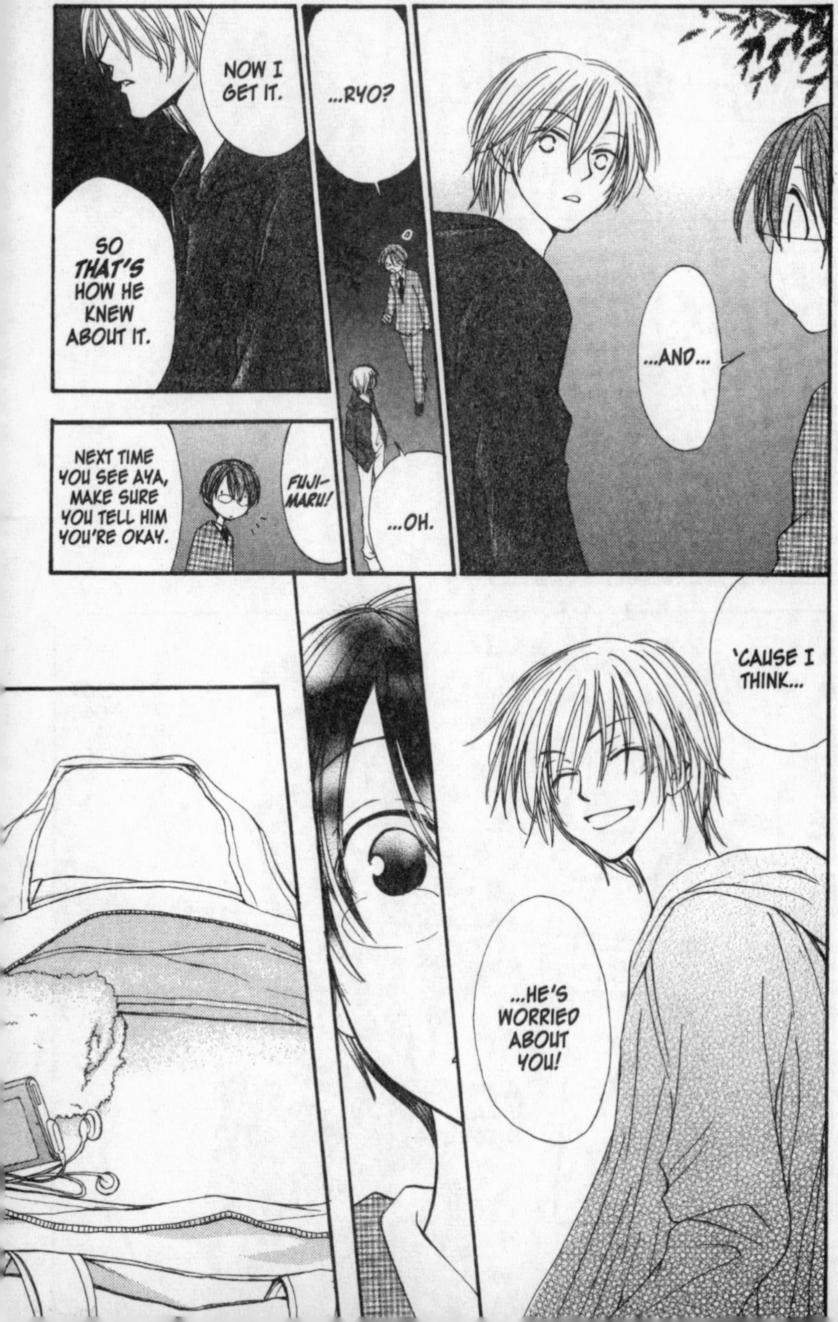
...AND...
...RYO?
FUJI-MARU!
...OH.
NOW I GET IT.
SO THAT'S HOW HE KNEW ABOUT IT.
NEXT TIME YOU SEE AYA, MAKE SURE YOU TELL HIM YOU'RE OKAY.
'CAUSE I THINK...
...HE'S WORRIED ABOUT YOU!

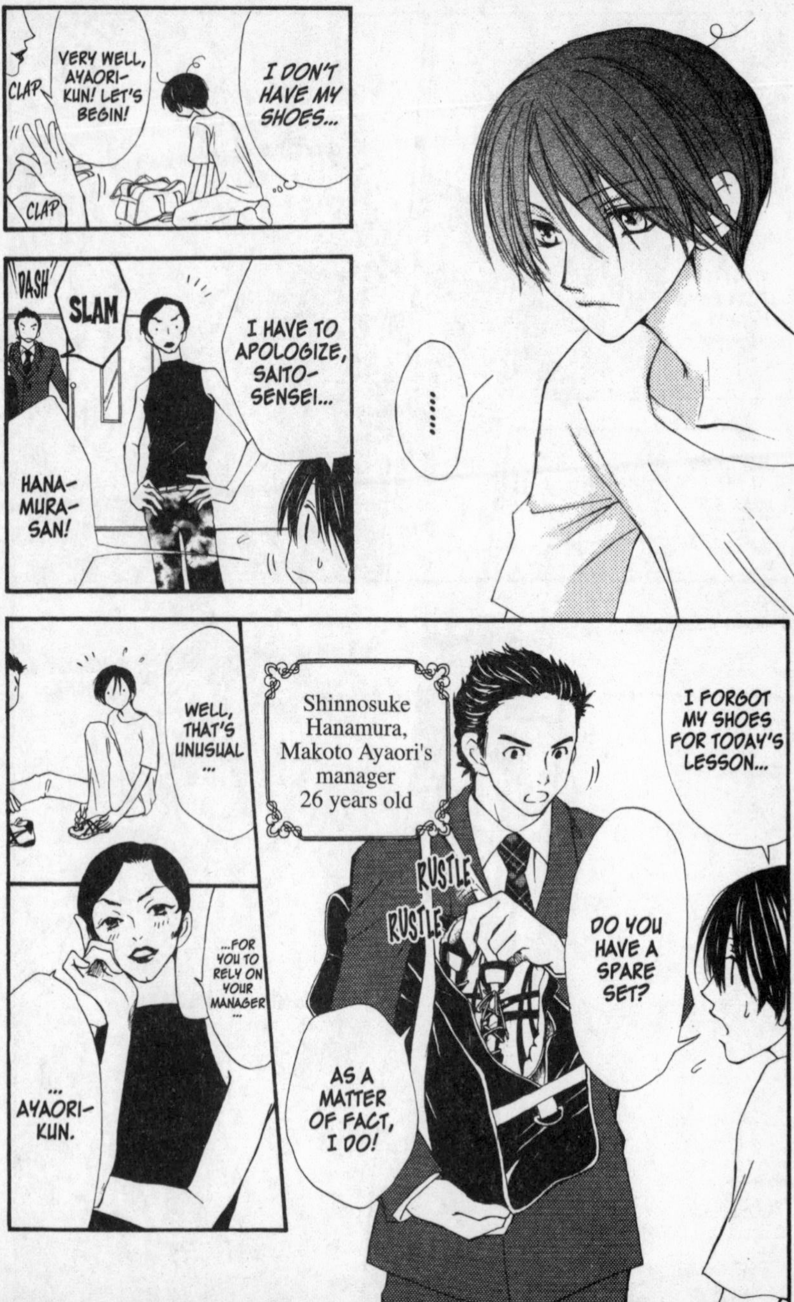
......
I DON'T HAVE MY SHOES...
VERY WELL, AYAORI-KUN! LET'S BEGIN!
CLAP
CLAP
I HAVE TO APOLOGIZE, SAITO-SENSEI...
SLAM
DASH
HANAMURA-SAN!
I FORGOT MY SHOES FOR TODAY'S LESSON...
DO YOU HAVE A SPARE SET?
Shinnosuke Hanamura, Makoto Ayaori's manager 26 years old
RUSTLE
RUSTLE
AS A MATTER OF FACT, I DO!
WELL, THAT'S UNUSUAL...
...FOR YOU TO RELY ON YOUR MANAGER...
...AYAORI-KUN.

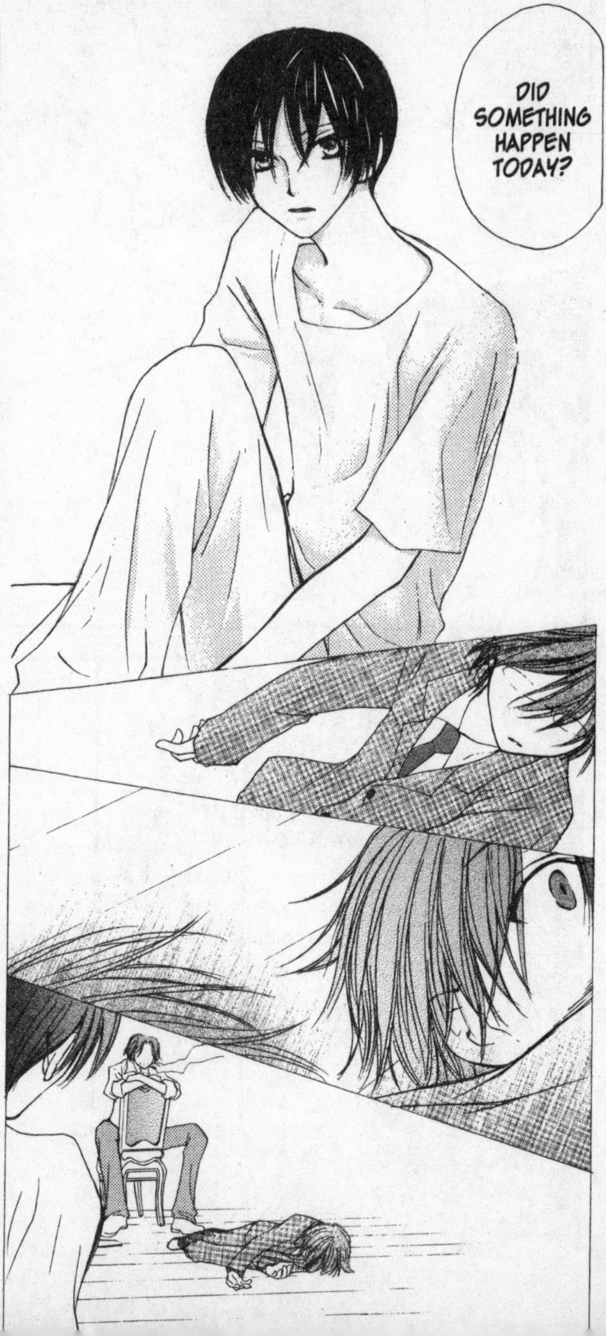
DID SOMETHING HAPPEN TODAY?

1/4 Sakura Mail

part 5

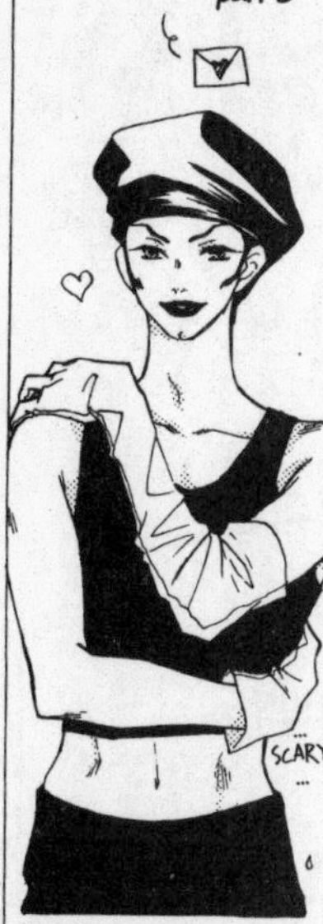
...SCARY...

In this episode, we get to see the unusual sight of "Peacock Aya" becoming unruffled. The out-of-it "school Aya" is a real part of his personality, so it doesn't look like he'd be the type to have mood swings. In fact, one glance at "Makoto Ayaori" appears to reveal a cool-headedness, a trait that many people would credit for his success at being a star. Good for you, Aya.

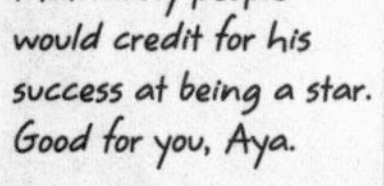
DAZ ED
HE HAS NO AWARENESS OF THIS POINT, THOUGH.

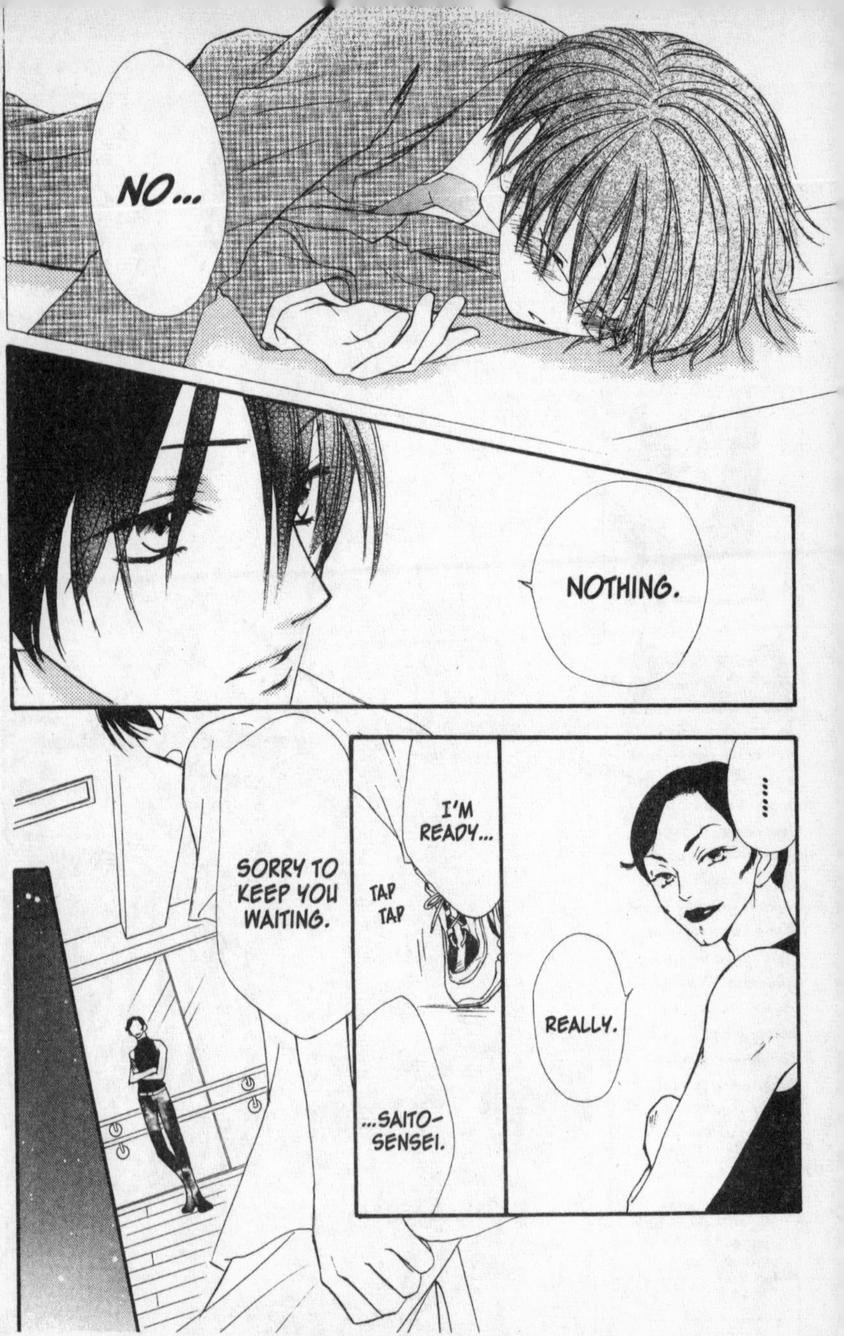
NO...
NOTHING.
......
REALLY.
I'M READY...
TAP TAP
SORRY TO KEEP YOU WAITING.
...SAITO-SENSEI.

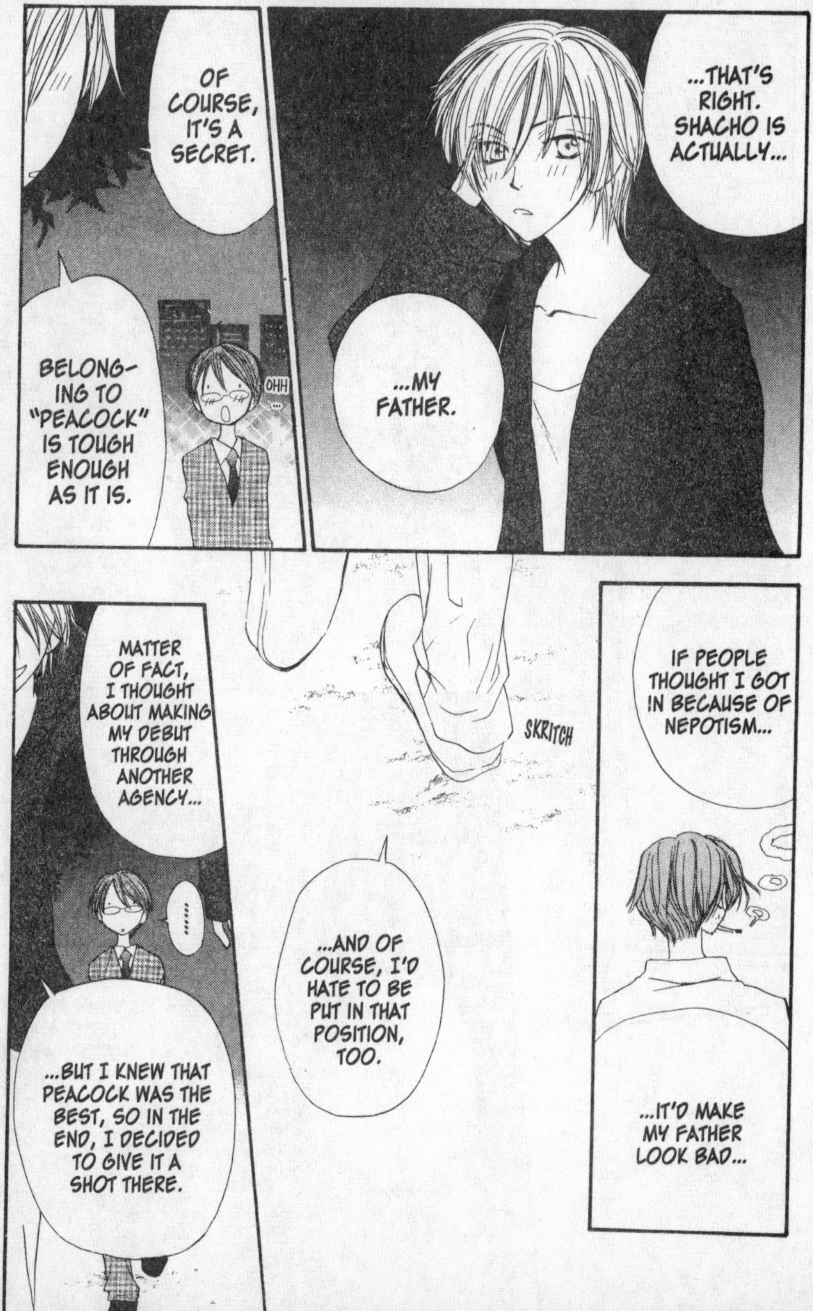
...THAT'S RIGHT. SHACHO IS ACTUALLY...
...MY FATHER.
OF COURSE, IT'S A SECRET.
OHH...
BELONG-ING TO "PEACOCK" IS TOUGH ENOUGH AS IT IS.
IF PEOPLE THOUGHT I GOT IN BECAUSE OF NEPOTISM...
...IT'D MAKE MY FATHER LOOK BAD...
SKRITCH
...AND OF COURSE, I'D HATE TO BE PUT IN THAT POSITION, TOO.
MATTER OF FACT, I THOUGHT ABOUT MAKING MY DEBUT THROUGH ANOTHER AGENCY...
......
...BUT I KNEW THAT PEACOCK WAS THE BEST, SO IN THE END, I DECIDED TO GIVE IT A SHOT THERE.

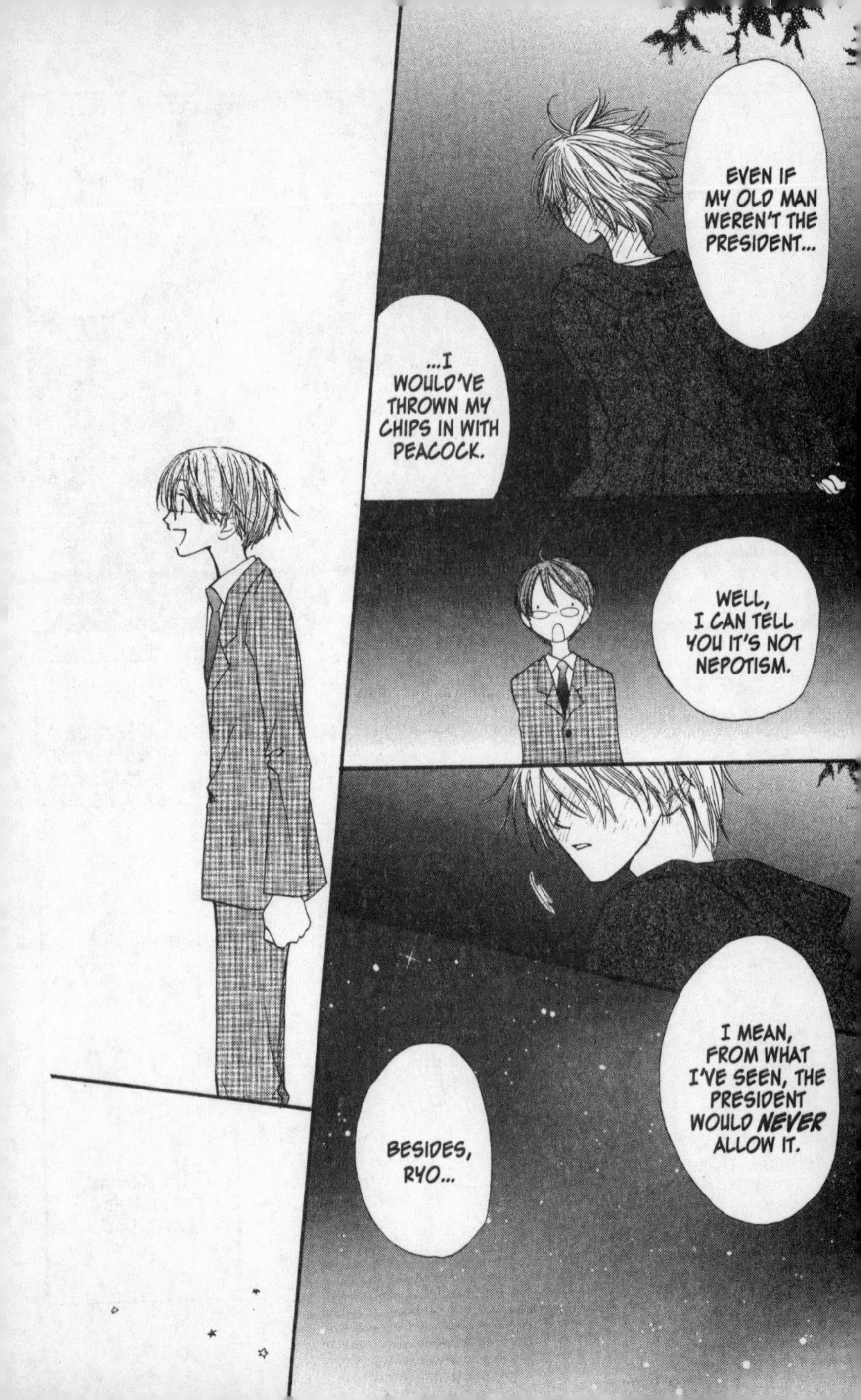
EVEN IF MY OLD MAN WEREN'T THE PRESIDENT...
...I WOULD'VE THROWN MY CHIPS IN WITH PEACOCK.
WELL, I CAN TELL YOU IT'S NOT NEPOTISM.
I MEAN, FROM WHAT I'VE SEEN, THE PRESIDENT WOULD **NEVER** ALLOW IT.
BESIDES, RYO...

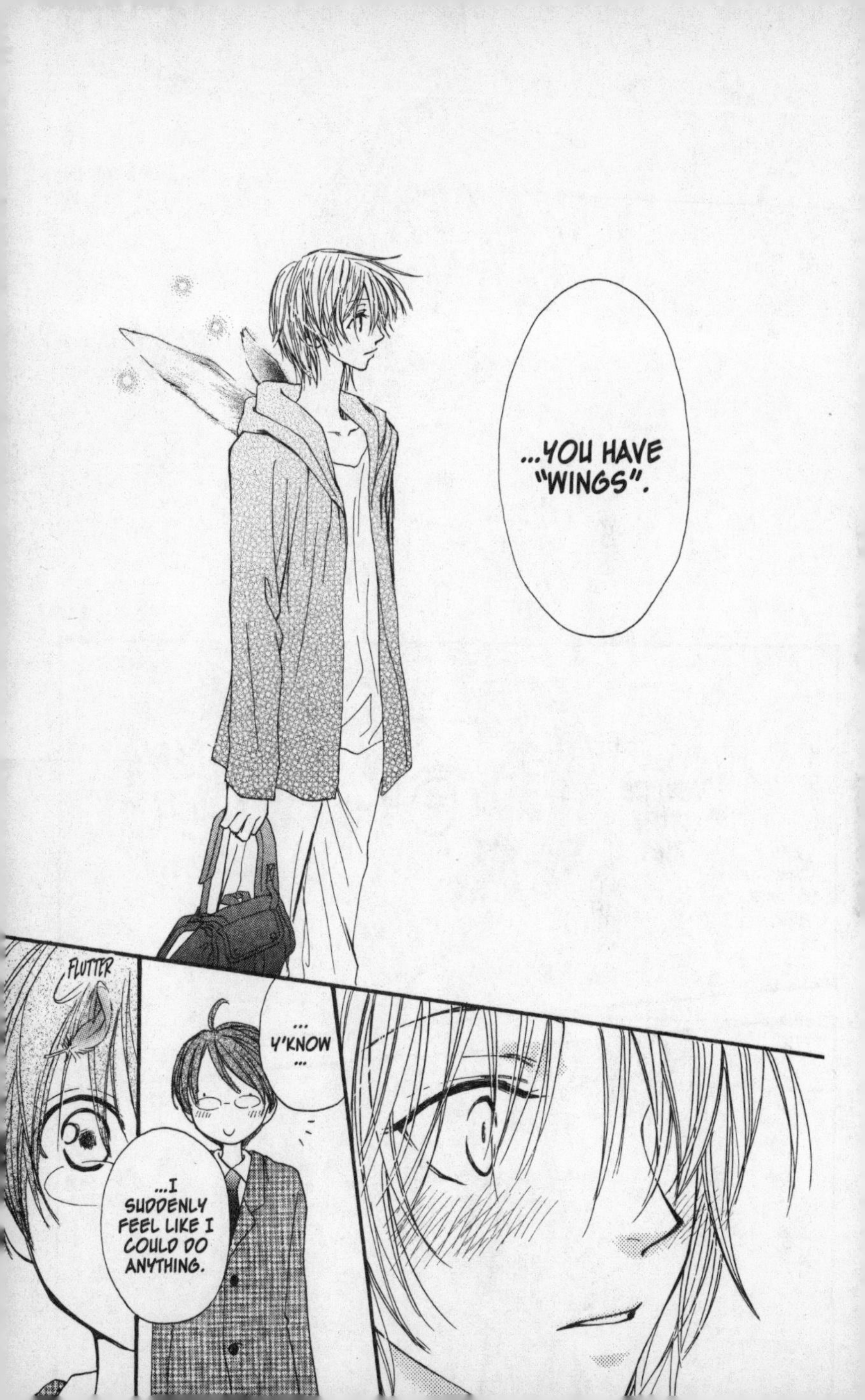
...YOU HAVE "WINGS".
... Y'KNOW ...
...I SUDDENLY FEEL LIKE I COULD DO ANYTHING.
FLUTTER

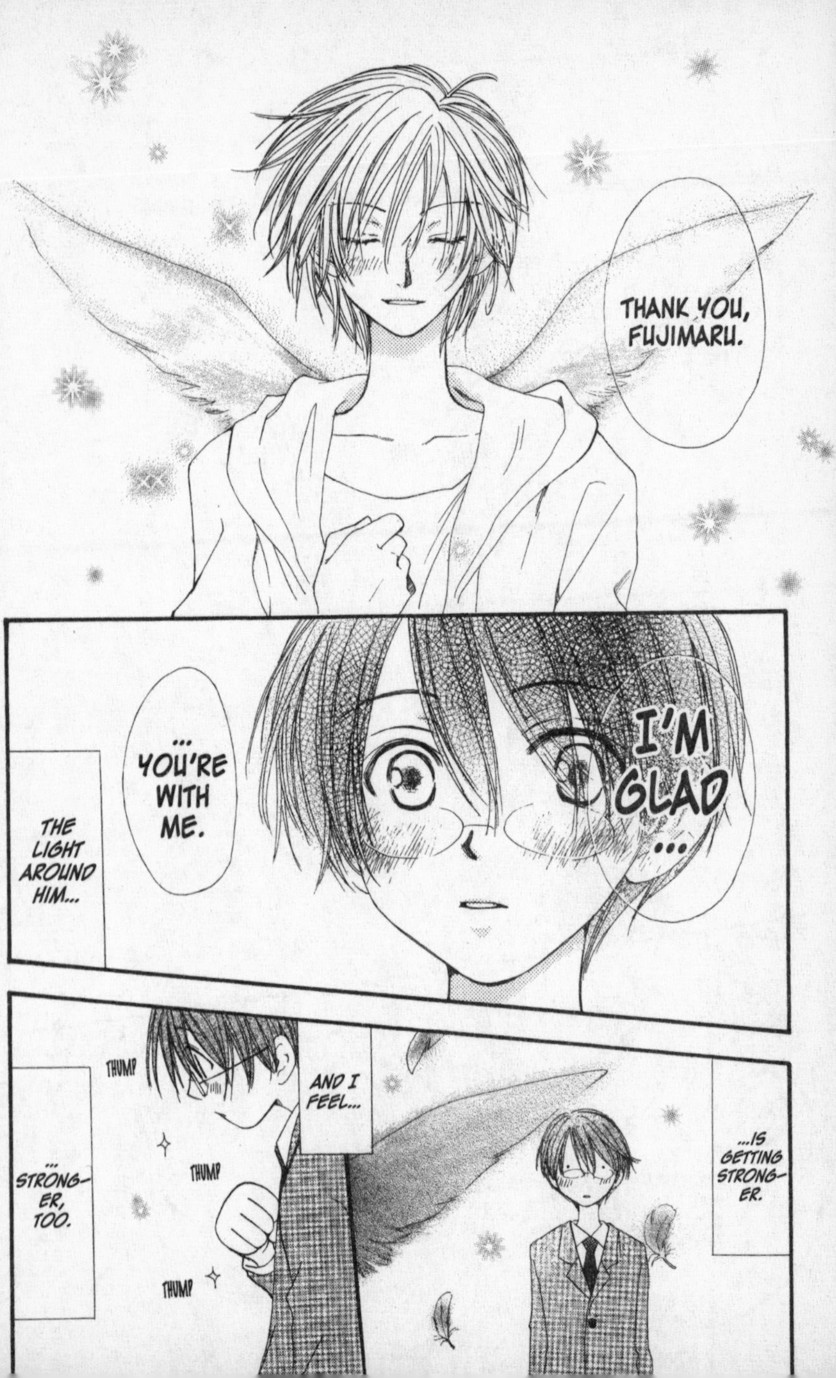
THANK YOU, FUJIMARU.
I'M GLAD ...
... YOU'RE WITH ME.
THE LIGHT AROUND HIM...
...IS GETTING STRONG-ER.
AND I FEEL...
THUMP
THUMP
... STRONG-ER, TOO.
THUMP

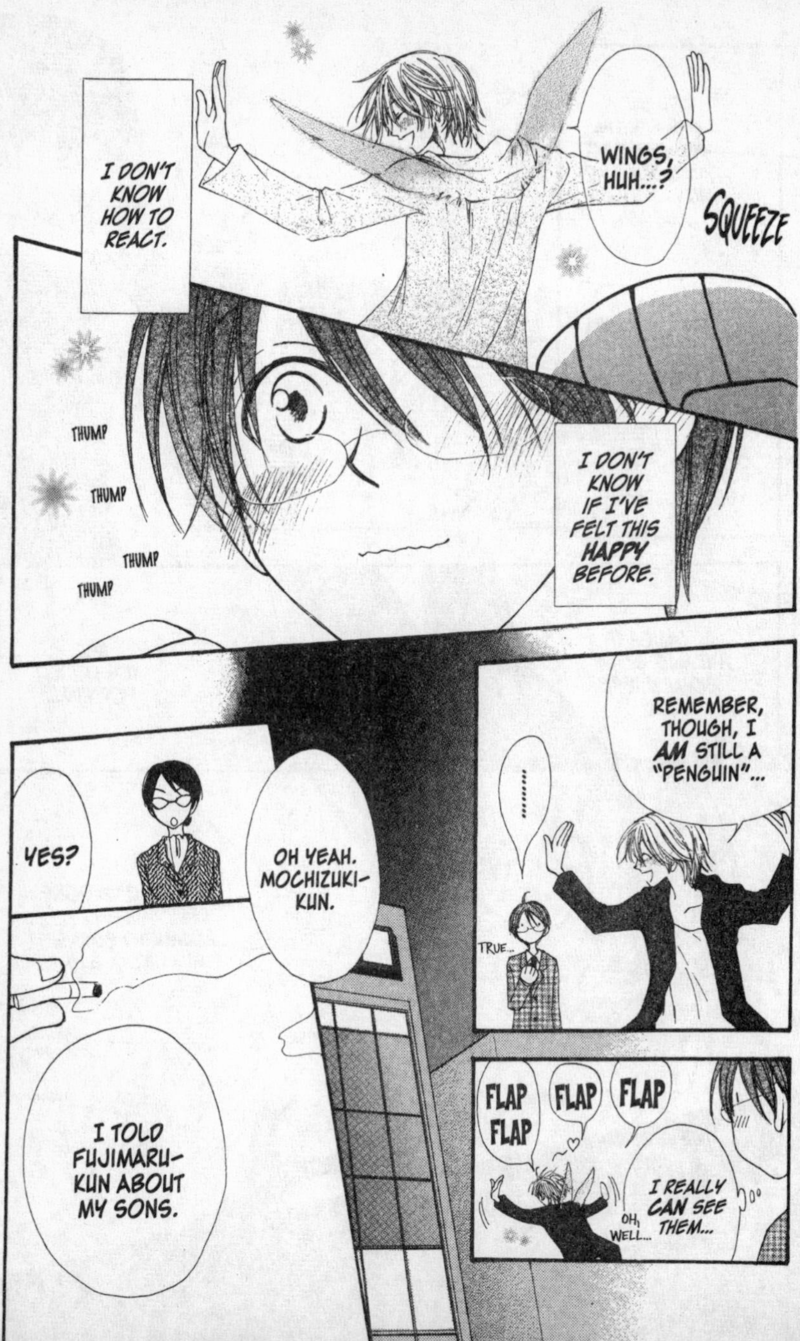
WINGS, HUH...?
SQUEEZE
I DON'T KNOW HOW TO REACT.
I DON'T KNOW IF I'VE FELT THIS HAPPY BEFORE.
THUMP
THUMP
THUMP
THUMP
REMEMBER, THOUGH, I AM STILL A "PENGUIN"...
......
TRUE...
FLAP
FLAP
FLAP FLAP
I REALLY CAN SEE THEM...
OH, WELL...
OH YEAH. MOCHIZUKI-KUN.
YES?
I TOLD FUJIMARU-KUN ABOUT MY SONS.

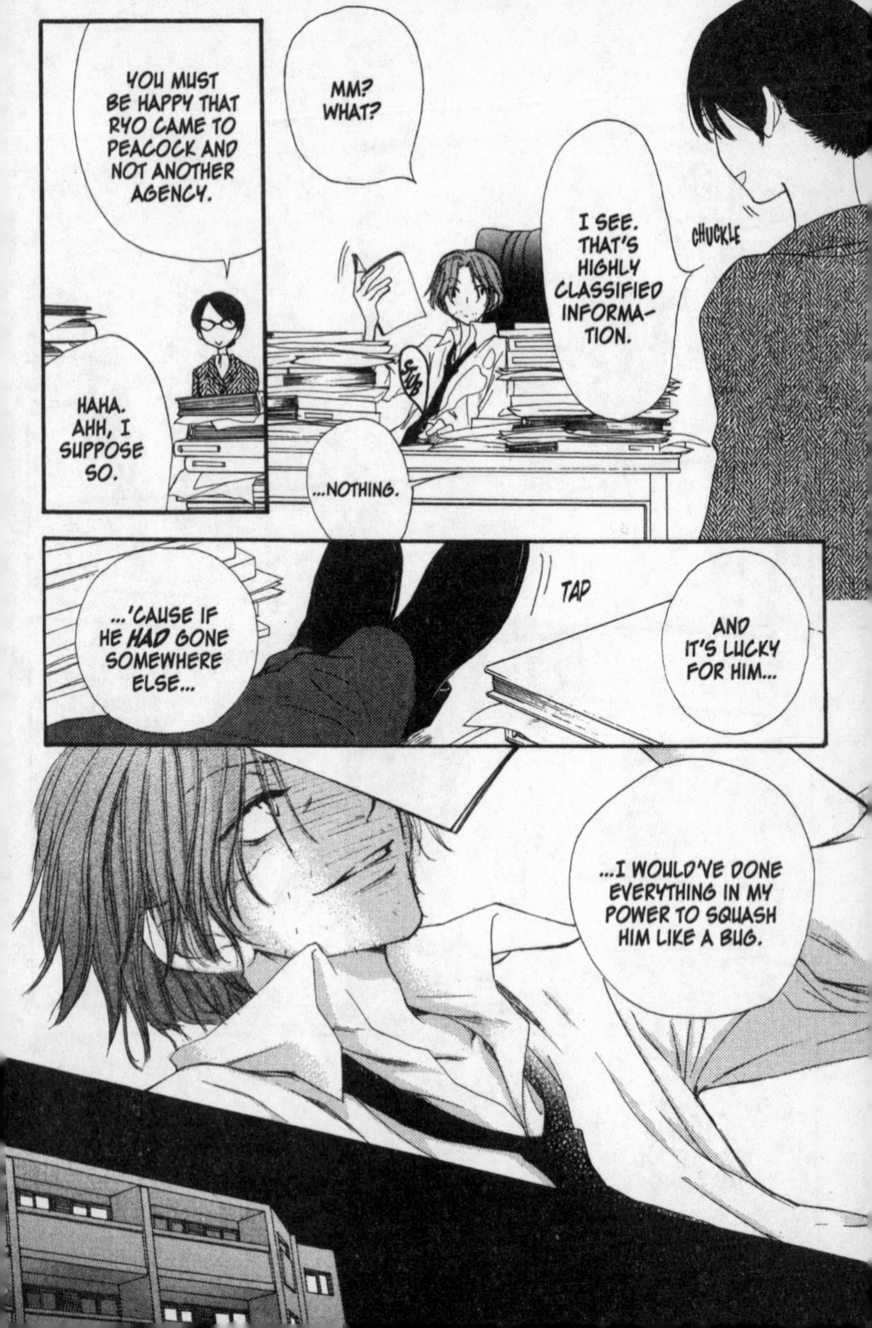
MM? WHAT?
I SEE. THAT'S HIGHLY CLASSIFIED INFORMATION.
CHUCKLE
SLUB
...NOTHING.
YOU MUST BE HAPPY THAT RYO CAME TO PEACOCK AND NOT ANOTHER AGENCY.
HAHA. AHH, I SUPPOSE SO.
AND IT'S LUCKY FOR HIM...
TAP
...'CAUSE IF HE *HAD* GONE SOMEWHERE ELSE...
...I WOULD'VE DONE EVERYTHING IN MY POWER TO SQUASH HIM LIKE A BUG.

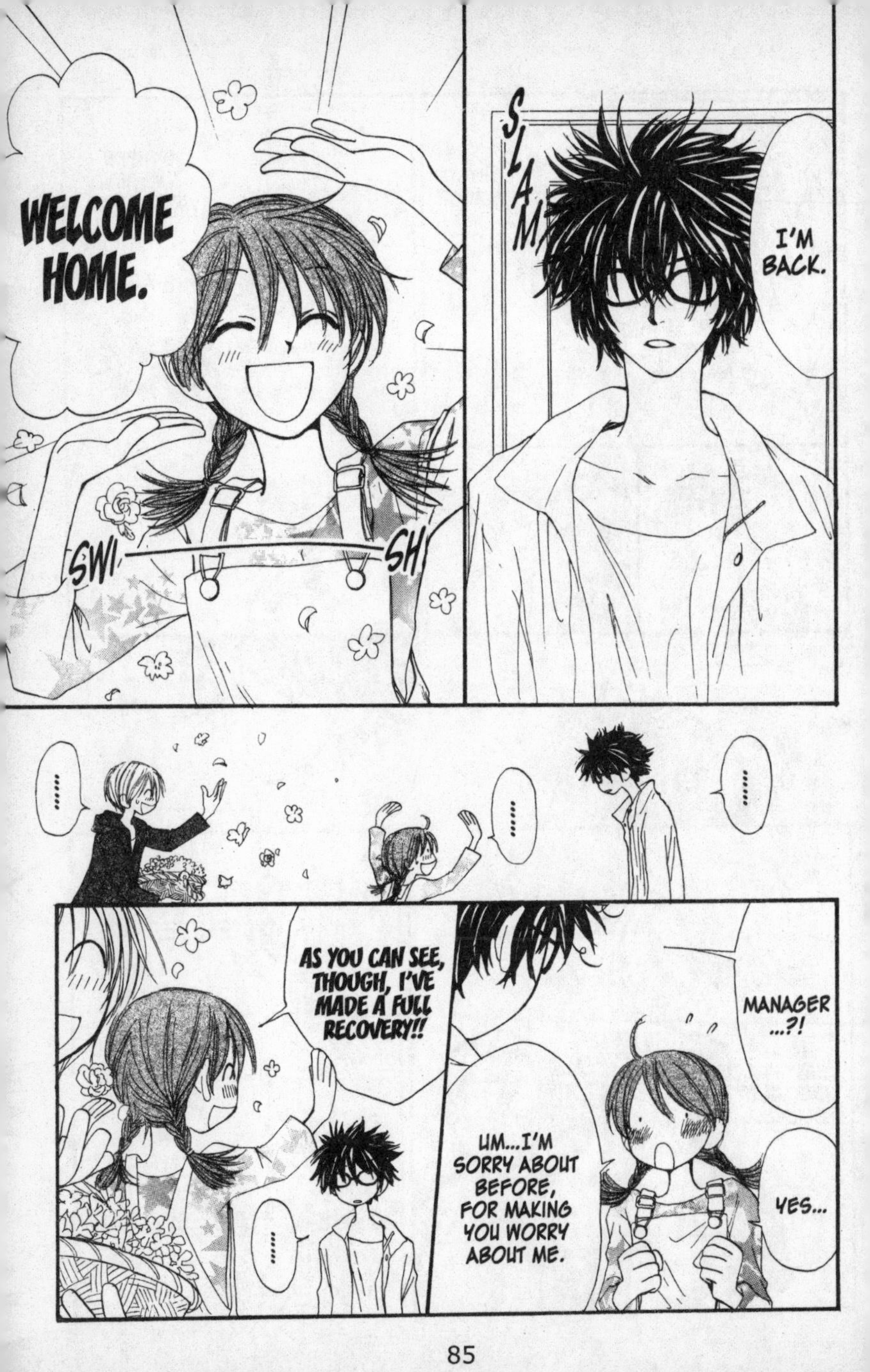
SLAM
I'M BACK.
WELCOME HOME.
SWISH
......
......
......
MANAGER ...?!
YES...
UM...I'M SORRY ABOUT BEFORE, FOR MAKING YOU WORRY ABOUT ME.
AS YOU CAN SEE, THOUGH, I'VE MADE A FULL RECOVERY!!
......

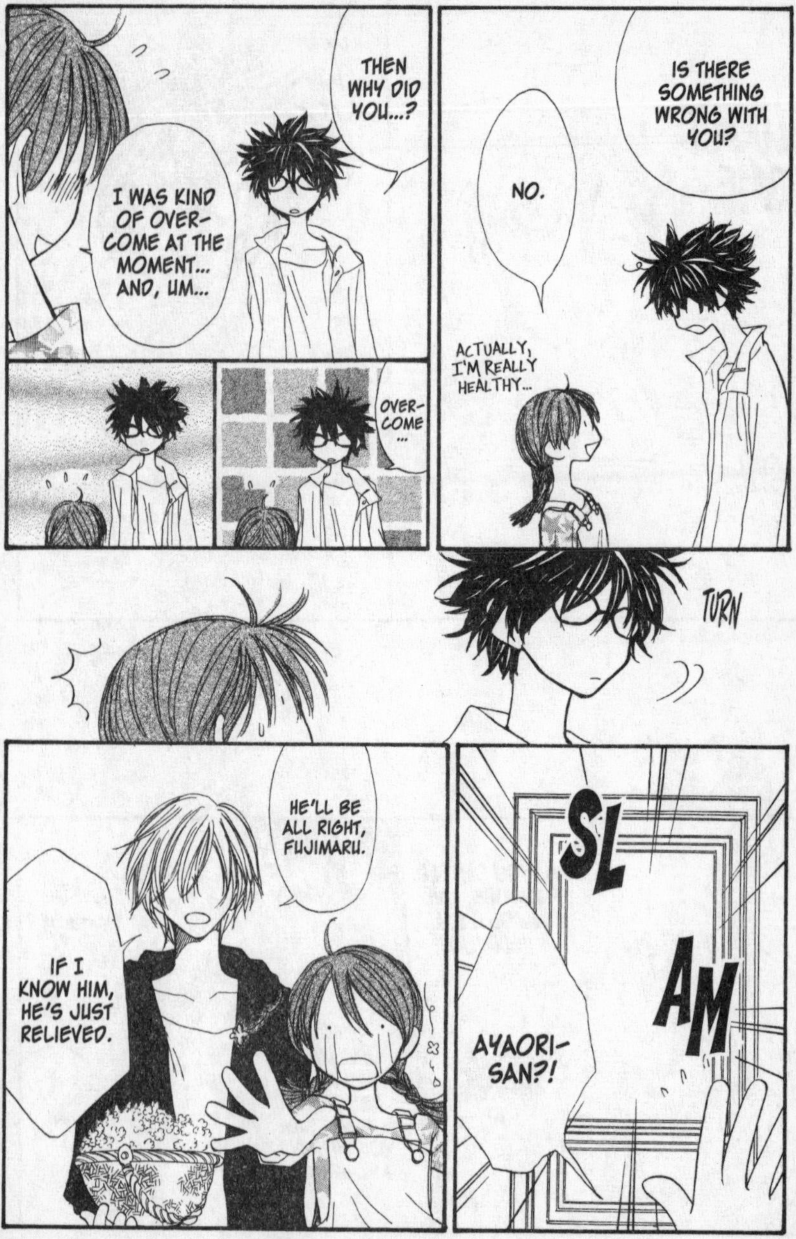
IS THERE SOMETHING WRONG WITH YOU?
NO.
ACTUALLY, I'M REALLY HEALTHY...
THEN WHY DID YOU...?
I WAS KIND OF OVER-COME AT THE MOMENT... AND, UM...
OVER-COME ...
TURN
SL AM
AYAORI-SAN?!
HE'LL BE ALL RIGHT, FUJIMARU.
IF I KNOW HIM, HE'S JUST RELIEVED.

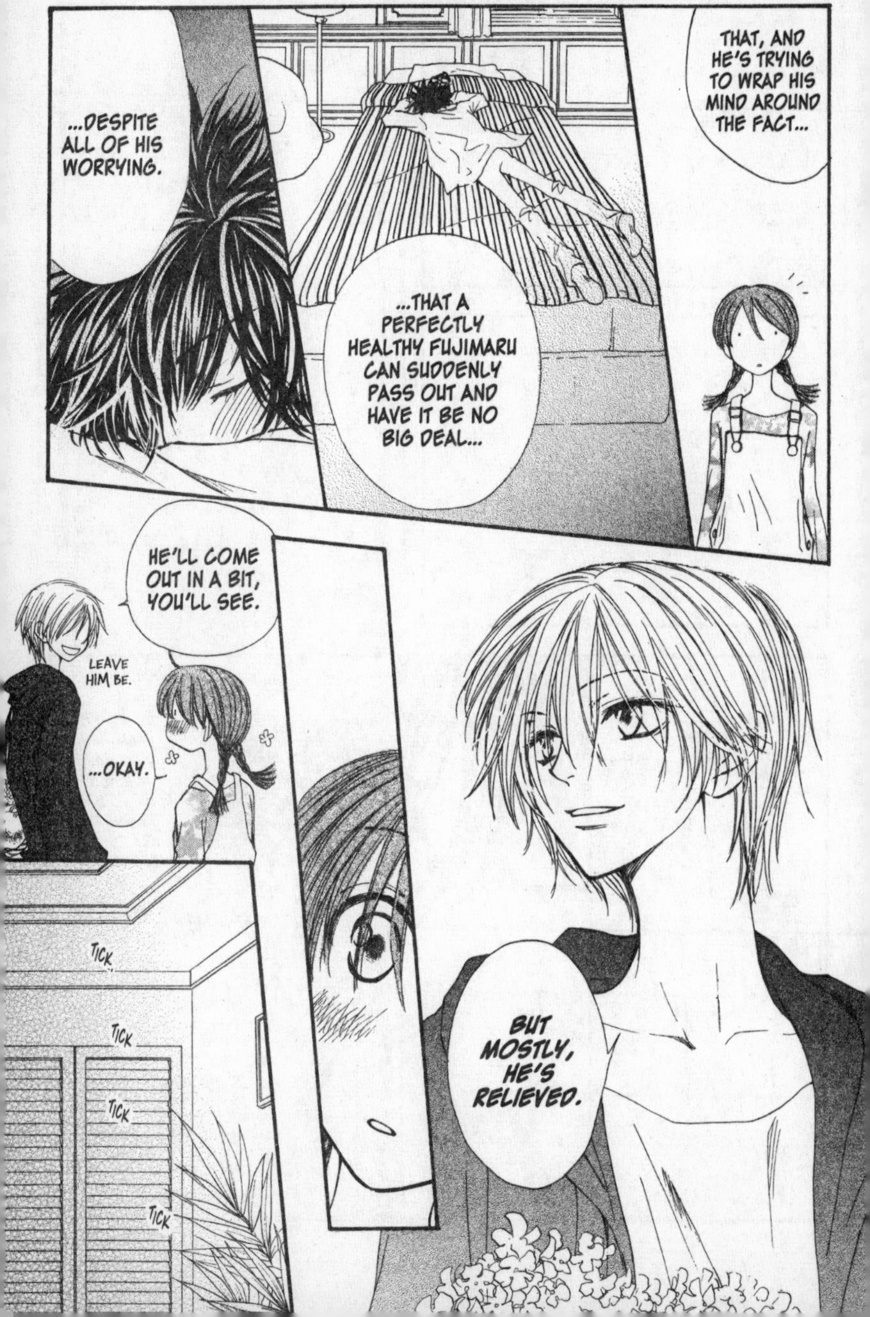
THAT, AND HE'S TRYING TO WRAP HIS MIND AROUND THE FACT...
...THAT A PERFECTLY HEALTHY FUJIMARU CAN SUDDENLY PASS OUT AND HAVE IT BE NO BIG DEAL...
...DESPITE ALL OF HIS WORRYING.
BUT MOSTLY, HE'S RELIEVED.
HE'LL COME OUT IN A BIT, YOU'LL SEE.
LEAVE HIM BE.
...OKAY.
TICK
TICK
TICK
TICK

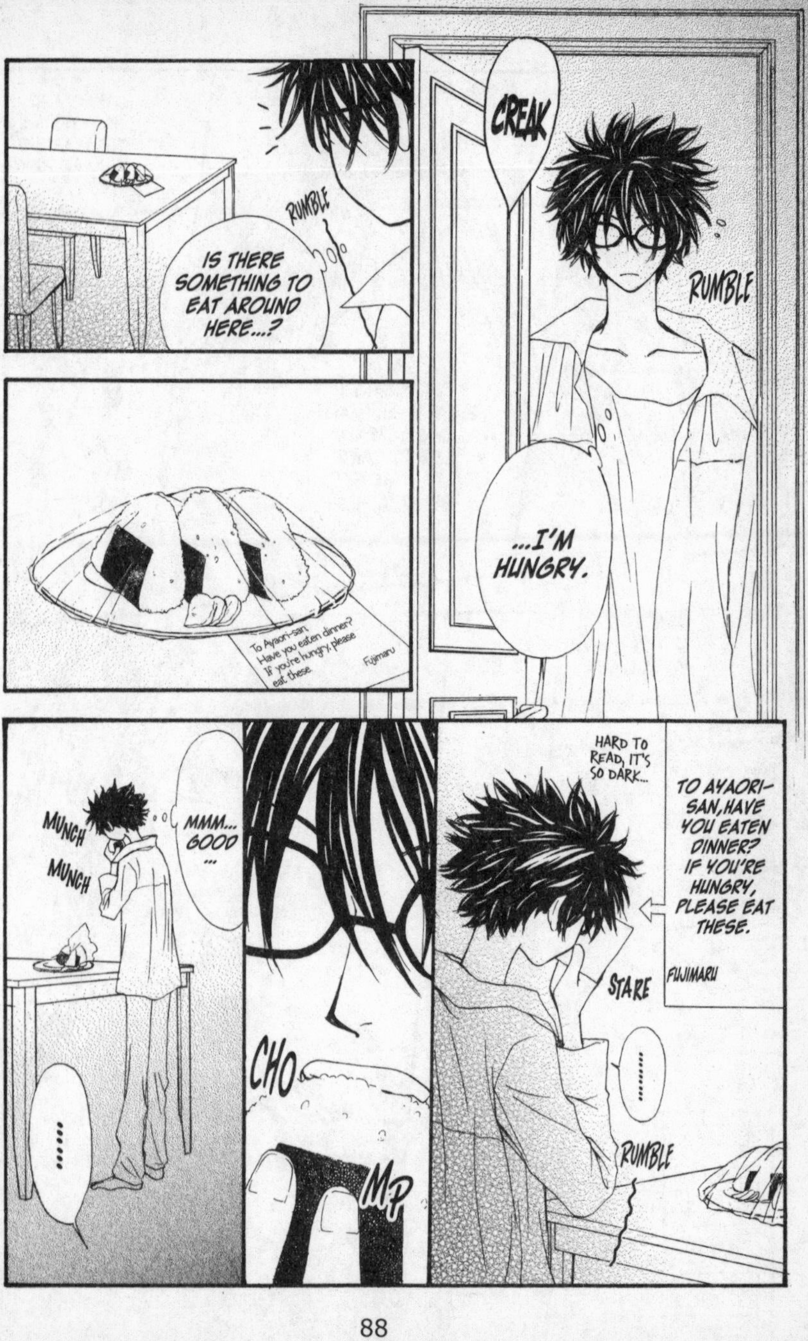
CREAK
RUMBLE
...I'M HUNGRY.
RUMBLE
IS THERE SOMETHING TO EAT AROUND HERE...?
To Ayaori-san
Have you eaten dinner?
If you're hungry, please eat these
Fujimaru
HARD TO READ, IT'S SO DARK...
TO AYAORI-SAN, HAVE YOU EATEN DINNER? IF YOU'RE HUNGRY, PLEASE EAT THESE.
FUJIMARU
STARE
......
RUMBLE
CHO
MP
MUNCH
MUNCH
MMM... GOOD...
......

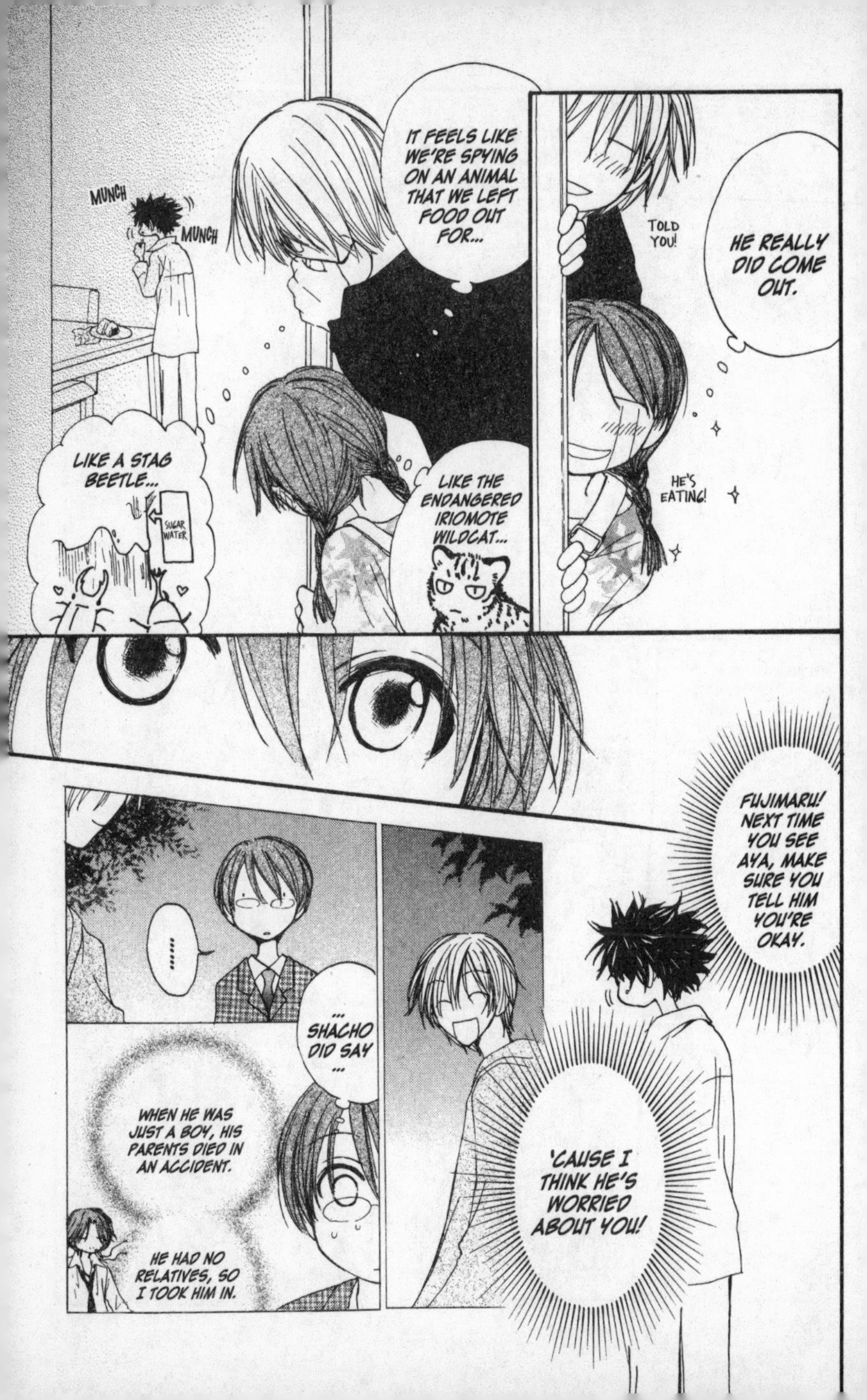
HE REALLY DID COME OUT.
TOLD YOU!
HE'S EATING!
IT FEELS LIKE WE'RE SPYING ON AN ANIMAL THAT WE LEFT FOOD OUT FOR...
MUNCH
MUNCH
LIKE THE ENDANGERED IRIOMOTE WILDCAT...
LIKE A STAG BEETLE...
SUGAR WATER
FUJIMARU! NEXT TIME YOU SEE AYA, MAKE SURE YOU TELL HIM YOU'RE OKAY.
'CAUSE I THINK HE'S WORRIED ABOUT YOU!
......
... SHACHO DID SAY ...
WHEN HE WAS JUST A BOY, HIS PARENTS DIED IN AN ACCIDENT.
HE HAD NO RELATIVES, SO I TOOK HIM IN.

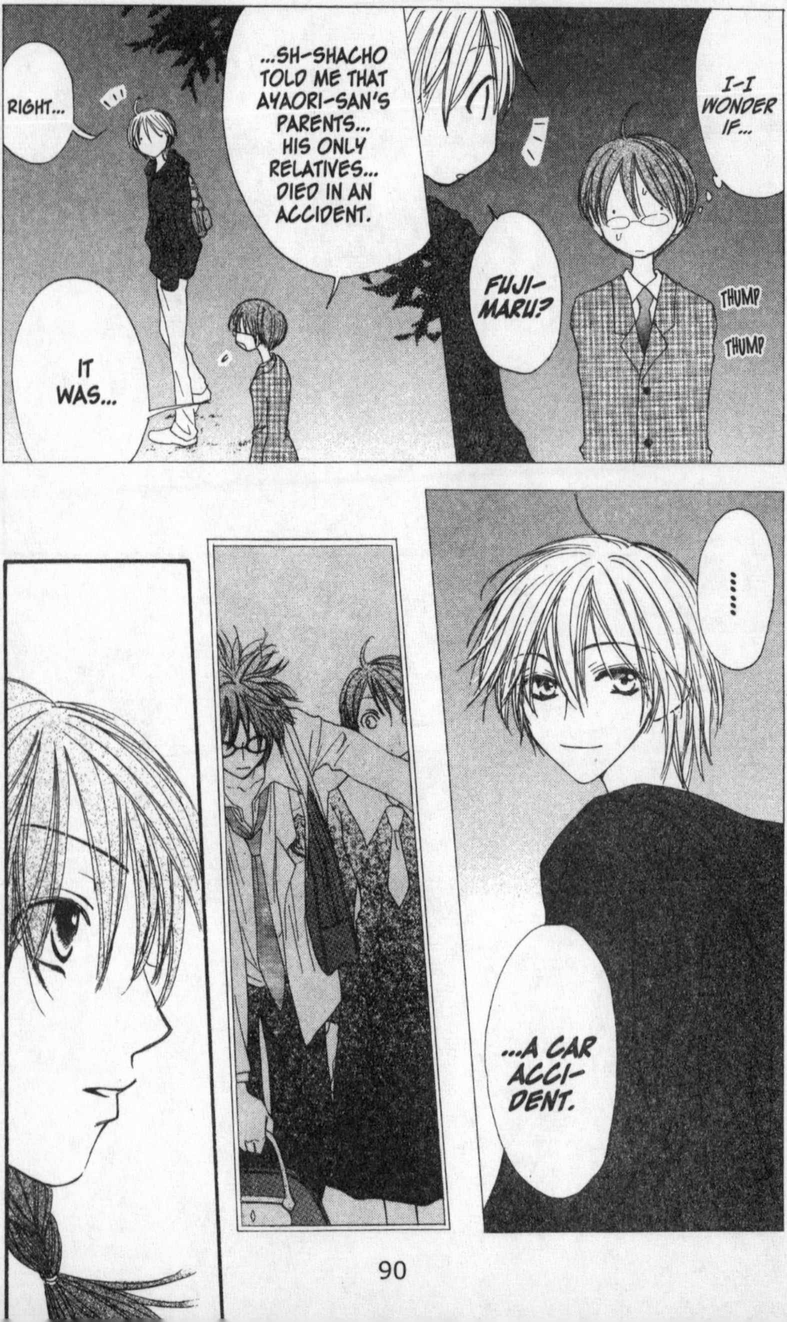
I-I WONDER IF...
THUMP
THUMP
FUJI-MARU?
...SH-SHACHO TOLD ME THAT AYAORI-SAN'S PARENTS... HIS ONLY RELATIVES... DIED IN AN ACCIDENT.
RIGHT...
IT WAS...
......
...A CAR ACCI-DENT.

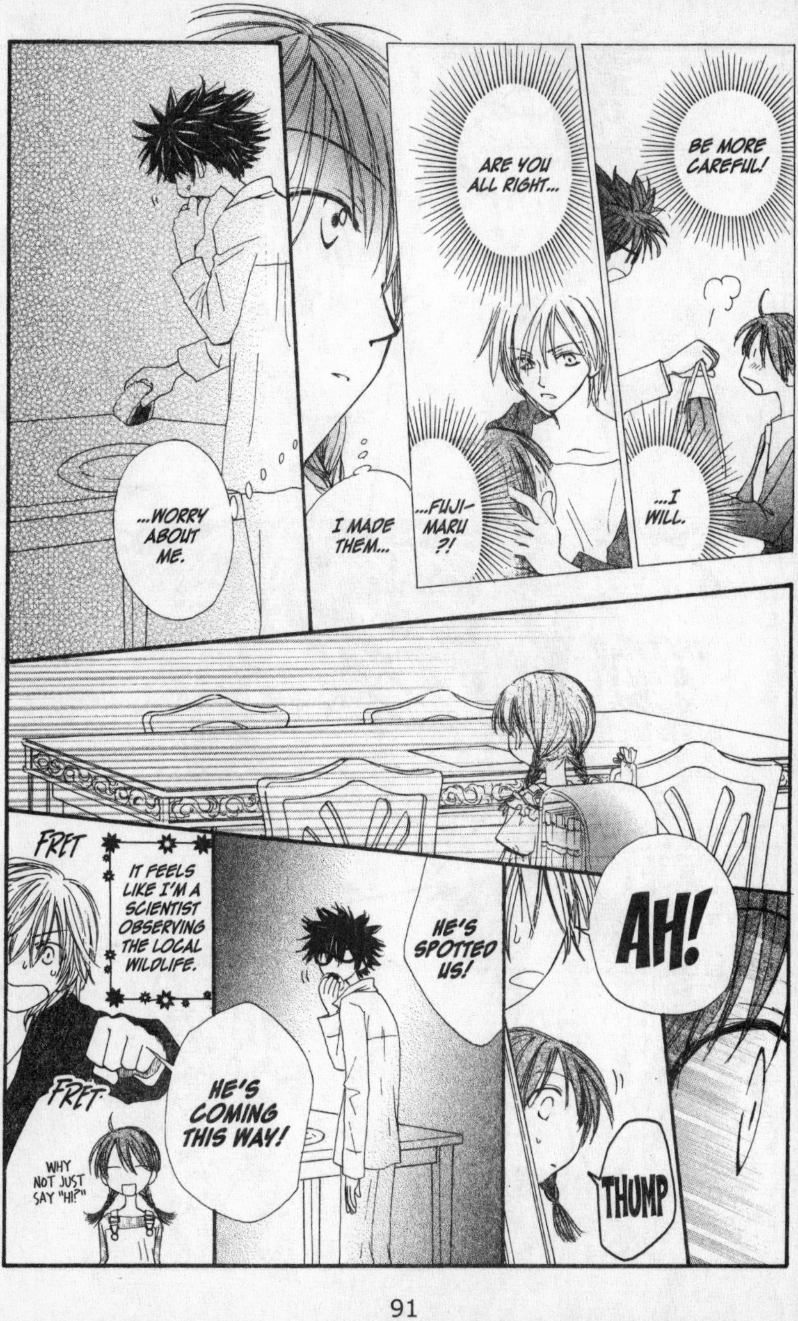
BE MORE CAREFUL!
...I WILL.
ARE YOU ALL RIGHT...
...FUJI-MARU?!
I MADE THEM...
...WORRY ABOUT ME.
AH!
THUMP
HE'S SPOTTED US!
HE'S COMING THIS WAY!
FRET
IT FEELS LIKE I'M A SCIENTIST OBSERVING THE LOCAL WILDLIFE.
FRET
WHY NOT JUST SAY "HI!?"

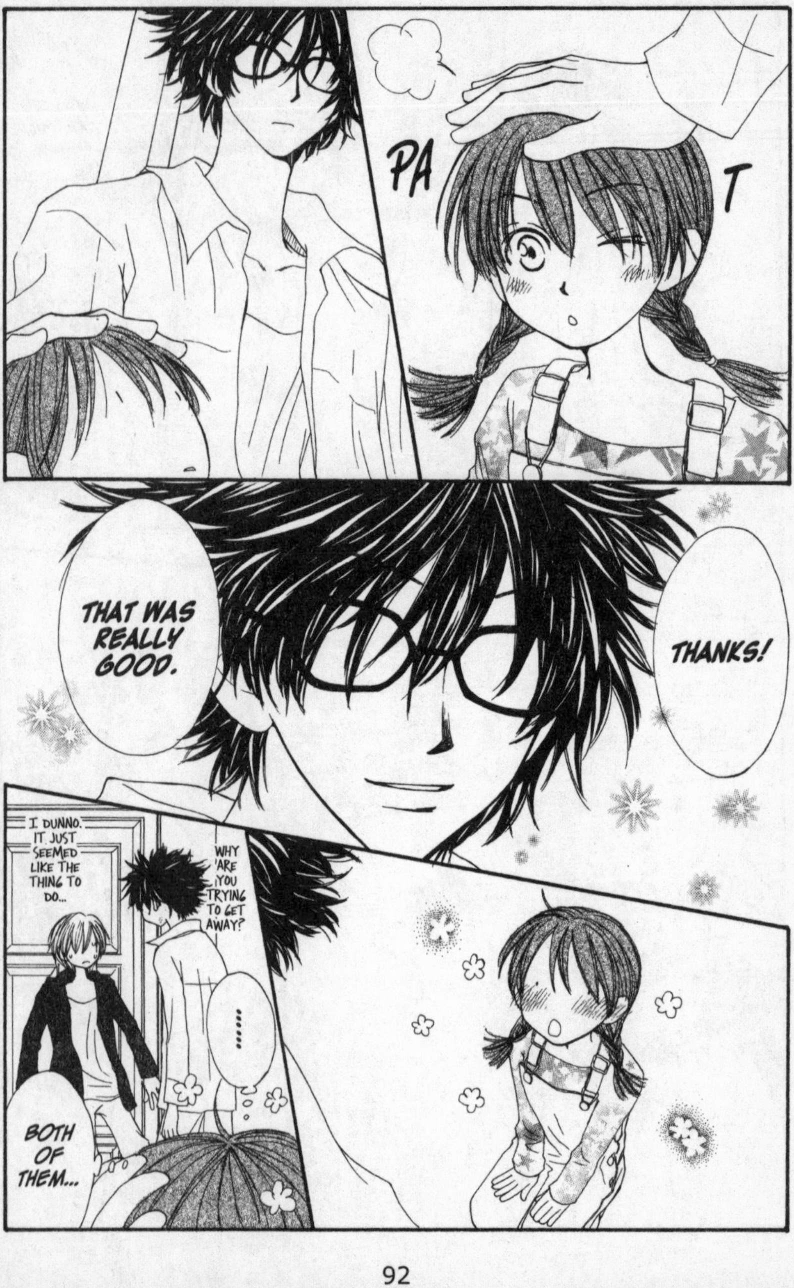
PA T
THANKS!
THAT WAS REALLY GOOD.
WHY ARE YOU TRYING TO GET AWAY?
I DUNNO. IT JUST SEEMED LIKE THE THING TO DO...
......
BOTH OF THEM...

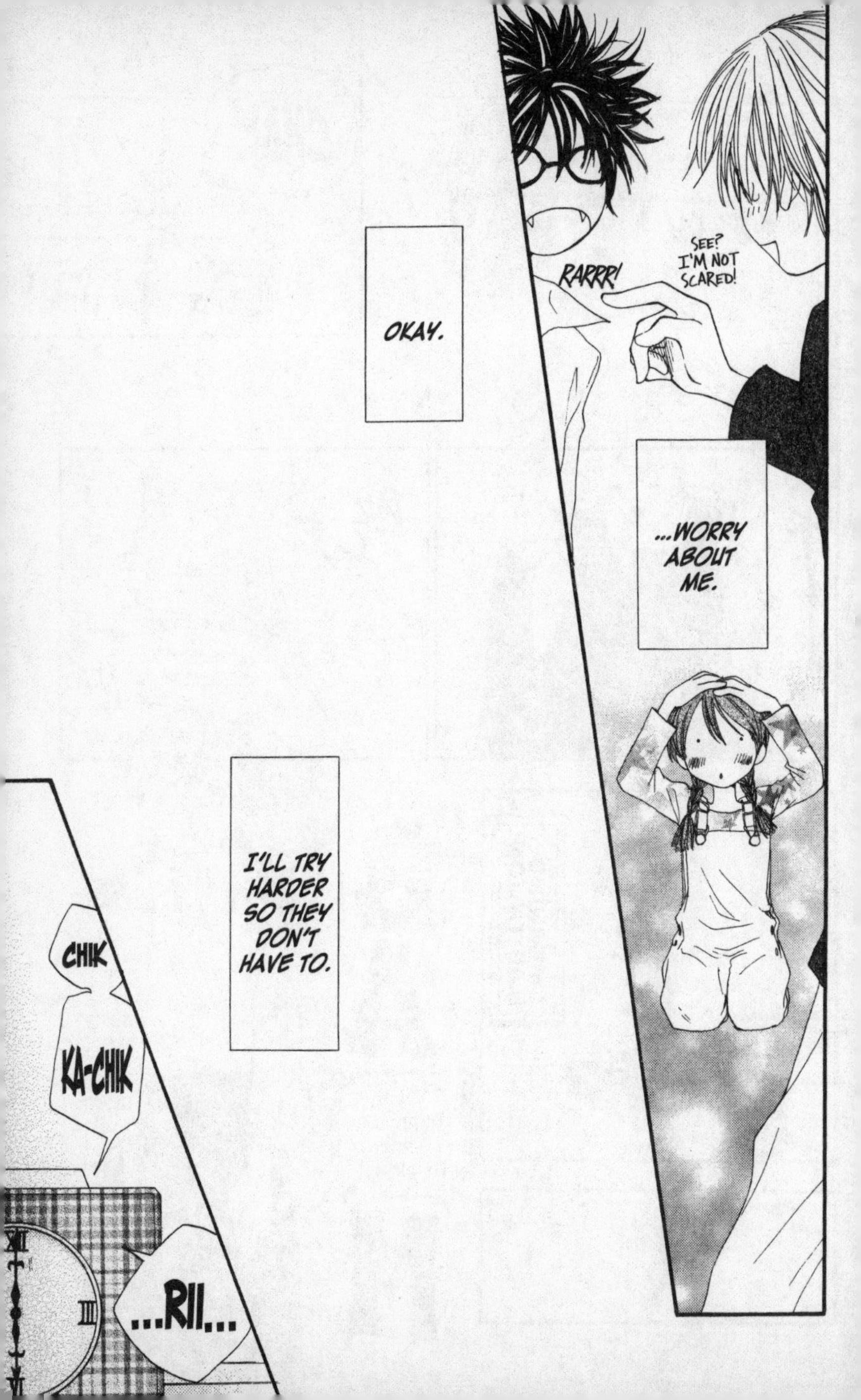
SEE? I'M NOT SCARED!
RARRR!
...WORRY ABOUT ME.
OKAY.
I'LL TRY HARDER SO THEY DON'T HAVE TO.
CHIK
KA-CHIK
...RII...

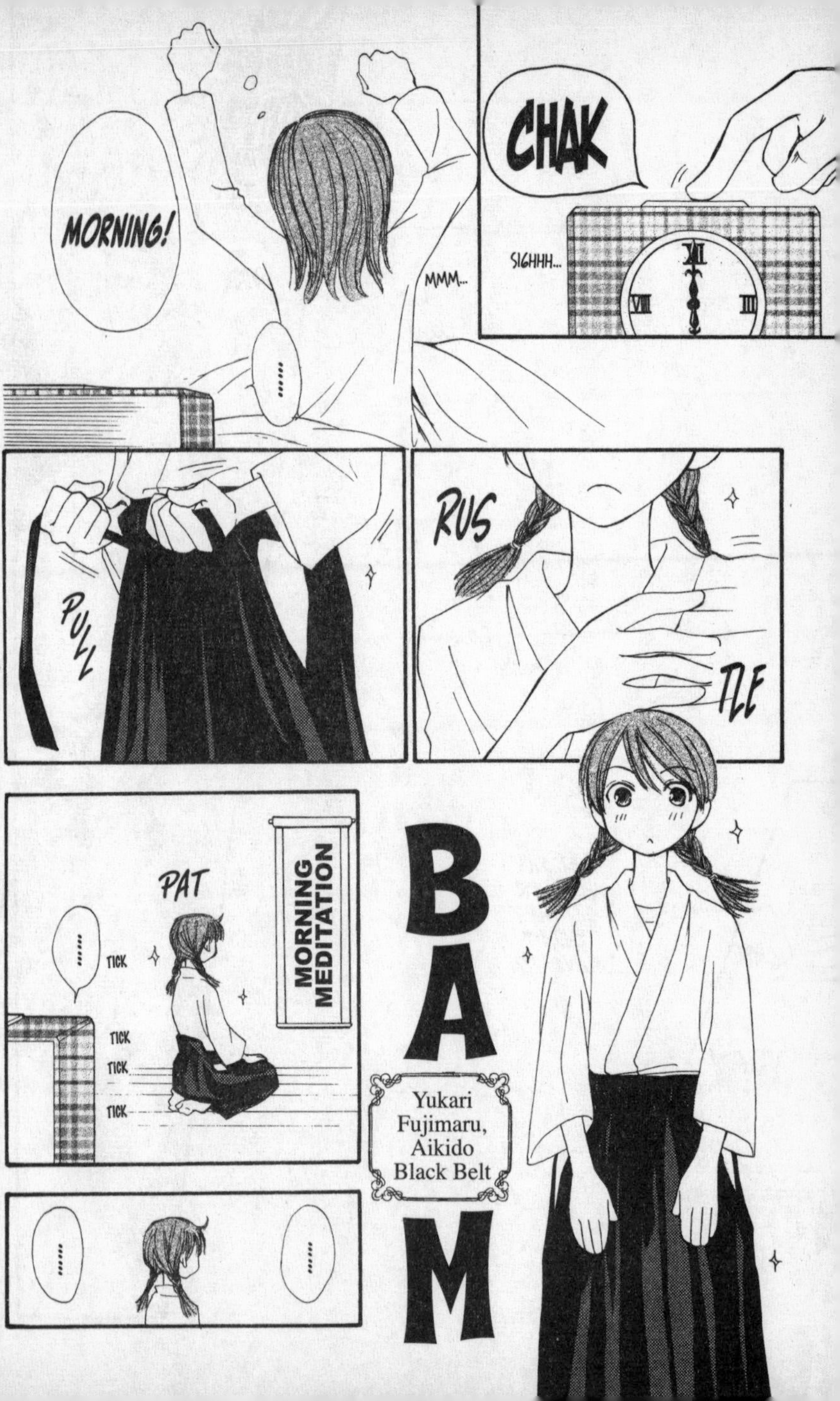
CHAK
SIGHHH...
MORNING!
MMM...
......
RUS
TLE
PULL
BAM
Yukari Fujimaru, Aikido Black Belt
MORNING MEDITATION
PAT
......
TICK
TICK
TICK
TICK
......
......

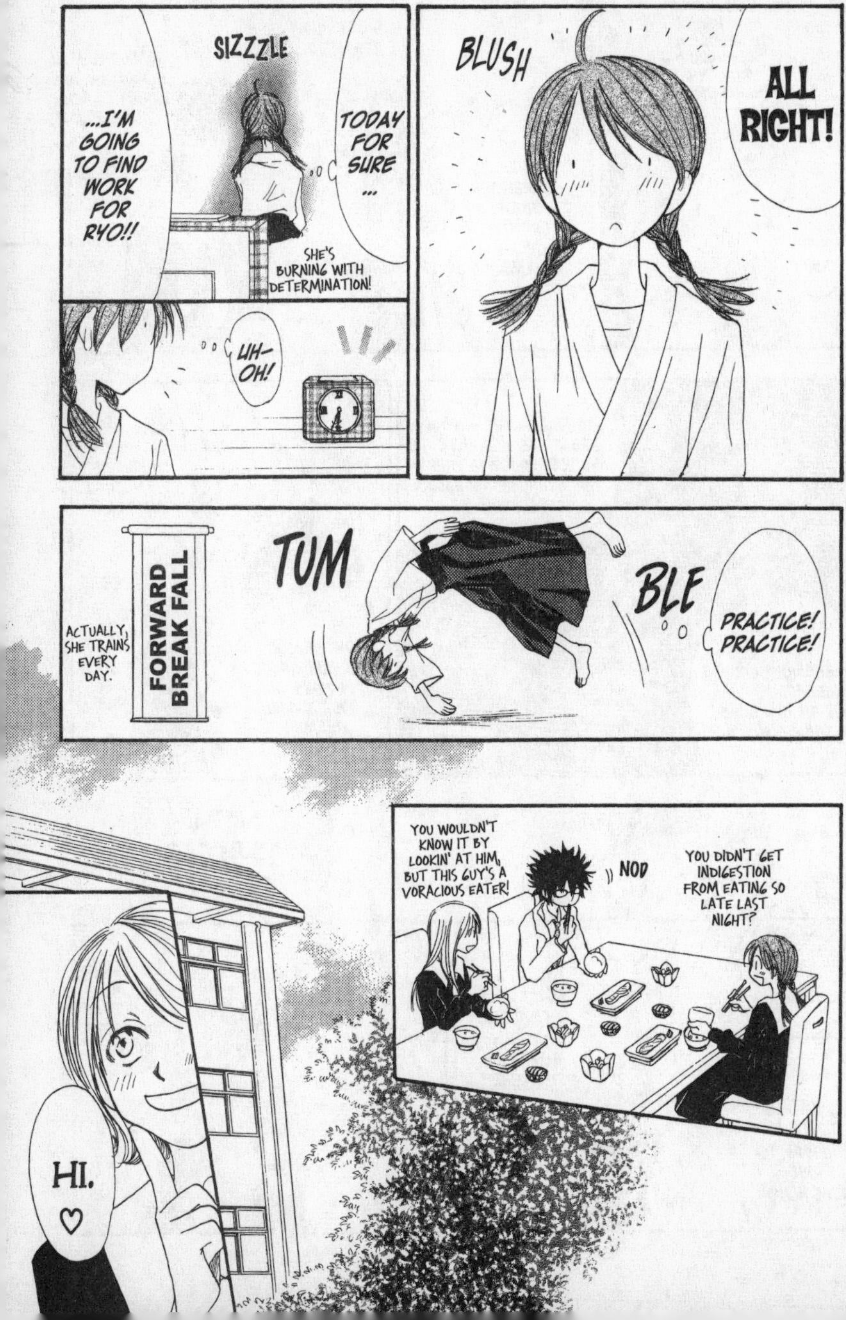
BLUSH
ALL RIGHT!
SIZZZLE
TODAY FOR SURE...
...I'M GOING TO FIND WORK FOR RYO!!
SHE'S BURNING WITH DETERMINATION!
UH-OH!
TUM
BLE
PRACTICE! PRACTICE!
FORWARD BREAK FALL
ACTUALLY, SHE TRAINS EVERY DAY.
YOU DIDN'T GET INDIGESTION FROM EATING SO LATE LAST NIGHT?
NOD
YOU WOULDN'T KNOW IT BY LOOKIN' AT HIM, BUT THIS GUY'S A VORACIOUS EATER!
HI. ♡

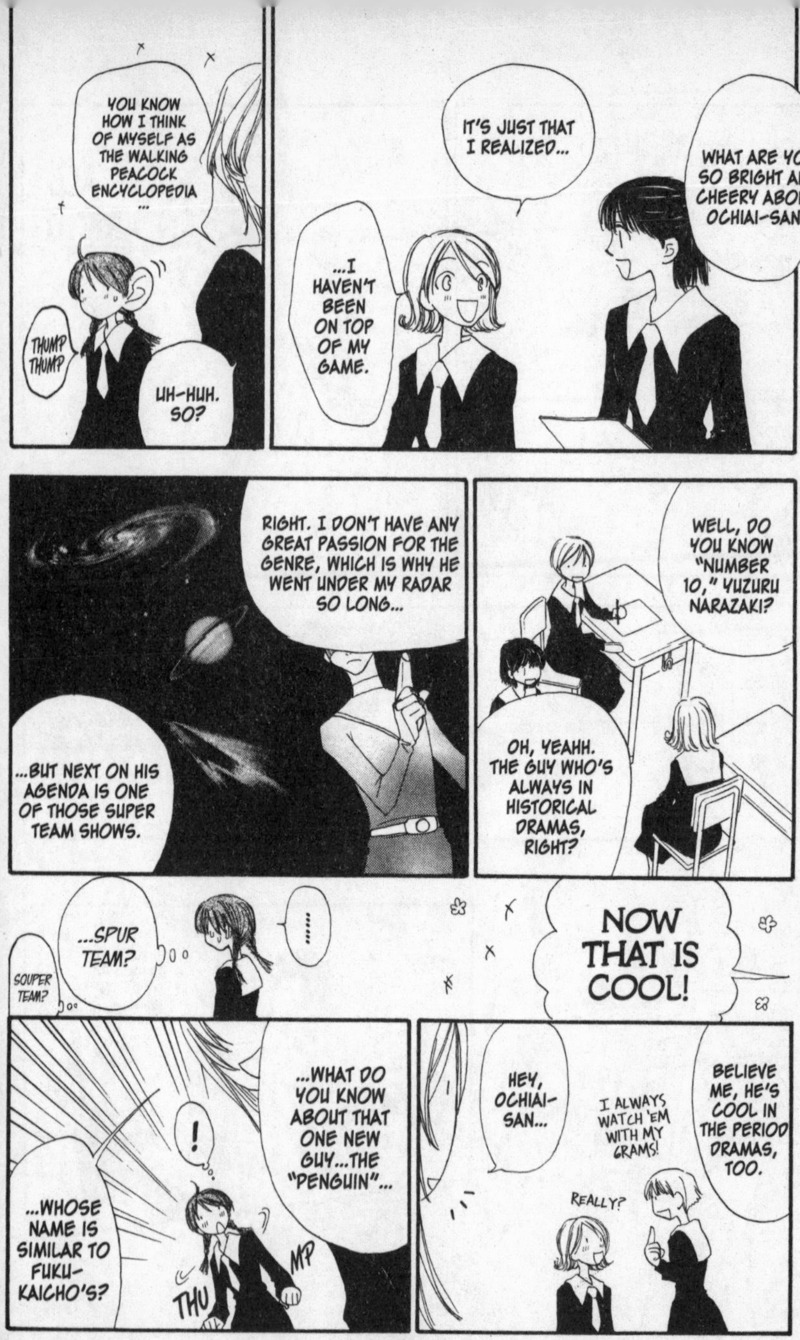
WHAT ARE YOU SO BRIGHT AND CHEERY ABOUT, OCHIAI-SAN?
IT'S JUST THAT I REALIZED...
...I HAVEN'T BEEN ON TOP OF MY GAME.
YOU KNOW HOW I THINK OF MYSELF AS THE WALKING PEACOCK ENCYCLOPEDIA...
THUMP THUMP
UH-HUH. SO?
WELL, DO YOU KNOW "NUMBER 10," YUZURU NARAZAKI?
OH, YEAHH. THE GUY WHO'S ALWAYS IN HISTORICAL DRAMAS, RIGHT?
RIGHT. I DON'T HAVE ANY GREAT PASSION FOR THE GENRE, WHICH IS WHY HE WENT UNDER MY RADAR SO LONG...
...BUT NEXT ON HIS AGENDA IS ONE OF THOSE SUPER TEAM SHOWS.
NOW THAT IS COOL!
......
...SPUR TEAM?
SOUPER TEAM?
BELIEVE ME, HE'S COOL IN THE PERIOD DRAMAS, TOO.
I ALWAYS WATCH 'EM WITH MY GRAMS!
REALLY?
HEY, OCHIAI-SAN...
...WHAT DO YOU KNOW ABOUT THAT ONE NEW GUY...THE "PENGUIN"...
!
...WHOSE NAME IS SIMILAR TO FUKU-KAICHO'S?
THU
MP

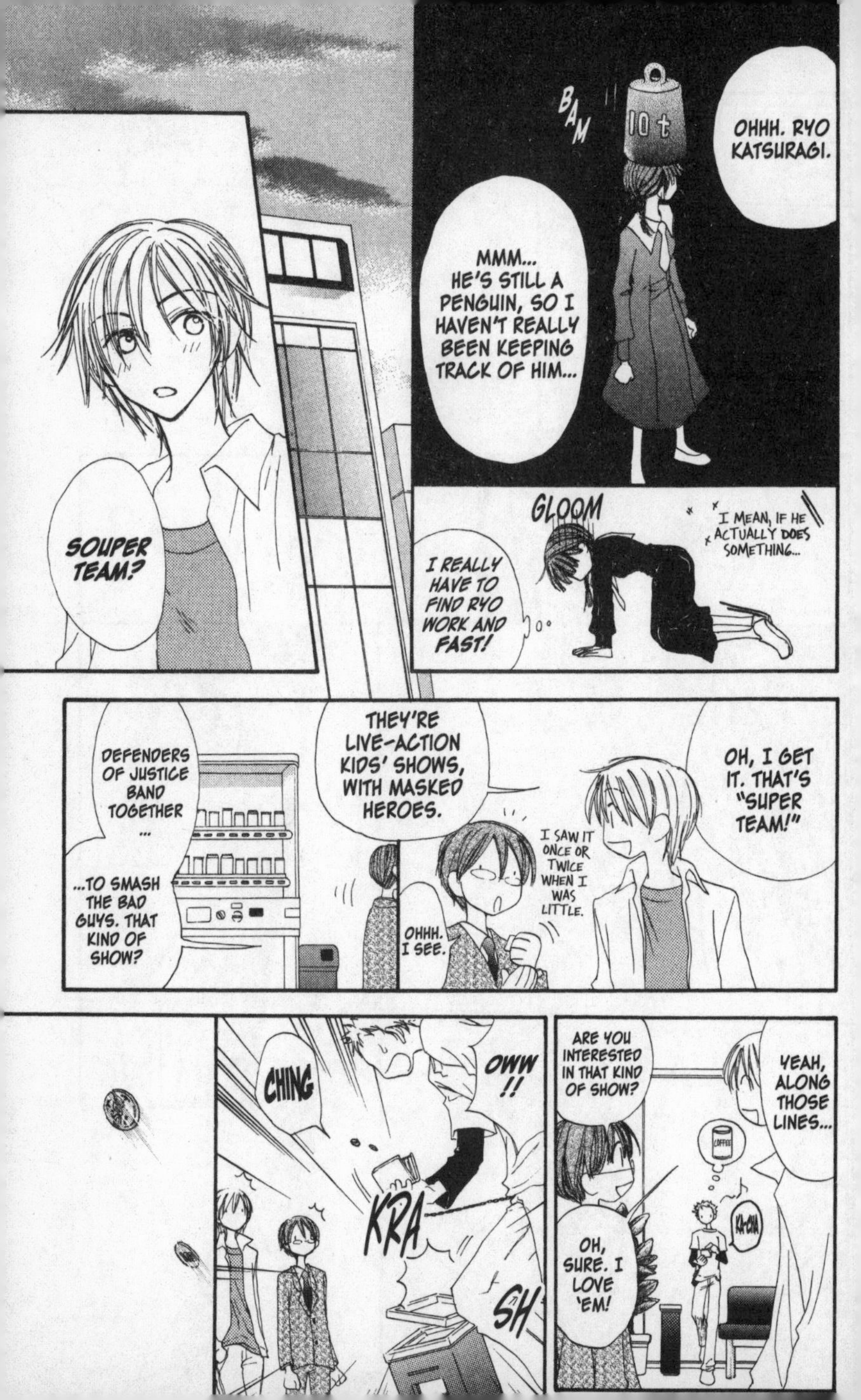
OHHH. RYO KATSURAGI.
BAM
10t
MMM... HE'S STILL A PENGUIN, SO I HAVEN'T REALLY BEEN KEEPING TRACK OF HIM...
I MEAN, IF HE ACTUALLY DOES SOMETHING...
GLOOM
I REALLY HAVE TO FIND RYO WORK AND FAST!
SOUPER TEAM?
OH, I GET IT. THAT'S "SUPER TEAM!"
THEY'RE LIVE-ACTION KIDS' SHOWS, WITH MASKED HEROES.
I SAW IT ONCE OR TWICE WHEN I WAS LITTLE.
OHHH. I SEE.
DEFENDERS OF JUSTICE BAND TOGETHER ...
...TO SMASH THE BAD GUYS. THAT KIND OF SHOW?
YEAH, ALONG THOSE LINES...
ARE YOU INTERESTED IN THAT KIND OF SHOW?
COFFEE
KA-CHA
OH, SURE. I LOVE 'EM!
OWW !!
CHING
KRA
SH

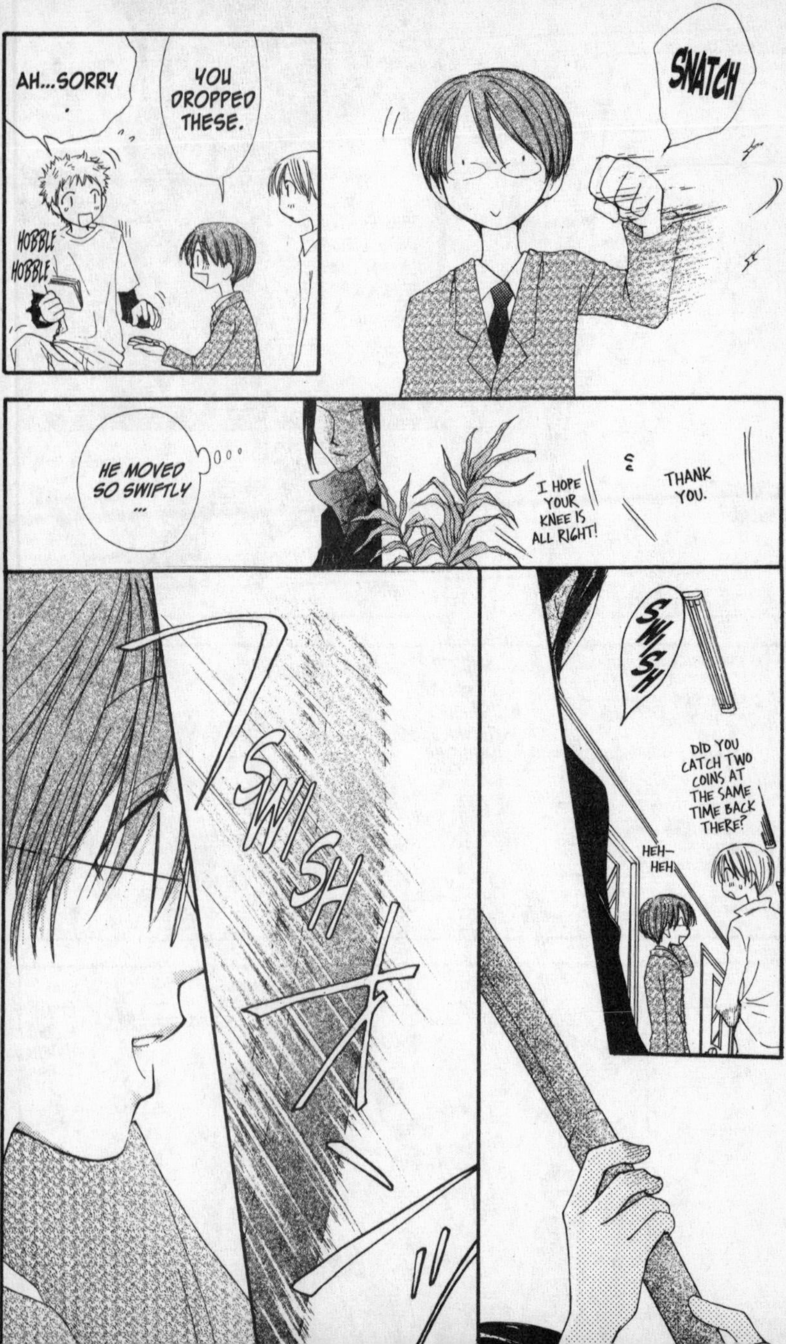
SNATCH
YOU DROPPED THESE.
AH...SORRY.
HOBBLE HOBBLE
THANK YOU.
I HOPE YOUR KNEE IS ALL RIGHT!
HE MOVED SO SWIFTLY...
SWISH
DID YOU CATCH TWO COINS AT THE SAME TIME BACK THERE?
HEH-HEH.
SWISH

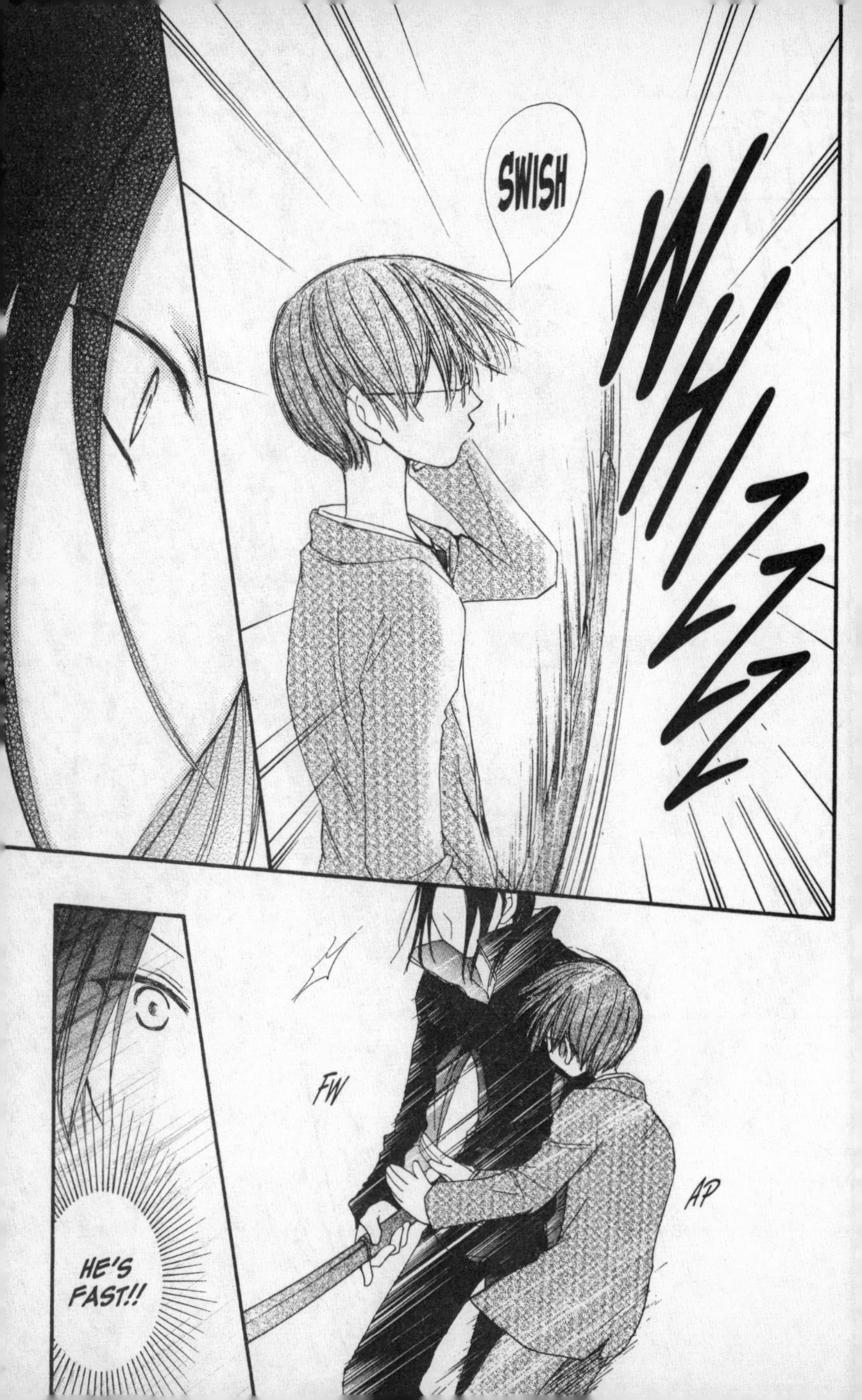
WHIZZZ
SWISH
FW
AP
HE'S FAST!!

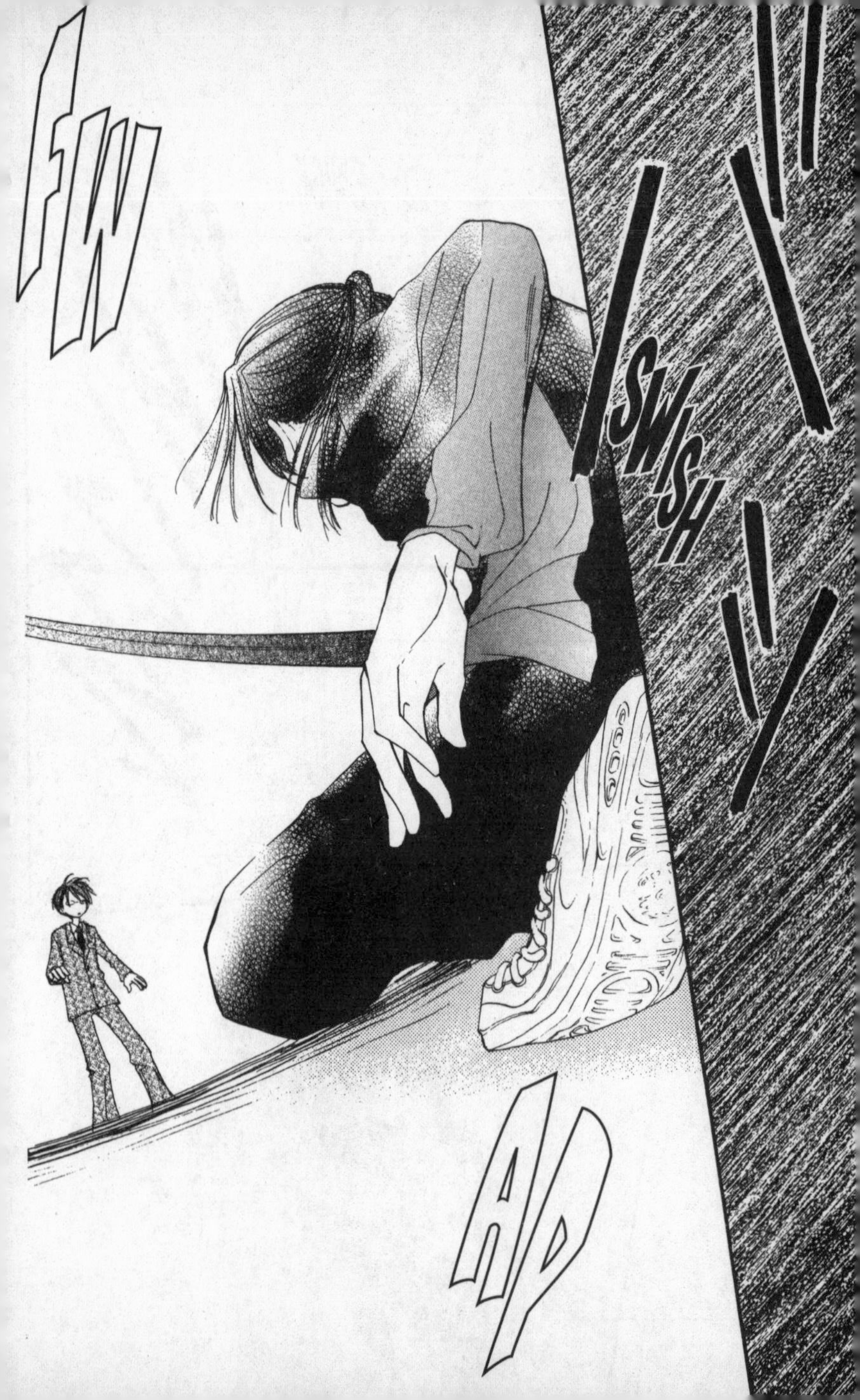
SWISH
FWN
AH

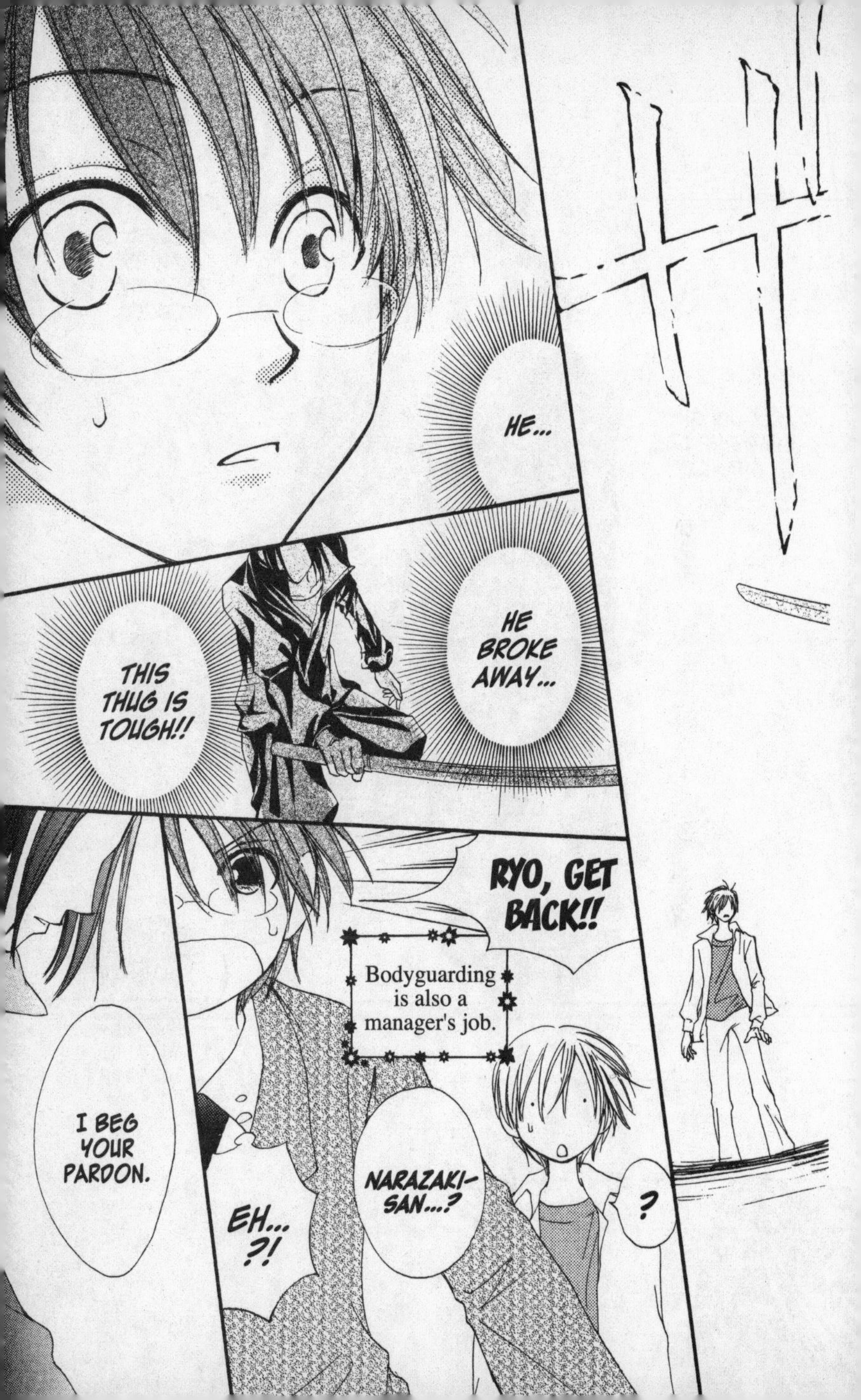
HE...
HE BROKE AWAY...
THIS THUG IS TOUGH!!
RYO, GET BACK!!
Bodyguarding is also a manager's job.
?
NARAZAKI-SAN...?
EH...?!
I BEG YOUR PARDON.

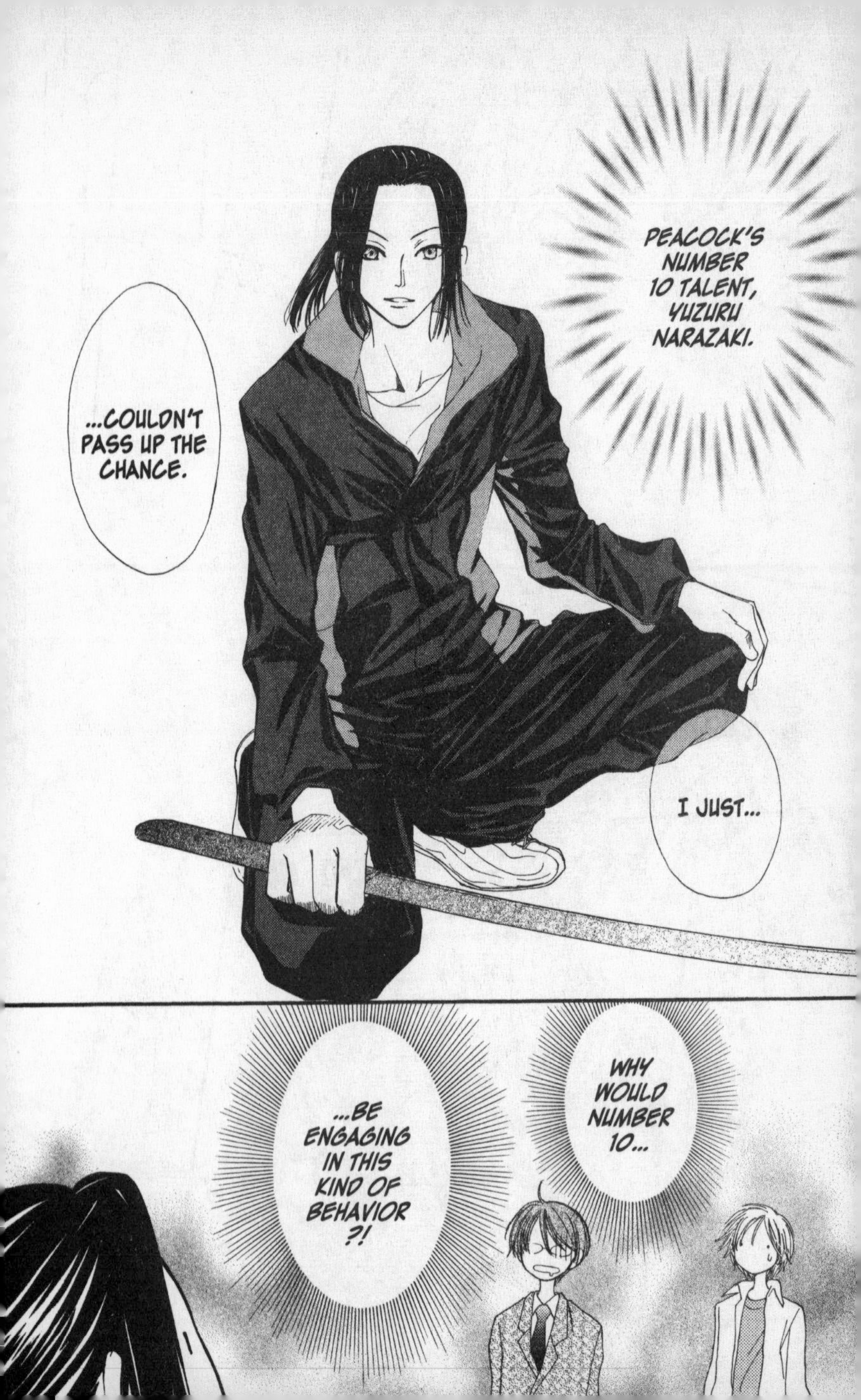
PEACOCK'S NUMBER 10 TALENT, YUZURU NARAZAKI.
I JUST...
...COULDN'T PASS UP THE CHANCE.
WHY WOULD NUMBER 10...
...BE ENGAGING IN THIS KIND OF BEHAVIOR ?!

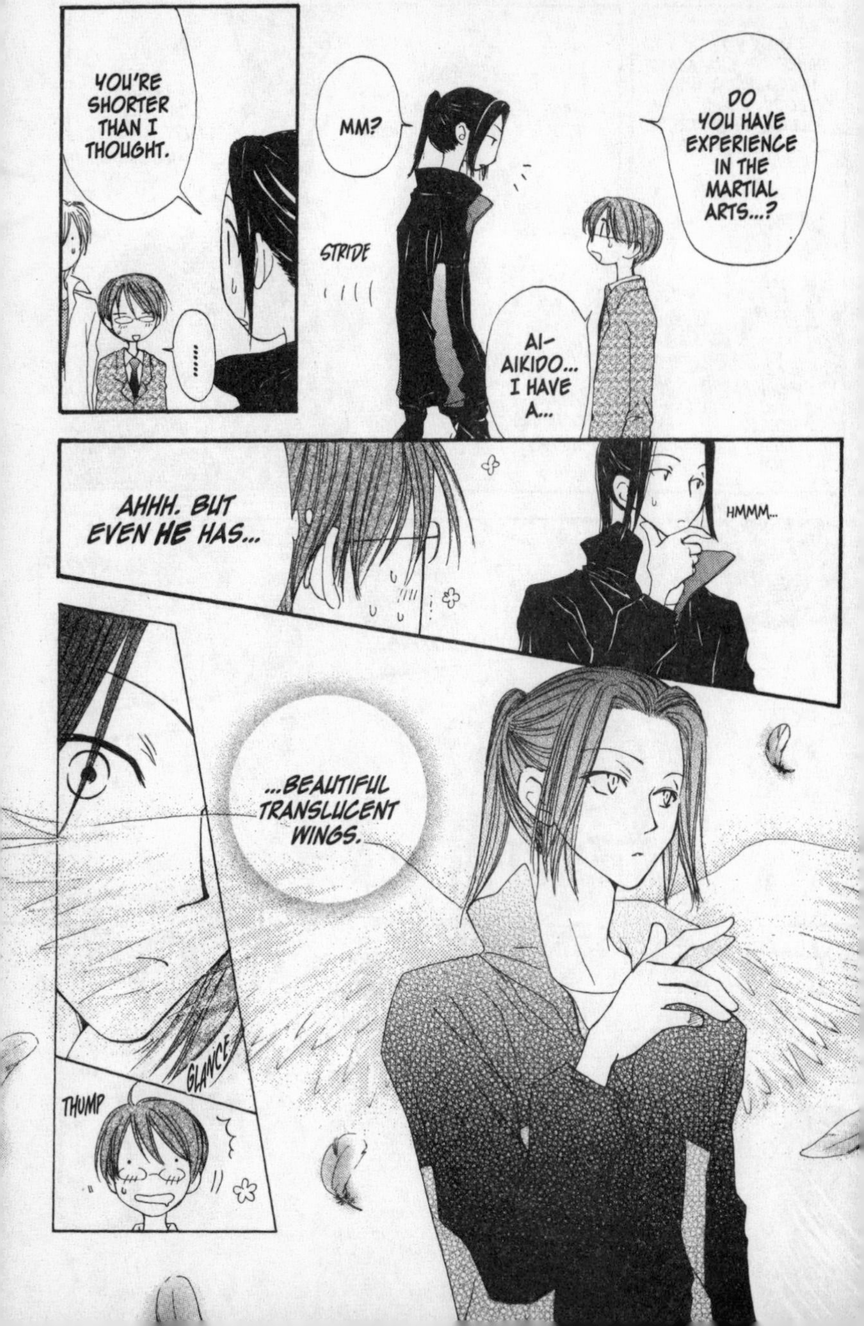
DO YOU HAVE EXPERIENCE IN THE MARTIAL ARTS...?
MM?
AI- AIKIDO... I HAVE A...
STRIDE
YOU'RE SHORTER THAN I THOUGHT.
......
HMMM...
AHHH. BUT EVEN HE HAS...
...BEAUTIFUL TRANSLUCENT WINGS.
GLANCE
THUMP

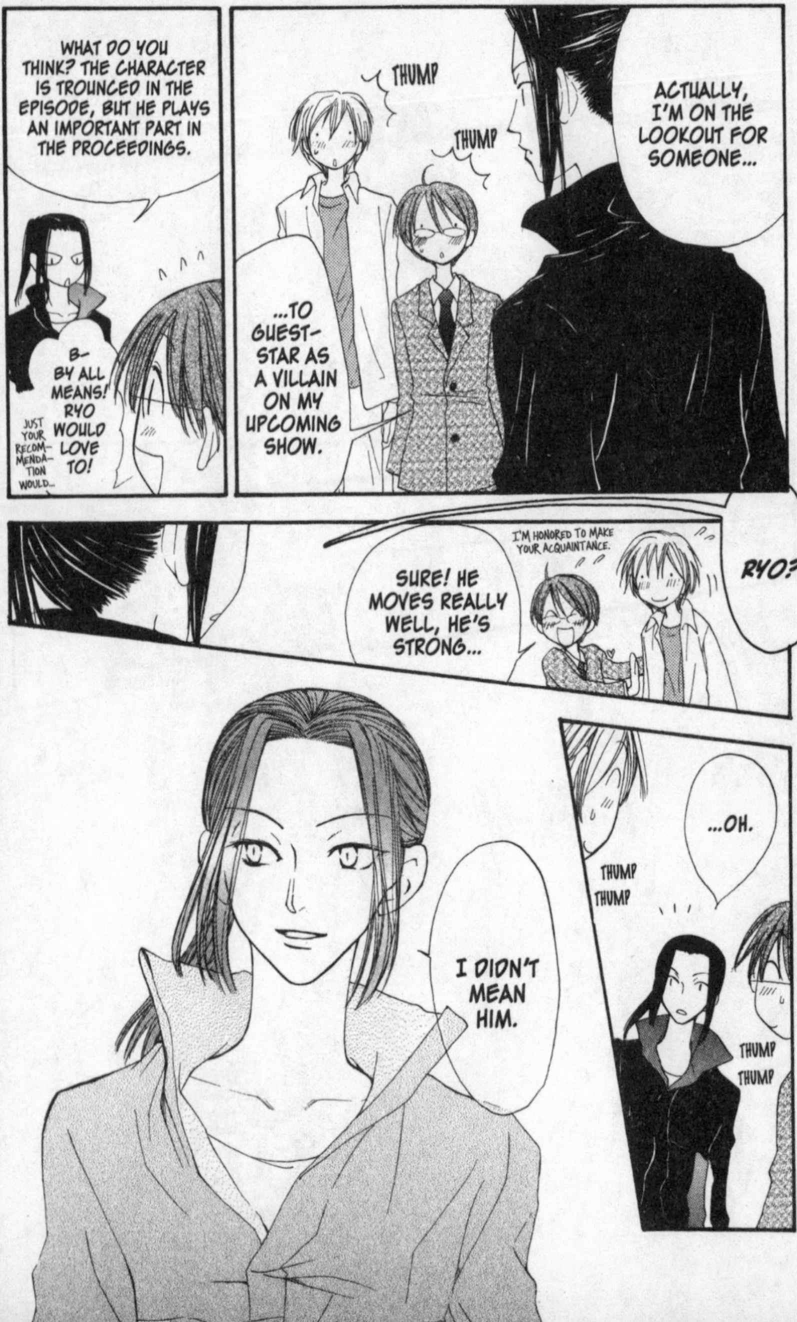
ACTUALLY, I'M ON THE LOOKOUT FOR SOMEONE...
THUMP
THUMP
...TO GUEST-STAR AS A VILLAIN ON MY UPCOMING SHOW.
WHAT DO YOU THINK? THE CHARACTER IS TROUNCED IN THE EPISODE, BUT HE PLAYS AN IMPORTANT PART IN THE PROCEEDINGS.
B- BY ALL MEANS! RYO WOULD LOVE TO!
JUST YOUR RECOMMENDATION WOULD...
RYO?
I'M HONORED TO MAKE YOUR ACQUAINTANCE.
SURE! HE MOVES REALLY WELL, HE'S STRONG...
...OH.
THUMP THUMP
THUMP THUMP
I DIDN'T MEAN HIM.

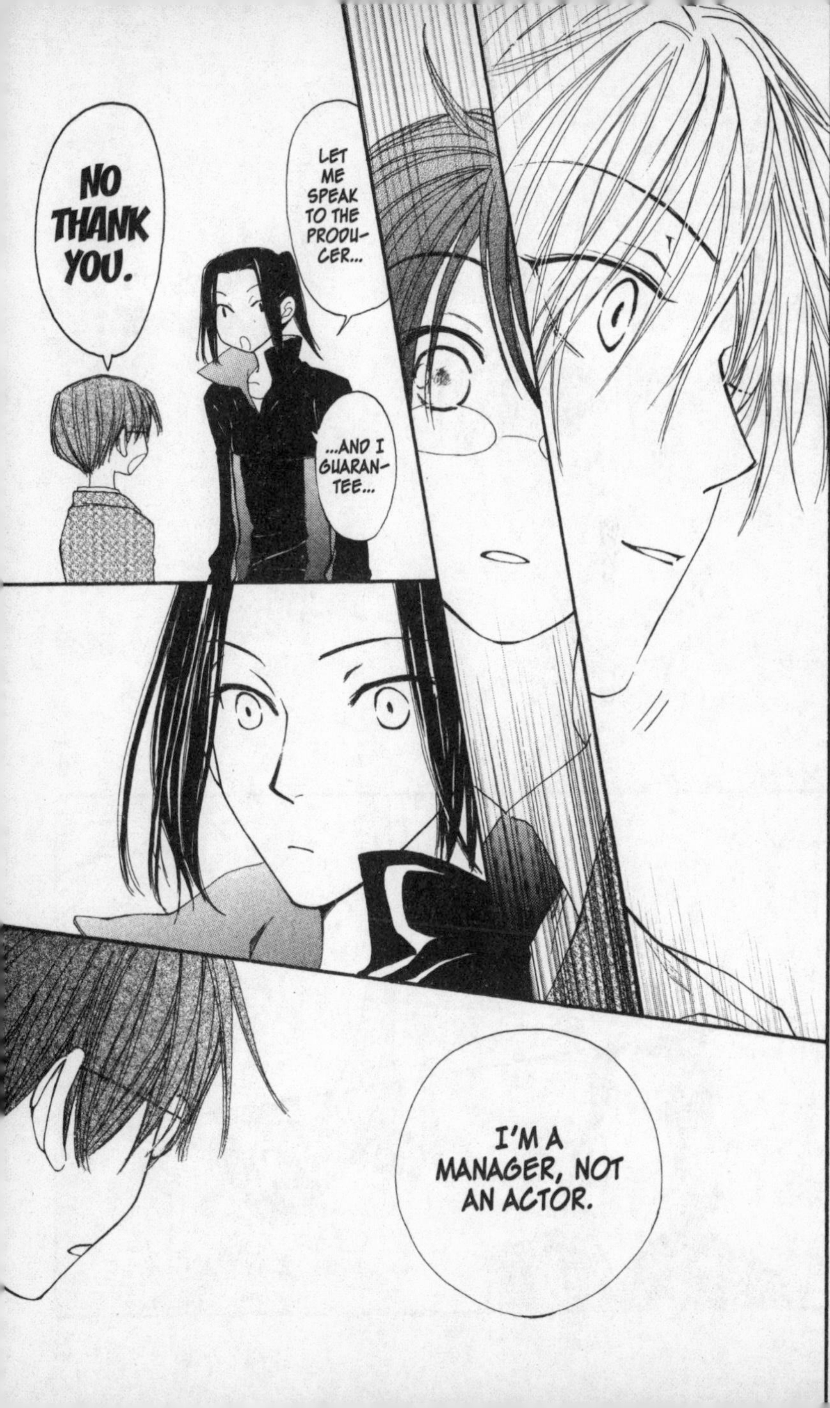
LET ME SPEAK TO THE PRODUCER...
...AND I GUARANTEE...
NO THANK YOU.
I'M A MANAGER, NOT AN ACTOR.

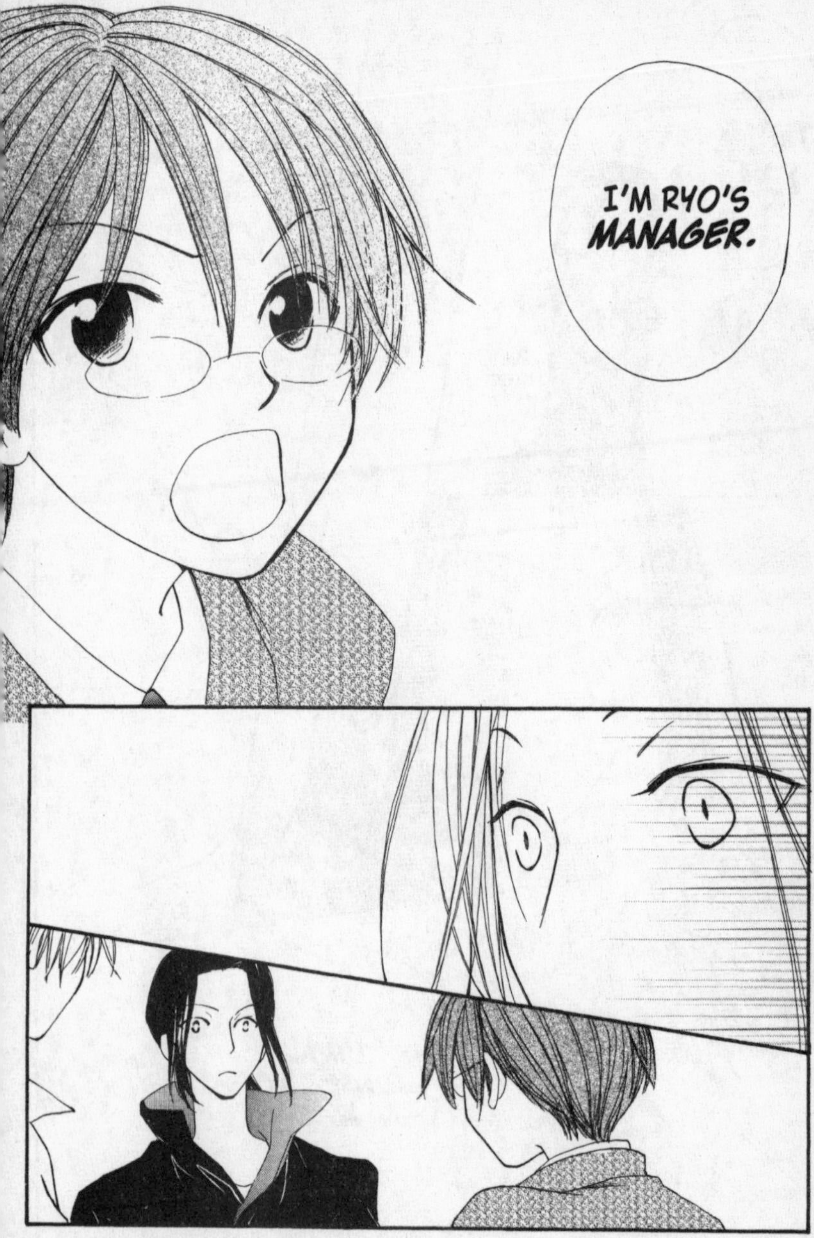
I'M RYO'S MANAGER.

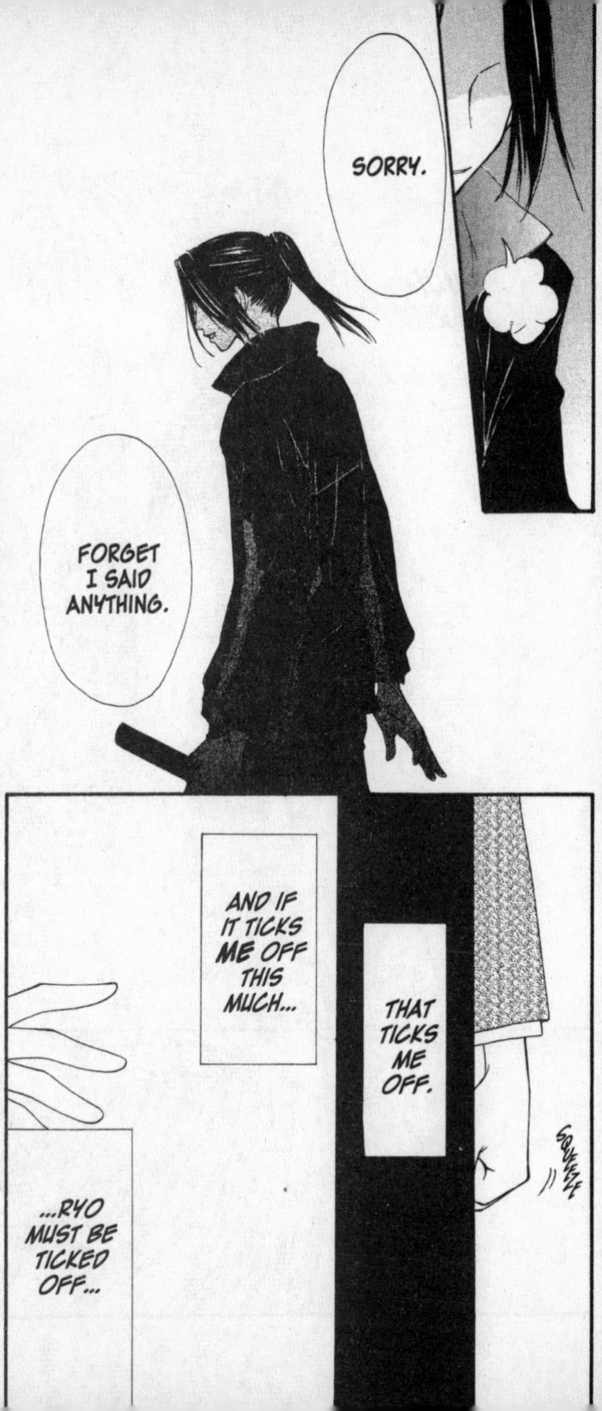
SORRY.
FORGET I SAID ANYTHING.
THAT TICKS ME OFF.
SQUEEZE
AND IF IT TICKS ME OFF THIS MUCH...
...RYO MUST BE TICKED OFF...

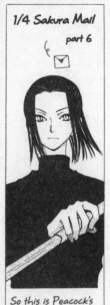

1/4 Sakura Mail
part 6

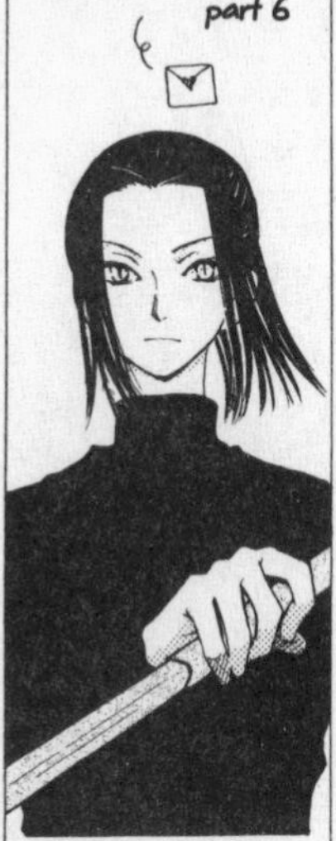

So this is Peacock's Number 10 man, Yuzuru Narazaki-san. I feel a little sorry for Ryo, who has longed to be one of the "Numbers" from the very beginning, yet they act like he doesn't exist. Ah, well, this too is a kind of training, so keep an eye on Ryo.
One thing I really like about Yuzuru Narazaki-san's debut here is that it gives me a chance to focus on Yuka-chin's own martial arts abilities.

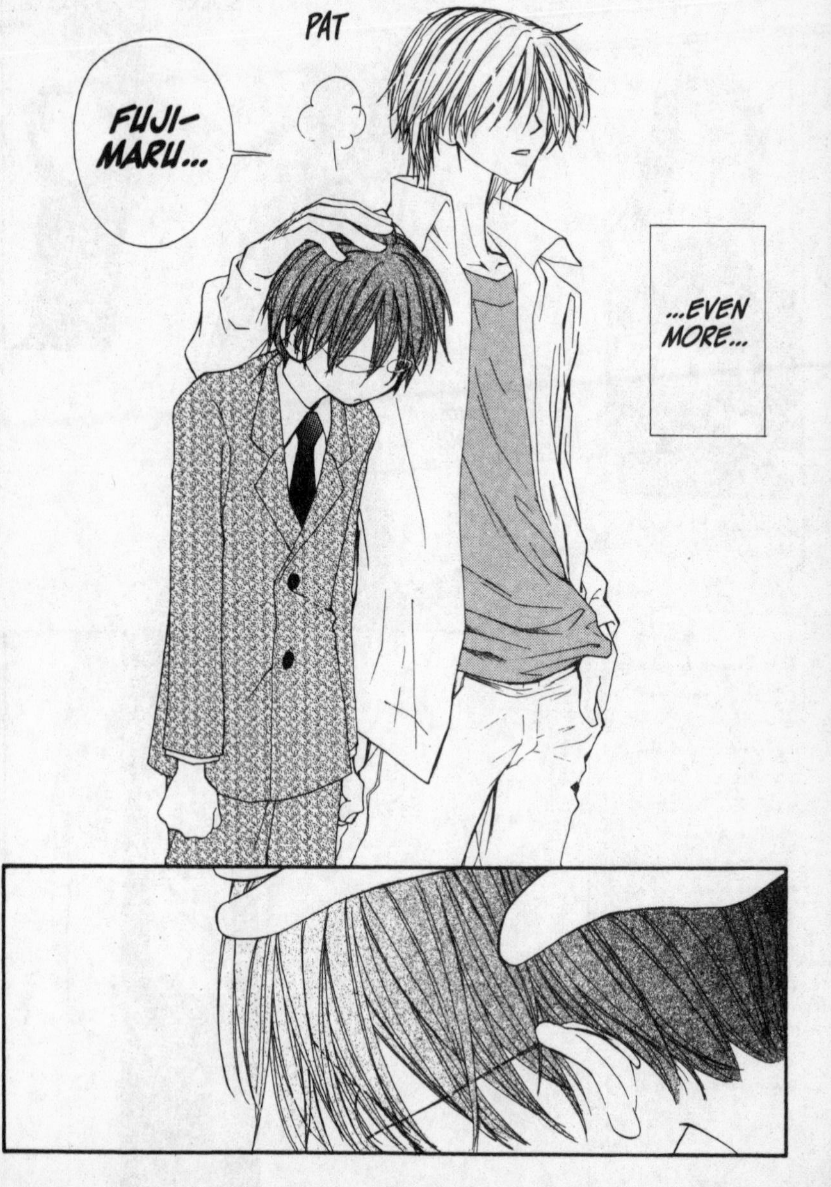
PAT
FUJI-MARU...
...EVEN MORE...

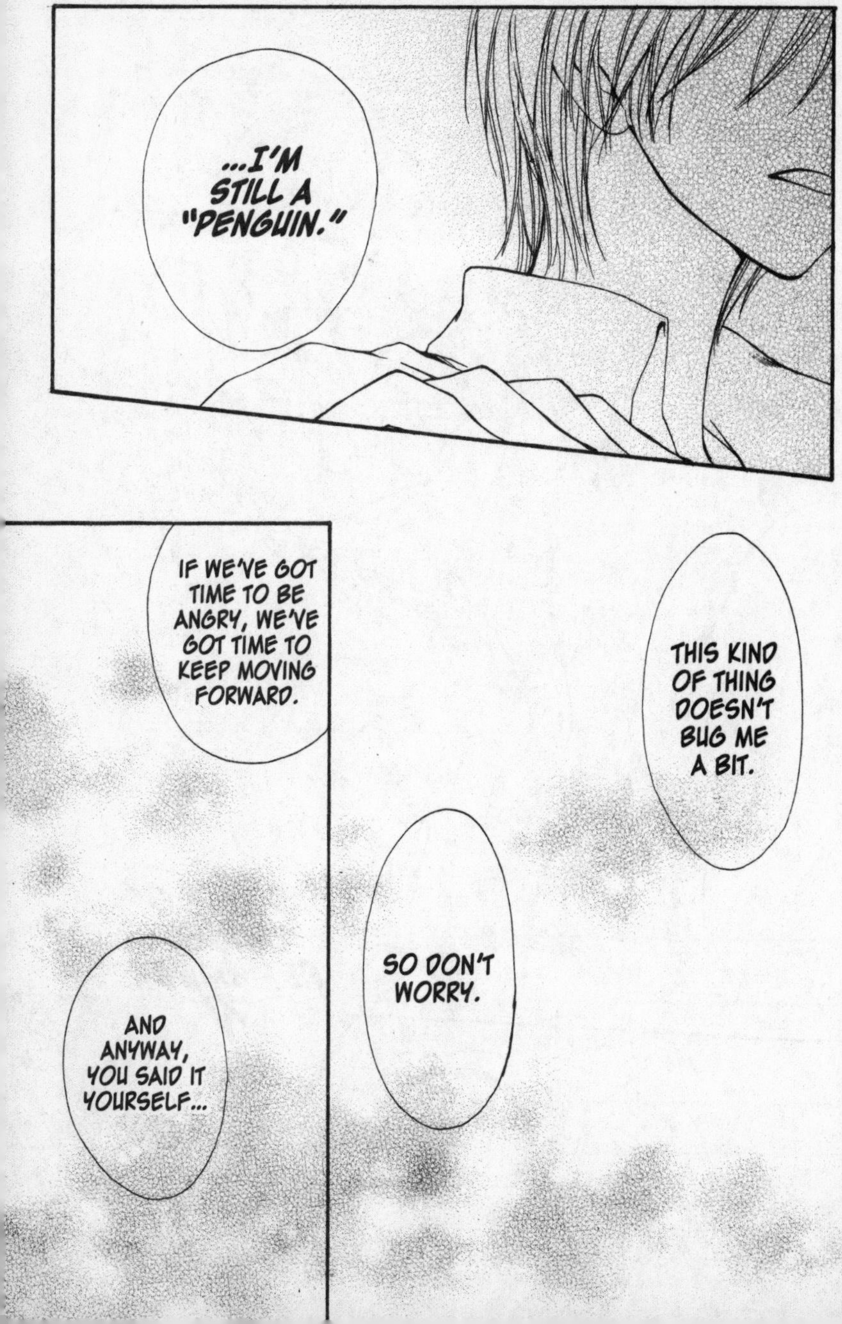
...I'M STILL A "PENGUIN."
THIS KIND OF THING DOESN'T BUG ME A BIT.
SO DON'T WORRY.
IF WE'VE GOT TIME TO BE ANGRY, WE'VE GOT TIME TO KEEP MOVING FORWARD.
AND ANYWAY, YOU SAID IT YOURSELF...

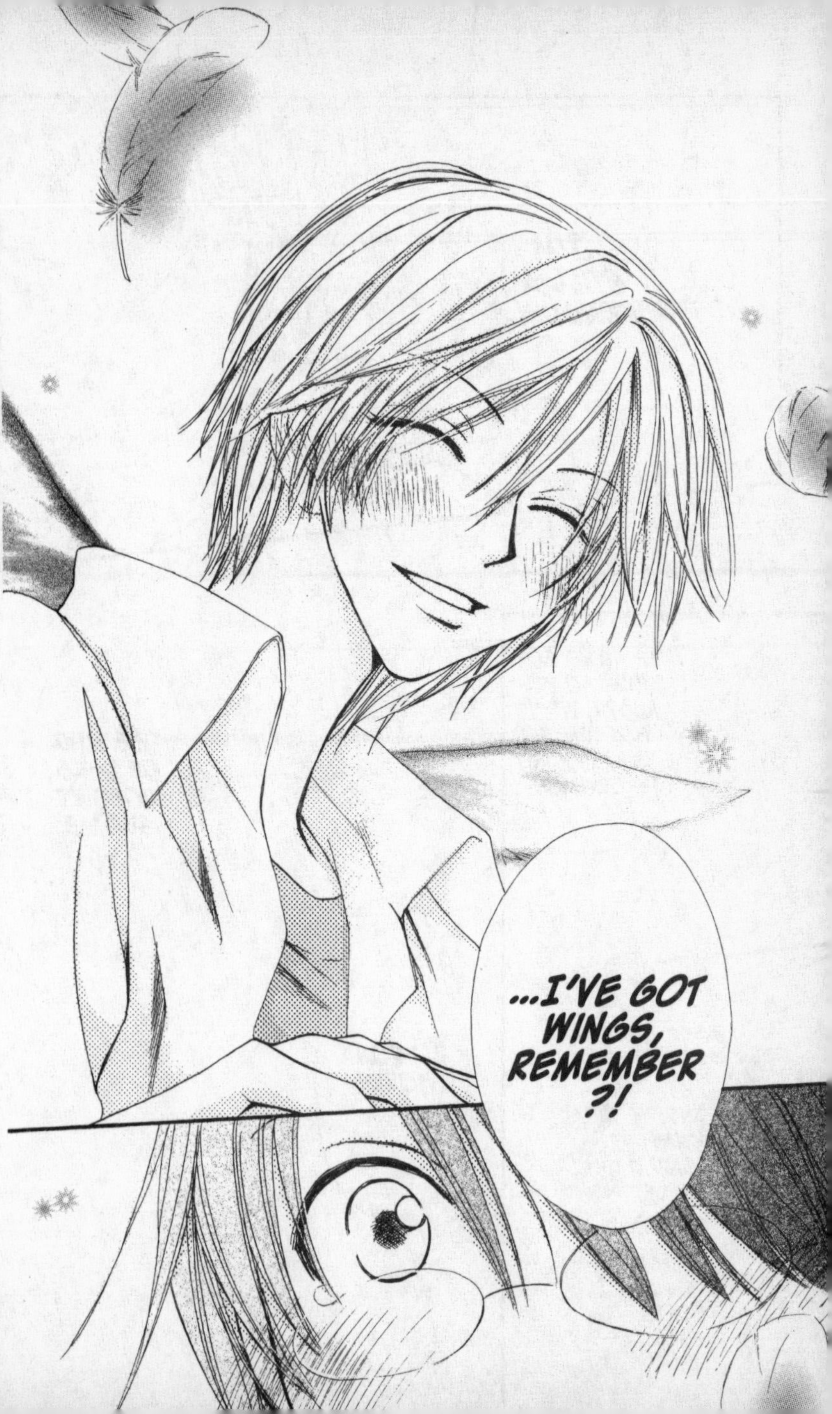
...I'VE GOT WINGS, REMEMBER ?!

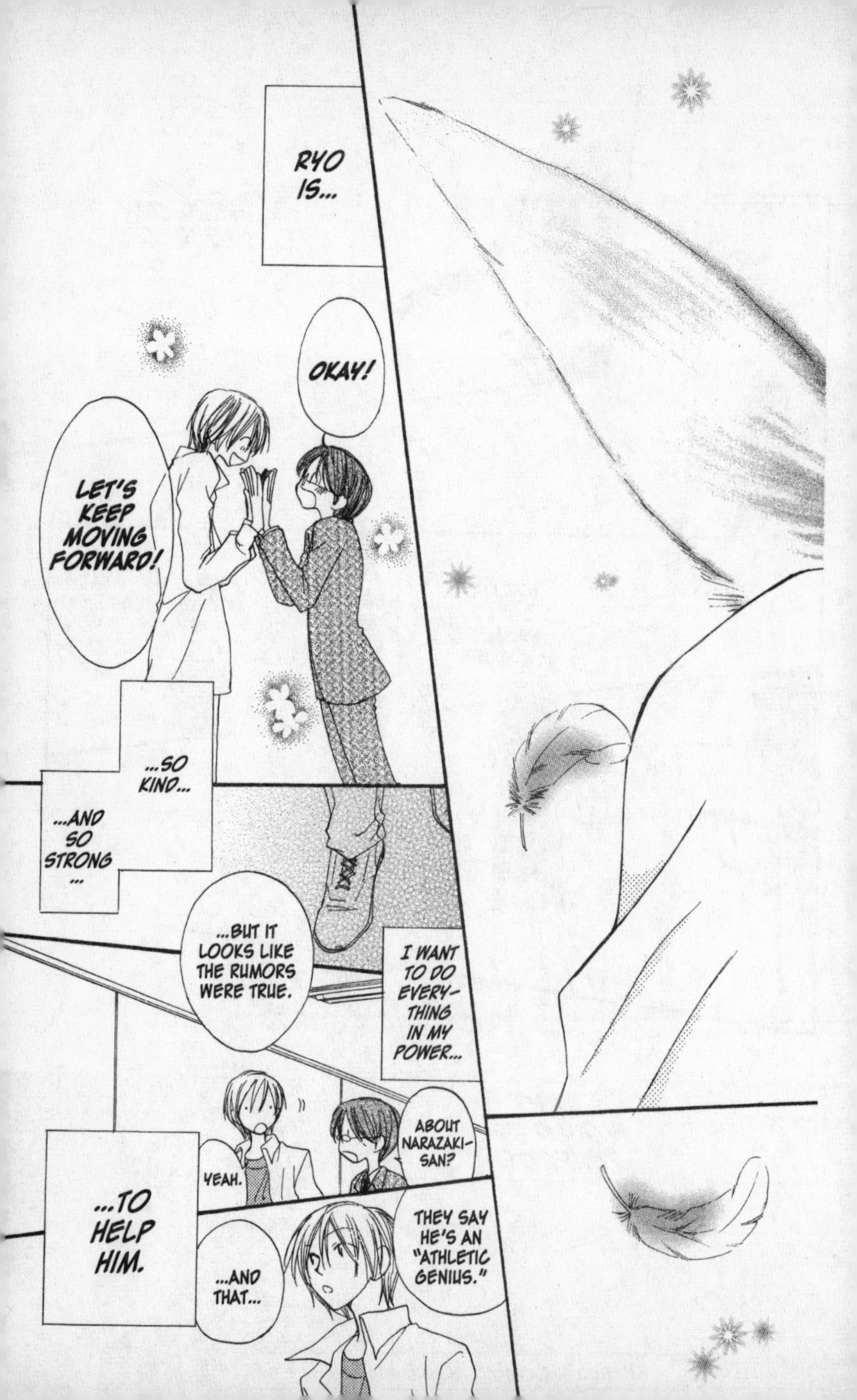
RYO IS...
OKAY!
LET'S KEEP MOVING FORWARD!
...SO KIND...
...AND SO STRONG...
I WANT TO DO EVERY-THING IN MY POWER...
...BUT IT LOOKS LIKE THE RUMORS WERE TRUE.
ABOUT NARAZAKI-SAN?
YEAH.
...TO HELP HIM.
THEY SAY HE'S AN "ATHLETIC GENIUS."
...AND THAT...

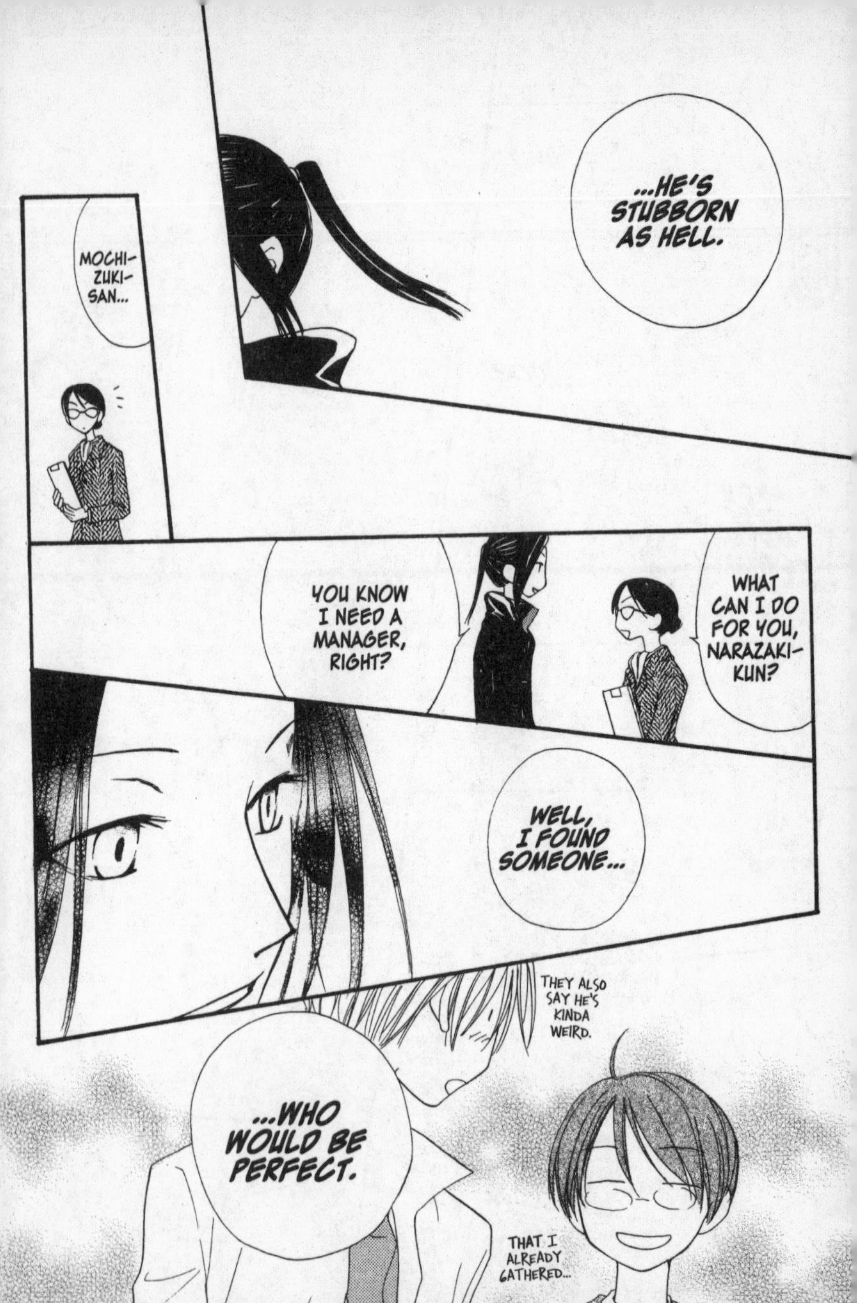
...HE'S STUBBORN AS HELL.
MOCHI-ZUKI-SAN...
WHAT CAN I DO FOR YOU, NARAZAKI-KUN?
YOU KNOW I NEED A MANAGER, RIGHT?
WELL, I FOUND SOMEONE...
...WHO WOULD BE PERFECT.
THEY ALSO SAY HE'S KINDA WEIRD.
THAT I ALREADY GATHERED...

Penguin Revolution Episode 8: The End

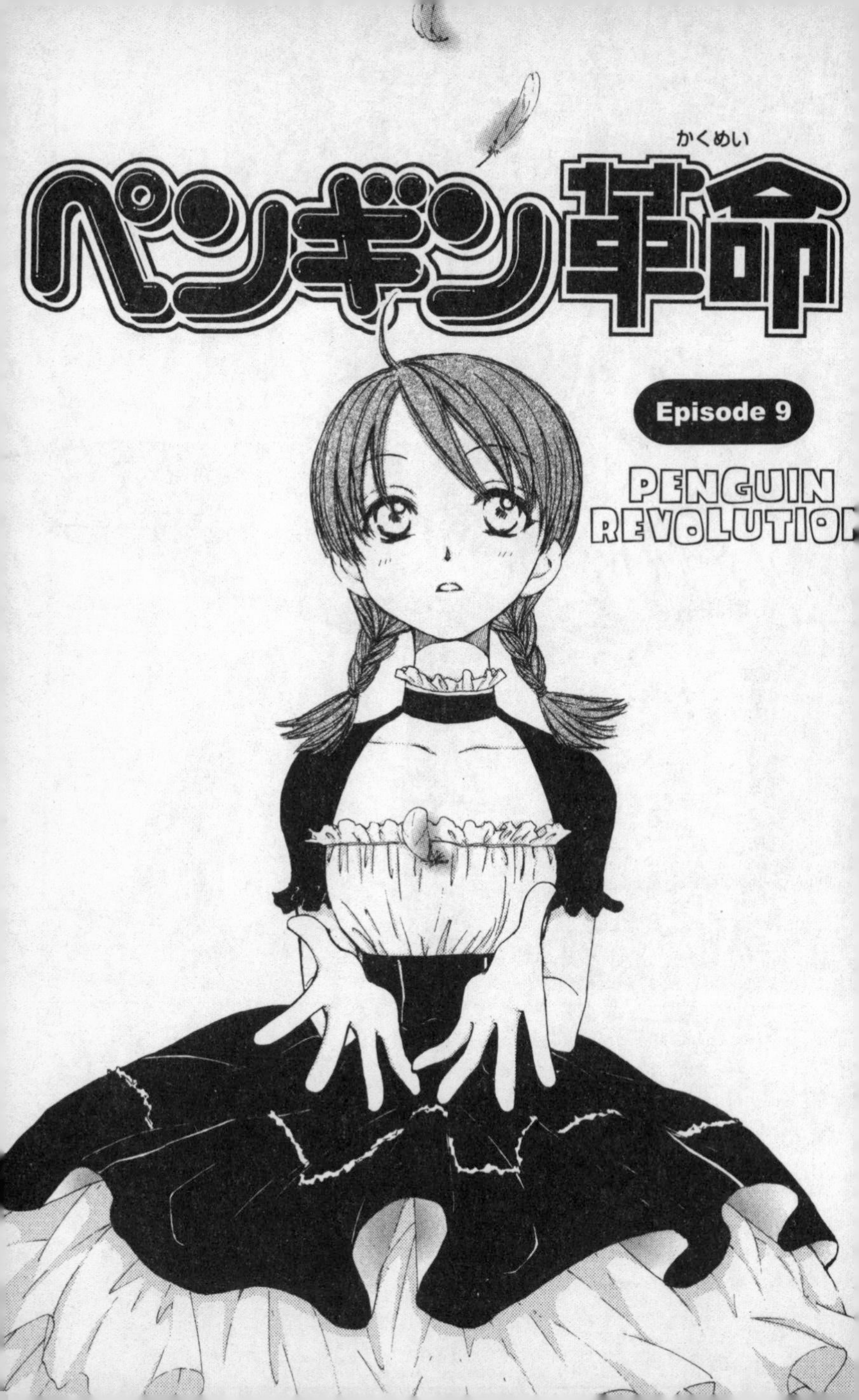
かくめい
ペンギン革命
Episode 9
PENGUIN
REVOLUTION

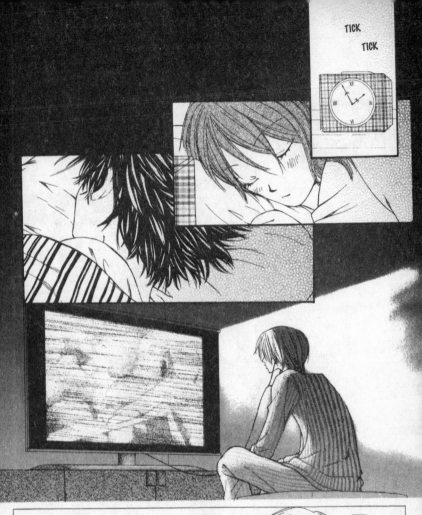

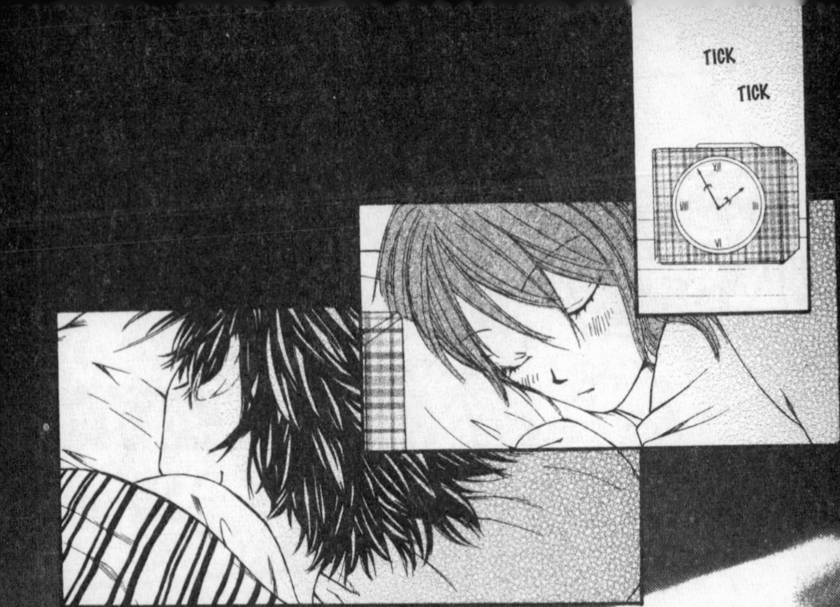
TICK
TICK

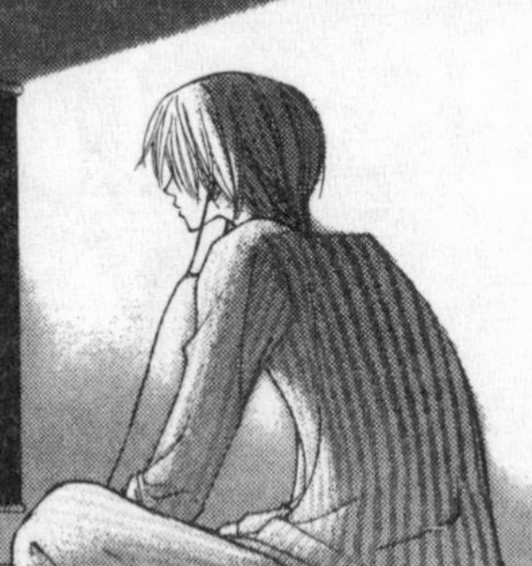

1/4 Sakura Mail

part 7

In this episode, I drew Yuka-chan's plain, everyday activities. I went back to the books to do research for her high school mathematics class in the story and ugh, was it difficult! I totally forgot all of the formulas I "learned" when I went to school. But boy, Yuka-chan is busy, isn't she, what with school and work? She's gotta be a whiz at time management.

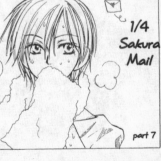

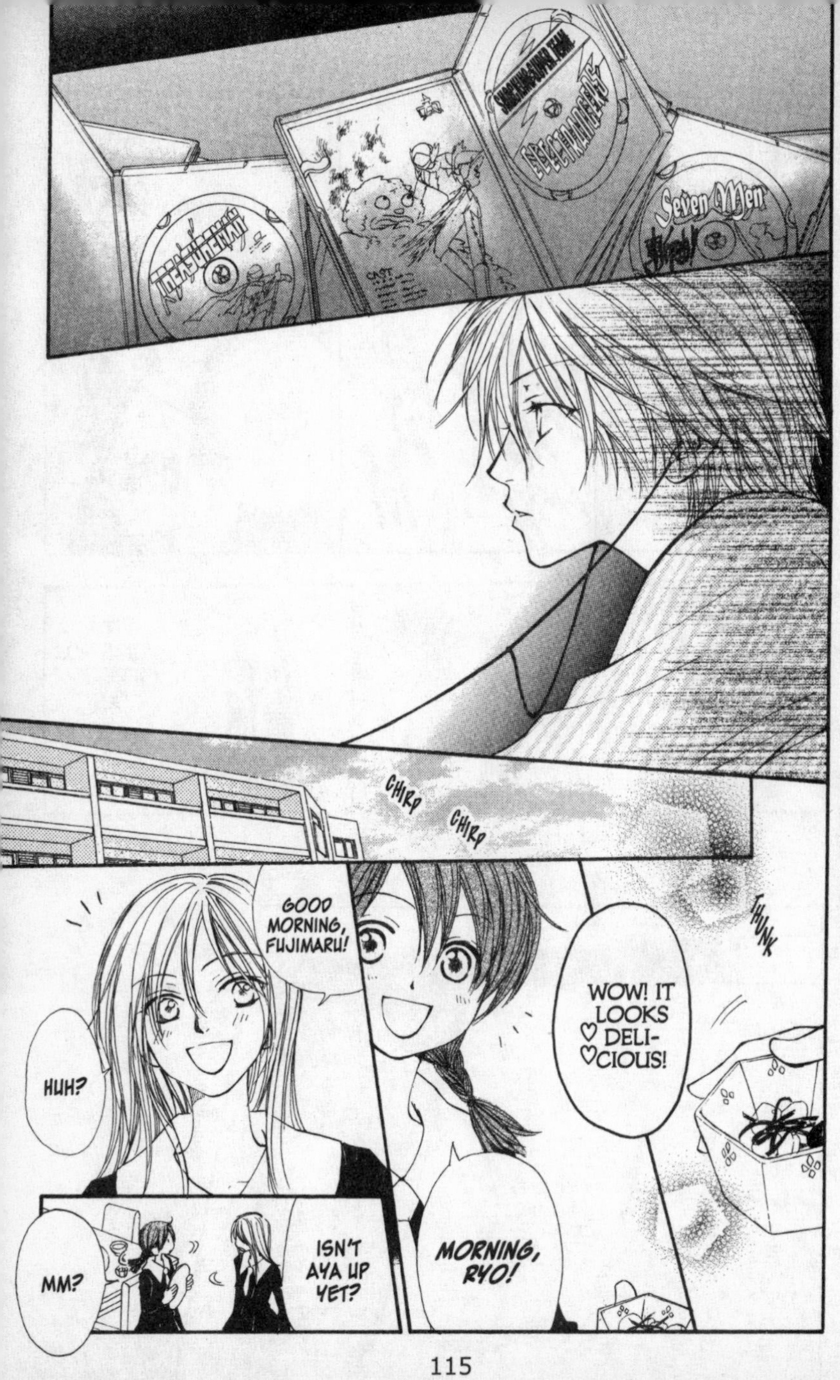
Seven Men
CHIRP
CHIRP
THUNK
WOW! IT LOOKS ♡ DELI- ♡CIOUS!
GOOD MORNING, FUJIMARU!
MORNING, RYO!
HUH?
ISN'T AYA UP YET?
MM?

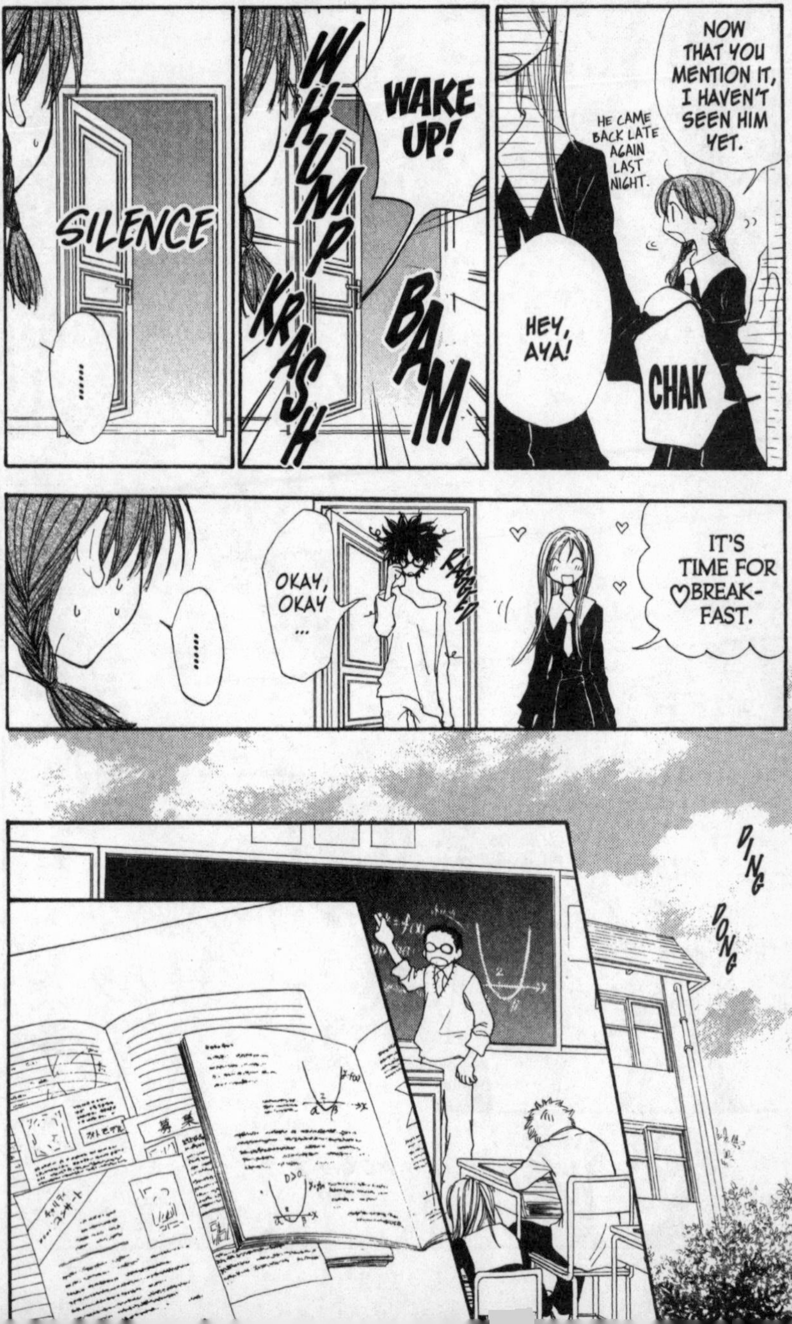
NOW THAT YOU MENTION IT, I HAVEN'T SEEN HIM YET.
HE CAME BACK LATE AGAIN LAST NIGHT.
HEY, AYA!
CHAK
WAKE UP!
WHUMP
BAM
KRASH
SILENCE
......
IT'S TIME FOR ♡BREAK-FAST.
OKAY, OKAY ...
......
DING
DONG

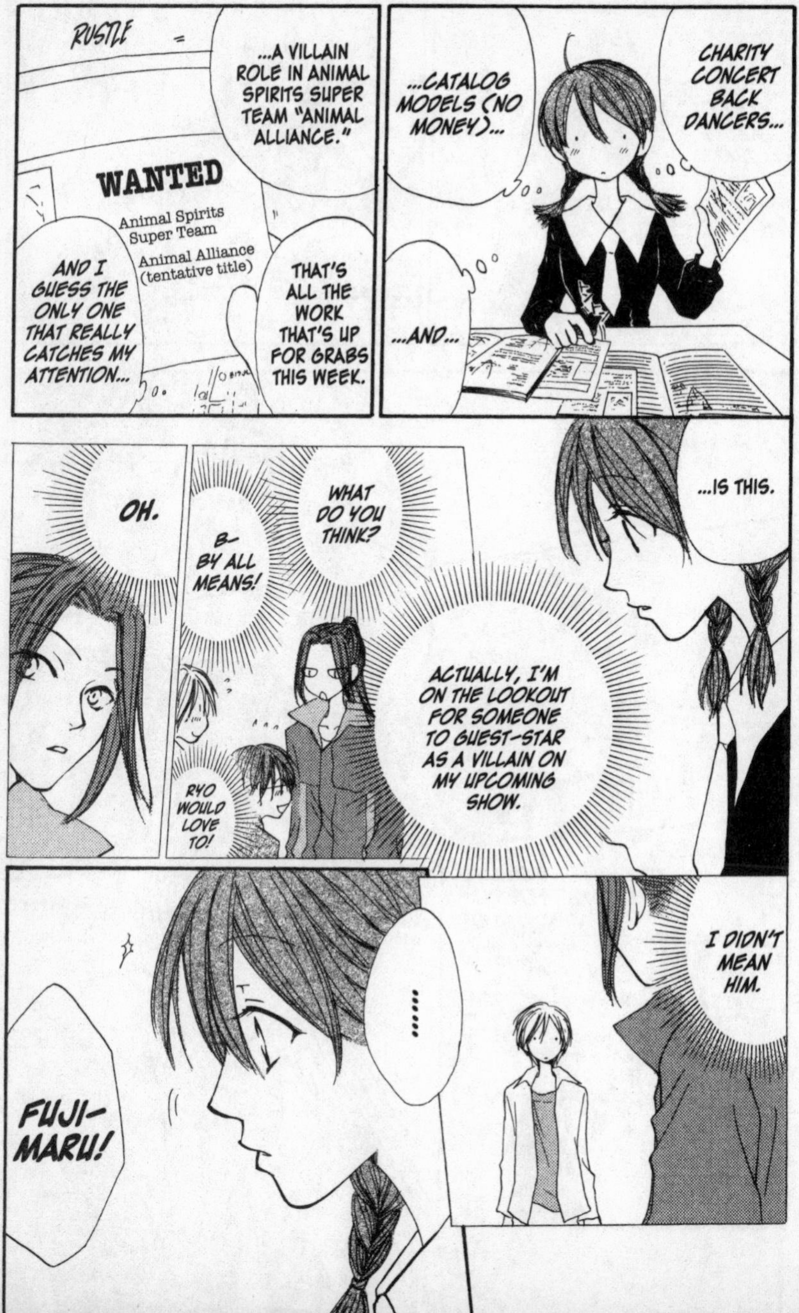
CHARITY CONCERT BACK DANCERS...
...CATALOG MODELS (NO MONEY)...
...AND...
RUSTLE
...A VILLAIN ROLE IN ANIMAL SPIRITS SUPER TEAM "ANIMAL ALLIANCE."
WANTED
Animal Spirits Super Team
Animal Alliance (tentative title)
THAT'S ALL THE WORK THAT'S UP FOR GRABS THIS WEEK.
AND I GUESS THE ONLY ONE THAT REALLY CATCHES MY ATTENTION...
...IS THIS.
ACTUALLY, I'M ON THE LOOKOUT FOR SOMEONE TO GUEST-STAR AS A VILLAIN ON MY UPCOMING SHOW.
WHAT DO YOU THINK?
B- BY ALL MEANS!
RYO WOULD LOVE TO!
OH.
I DIDN'T MEAN HIM.
......
FUJI-MARU!

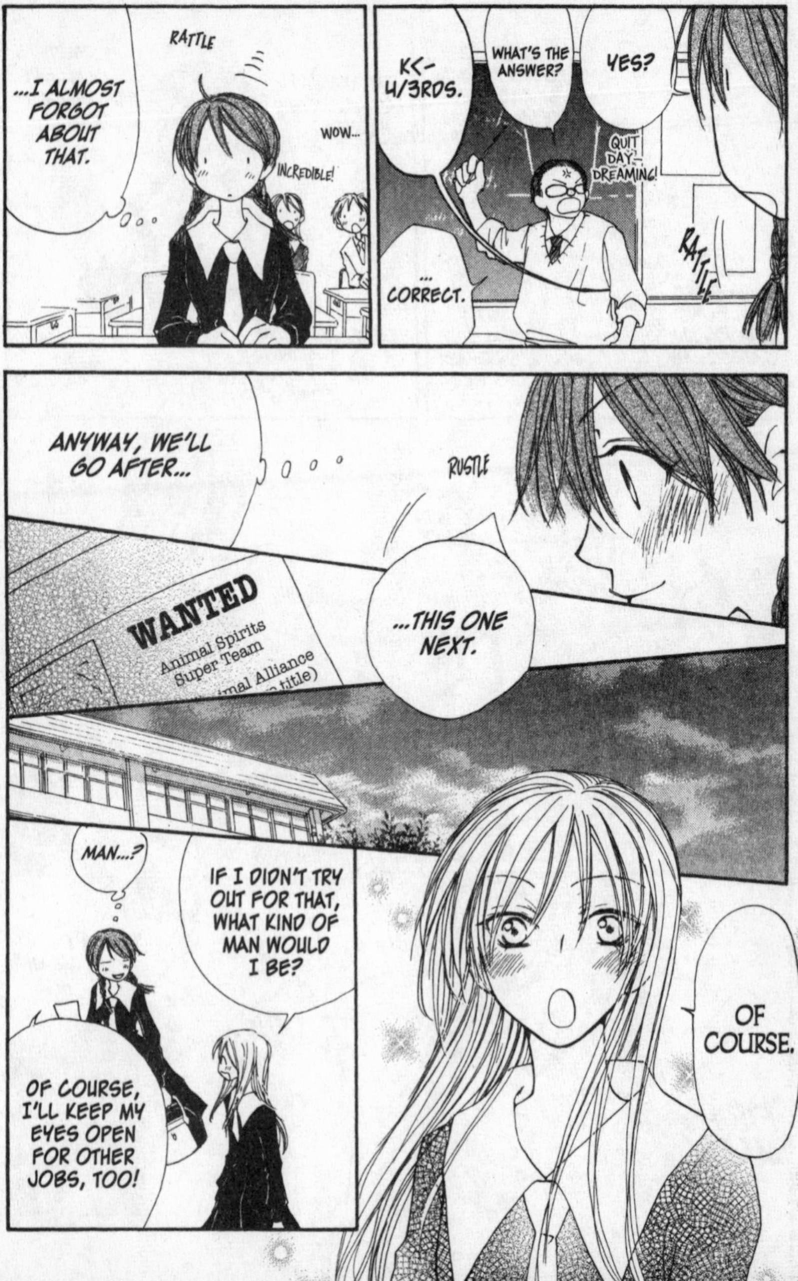
YES?
WHAT'S THE ANSWER?
QUIT DAY-DREAMING!
K<- 4/3RDS.
RATTLE
...CORRECT.
RATTLE
...I ALMOST FORGOT ABOUT THAT.
WOW...
INCREDIBLE!
ANYWAY, WE'LL GO AFTER...
RUSTLE
...THIS ONE NEXT.
WANTED
Animal Spirits Super Team
OF COURSE.
IF I DIDN'T TRY OUT FOR THAT, WHAT KIND OF MAN WOULD I BE?
MAN...?
OF COURSE, I'LL KEEP MY EYES OPEN FOR OTHER JOBS, TOO!

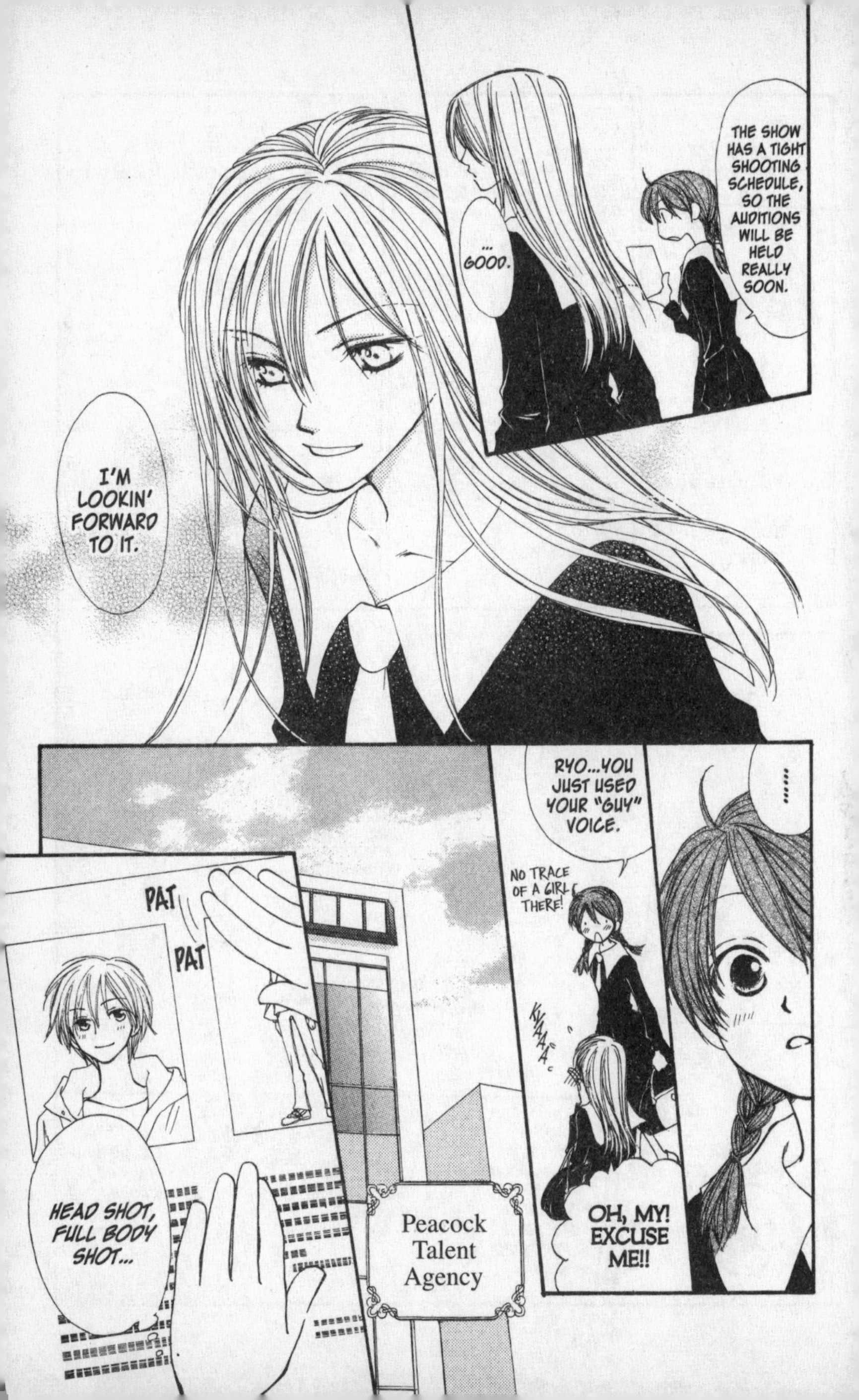
THE SHOW HAS A TIGHT SHOOTING SCHEDULE, SO THE AUDITIONS WILL BE HELD REALLY SOON.
...GOOD.
I'M LOOKIN' FORWARD TO IT.
......
RYO...YOU JUST USED YOUR "GUY" VOICE.
NO TRACE OF A GIRL THERE!
KYAAA
OH, MY! EXCUSE ME!!
Peacock Talent Agency
PAT
PAT
HEAD SHOT, FULL BODY SHOT...

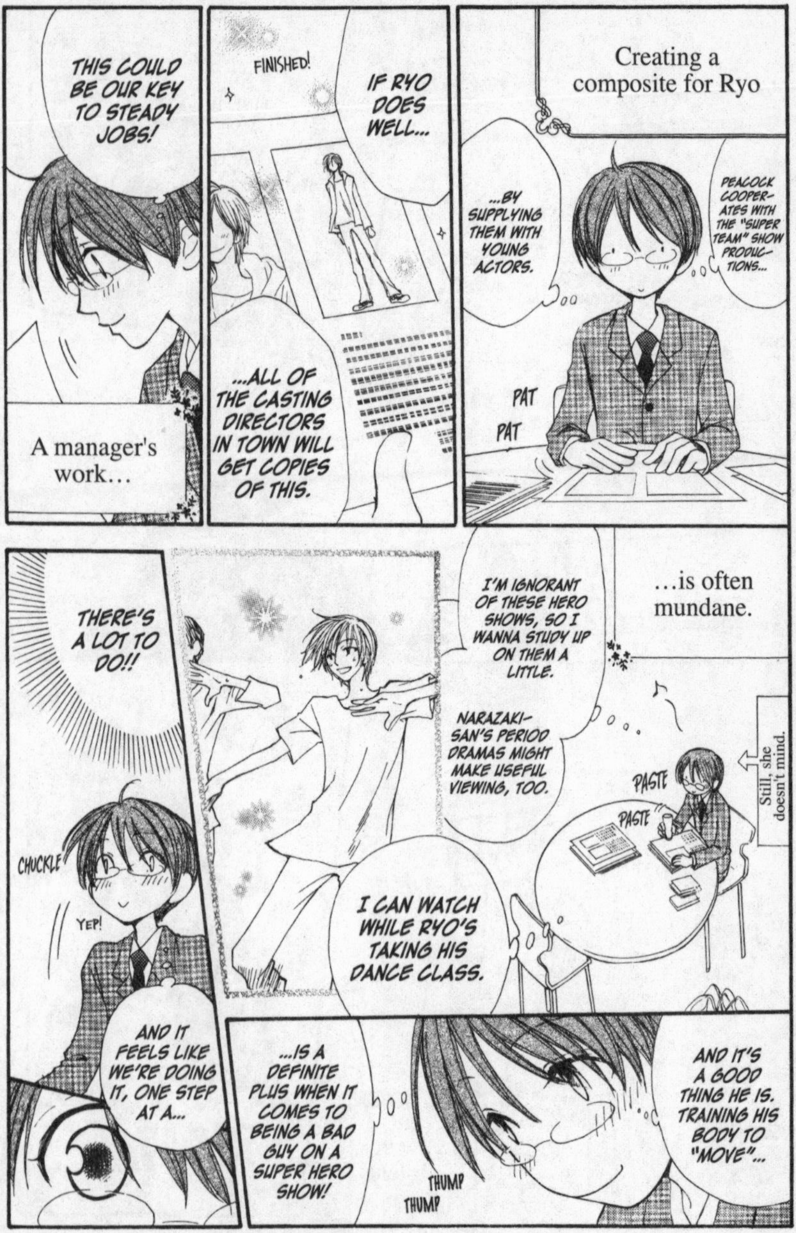
Creating a composite for Ryo
PEACOCK COOPERATES WITH THE "SUPER TEAM" SHOW PRODUCTIONS...
...BY SUPPLYING THEM WITH YOUNG ACTORS.
PAT
PAT
FINISHED!
IF RYO DOES WELL...
...ALL OF THE CASTING DIRECTORS IN TOWN WILL GET COPIES OF THIS.
THIS COULD BE OUR KEY TO STEADY JOBS!
A manager's work…
…is often mundane.
Still, she doesn't mind.
I'M IGNORANT OF THESE HERO SHOWS, SO I WANNA STUDY UP ON THEM A LITTLE.
NARAZAKI-SAN'S PERIOD DRAMAS MIGHT MAKE USEFUL VIEWING, TOO.
PASTE
PASTE
I CAN WATCH WHILE RYO'S TAKING HIS DANCE CLASS.
THERE'S A LOT TO DO!!
CHUCKLE
YEP!
AND IT'S A GOOD THING HE IS. TRAINING HIS BODY TO "MOVE"...
...IS A DEFINITE PLUS WHEN IT COMES TO BEING A BAD GUY ON A SUPER HERO SHOW!
THUMP
THUMP
AND IT FEELS LIKE WE'RE DOING IT, ONE STEP AT A...

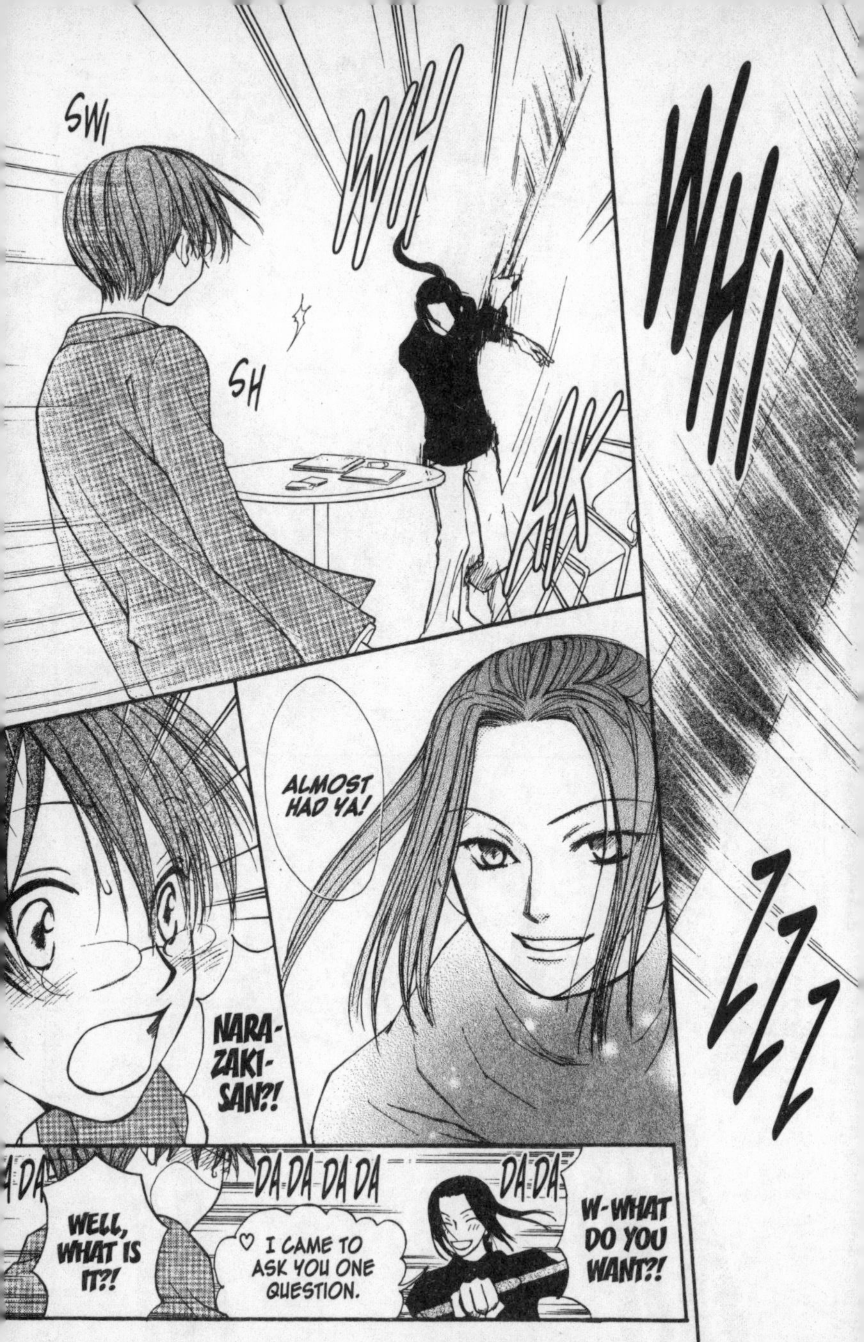
WHI
ZZZ
SWI
WH
SH
AK
ALMOST HAD YA!
NARA-ZAKI-SAN?!
W-WHAT DO YOU WANT?!
DA DA
♡ I CAME TO ASK YOU ONE QUESTION.
DA DA DA DA
WELL, WHAT IS IT?!
DA

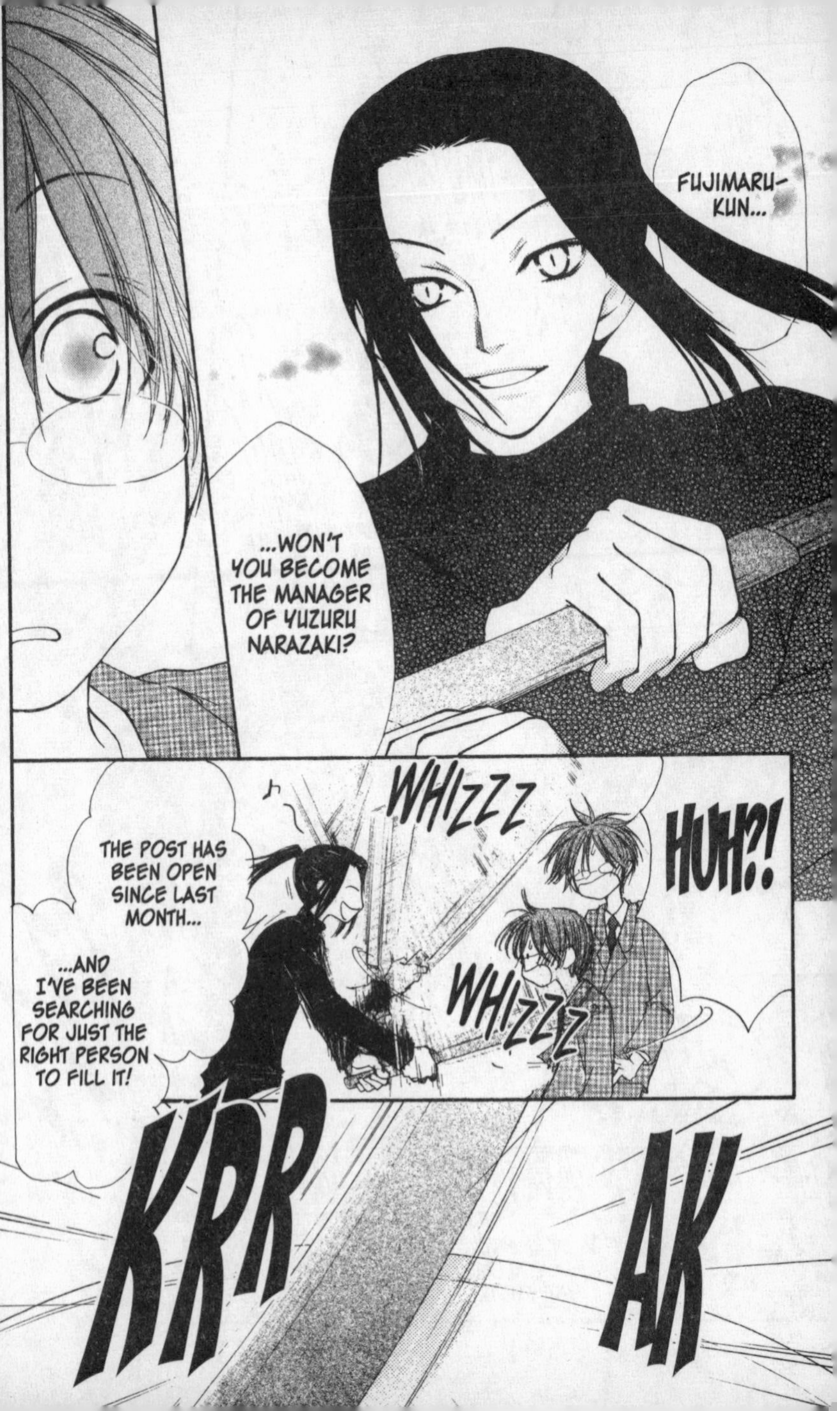
FUJIMARU-KUN...
...WON'T YOU BECOME THE MANAGER OF YUZURU NARAZAKI?
HUH?!
WHIZZZ
WHIZZZ
THE POST HAS BEEN OPEN SINCE LAST MONTH...
...AND I'VE BEEN SEARCHING FOR JUST THE RIGHT PERSON TO FILL IT!
KRR
AK

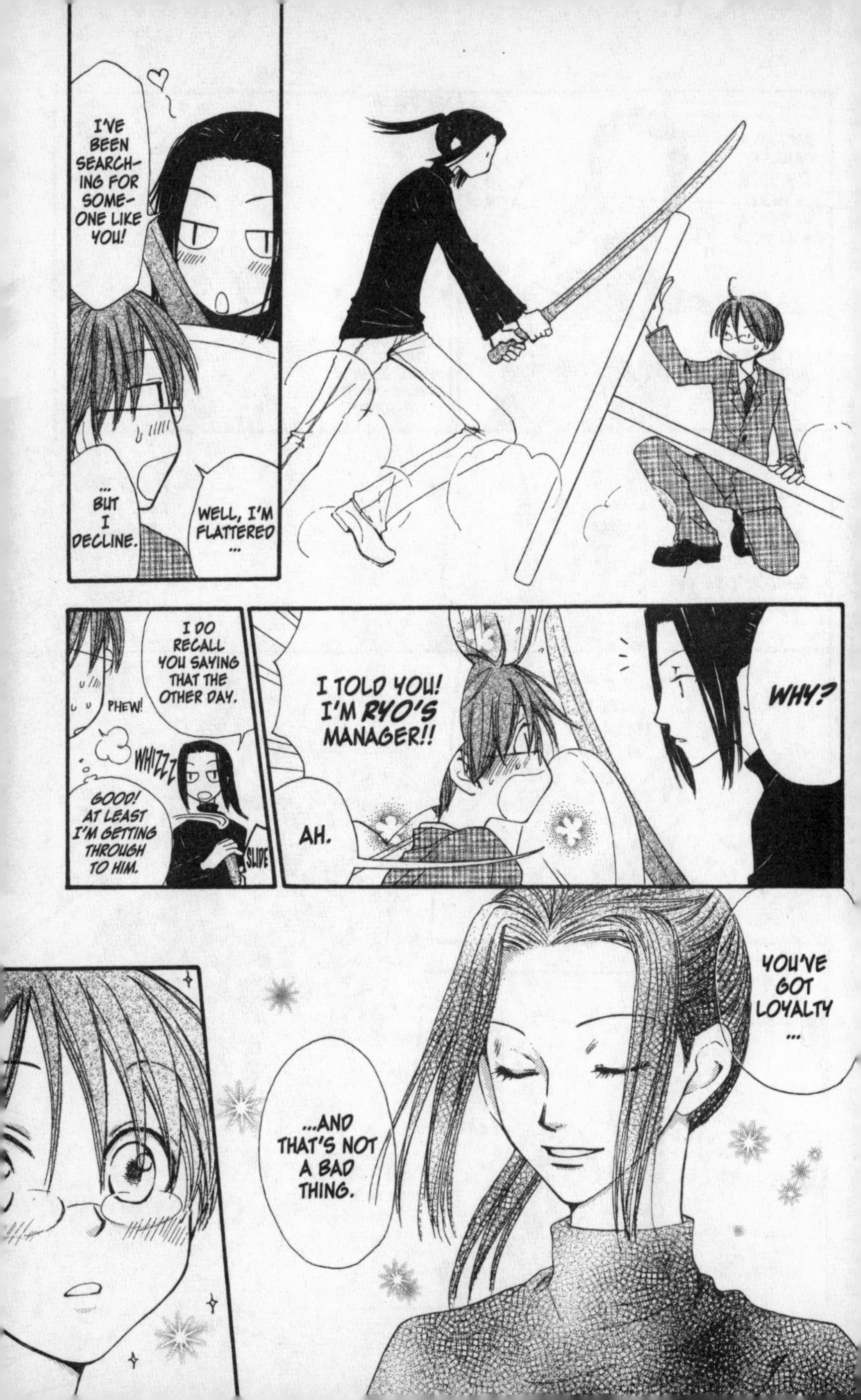
I'VE BEEN SEARCHING FOR SOMEONE LIKE YOU!
WELL, I'M FLATTERED...
...BUT I DECLINE.
WHY?
I TOLD YOU! I'M RYO'S MANAGER!!
AH.
I DO RECALL YOU SAYING THAT THE OTHER DAY.
PHEW!
WHIZZZ
GOOD! AT LEAST I'M GETTING THROUGH TO HIM.
SLIDE
YOU'VE GOT LOYALTY...
...AND THAT'S NOT A BAD THING.

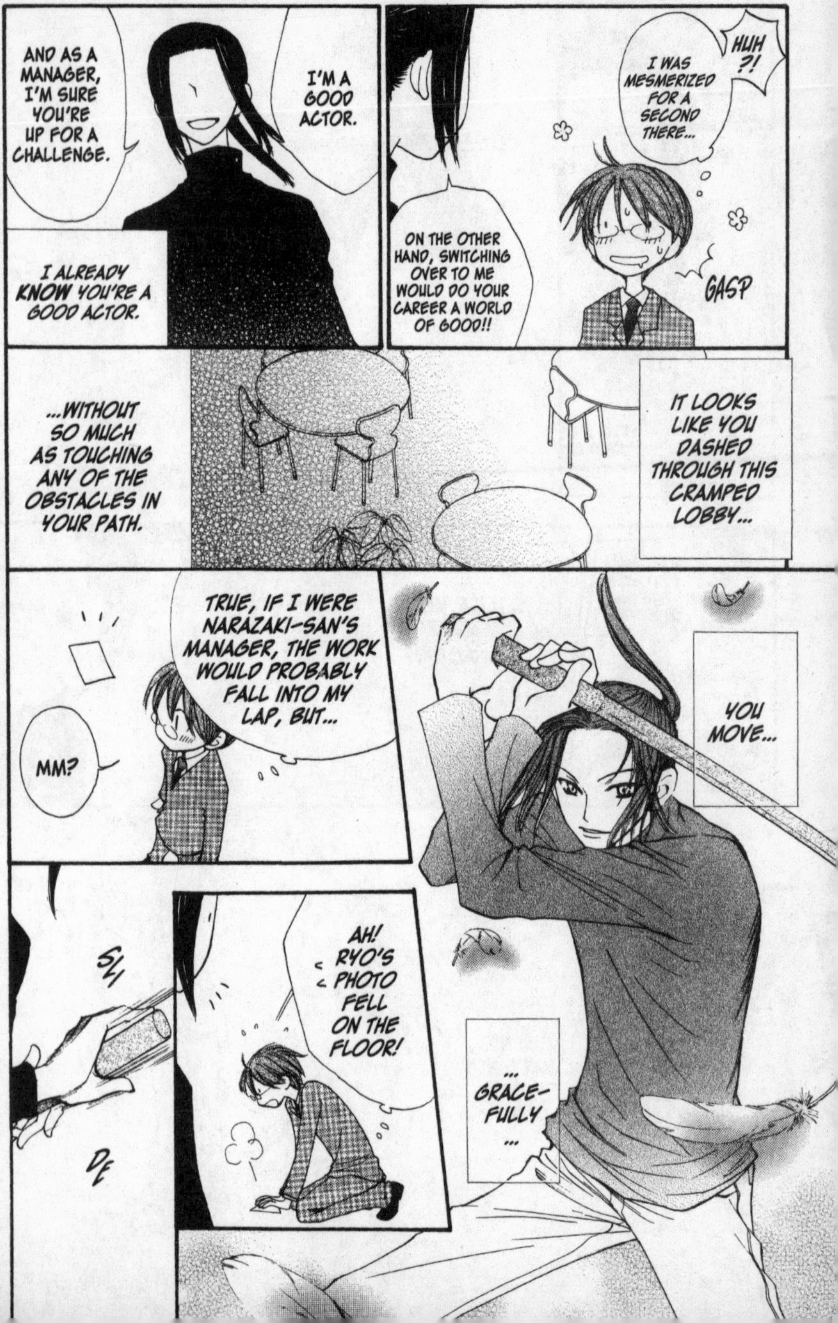
HUH ?!
I WAS MESMERIZED FOR A SECOND THERE...
ON THE OTHER HAND, SWITCHING OVER TO ME WOULD DO YOUR CAREER A WORLD OF GOOD!!
GASP
I'M A GOOD ACTOR.
AND AS A MANAGER, I'M SURE YOU'RE UP FOR A CHALLENGE.
I ALREADY KNOW YOU'RE A GOOD ACTOR.
IT LOOKS LIKE YOU DASHED THROUGH THIS CRAMPED LOBBY...
...WITHOUT SO MUCH AS TOUCHING ANY OF THE OBSTACLES IN YOUR PATH.
YOU MOVE...
...GRACEFULLY...
TRUE, IF I WERE NARAZAKI-SAN'S MANAGER, THE WORK WOULD PROBABLY FALL INTO MY LAP, BUT...
MM?
AH! RYO'S PHOTO FELL ON THE FLOOR!
SLI
DE

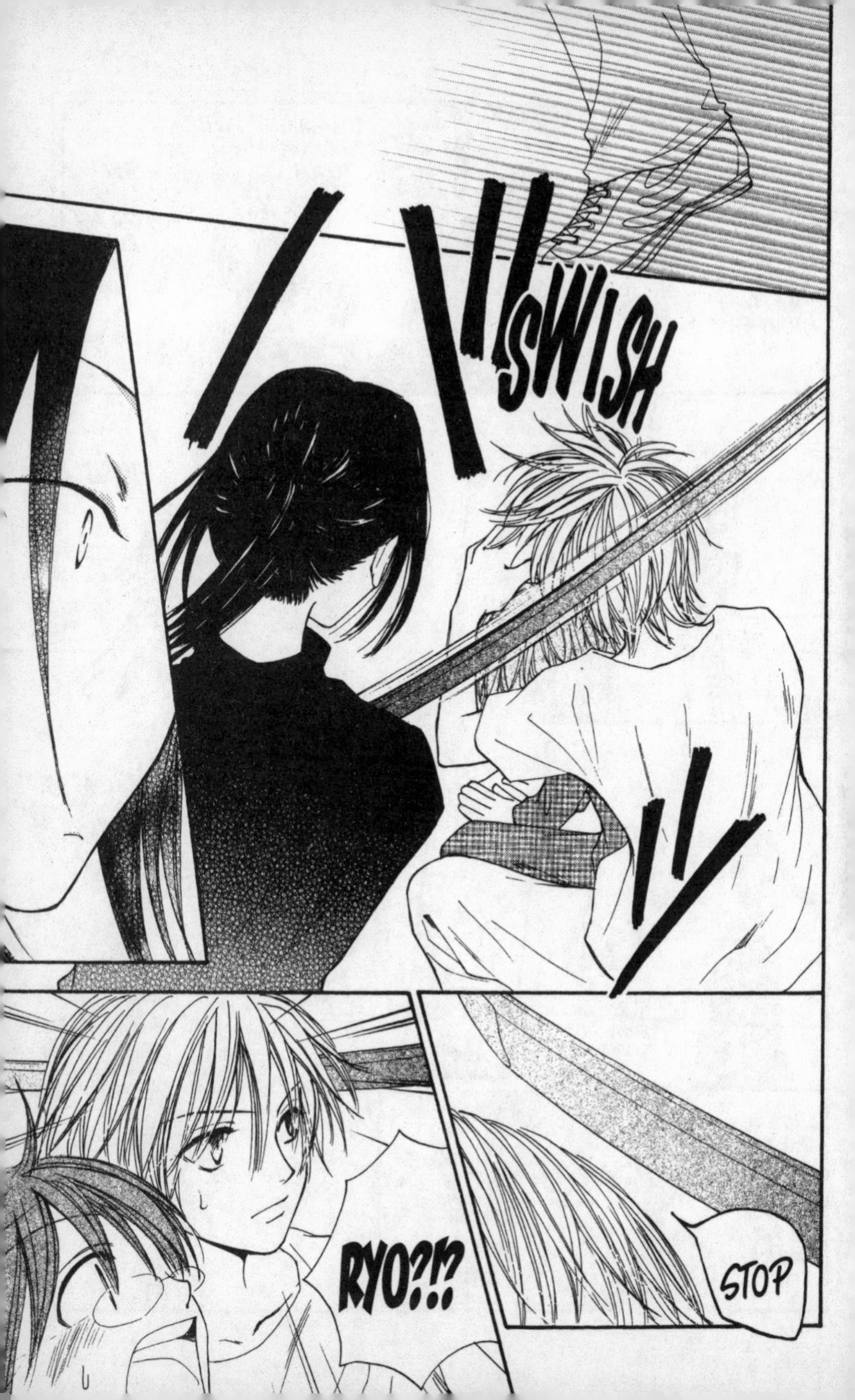
SWISH
STOP
RYO?!?

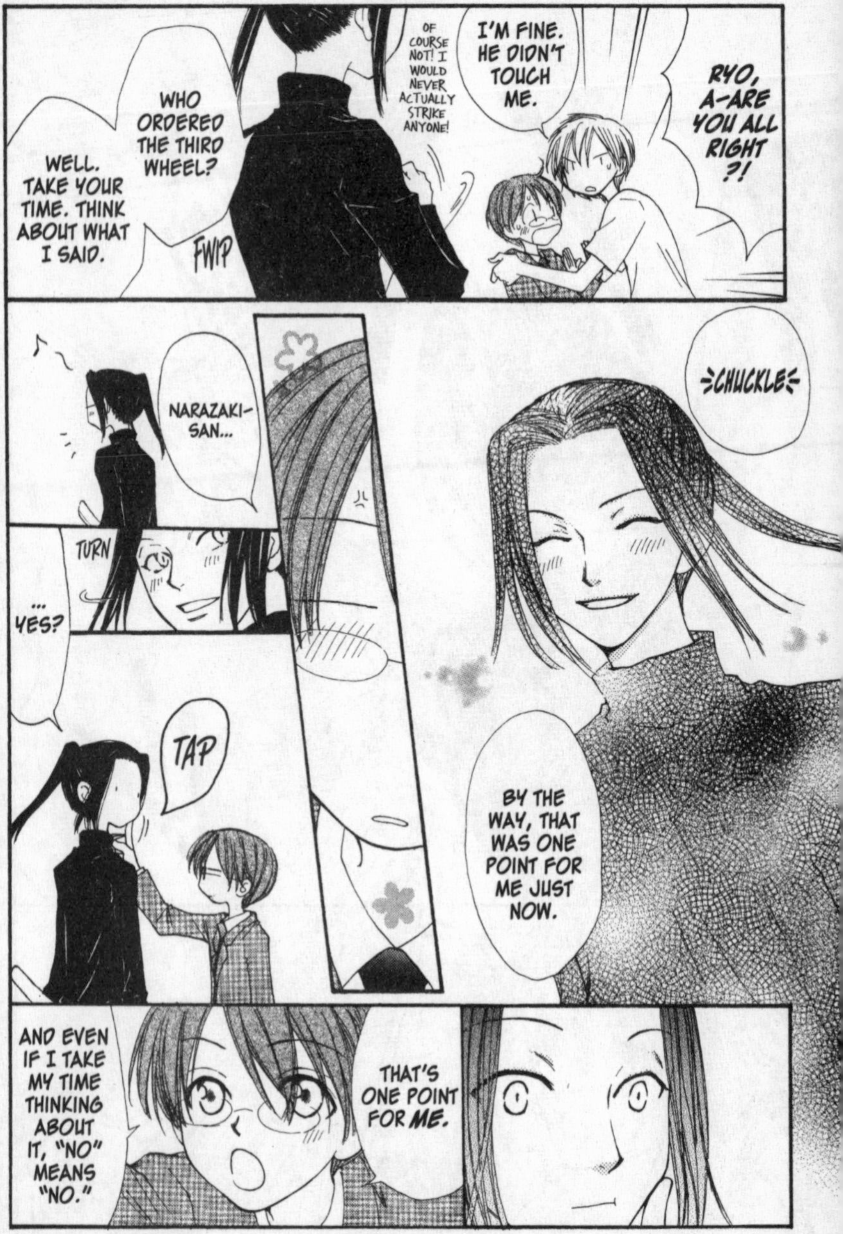
RYO, A-ARE YOU ALL RIGHT?!
I'M FINE. HE DIDN'T TOUCH ME.
OF COURSE NOT! I WOULD NEVER ACTUALLY STRIKE ANYONE!
WHO ORDERED THE THIRD WHEEL?
FWIP
WELL. TAKE YOUR TIME. THINK ABOUT WHAT I SAID.
CHUCKLE
BY THE WAY, THAT WAS ONE POINT FOR ME JUST NOW.
NARAZAKI-SAN...
TURN
...YES?
TAP
AND EVEN IF I TAKE MY TIME THINKING ABOUT IT, "NO" MEANS "NO."
THAT'S ONE POINT FOR ME.

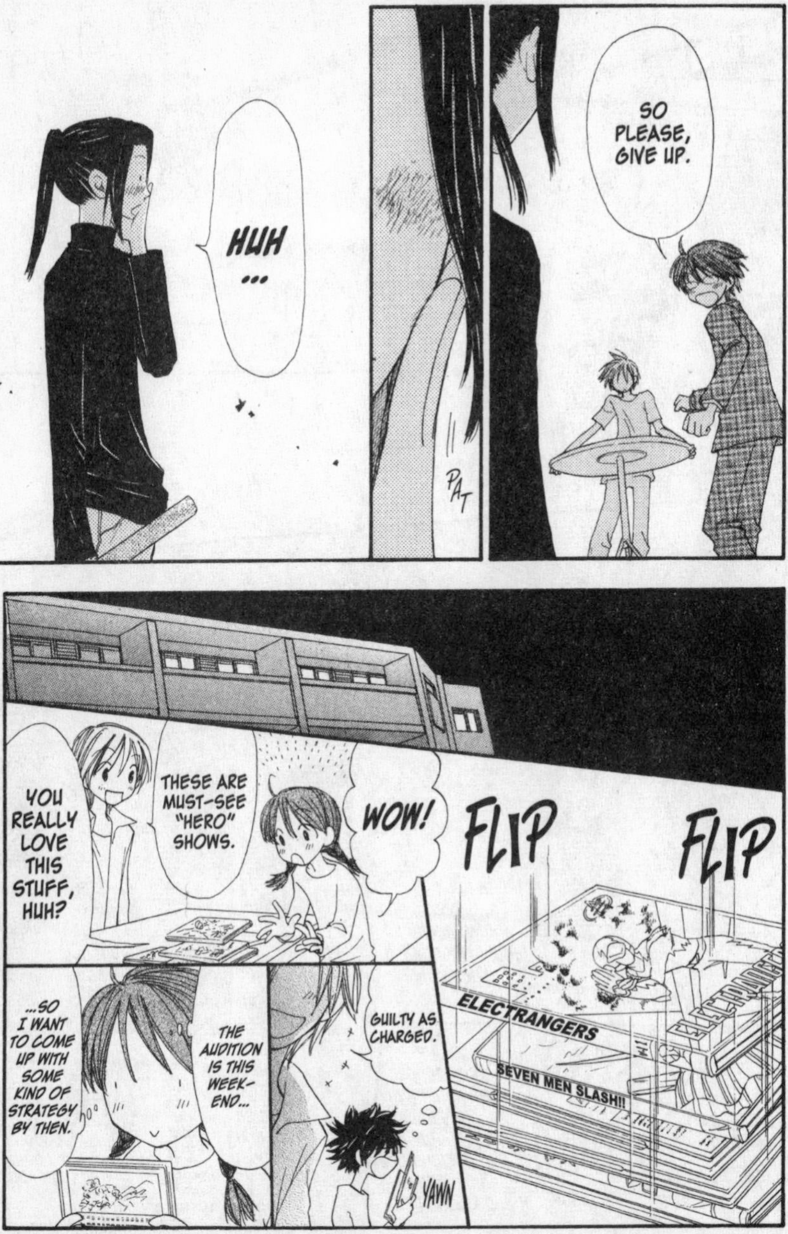
SO PLEASE, GIVE UP.
PAT
HUH ...
FLIP
FLIP
ELECTRANGERS
SEVEN MEN SLASH!!
WOW!
THESE ARE MUST-SEE "HERO" SHOWS.
YOU REALLY LOVE THIS STUFF, HUH?
GUILTY AS CHARGED.
YAWN
THE AUDITION IS THIS WEEK-END...
...SO I WANT TO COME UP WITH SOME KIND OF STRATEGY BY THEN.

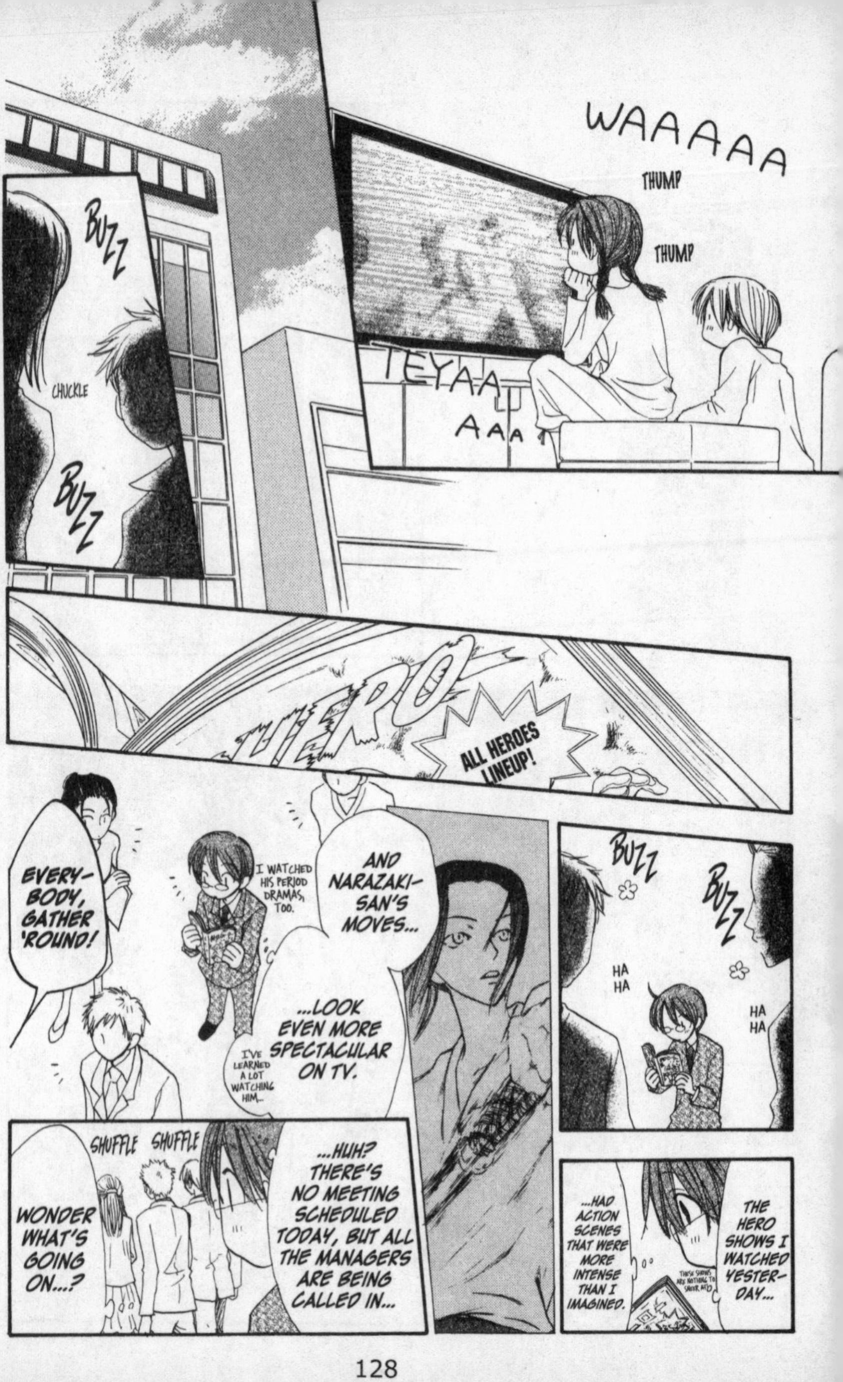
WAAAAAA
THUMP
THUMP
TEYAA
AAA
BUZZ
CHUCKLE
BUZZ
ALL HEROES LINEUP!
BUZZ
BUZZ
HA HA
HA HA
THE HERO SHOWS I WATCHED YESTER-DAY...
...HAD ACTION SCENES THAT WERE MORE INTENSE THAN I IMAGINED.
THESE SHOWS ARE NOTHING TO SNEER AT!
AND NARAZAKI-SAN'S MOVES...
...LOOK EVEN MORE SPECTACULAR ON TV.
I'VE LEARNED A LOT WATCHING HIM...
I WATCHED HIS PERIOD DRAMAS, TOO.
EVERY-BODY, GATHER 'ROUND!
...HUH? THERE'S NO MEETING SCHEDULED TODAY, BUT ALL THE MANAGERS ARE BEING CALLED IN...
SHUFFLE SHUFFLE
WONDER WHAT'S GOING ON...?

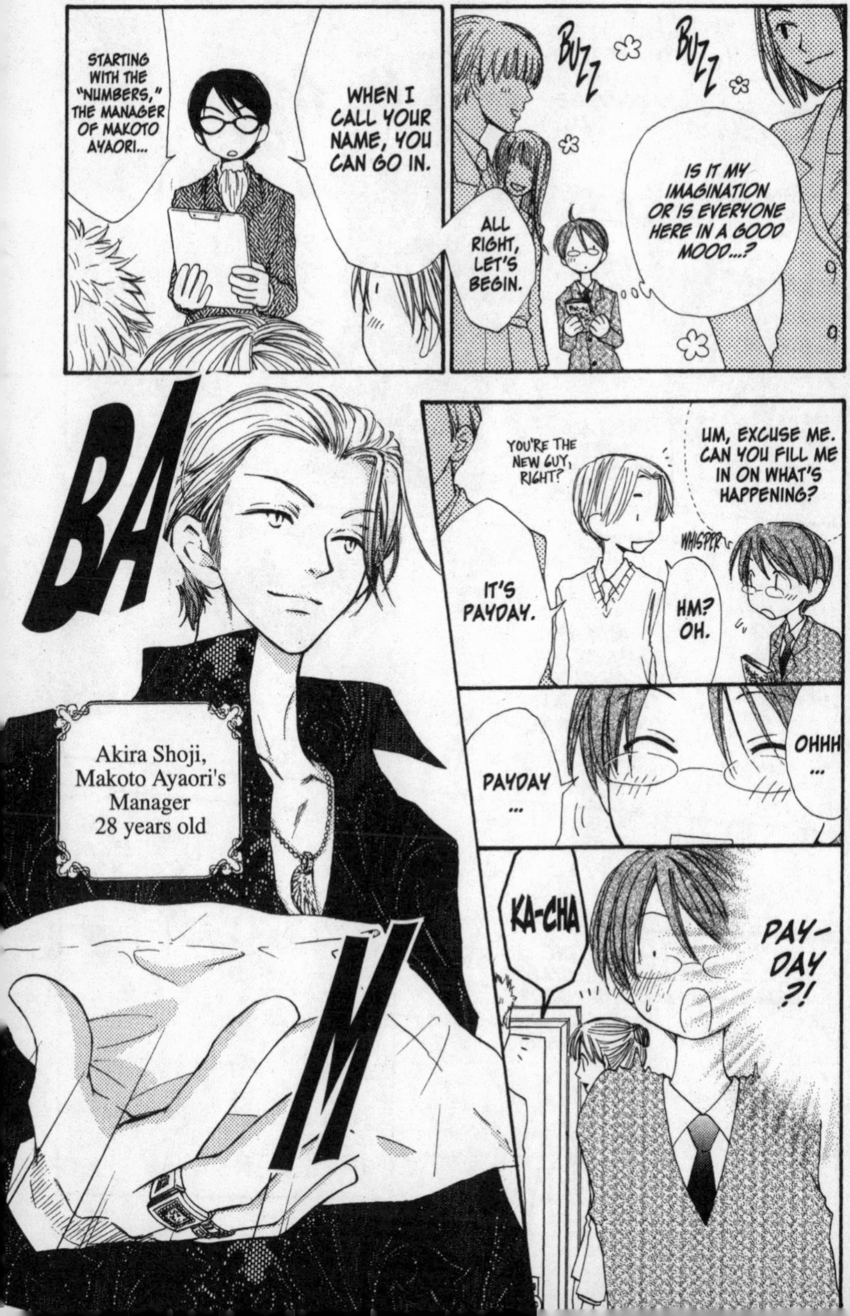
BUZZ
BUZZ
IS IT MY IMAGINATION OR IS EVERYONE HERE IN A GOOD MOOD...?
ALL RIGHT, LET'S BEGIN.
STARTING WITH THE "NUMBERS," THE MANAGER OF MAKOTO AYAORI...
WHEN I CALL YOUR NAME, YOU CAN GO IN.
UM, EXCUSE ME. CAN YOU FILL ME IN ON WHAT'S HAPPENING?
WHISPER
YOU'RE THE NEW GUY, RIGHT?
HM? OH.
IT'S PAYDAY.
OHHH...
PAYDAY...
PAY-DAY?!
KA-CHA
BAM
Akira Shoji, Makoto Ayaori's Manager 28 years old

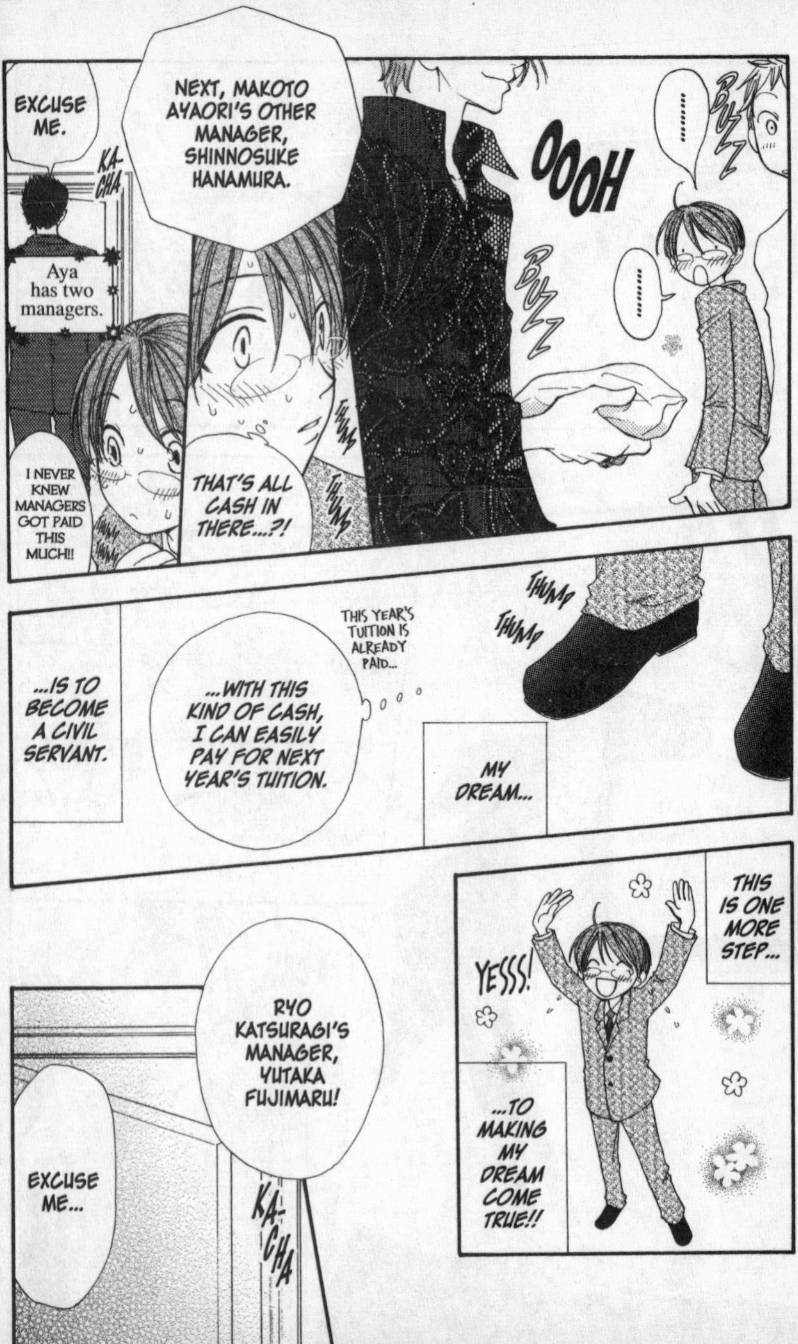
......
BUZZ
OOOH
......
BUZZ
NEXT, MAKOTO AYAORI'S OTHER MANAGER, SHINNOSUKE HANAMURA.
EXCUSE ME.
KA-CHA
Aya has two managers.
THUMP THUMP
THAT'S ALL CASH IN THERE...?!
I NEVER KNEW MANAGERS GOT PAID THIS MUCH!!
THUMP THUMP
MY DREAM...
THIS YEAR'S TUITION IS ALREADY PAID...
...WITH THIS KIND OF CASH, I CAN EASILY PAY FOR NEXT YEAR'S TUITION.
...IS TO BECOME A CIVIL SERVANT.
THIS IS ONE MORE STEP...
YESSS!
...TO MAKING MY DREAM COME TRUE!!
RYO KATSURAGI'S MANAGER, YUTAKA FUJIMARU!
EXCUSE ME...
KA-CHA

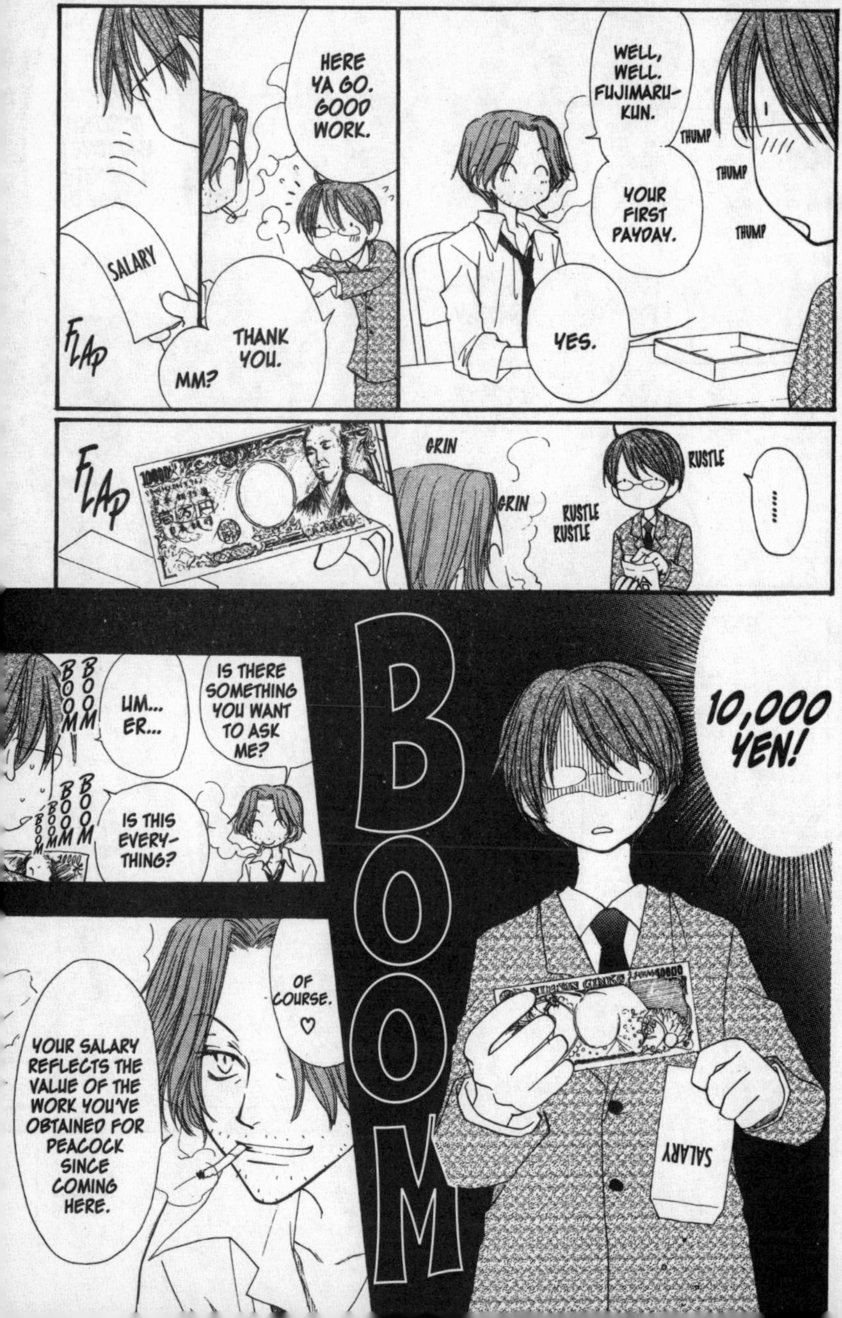
WELL, WELL. FUJIMARU-KUN.
THUMP
THUMP
THUMP
YOUR FIRST PAYDAY.
YES.
HERE YA GO. GOOD WORK.
THANK YOU.
MM?
SALARY
FLAP
......
RUSTLE
RUSTLE RUSTLE
GRIN
GRIN
FLAP
10,000 YEN!
BOOM
SALARY
IS THERE SOMETHING YOU WANT TO ASK ME?
UM... ER...
BOOM BOOM
IS THIS EVERY-THING?
BOOM BOOM BOOM
OF COURSE. ♡
YOUR SALARY REFLECTS THE VALUE OF THE WORK YOU'VE OBTAINED FOR PEACOCK SINCE COMING HERE.

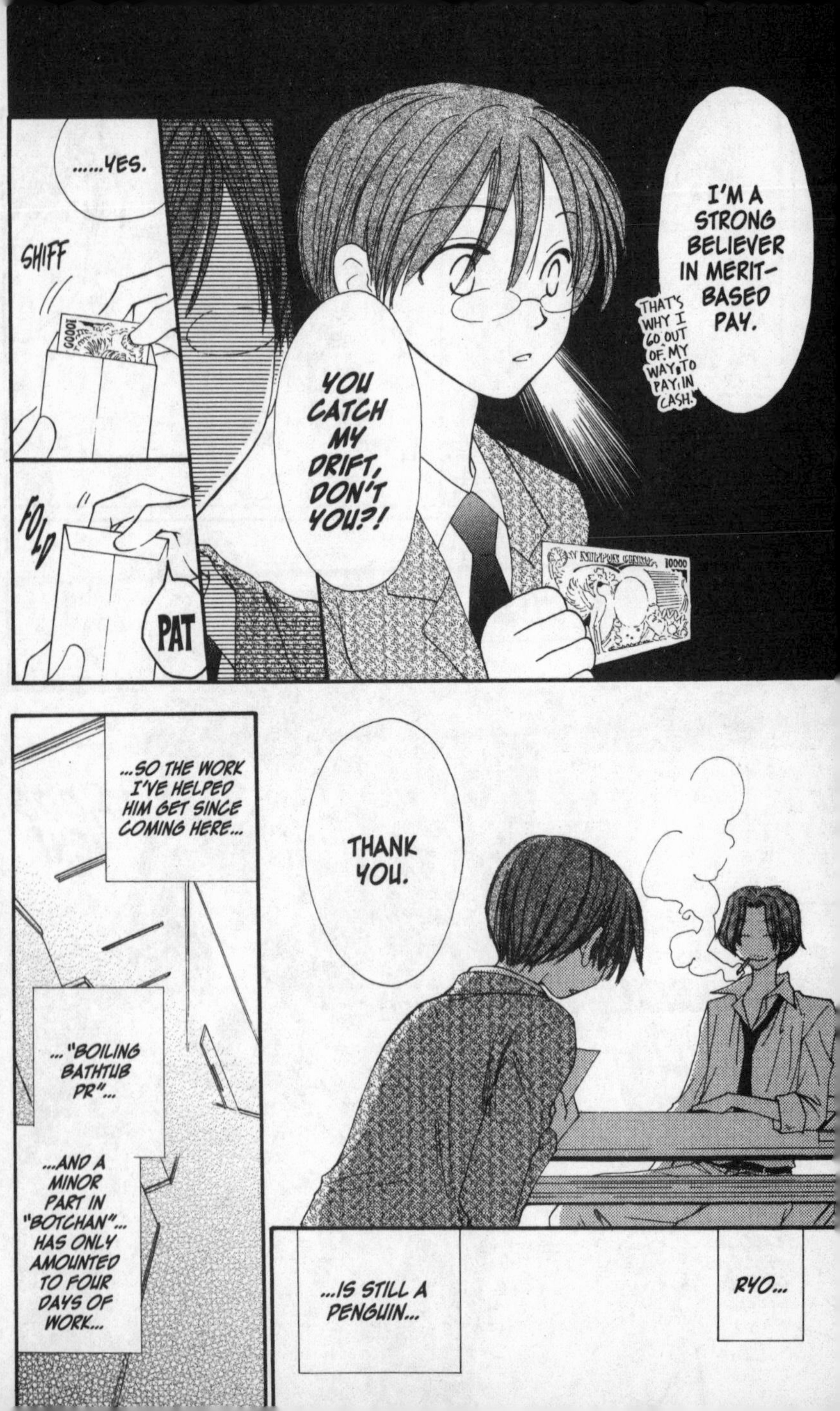
I'M A STRONG BELIEVER IN MERIT-BASED PAY.
THAT'S WHY I GO OUT OF MY WAY TO PAY IN CASH.
YOU CATCH MY DRIFT, DON'T YOU?!
......YES.
SHIFF
FOLD
PAT
THANK YOU.
...SO THE WORK I'VE HELPED HIM GET SINCE COMING HERE...
..."BOILING BATHTUB PR"...
...AND A MINOR PART IN "BOTCHAN"... HAS ONLY AMOUNTED TO FOUR DAYS OF WORK...
RYO...
...IS STILL A PENGUIN...

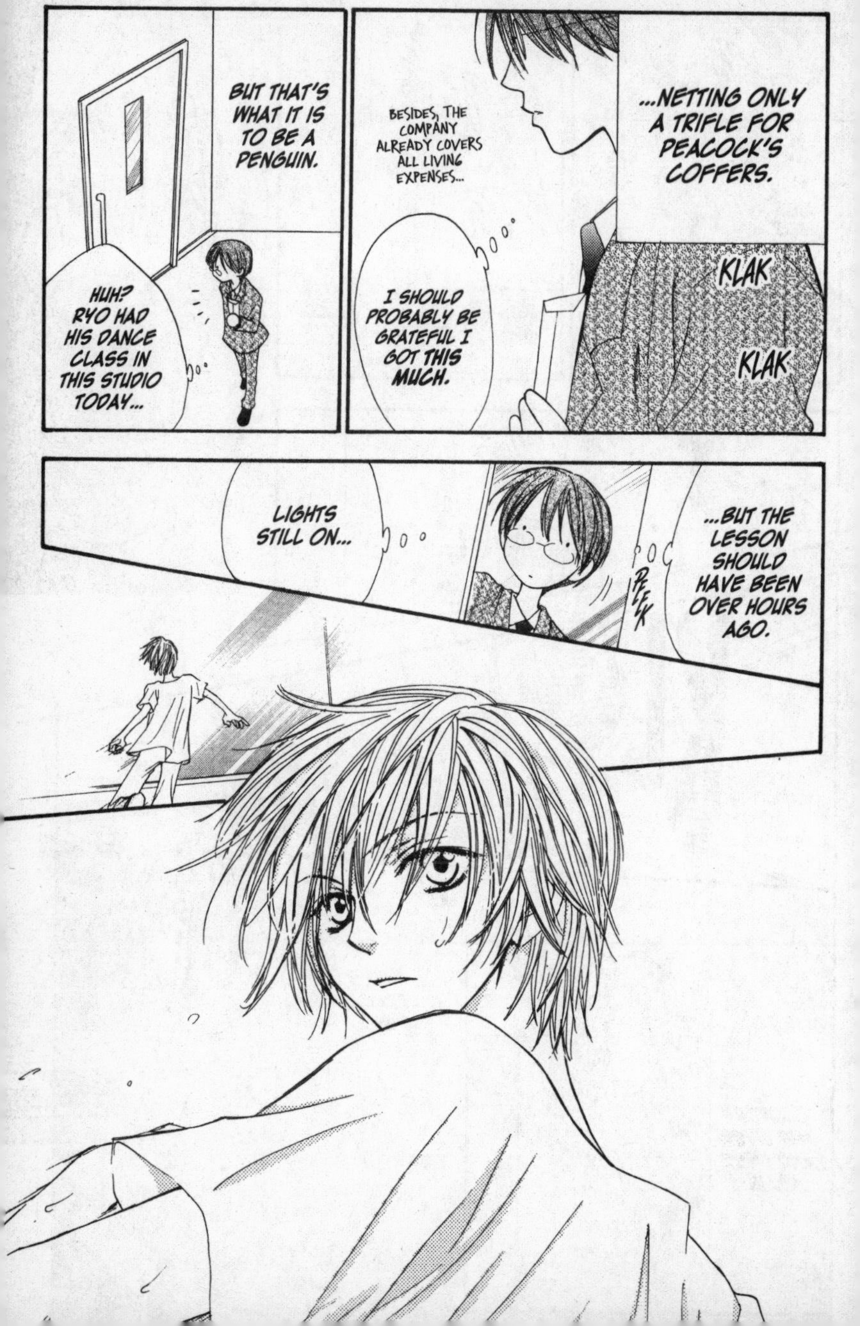
...NETTING ONLY A TRIFLE FOR PEACOCK'S COFFERS.
BESIDES, THE COMPANY ALREADY COVERS ALL LIVING EXPENSES...
KLAK
KLAK
I SHOULD PROBABLY BE GRATEFUL I GOT THIS MUCH.
BUT THAT'S WHAT IT IS TO BE A PENGUIN.
HUH? RYO HAD HIS DANCE CLASS IN THIS STUDIO TODAY...
...BUT THE LESSON SHOULD HAVE BEEN OVER HOURS AGO.
PEEK
LIGHTS STILL ON...

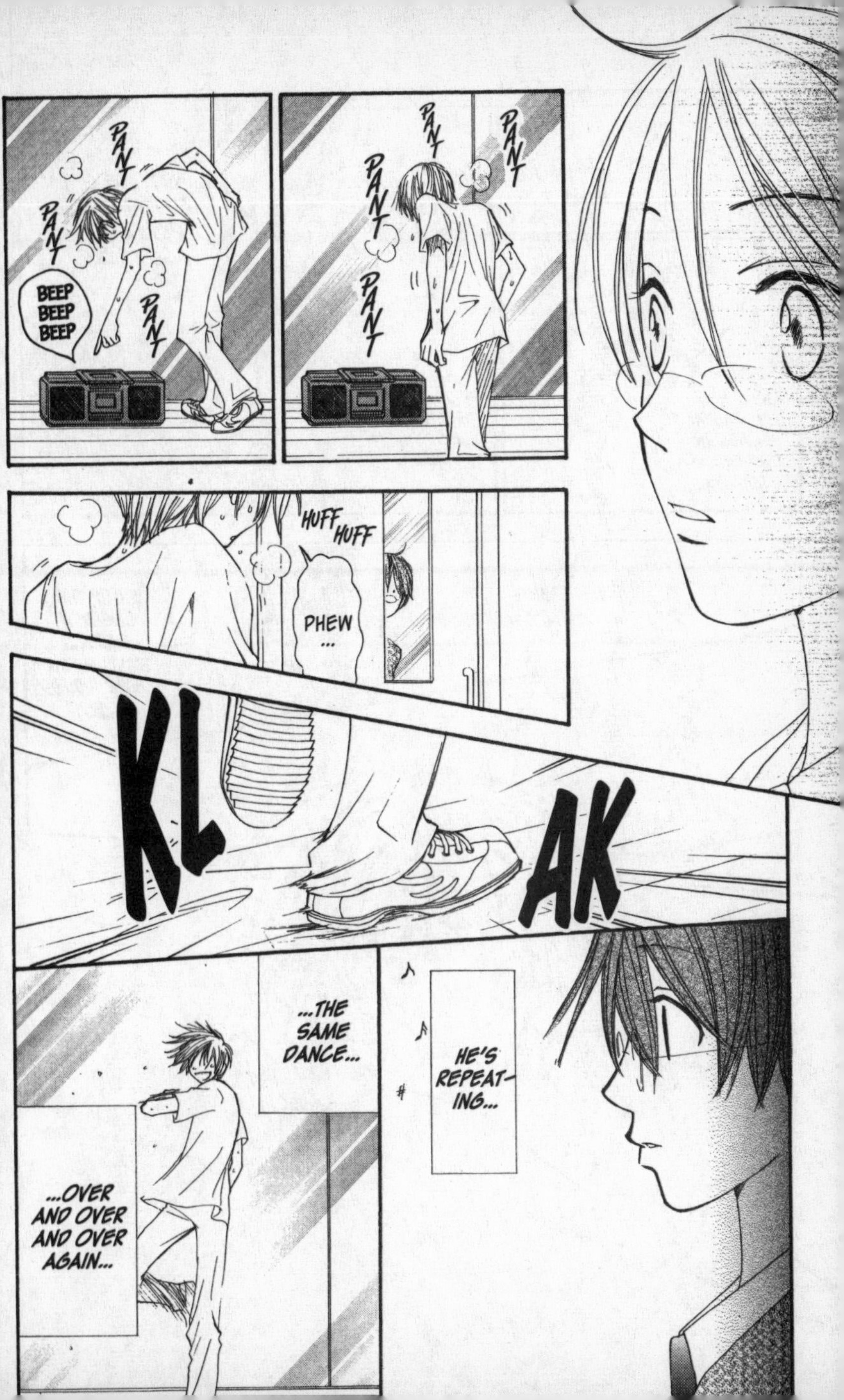

PANT
PANT
PANT
PANT
PANT
PANT
BEEP BEEP BEEP
PANT
HUFF HUFF
PHEW...
KLAK
HE'S REPEAT-ING...
...THE SAME DANCE...
...OVER AND OVER AND OVER AGAIN...

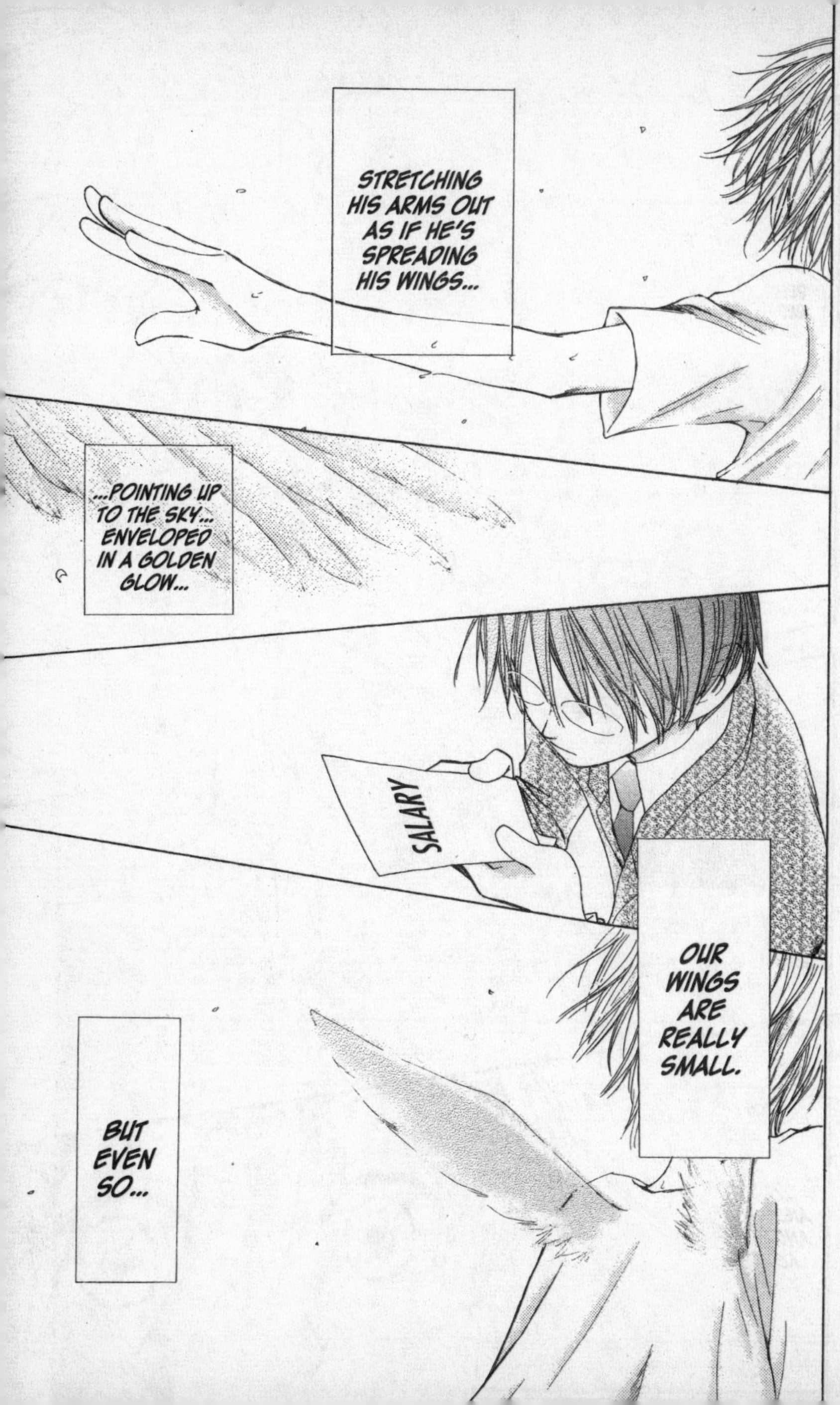
STRETCHING HIS ARMS OUT AS IF HE'S SPREADING HIS WINGS...
...POINTING UP TO THE SKY... ENVELOPED IN A GOLDEN GLOW...
SALARY
OUR WINGS ARE REALLY SMALL.
BUT EVEN SO...

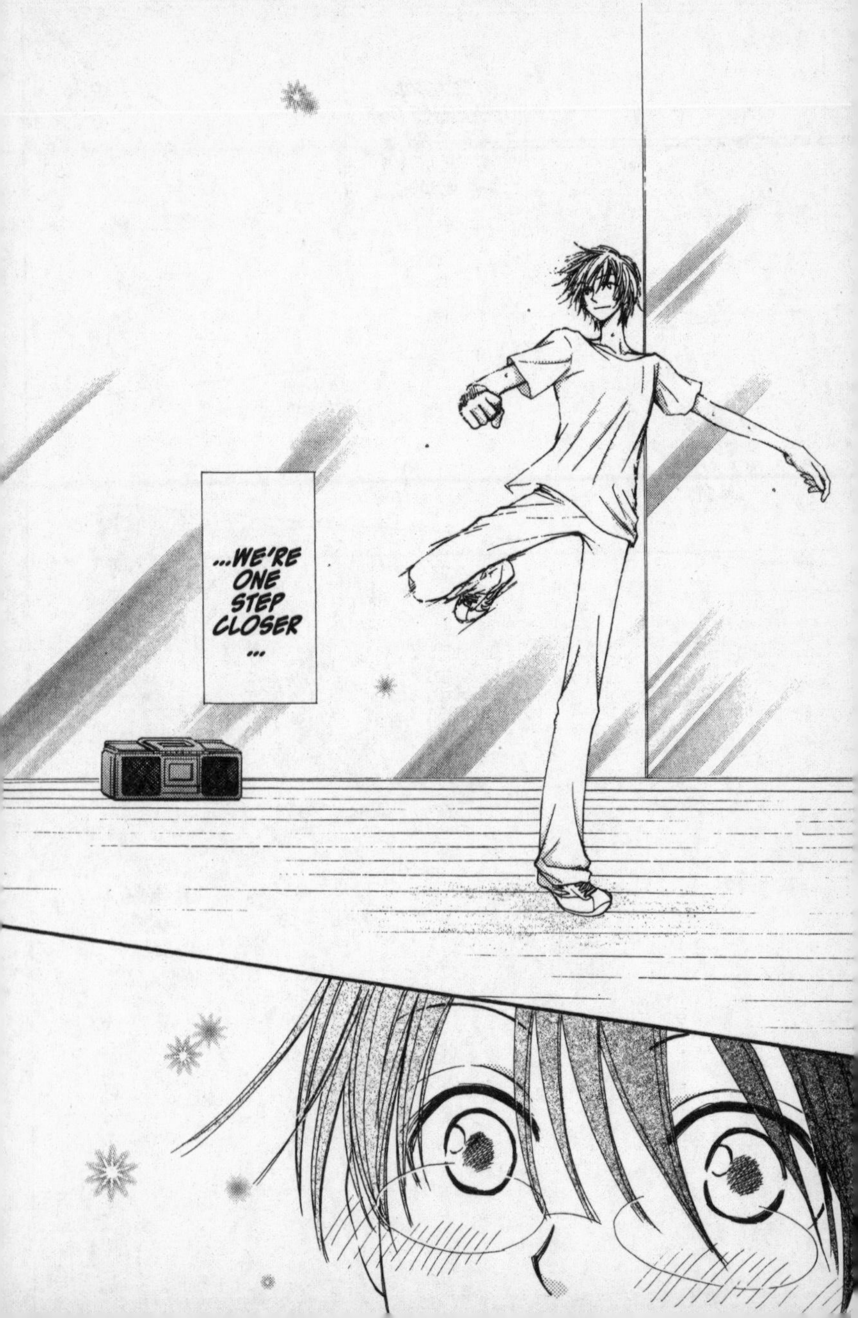
...WE'RE ONE STEP CLOSER ...

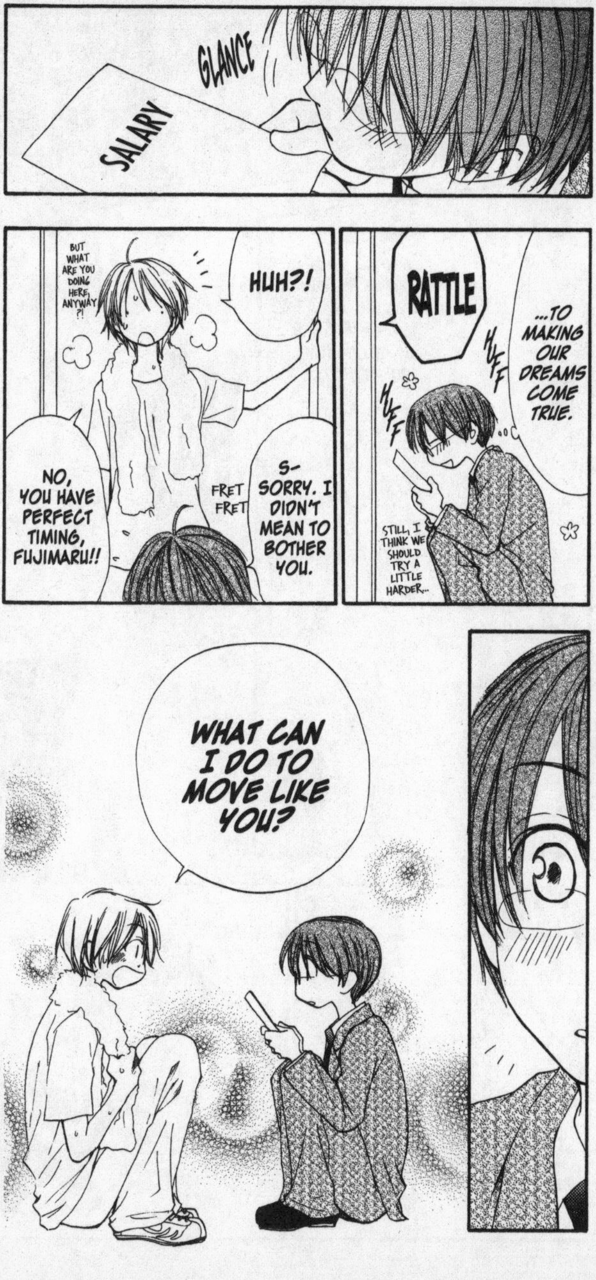
GLANCE
SALARY
...TO MAKING OUR DREAMS COME TRUE.
RATTLE
HUFF
HUFF
STILL, I THINK WE SHOULD TRY A LITTLE HARDER...
HUH?!
BUT WHAT ARE YOU DOING HERE, ANYWAY?!
S-SORRY. I DIDN'T MEAN TO BOTHER YOU.
FRET FRET
NO, YOU HAVE PERFECT TIMING, FUJIMARU!!
WHAT CAN I DO TO MOVE LIKE YOU?

1/4 Sakura Mail

part 8

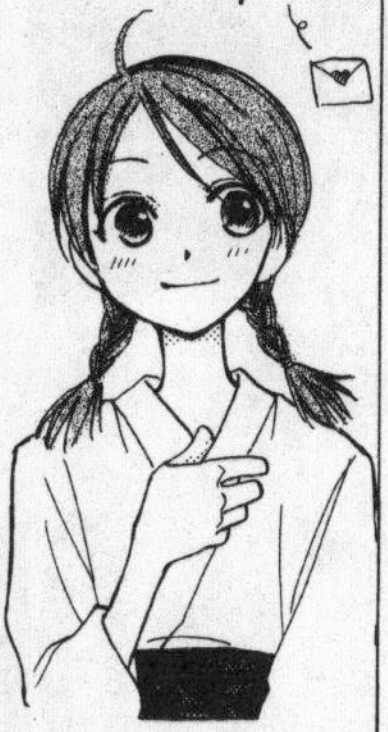

So Yuka-chan got her first salary. As it's noted in the story, the company covers all necessary expenses, so she's not going to go hungry, even in a lean month. Still, she's a long way from being able to pay her school tuition for next year, so do your best, Yuka-chan!! By the way, the proper name for the "break fall" portrayed in this and last episode is the "forward turning break fall." It's the basic break fall.

♡

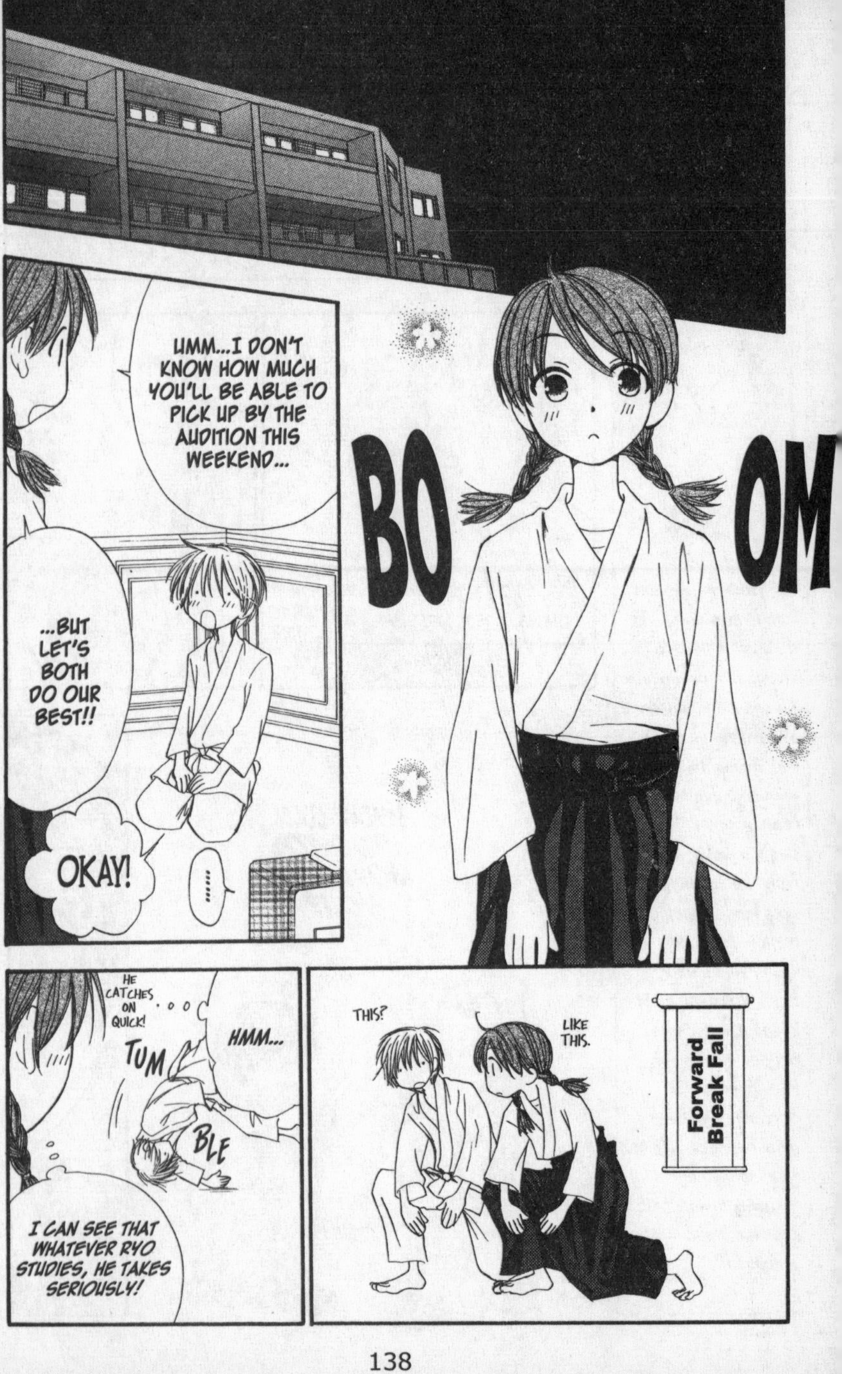
BO
OM
UMM...I DON'T KNOW HOW MUCH YOU'LL BE ABLE TO PICK UP BY THE AUDITION THIS WEEKEND...
...BUT LET'S BOTH DO OUR BEST!!
OKAY!
......
Forward Break Fall
LIKE THIS.
THIS?
HMM...
HE CATCHES ON QUICK!
. . .
TUM
BLE
I CAN SEE THAT WHATEVER RYO STUDIES, HE TAKES SERIOUSLY!

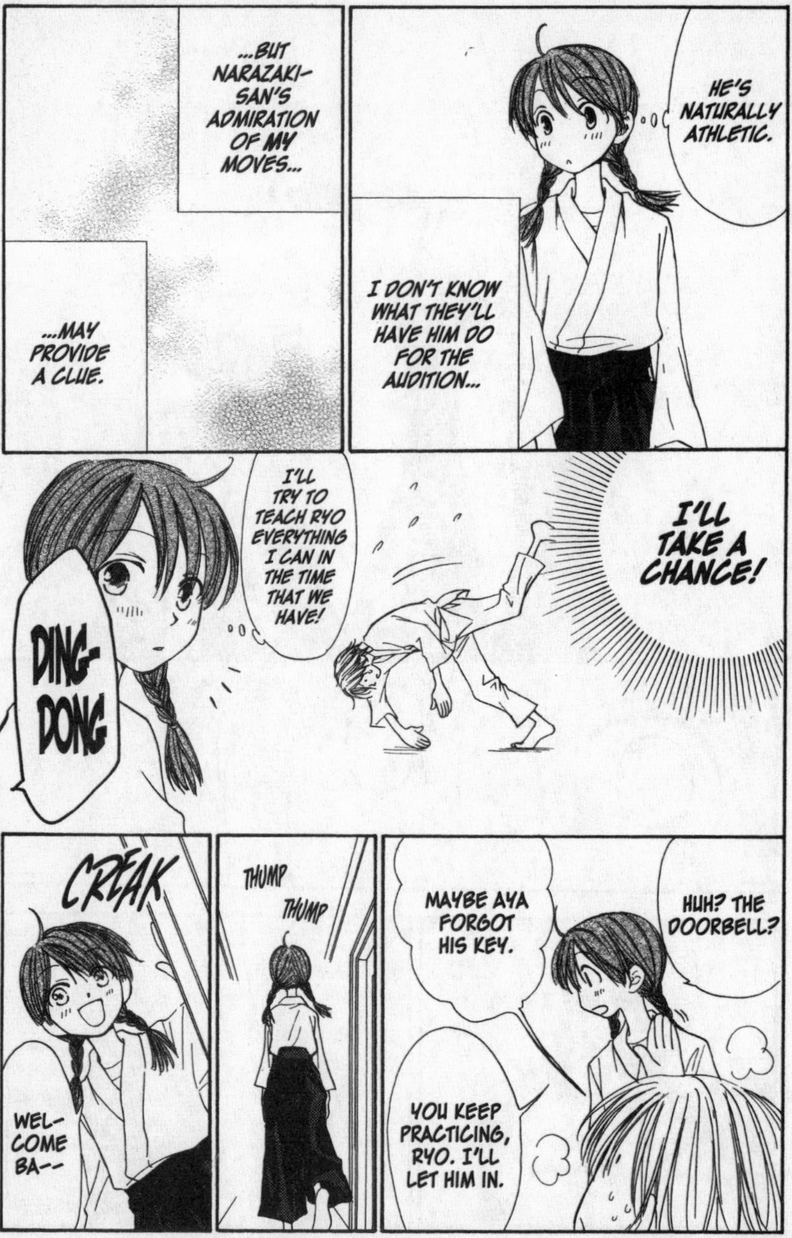
HE'S NATURALLY ATHLETIC.
I DON'T KNOW WHAT THEY'LL HAVE HIM DO FOR THE AUDITION...
...BUT NARAZAKI-SAN'S ADMIRATION OF MY MOVES...
...MAY PROVIDE A CLUE.
I'LL TAKE A CHANCE!
I'LL TRY TO TEACH RYO EVERYTHING I CAN IN THE TIME THAT WE HAVE!
DING-DONG
HUH? THE DOORBELL?
MAYBE AYA FORGOT HIS KEY.
YOU KEEP PRACTICING, RYO. I'LL LET HIM IN.
THUMP
THUMP
CREAK
WEL-COME BA--

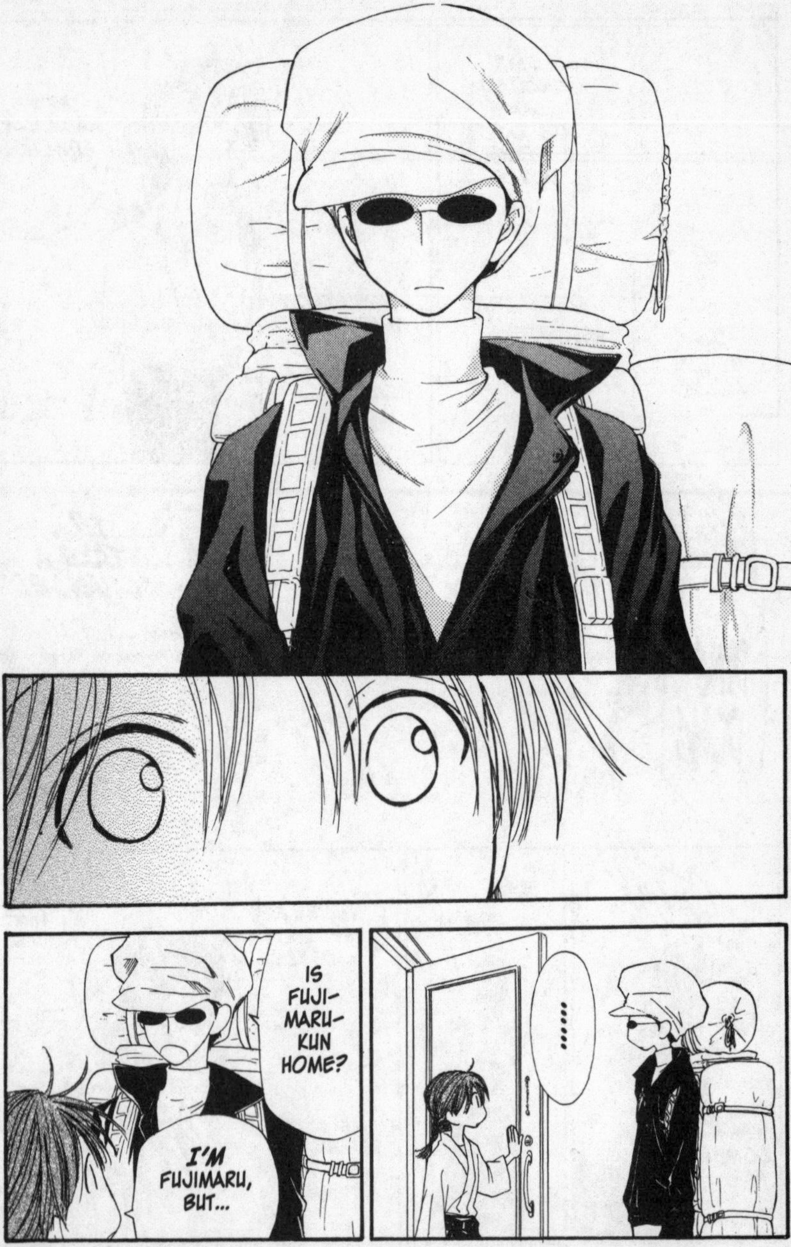
......
IS FUJI-MARU-KUN HOME?
I'M FUJIMARU, BUT...

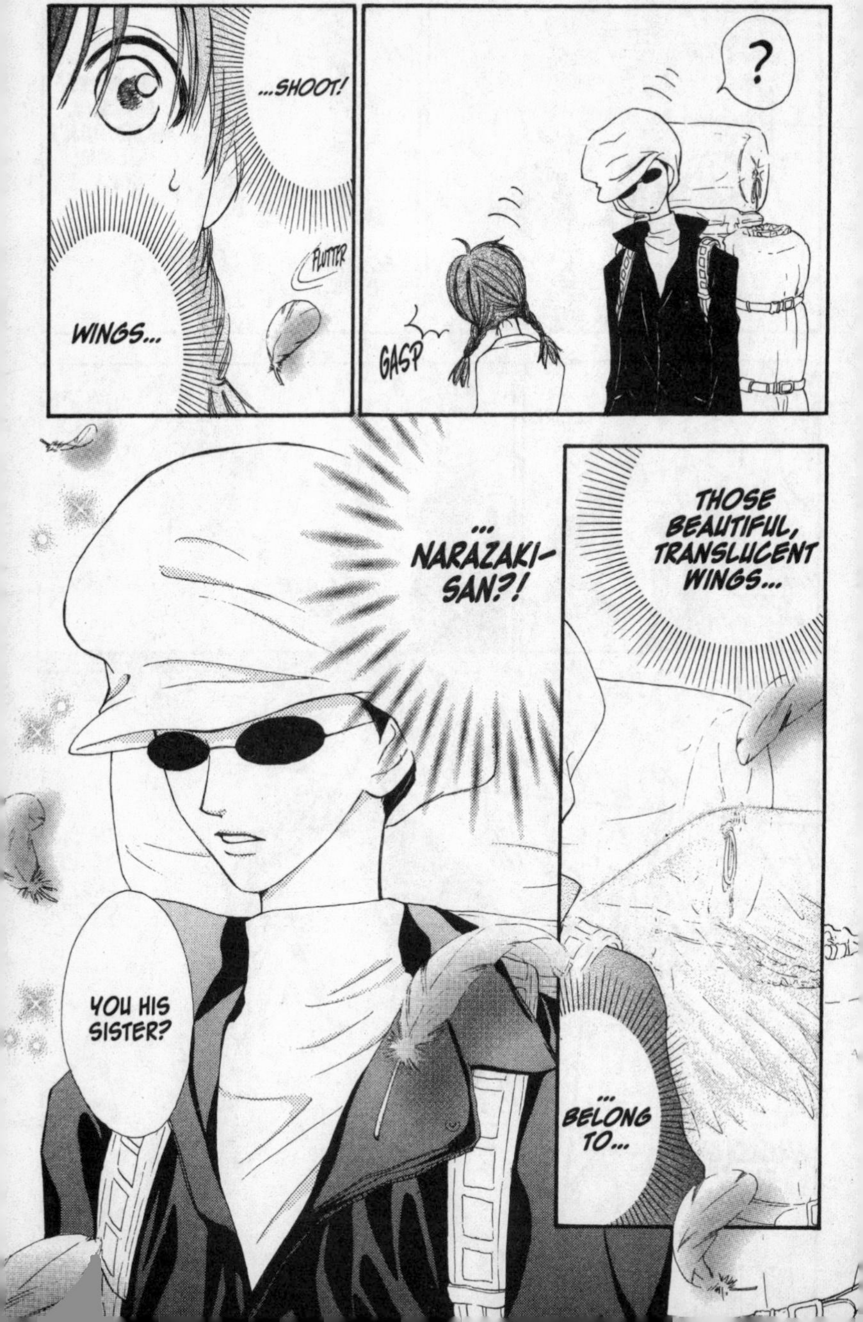
?
GASP
...SHOOT!
FLUTTER
WINGS...
THOSE BEAUTIFUL, TRANSLUCENT WINGS...
...BELONG TO...
...NARAZAKI-SAN?!
YOU HIS SISTER?

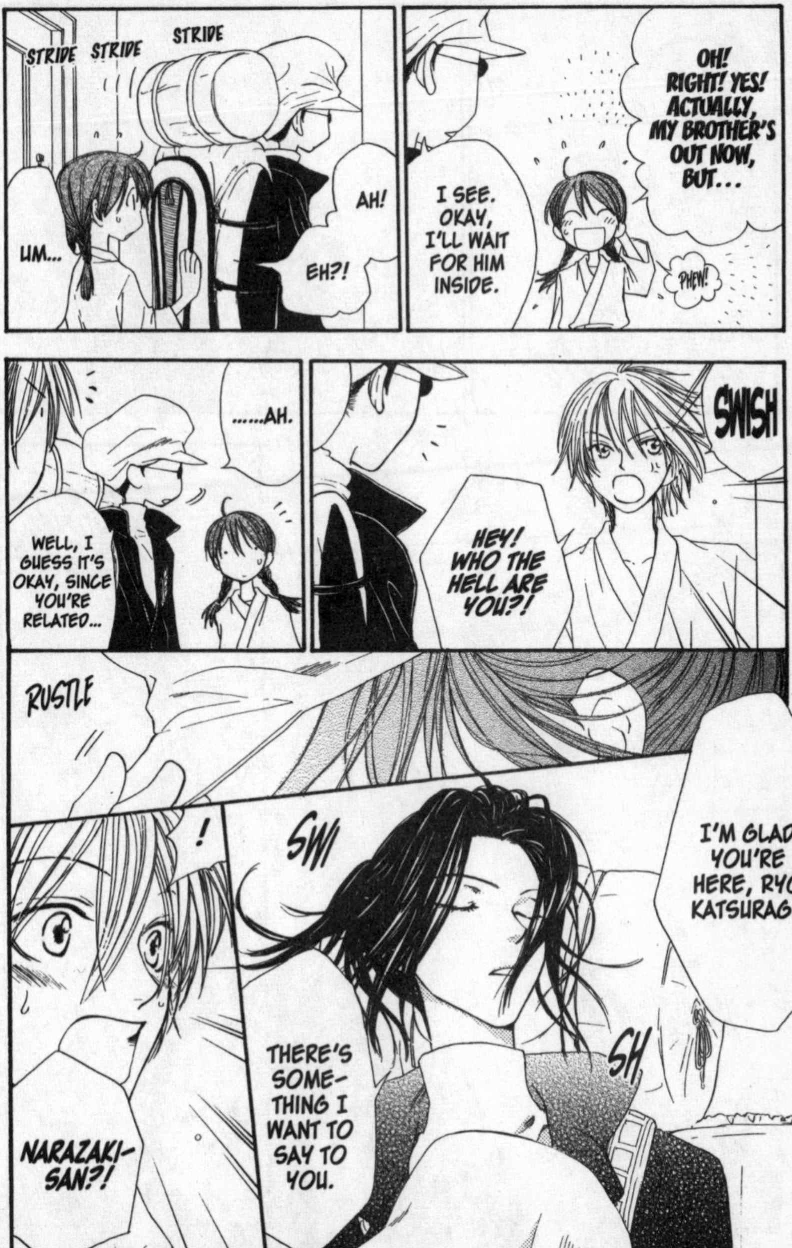
OH! RIGHT! YES! ACTUALLY, MY BROTHER'S OUT NOW, BUT...
PHEW!
I SEE. OKAY, I'LL WAIT FOR HIM INSIDE.
AH!
EH?!
STRIDE
STRIDE
STRIDE
UM...
SWISH
HEY! WHO THE HELL ARE YOU?!
......AH.
WELL, I GUESS IT'S OKAY, SINCE YOU'RE RELATED...
RUSTLE
I'M GLAD YOU'RE HERE, RYO KATSURAGI.
SWI
SH
THERE'S SOME-THING I WANT TO SAY TO YOU.
!
NARAZAKI-SAN?!

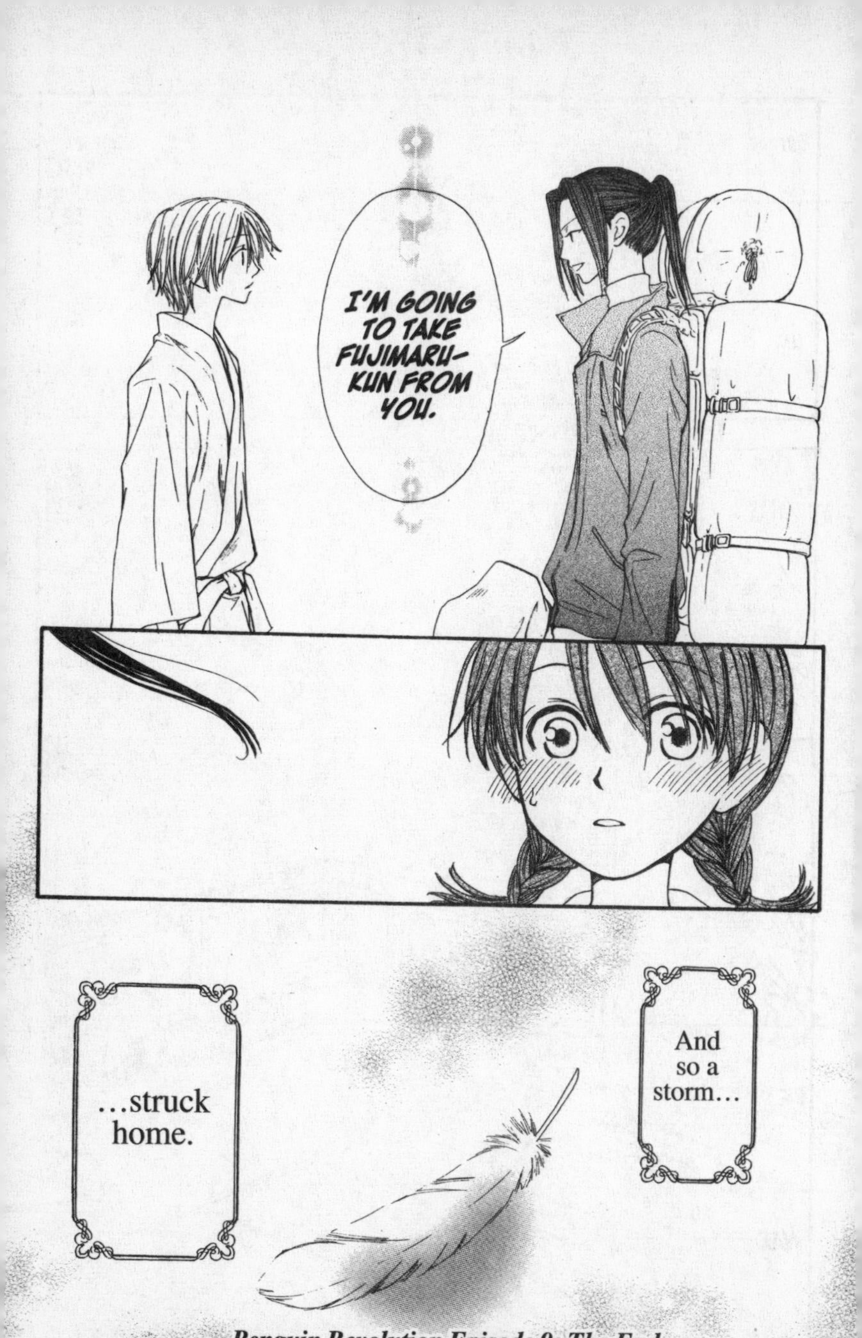
I'M GOING TO TAKE FUJIMARU-KUN FROM YOU.
And so a storm…
…struck home.

Penguin Revolution Episode 9: The End

Putting in tatami* in Yuka-chin's room.

* Tatami mats are traditional Japanese flooring, made of woven straw.

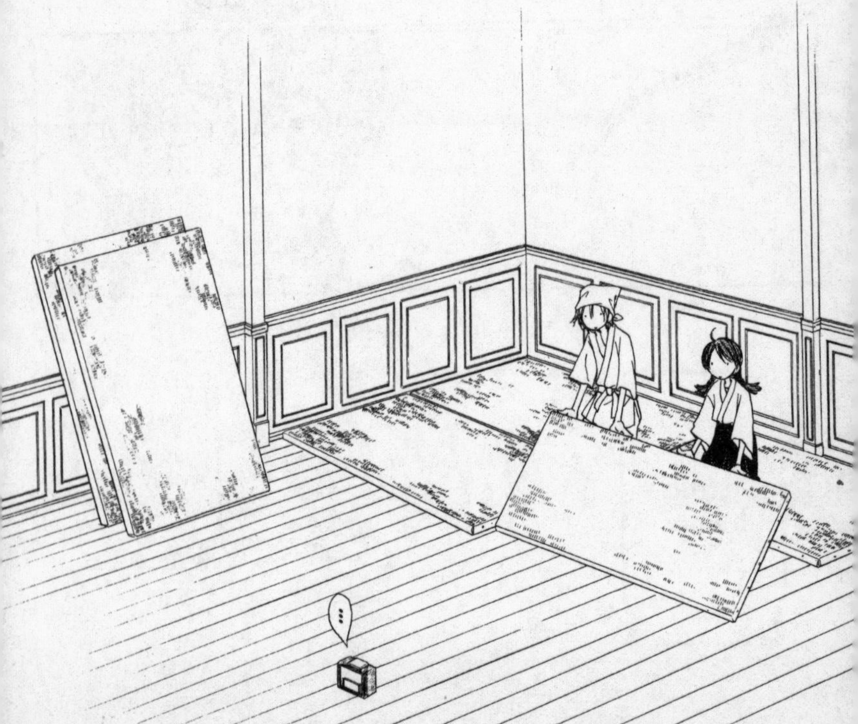

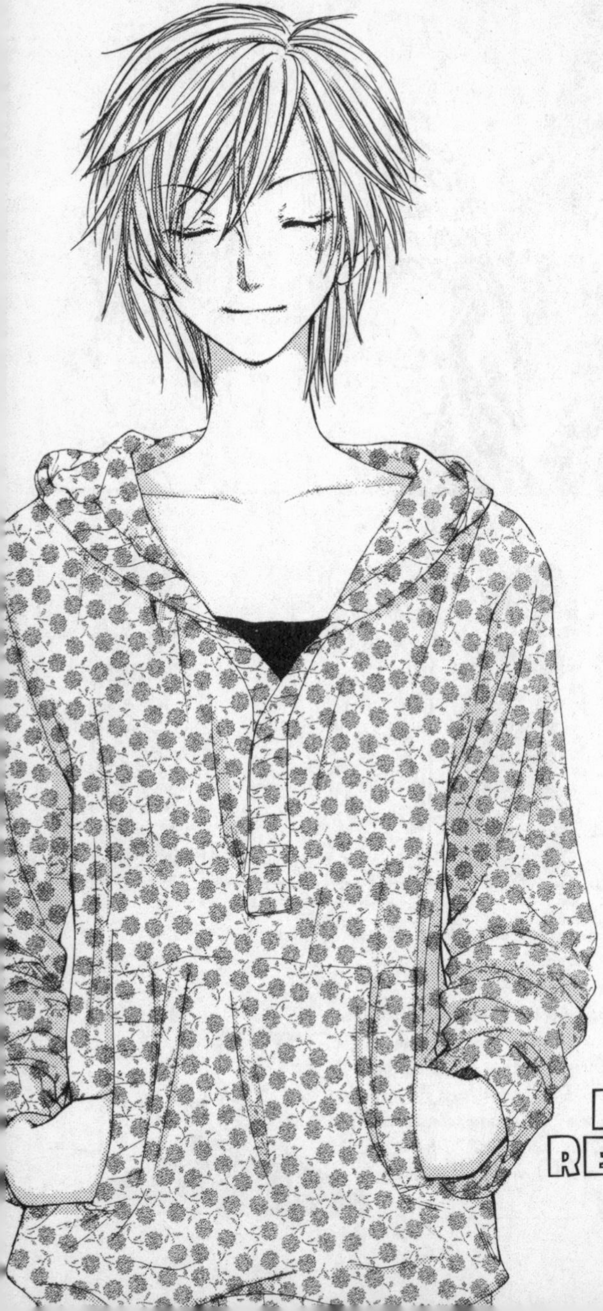

ペンギン革命(かくめい)

PENGUIN REVOLUTION

Episode 10

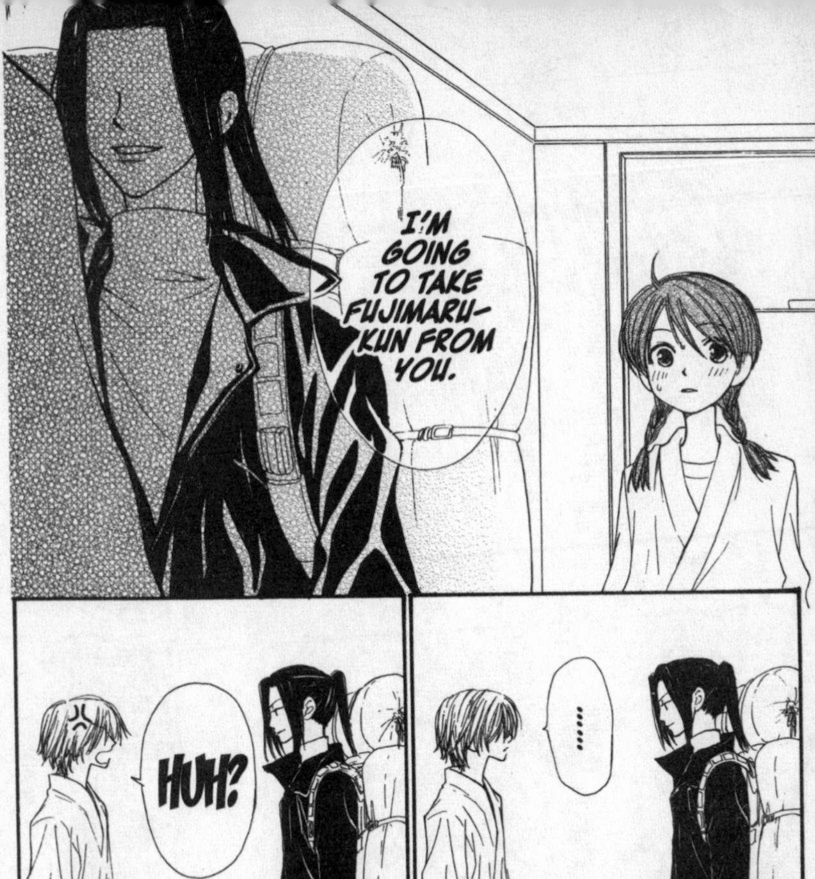
I'M GOING TO TAKE FUJIMARU-KUN FROM YOU.
......
HUH?

1/4 Sakura Mail

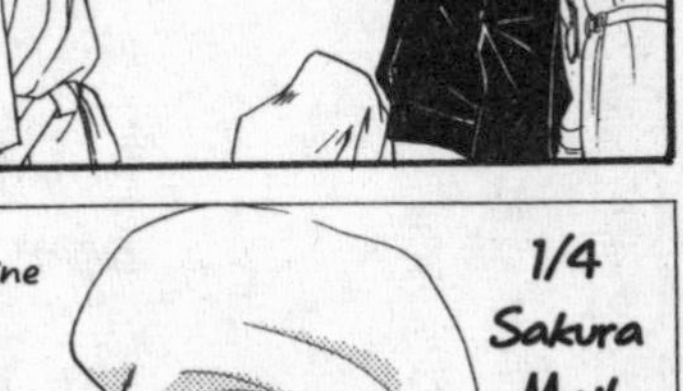

part 9

In this episode, Narazaki-san declares war. If you line up Ryo-chin's face with his, you can really see that Narazaki-san has a wolf-like face.
There must be a lot of good-looking guys at Peacock, so I know it's going to get increasingly tough for me to draw different-looking faces, but it's a challenge that I'm also looking forward to. Oh, and it's also fun for me to come up with the disguises the young talents have to wear when they're out in the "real world." I think their disguises say something about their personalities.

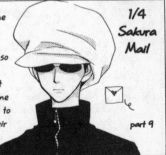

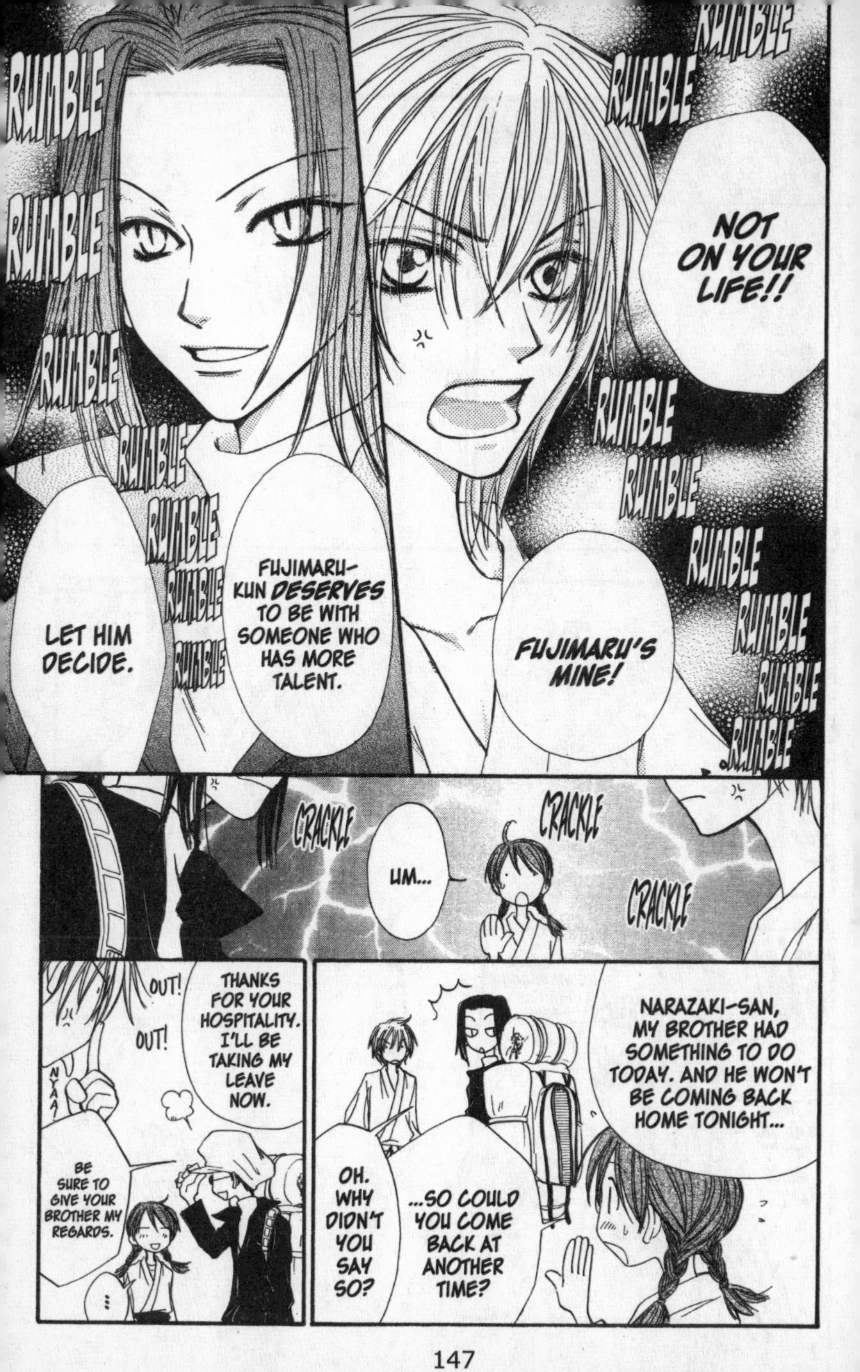
RUMBLE
RUMBLE
NOT ON YOUR LIFE!!
RUMBLE RUMBLE RUMBLE RUMBLE RUMBLE RUMBLE
FUJIMARU'S MINE!
RUMBLE
RUMBLE
RUMBLE
RUMBLE
RUMBLE RUMBLE RUMBLE
FUJIMARU-KUN DESERVES TO BE WITH SOMEONE WHO HAS MORE TALENT.
LET HIM DECIDE.
CRACKLE
CRACKLE
UM...
CRACKLE
NARAZAKI-SAN, MY BROTHER HAD SOMETHING TO DO TODAY. AND HE WON'T BE COMING BACK HOME TONIGHT...
...SO COULD YOU COME BACK AT ANOTHER TIME?
OH. WHY DIDN'T YOU SAY SO?
THANKS FOR YOUR HOSPITALITY. I'LL BE TAKING MY LEAVE NOW.
OUT!
OUT!
NYAA!
BE SURE TO GIVE YOUR BROTHER MY REGARDS.
...

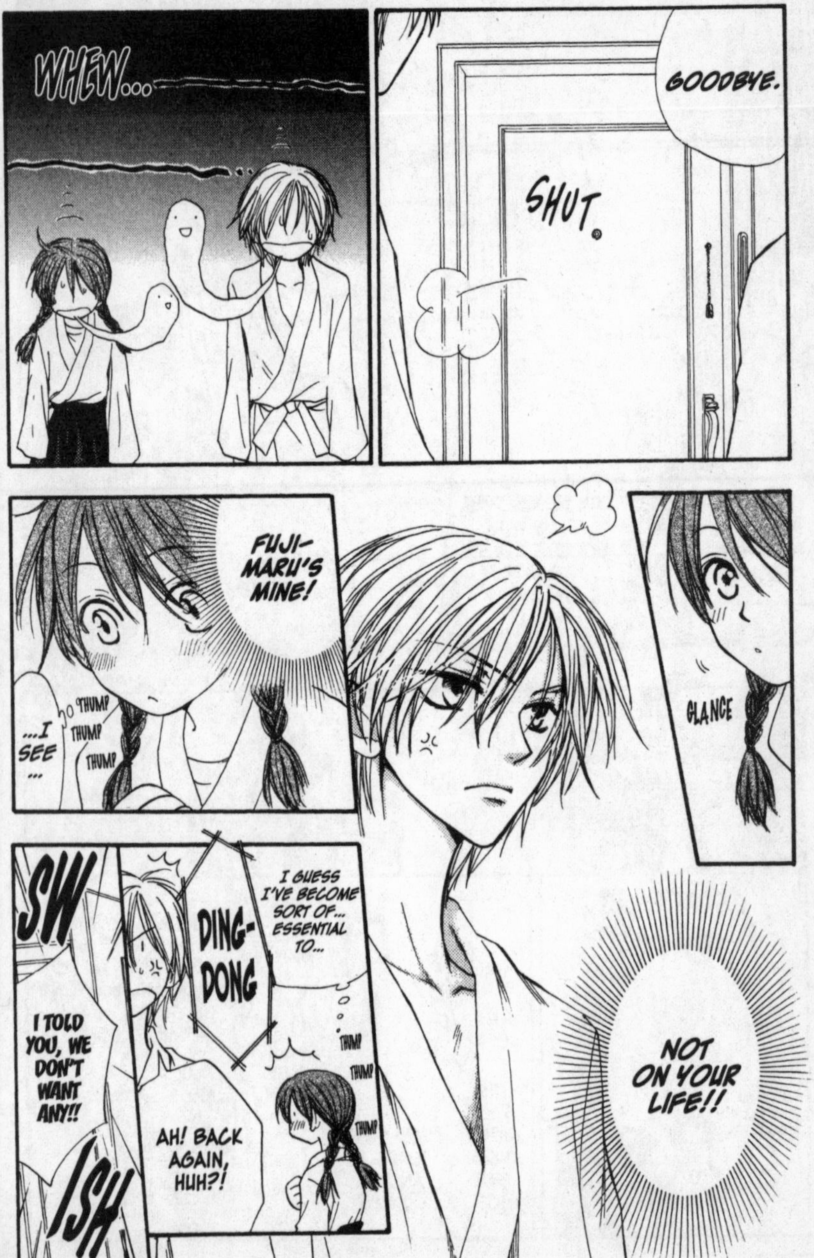
GOODBYE.
SHUT.
WHEW...
GLANCE
NOT ON YOUR LIFE!!
FUJI-MARU'S MINE!
THUMP THUMP THUMP
...I SEE...
I GUESS I'VE BECOME SORT OF... ESSENTIAL TO...
DING-DONG
THUMP THUMP THUMP
AH! BACK AGAIN, HUH?!
SWISH
I TOLD YOU, WE DON'T WANT ANY!!

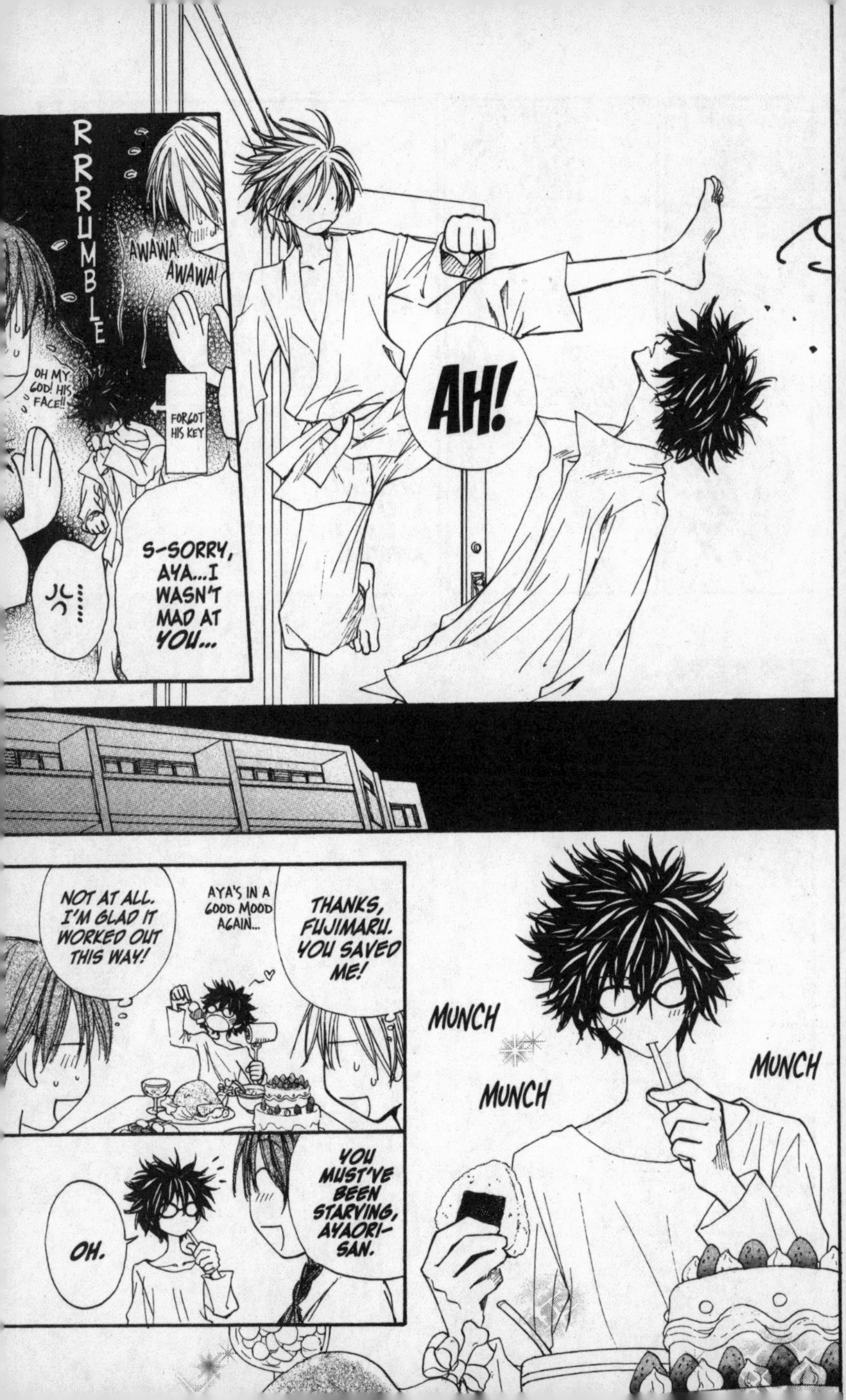
AH!
RRRUMBLE
AWAWA! AWAWA!
OH MY GOD! HIS FACE!!
FORGOT HIS KEY
S-SORRY, AYA...I WASN'T MAD AT YOU...
MUNCH
MUNCH
MUNCH
THANKS, FUJIMARU. YOU SAVED ME!
AYA'S IN A GOOD MOOD AGAIN...
NOT AT ALL. I'M GLAD IT WORKED OUT THIS WAY!
YOU MUST'VE BEEN STARVING, AYAORI-SAN.
OH.

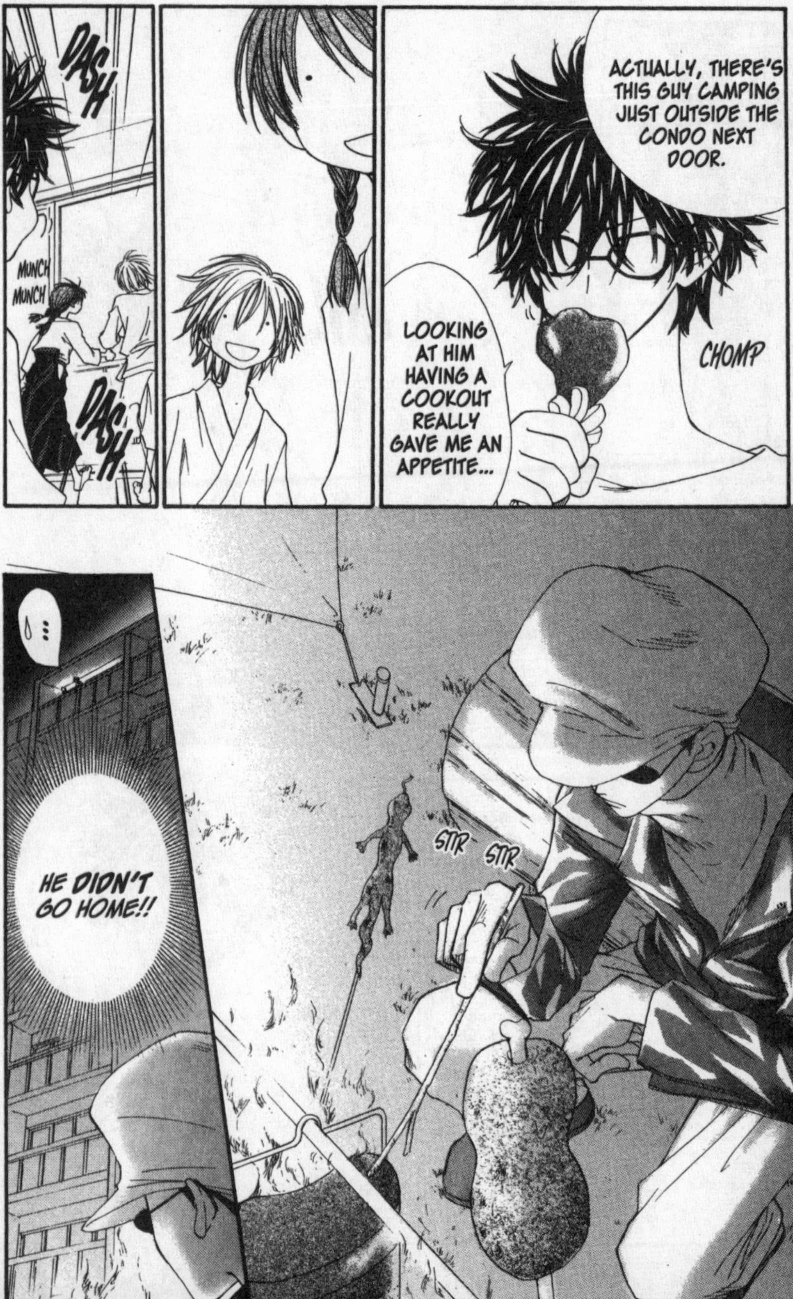
ACTUALLY, THERE'S THIS GUY CAMPING JUST OUTSIDE THE CONDO NEXT DOOR.
CHOMP
LOOKING AT HIM HAVING A COOKOUT REALLY GAVE ME AN APPETITE...
DASH
MUNCH MUNCH
DASH
STIR STIR
...
HE DIDN'T GO HOME!!

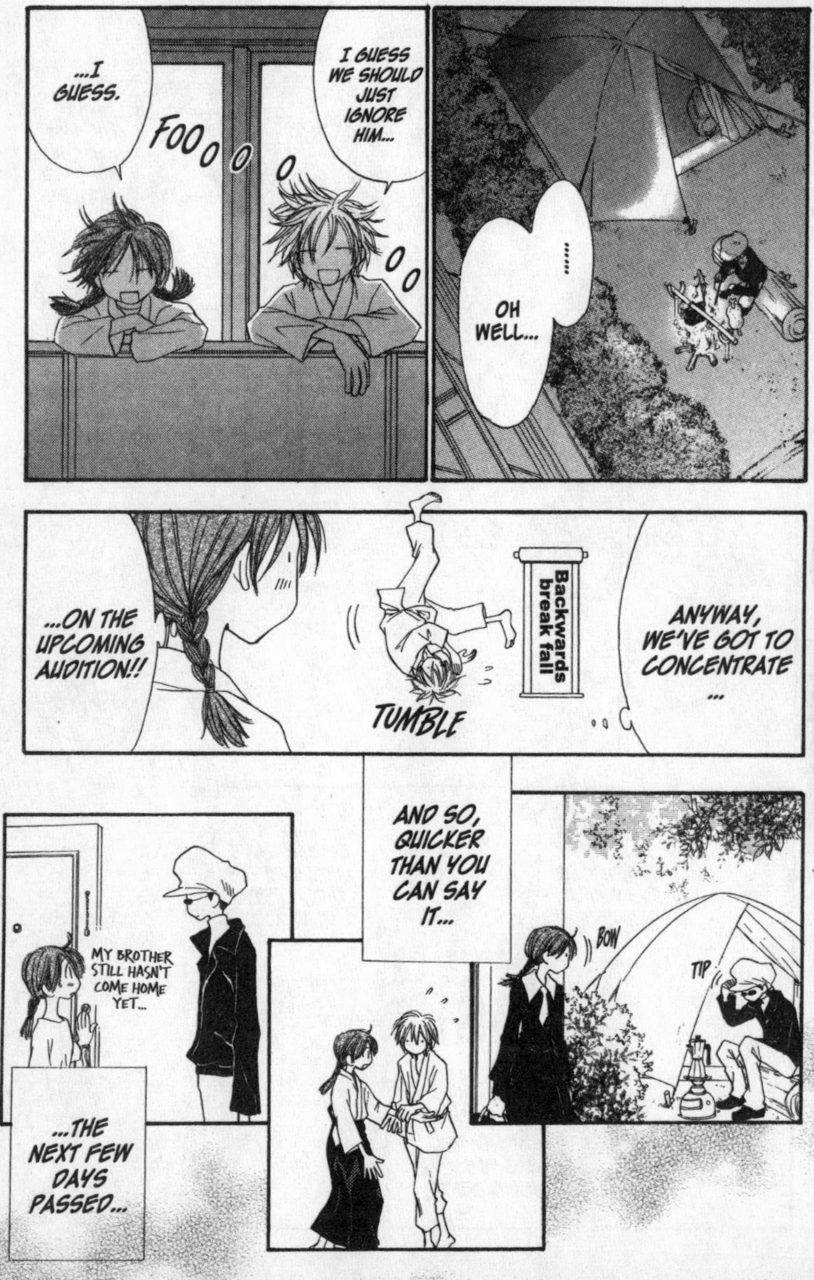
......
OH WELL...
I GUESS WE SHOULD JUST IGNORE HIM...
FOOOOOOOO
...I GUESS.
ANYWAY, WE'VE GOT TO CONCENTRATE ...
Backwards break fall
TUMBLE
...ON THE UPCOMING AUDITION!!
AND SO, QUICKER THAN YOU CAN SAY IT...
BOW
TIP
MY BROTHER STILL HASN'T COME HOME YET...
...THE NEXT FEW DAYS PASSED...

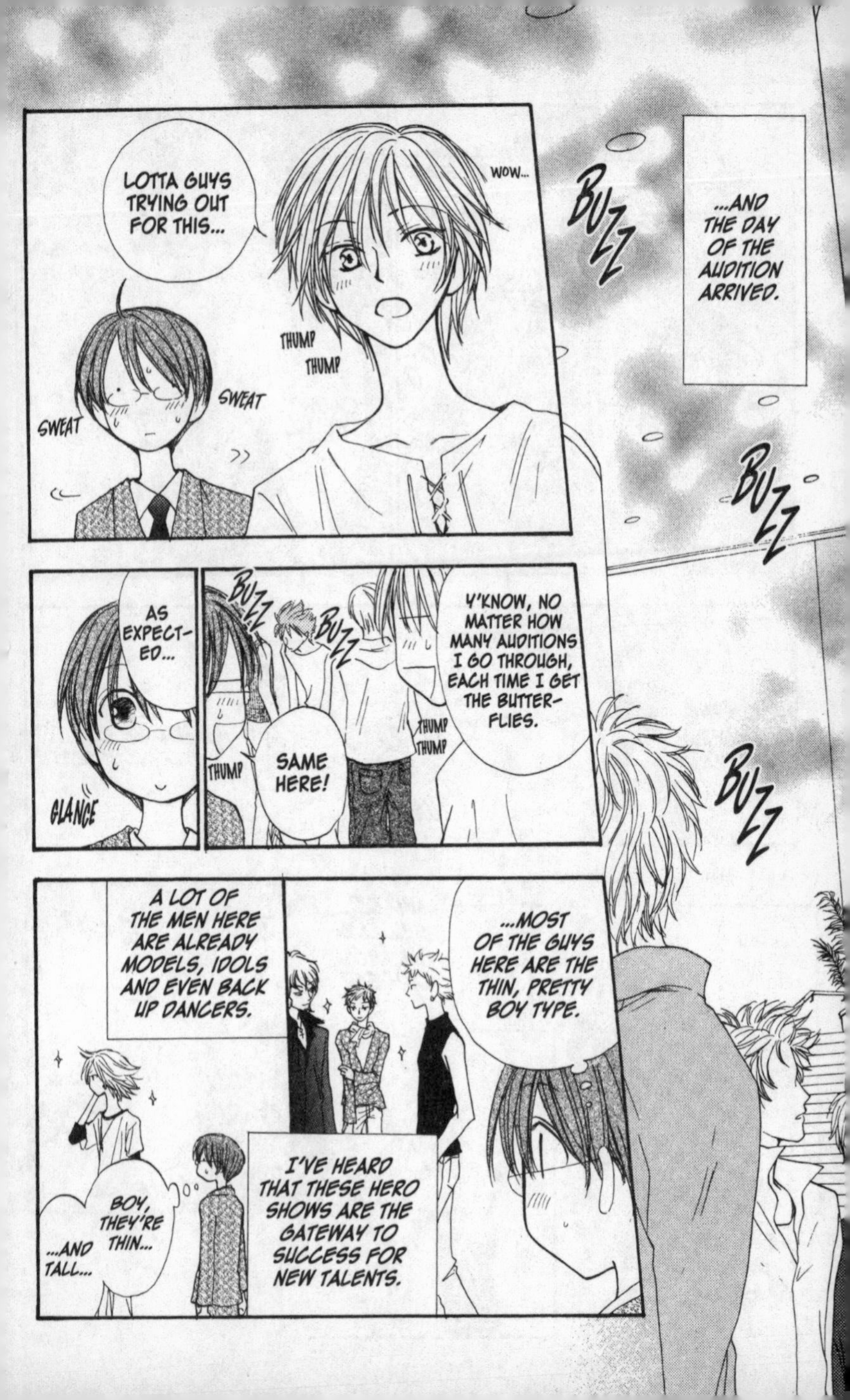
...AND THE DAY OF THE AUDITION ARRIVED.
BUZZ
BUZZ
BUZZ
WOW...
LOTTA GUYS TRYING OUT FOR THIS...
THUMP
THUMP
SWEAT
SWEAT
BUZZ
BUZZ
Y'KNOW, NO MATTER HOW MANY AUDITIONS I GO THROUGH, EACH TIME I GET THE BUTTER-FLIES.
THUMP
THUMP
SAME HERE!
THUMP
AS EXPECT-ED...
GLANCE
...MOST OF THE GUYS HERE ARE THE THIN, PRETTY BOY TYPE.
A LOT OF THE MEN HERE ARE ALREADY MODELS, IDOLS AND EVEN BACK UP DANCERS.
I'VE HEARD THAT THESE HERO SHOWS ARE THE GATEWAY TO SUCCESS FOR NEW TALENTS.
BOY, THEY'RE THIN...
...AND TALL...

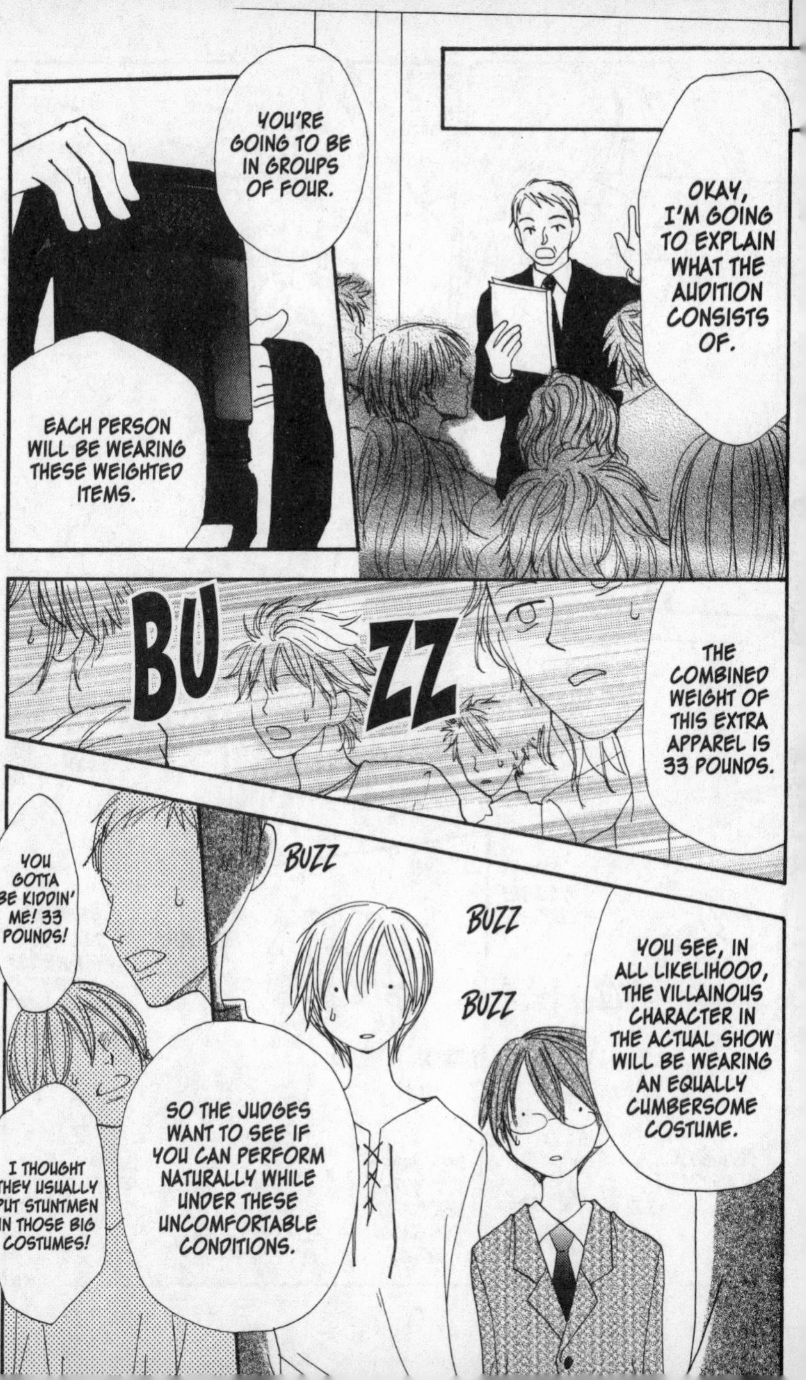
OKAY, I'M GOING TO EXPLAIN WHAT THE AUDITION CONSISTS OF.
YOU'RE GOING TO BE IN GROUPS OF FOUR.
EACH PERSON WILL BE WEARING THESE WEIGHTED ITEMS.
THE COMBINED WEIGHT OF THIS EXTRA APPAREL IS 33 POUNDS.
BU ZZ
YOU SEE, IN ALL LIKELIHOOD, THE VILLAINOUS CHARACTER IN THE ACTUAL SHOW WILL BE WEARING AN EQUALLY CUMBERSOME COSTUME.
BUZZ
BUZZ
BUZZ
SO THE JUDGES WANT TO SEE IF YOU CAN PERFORM NATURALLY WHILE UNDER THESE UNCOMFORTABLE CONDITIONS.
YOU GOTTA BE KIDDIN' ME! 33 POUNDS!
I THOUGHT THEY USUALLY PUT STUNTMEN IN THOSE BIG COSTUMES!

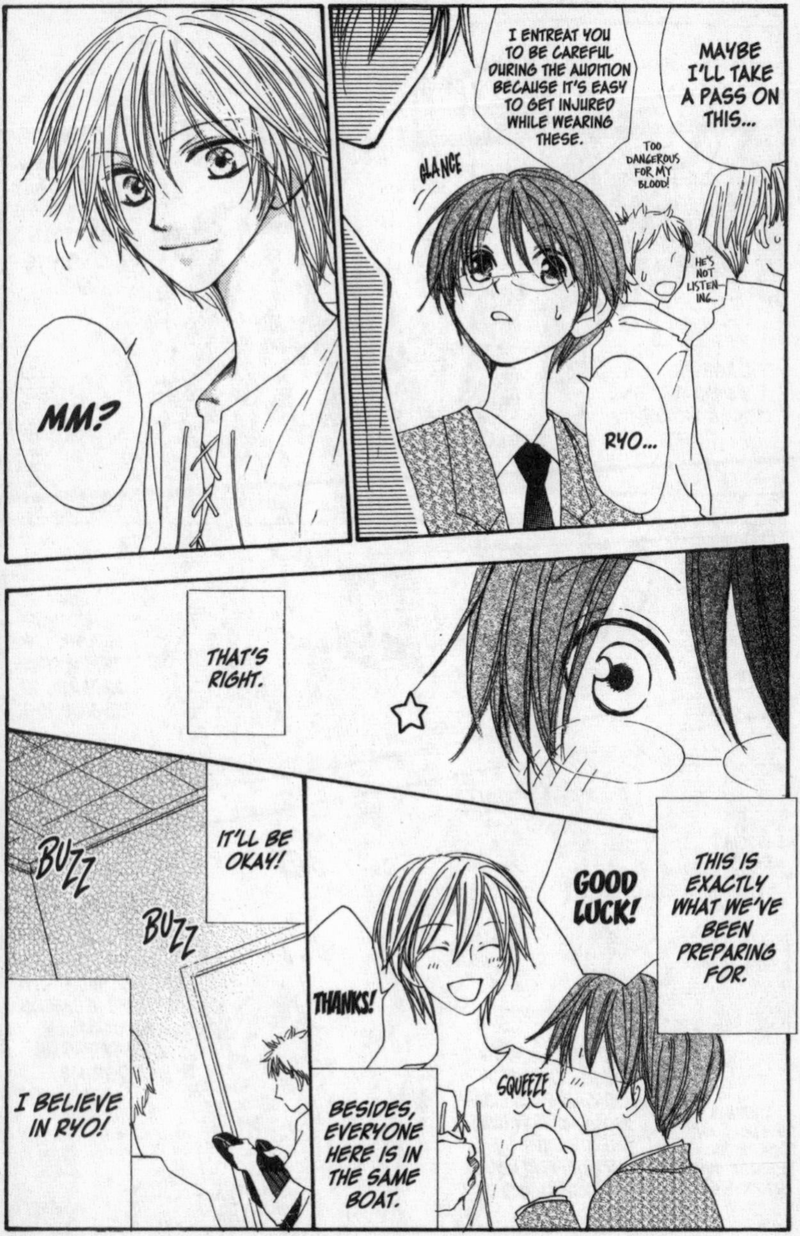
MAYBE I'LL TAKE A PASS ON THIS...
I ENTREAT YOU TO BE CAREFUL DURING THE AUDITION BECAUSE IT'S EASY TO GET INJURED WHILE WEARING THESE.
TOO DANGEROUS FOR MY BLOOD!
GLANCE
HE'S NOT LISTENING...
RYO...
MM?
THAT'S RIGHT.
THIS IS EXACTLY WHAT WE'VE BEEN PREPARING FOR.
GOOD LUCK!
THANKS!
SQUEEZE
BESIDES, EVERYONE HERE IS IN THE SAME BOAT.
IT'LL BE OKAY!
BUZZ
BUZZ
I BELIEVE IN RYO!

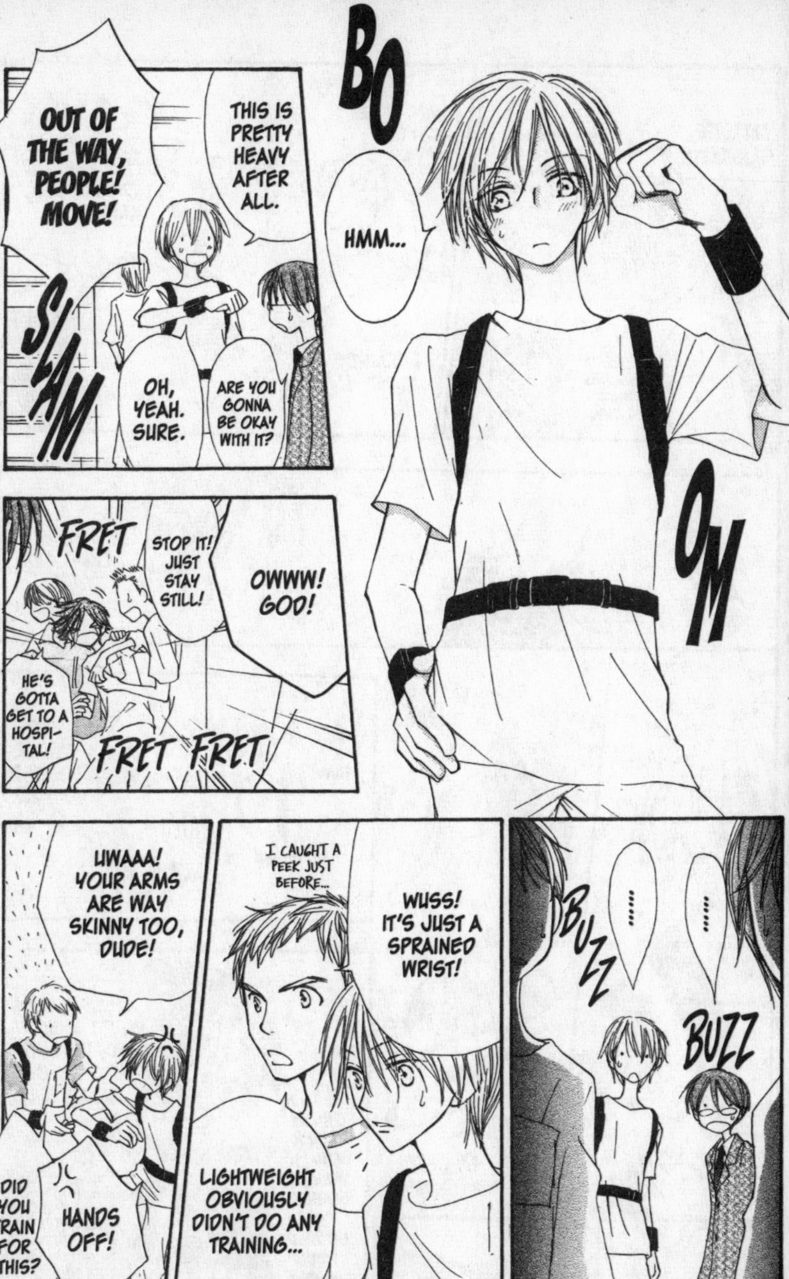
BO
HMM...
OM
THIS IS PRETTY HEAVY AFTER ALL.
OUT OF THE WAY, PEOPLE! MOVE!
ARE YOU GONNA BE OKAY WITH IT?
OH, YEAH. SURE.
SLAM
OWWW! GOD!
STOP IT! JUST STAY STILL!
FRET
HE'S GOTTA GET TO A HOSPITAL!
FRET FRET
.....
.....
BUZZ
BUZZ
WUSS! IT'S JUST A SPRAINED WRIST!
I CAUGHT A PEEK JUST BEFORE...
LIGHTWEIGHT OBVIOUSLY DIDN'T DO ANY TRAINING...
UWAAA! YOUR ARMS ARE WAY SKINNY TOO, DUDE!
HANDS OFF!
DID YOU TRAIN FOR THIS?

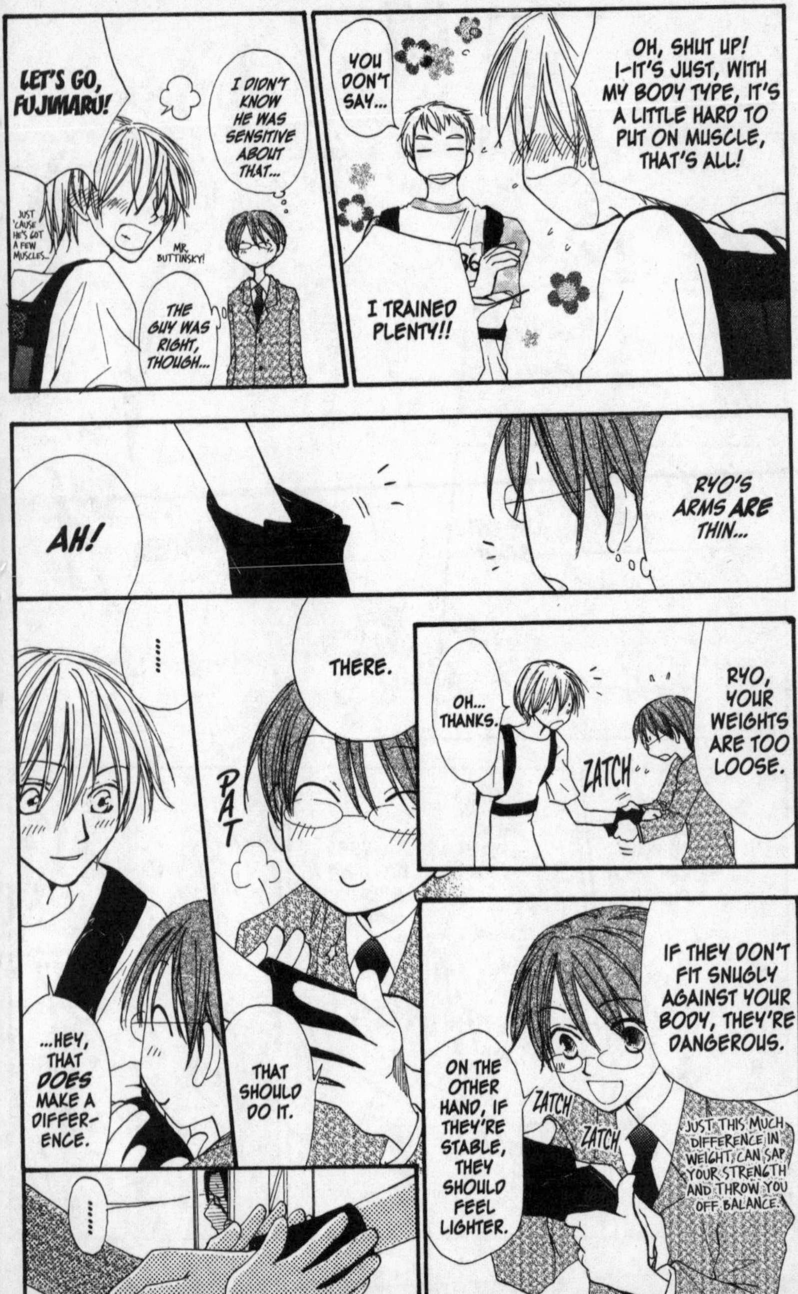

OH, SHUT UP! I-IT'S JUST, WITH MY BODY TYPE, IT'S A LITTLE HARD TO PUT ON MUSCLE, THAT'S ALL!
YOU DON'T SAY...
I TRAINED PLENTY!!
LET'S GO, FUJIMARU!
I DIDN'T KNOW HE WAS SENSITIVE ABOUT THAT...
JUST 'CAUSE HE'S GOT A FEW MUSCLES...
MR. BUTTINSKY!
THE GUY WAS RIGHT, THOUGH...
RYO'S ARMS ARE THIN...
AH!
RYO, YOUR WEIGHTS ARE TOO LOOSE.
ZATCH
OH... THANKS.
IF THEY DON'T FIT SNUGLY AGAINST YOUR BODY, THEY'RE DANGEROUS.
JUST THIS MUCH DIFFERENCE IN WEIGHT CAN SAP YOUR STRENGTH AND THROW YOU OFF BALANCE.
ZATCH
ZATCH
ON THE OTHER HAND, IF THEY'RE STABLE, THEY SHOULD FEEL LIGHTER.
THERE.
PAT
......
THAT SHOULD DO IT.
...HEY, THAT DOES MAKE A DIFFERENCE.
......

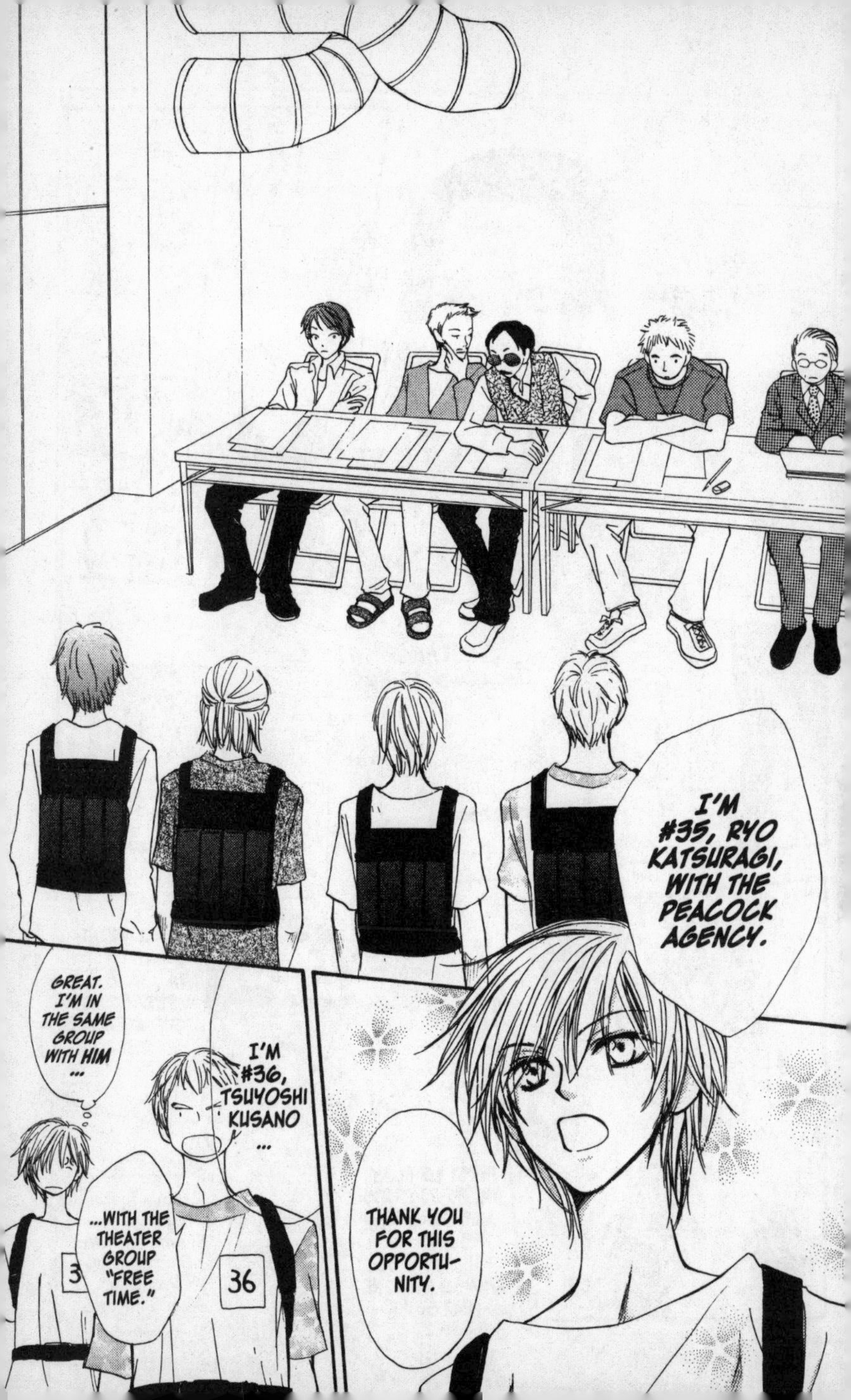
I'M #35, RYO KATSURAGI, WITH THE PEACOCK AGENCY.
THANK YOU FOR THIS OPPORTUNITY.
I'M #36, TSUYOSHI KUSANO ...
...WITH THE THEATER GROUP "FREE TIME."
GREAT. I'M IN THE SAME GROUP WITH HIM ...
36

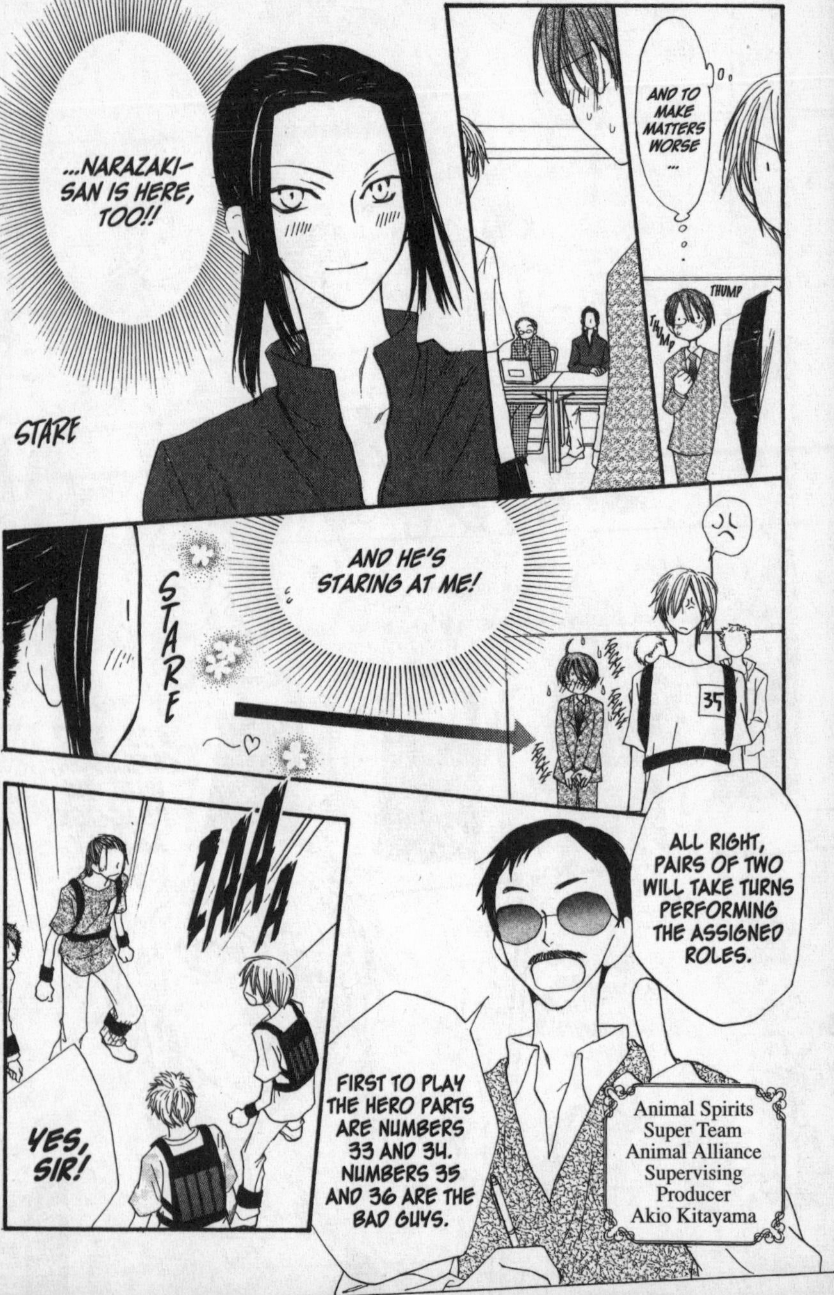
AND TO MAKE MATTERS WORSE ...
THUMP
THUMP
...NARAZAKI-SAN IS HERE, TOO!!
STARE
AND HE'S STARING AT ME!
STARE
ALL RIGHT, PAIRS OF TWO WILL TAKE TURNS PERFORMING THE ASSIGNED ROLES.
Animal Spirits Super Team Animal Alliance Supervising Producer Akio Kitayama
FIRST TO PLAY THE HERO PARTS ARE NUMBERS 33 AND 34. NUMBERS 35 AND 36 ARE THE BAD GUYS.
35
ZAHA
YES, SIR!

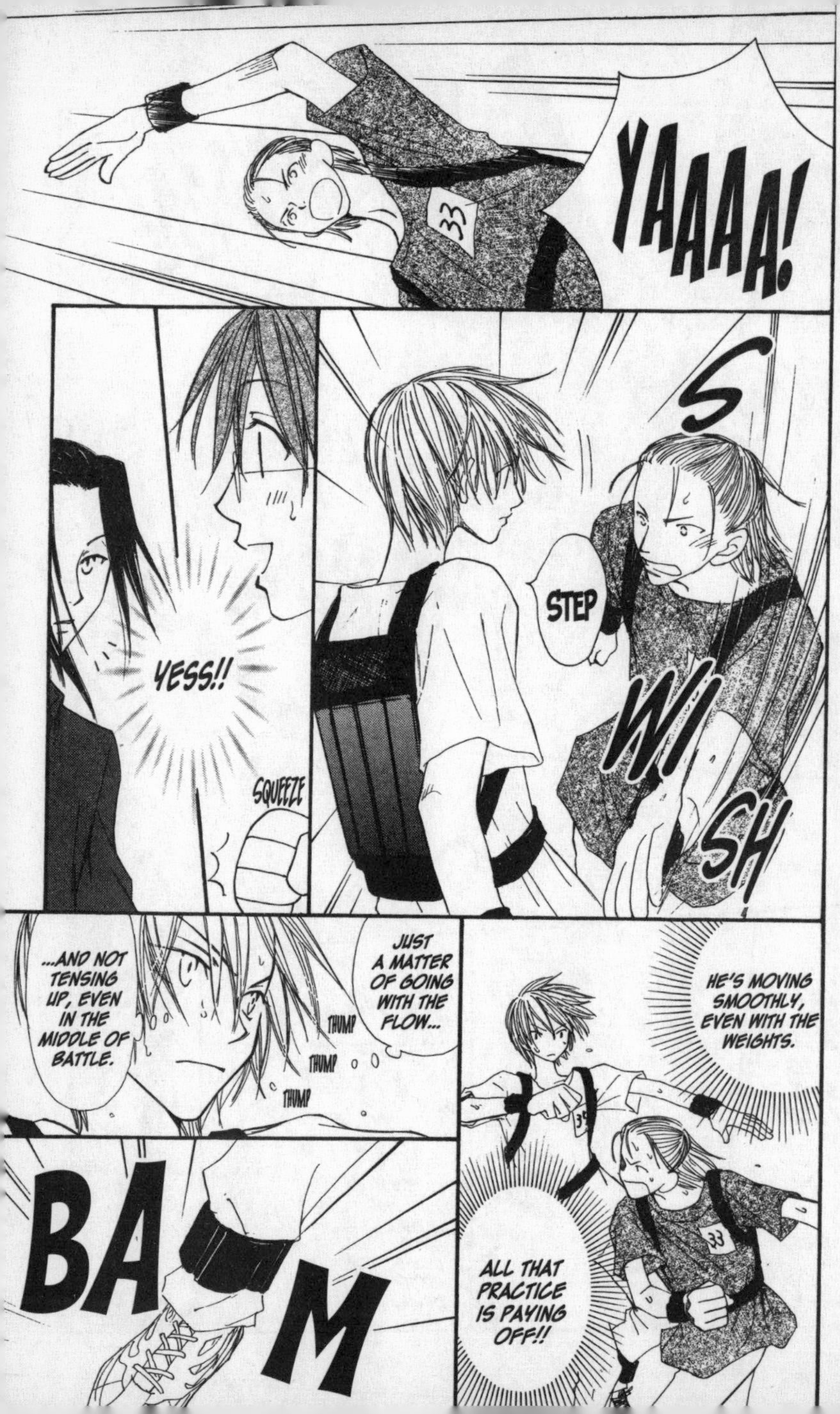
YAAAA!
SWISH
STEP
YESS!!
SQUEEZE
HE'S MOVING SMOOTHLY, EVEN WITH THE WEIGHTS.
ALL THAT PRACTICE IS PAYING OFF!!
JUST A MATTER OF GOING WITH THE FLOW...
THUMP
THUMP
THUMP
...AND NOT TENSING UP, EVEN IN THE MIDDLE OF BATTLE.
BAM

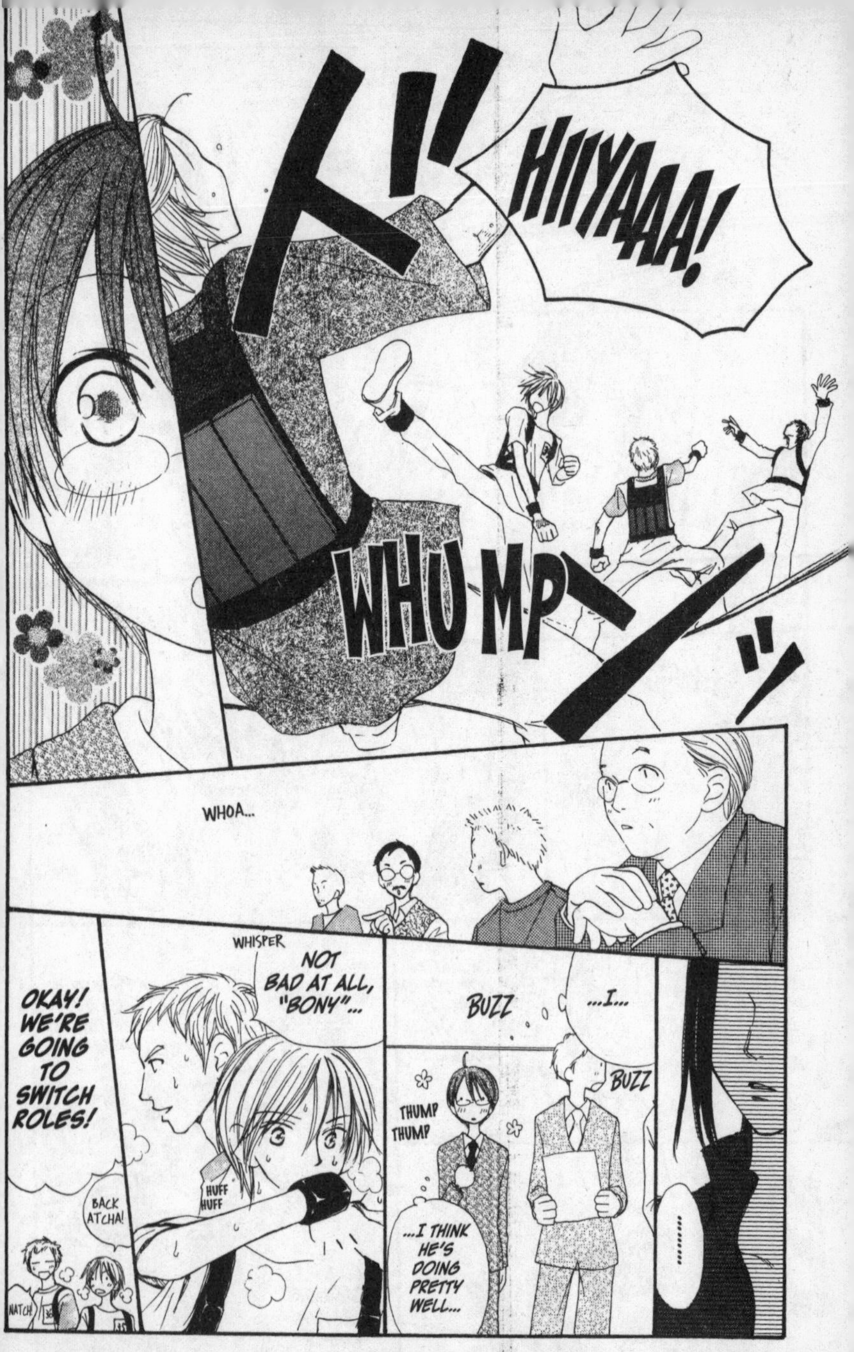
HIIYAAA!
WHUMP
WHOA...
....
...I...
BUZZ
BUZZ
THUMP THUMP
...I THINK HE'S DOING PRETTY WELL...
WHISPER
NOT BAD AT ALL, "BONY"...
OKAY! WE'RE GOING TO SWITCH ROLES!
HUFF HUFF
BACK ATCHA!
NATCH

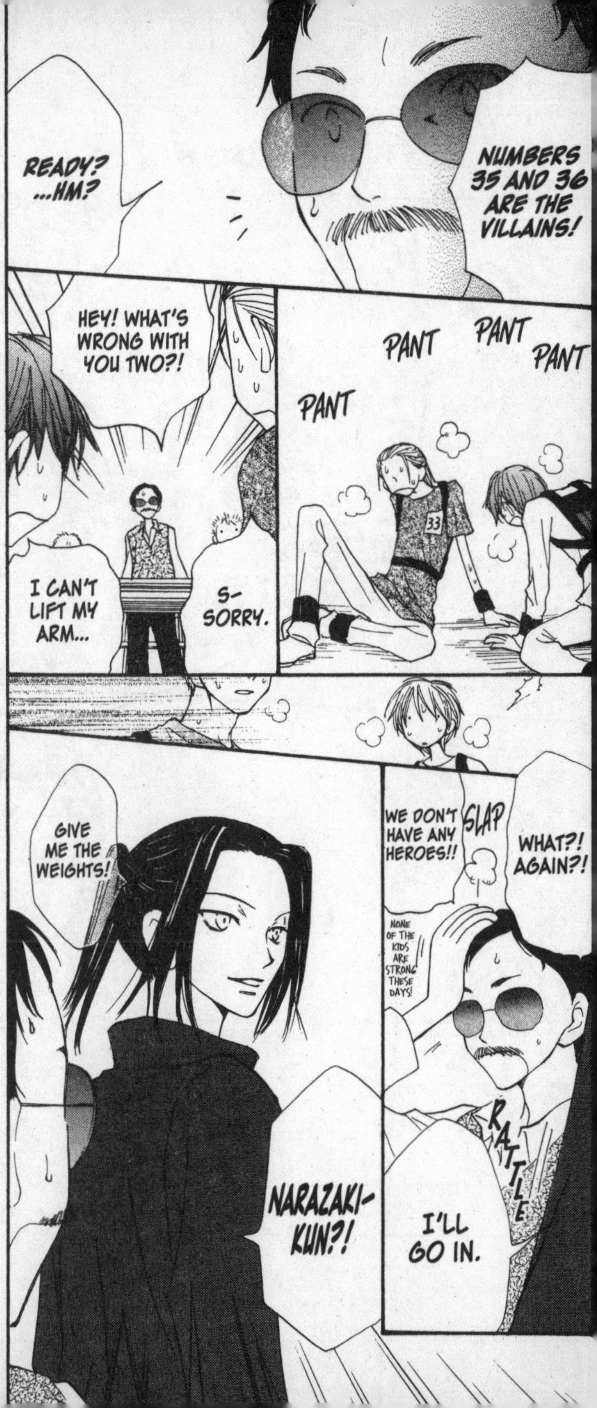
NUMBERS 35 AND 36 ARE THE VILLAINS!
READY? ...HM?
PANT PANT PANT PANT
HEY! WHAT'S WRONG WITH YOU TWO?!
S-SORRY.
I CAN'T LIFT MY ARM...
WHAT?! AGAIN?!
SLAP
WE DON'T HAVE ANY HEROES!!
NONE OF THE KIDS ARE STRONG THESE DAYS!
RATTLE
I'LL GO IN.
NARAZAKI-KUN?!
GIVE ME THE WEIGHTS!

1/4 Sakura Mail

part 10

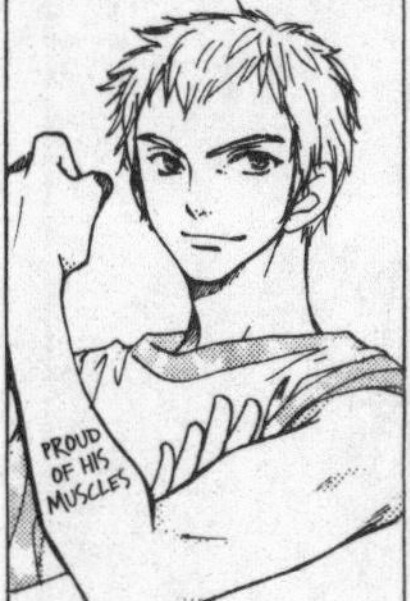
PROUD OF HIS MUSCLES

And so here we are at the "Animal Alliance" audition. No matter how easy the characters make it look, they've got a really heavy load strapped on, so they definitely gave it their all during the audition. Once Narazaki-san put his weights on, he suddenly looked so heroic that I just had to laugh.
By the way, the full name of the "break fall" that Ryo performs in this episode is a "backward turning break fall." Well, I'm out of room, so I'll wind it up here! See you again!!

Sakura Tsukba

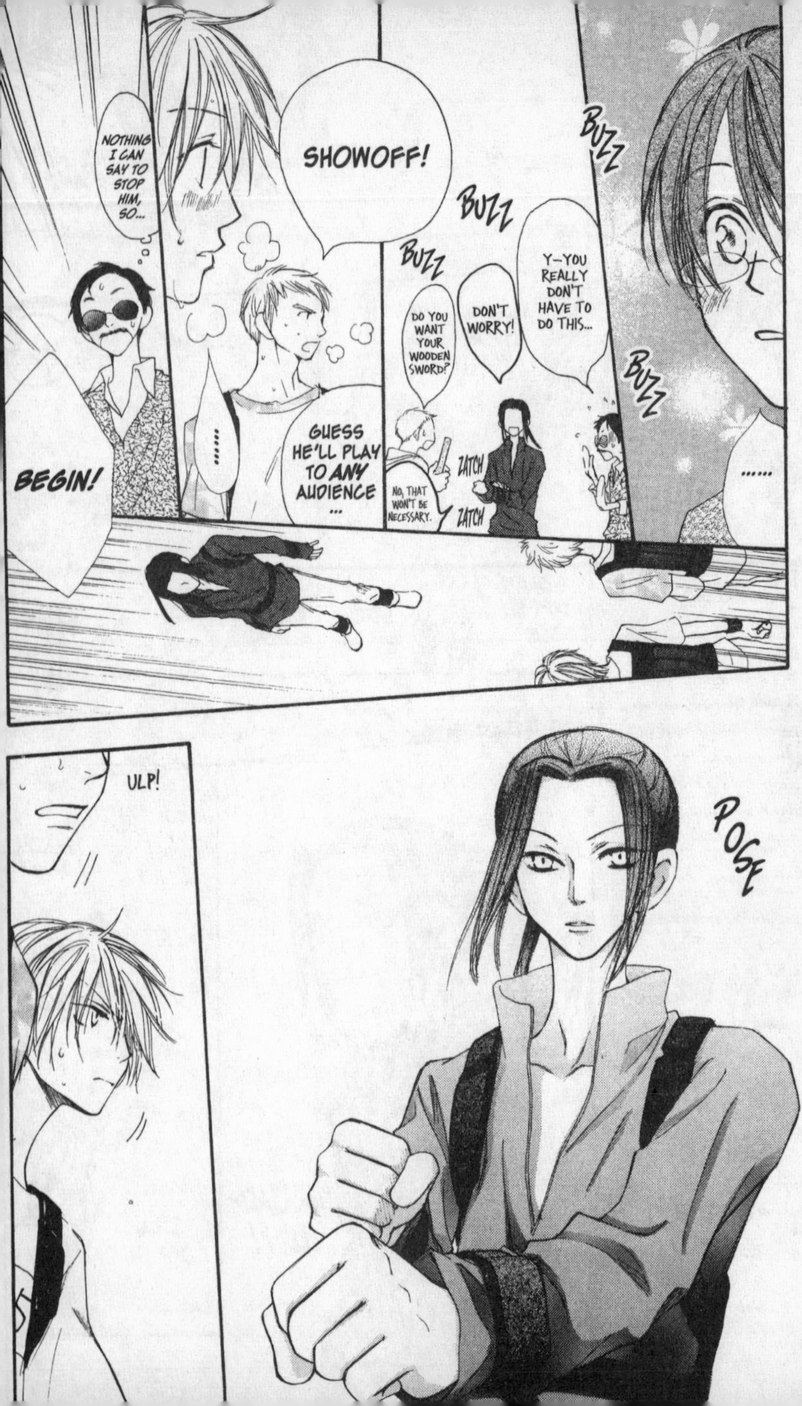
BUZZ
BUZZ
......
Y-YOU REALLY DON'T HAVE TO DO THIS...
BUZZ
DON'T WORRY!
BUZZ
DO YOU WANT YOUR WOODEN SWORD?
NO, THAT WON'T BE NECESSARY.
ZATCH
ZATCH
SHOWOFF!
GUESS HE'LL PLAY TO ANY AUDIENCE...
......
NOTHING I CAN SAY TO STOP HIM, SO...
BEGIN!
POSE
ULP!

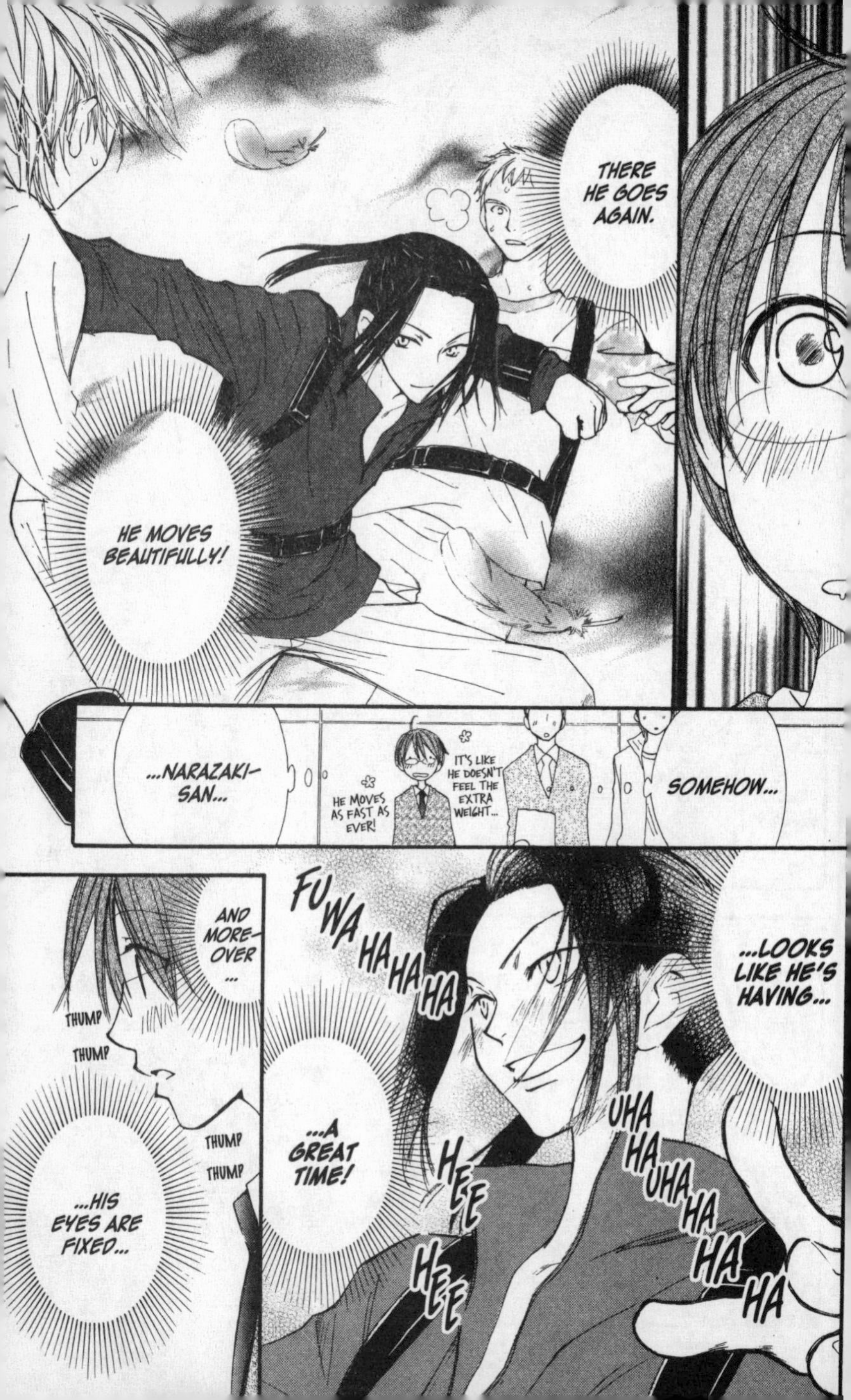
THERE HE GOES AGAIN.
HE MOVES BEAUTIFULLY!
SOMEHOW...
IT'S LIKE HE DOESN'T FEEL THE EXTRA WEIGHT...
HE MOVES AS FAST AS EVER!
...NARAZAKI-SAN...
...LOOKS LIKE HE'S HAVING...
FUWAHAHAHAHA
UHA HA UHAHA HA HA HA HA
HEE HEE
...A GREAT TIME!
AND MOREOVER...
THUMP THUMP
THUMP THUMP
...HIS EYES ARE FIXED...

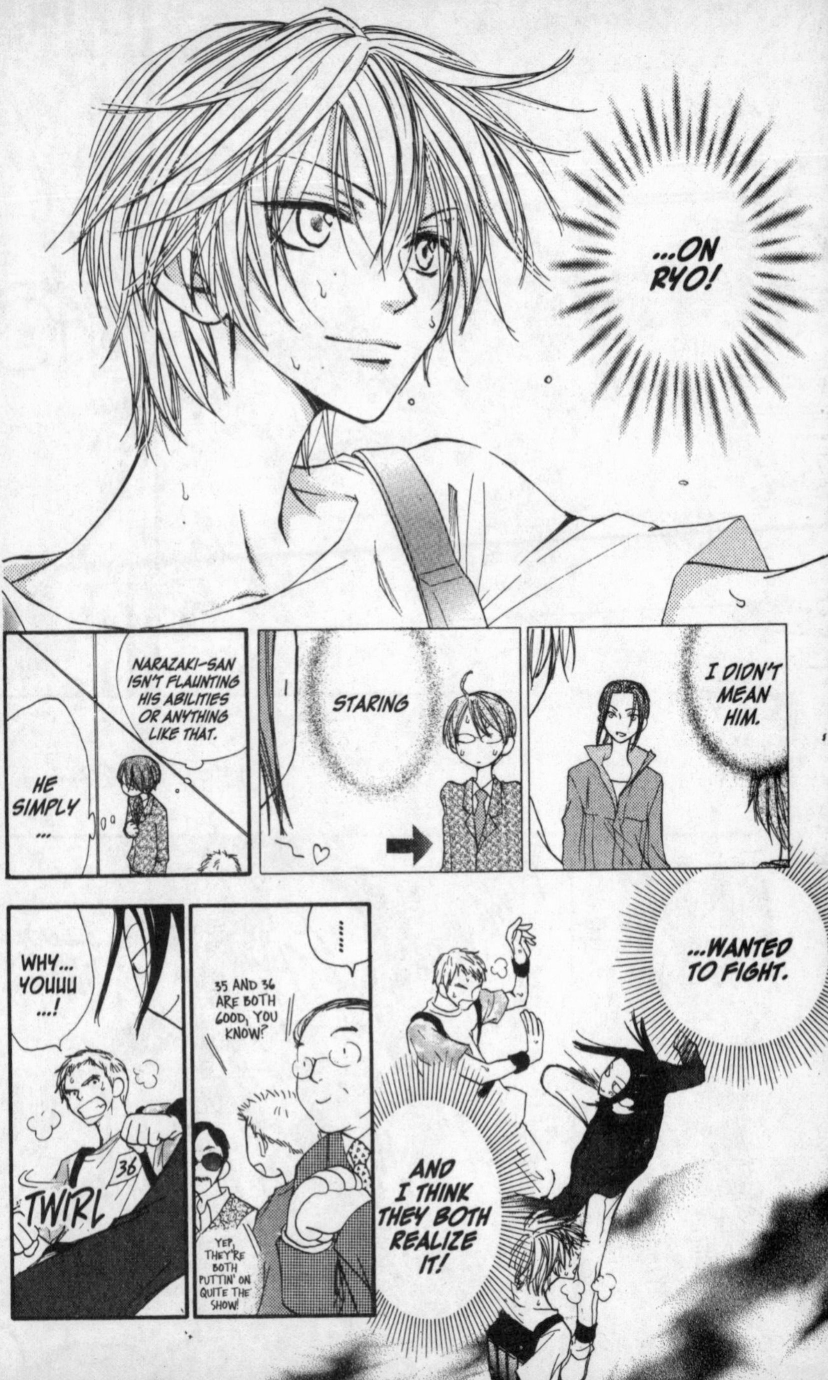
...ON RYO!
I DIDN'T MEAN HIM.
STARING
NARAZAKI-SAN ISN'T FLAUNTING HIS ABILITIES OR ANYTHING LIKE THAT.
HE SIMPLY ...
...WANTED TO FIGHT.
AND I THINK THEY BOTH REALIZE IT!
......
35 AND 36 ARE BOTH GOOD, YOU KNOW?
YEP, THEY'RE BOTH PUTTIN' ON QUITE THE SHOW!
WHY... YOUUU ...!
TWIRL

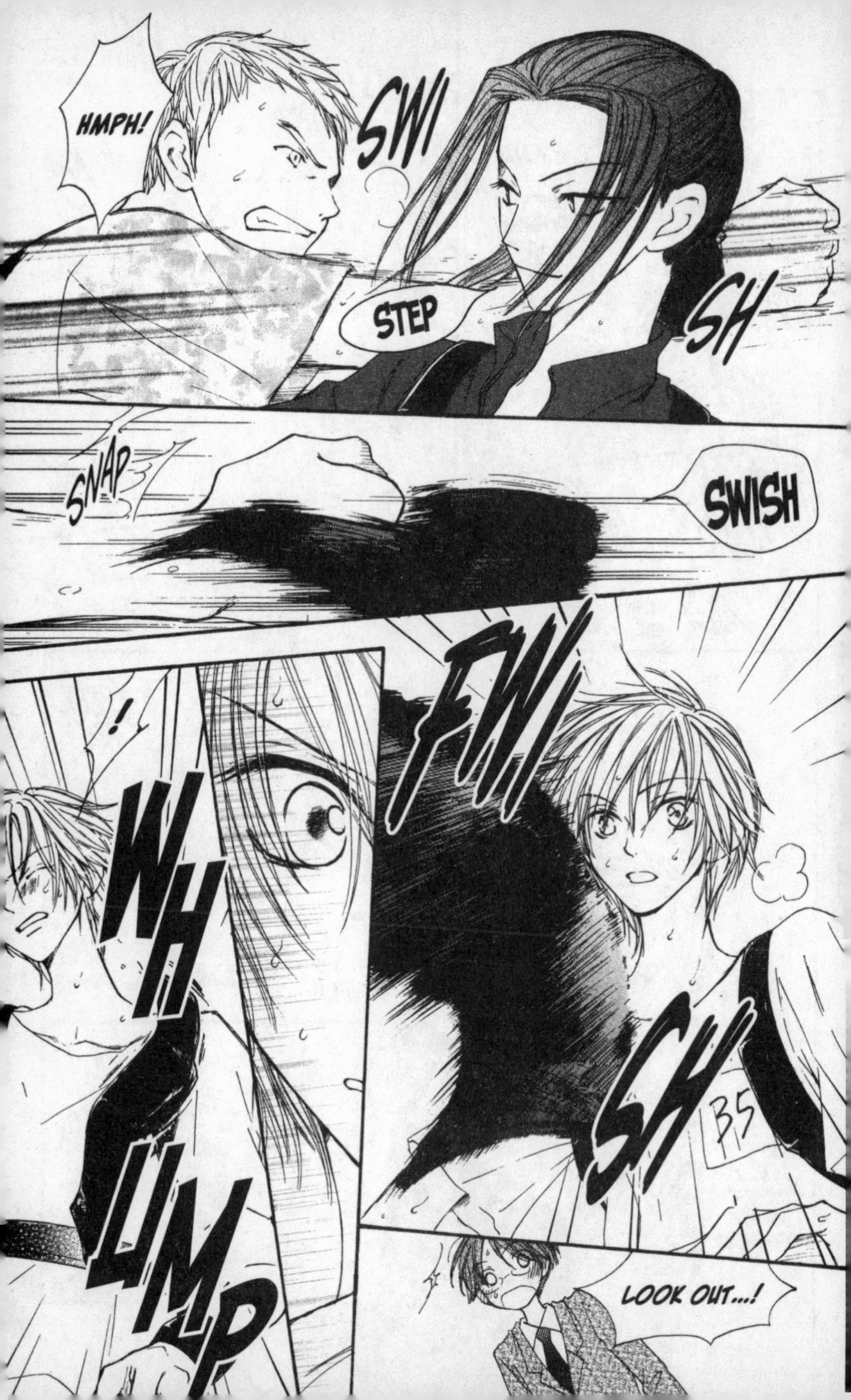
SWI
SH
STEP
HMPH!
SWISH
SNAP
FW
SCH
B5
LOOK OUT...!
!
WH
UMP

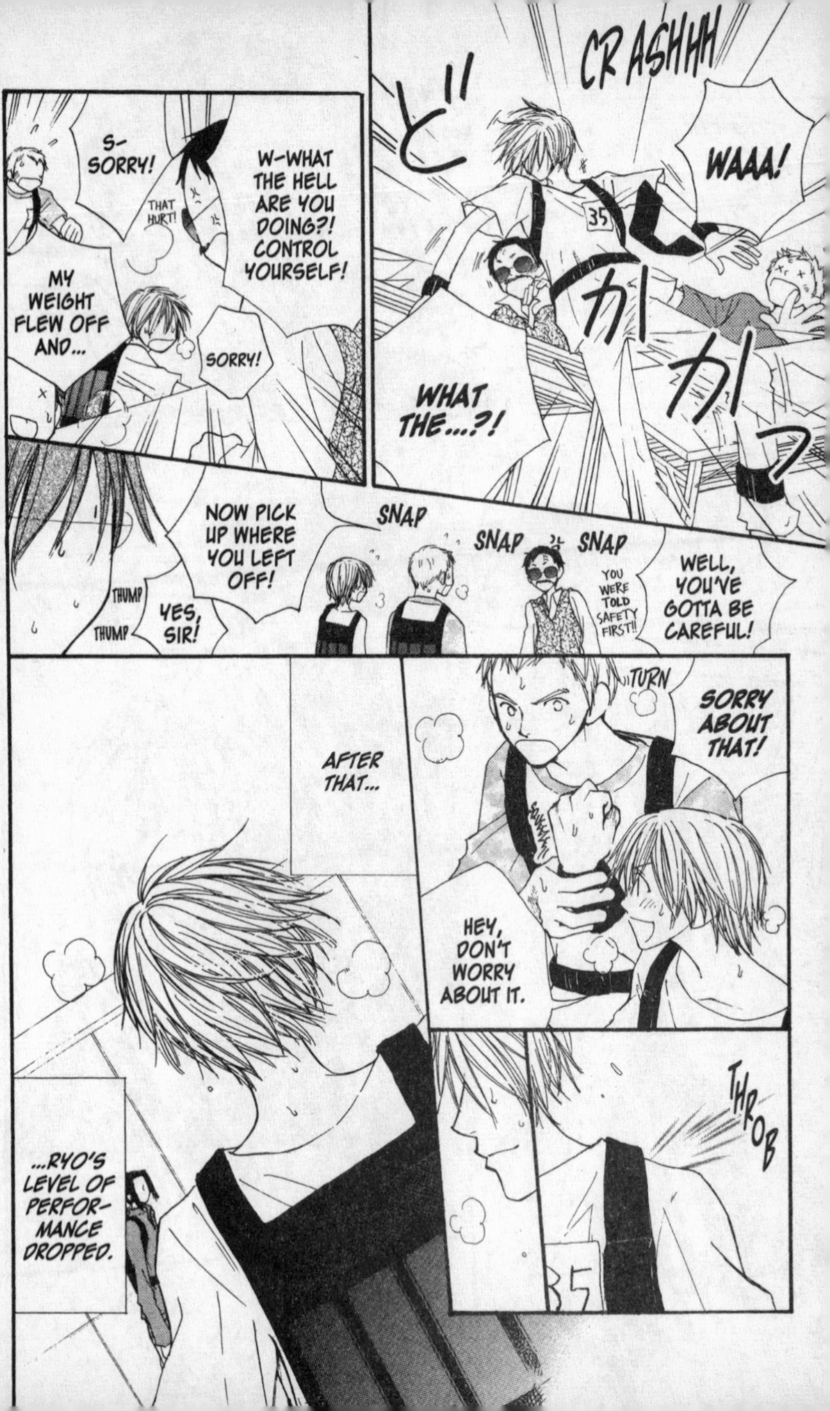

CRASHHH
WAAA!
WHAT THE...?!
W-WHAT THE HELL ARE YOU DOING?! CONTROL YOURSELF!
THAT HURT!
S-SORRY!
SORRY!
MY WEIGHT FLEW OFF AND...
WELL, YOU'VE GOTTA BE CAREFUL!
YOU WERE TOLD SAFETY FIRST!!
SNAP
SNAP
SNAP
NOW PICK UP WHERE YOU LEFT OFF!
YES, SIR!
THUMP
THUMP
SORRY ABOUT THAT!
TURN
HEY, DON'T WORRY ABOUT IT.
AFTER THAT...
THROB
...RYO'S LEVEL OF PERFORMANCE DROPPED.

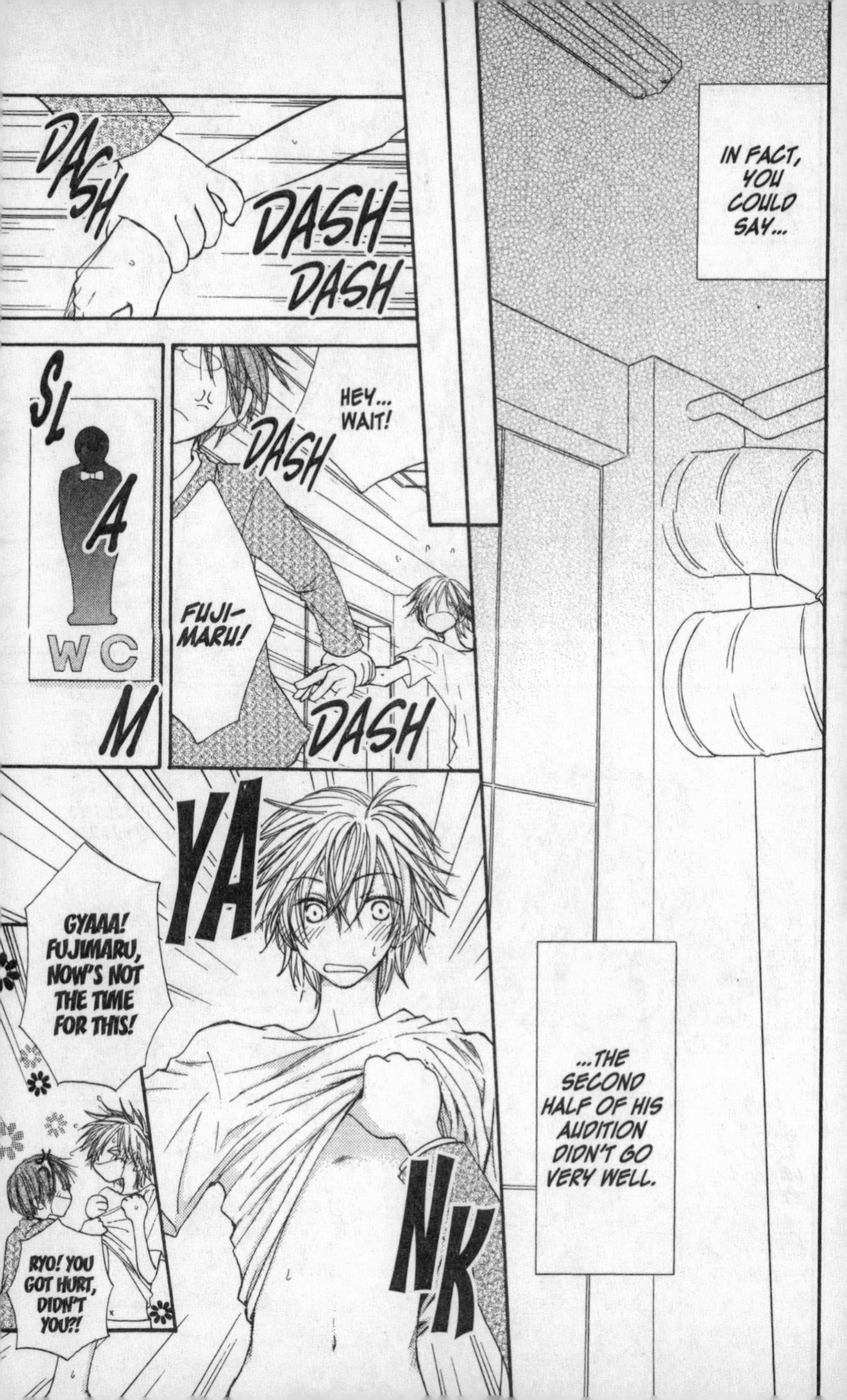
IN FACT, YOU COULD SAY...
...THE SECOND HALF OF HIS AUDITION DIDN'T GO VERY WELL.
DASH
DASH DASH
HEY... WAIT!
DASH
FUJI-MARU!
DASH
SLAM
WC
YANK
GYAAA! FUJIMARU, NOW'S NOT THE TIME FOR THIS!
RYO! YOU GOT HURT, DIDN'T YOU?!

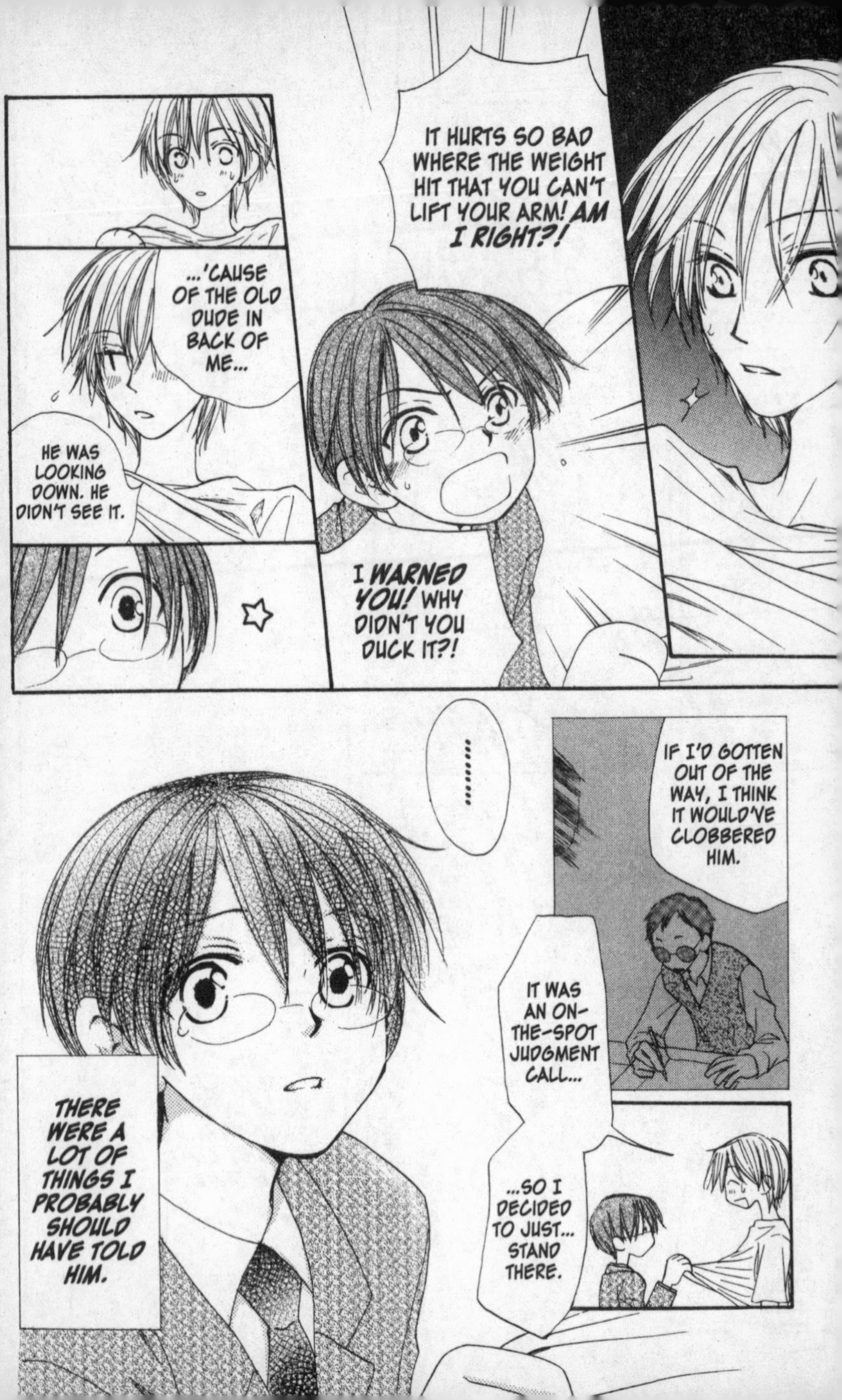
IT HURTS SO BAD WHERE THE WEIGHT HIT THAT YOU CAN'T LIFT YOUR ARM! AM I RIGHT?!
I WARNED YOU! WHY DIDN'T YOU DUCK IT?!
...'CAUSE OF THE OLD DUDE IN BACK OF ME...
HE WAS LOOKING DOWN. HE DIDN'T SEE IT.
IF I'D GOTTEN OUT OF THE WAY, I THINK IT WOULD'VE CLOBBERED HIM.
IT WAS AN ON-THE-SPOT JUDGMENT CALL...
...SO I DECIDED TO JUST... STAND THERE.
......
THERE WERE A LOT OF THINGS I PROBABLY SHOULD HAVE TOLD HIM.

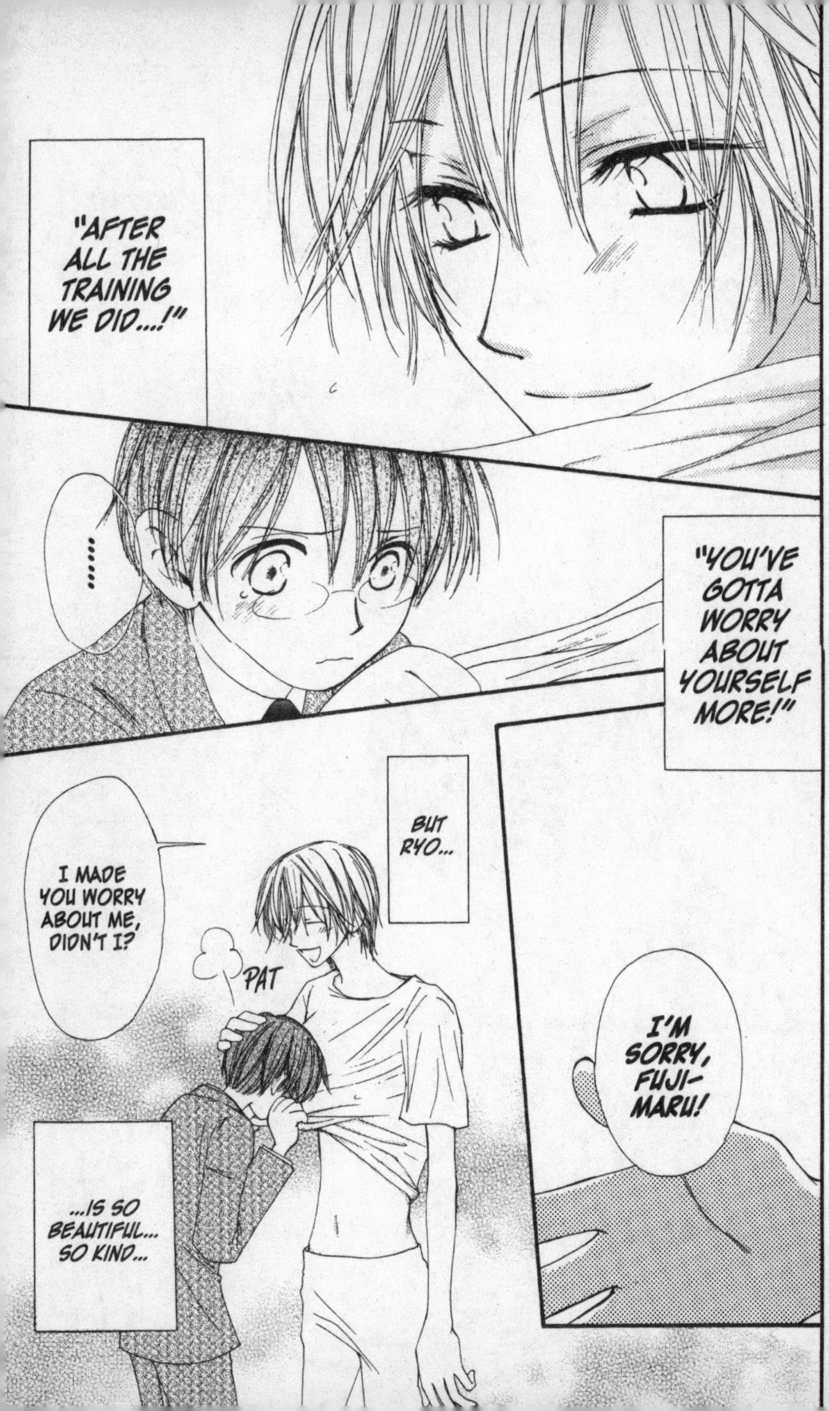
"AFTER ALL THE TRAINING WE DID...!"
"YOU'VE GOTTA WORRY ABOUT YOURSELF MORE!"
......
I'M SORRY, FUJI-MARU!
BUT RYO...
I MADE YOU WORRY ABOUT ME, DIDN'T I?
PAT
...IS SO BEAUTIFUL... SO KIND...

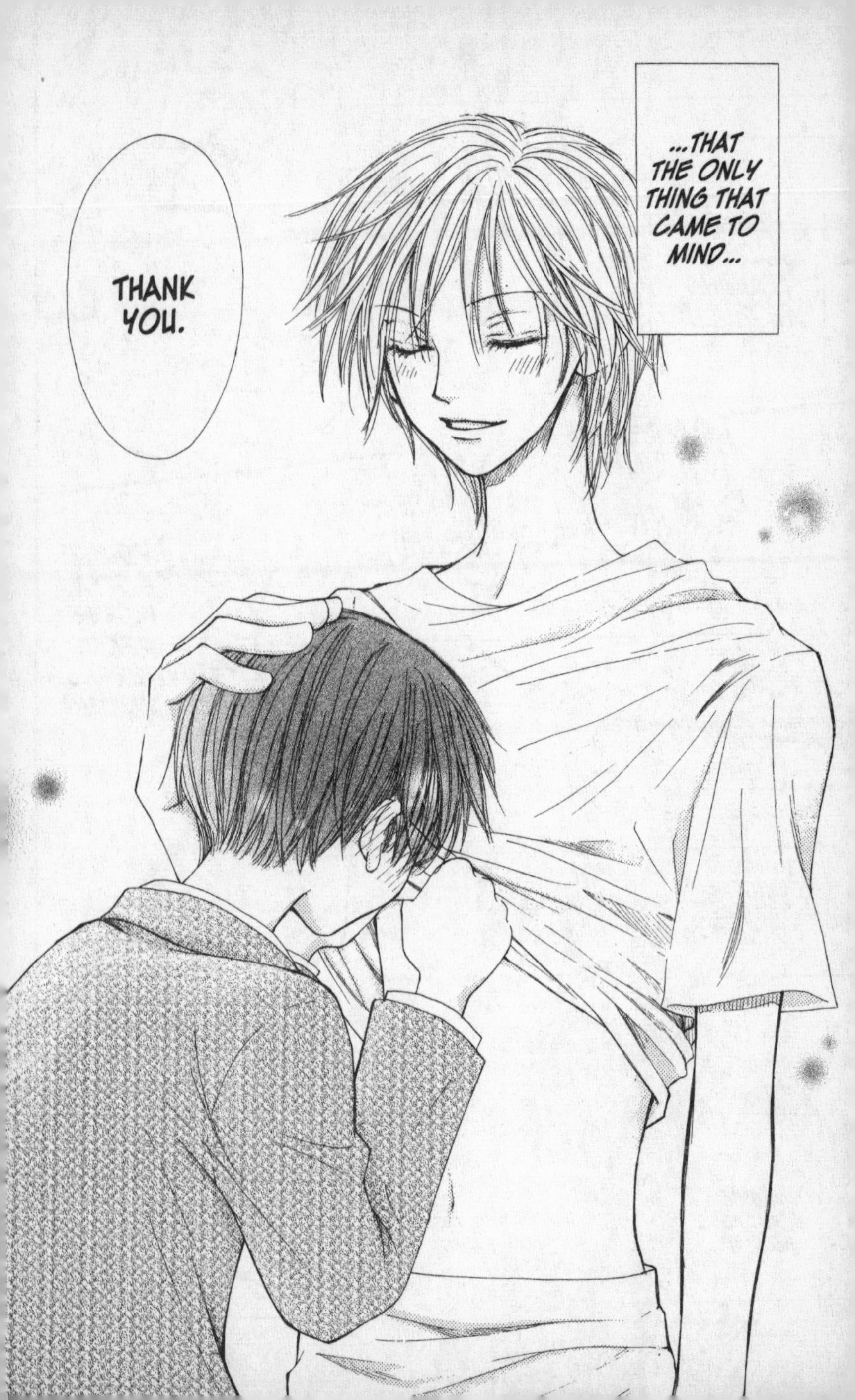
...THAT THE ONLY THING THAT CAME TO MIND...
THANK YOU.

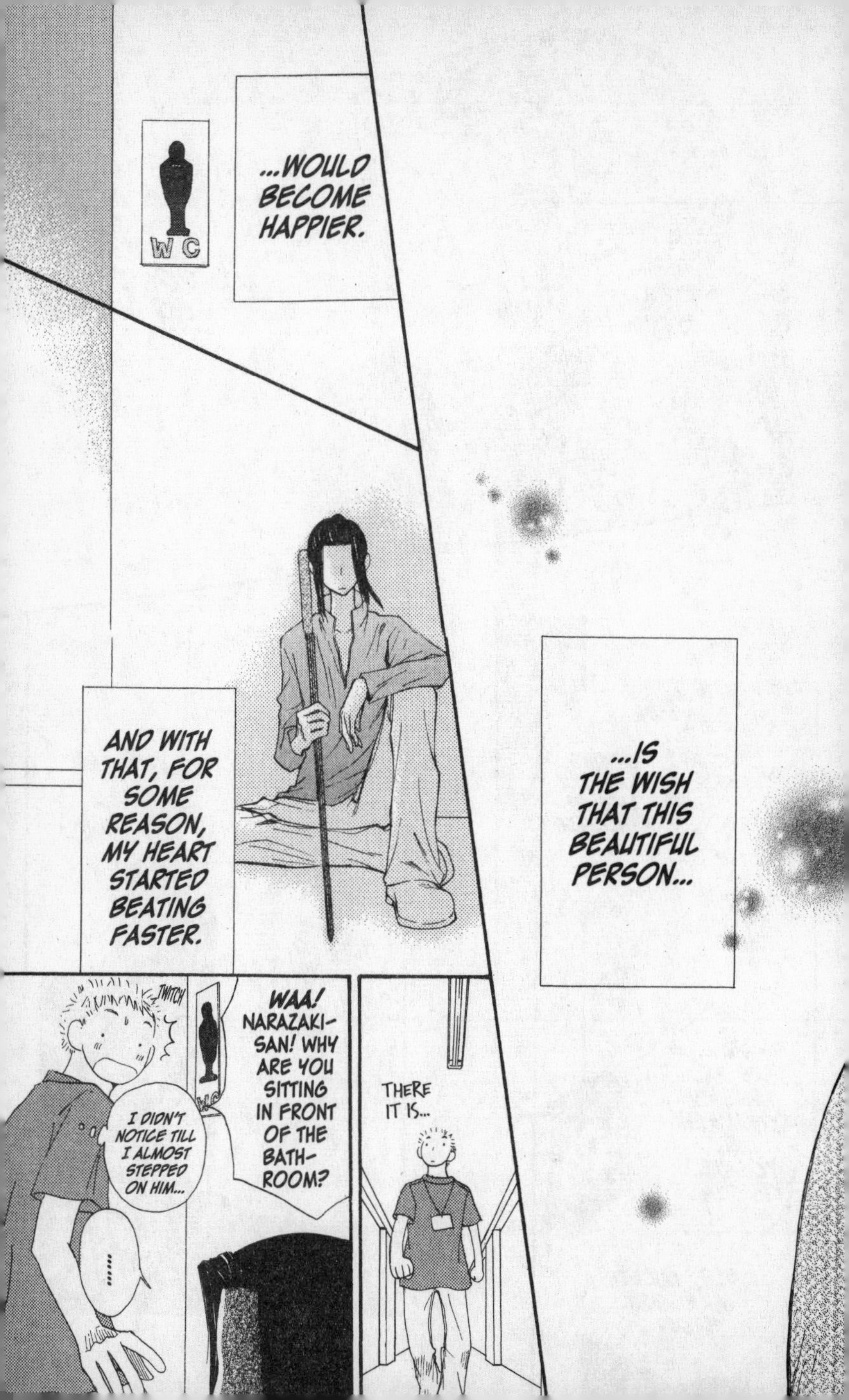
...IS THE WISH THAT THIS BEAUTIFUL PERSON...
...WOULD BECOME HAPPIER.
AND WITH THAT, FOR SOME REASON, MY HEART STARTED BEATING FASTER.
THERE IT IS...
WAA! NARAZAKI-SAN! WHY ARE YOU SITTING IN FRONT OF THE BATH-ROOM?
TWITCH
I DIDN'T NOTICE TILL I ALMOST STEPPED ON HIM...
......
W C

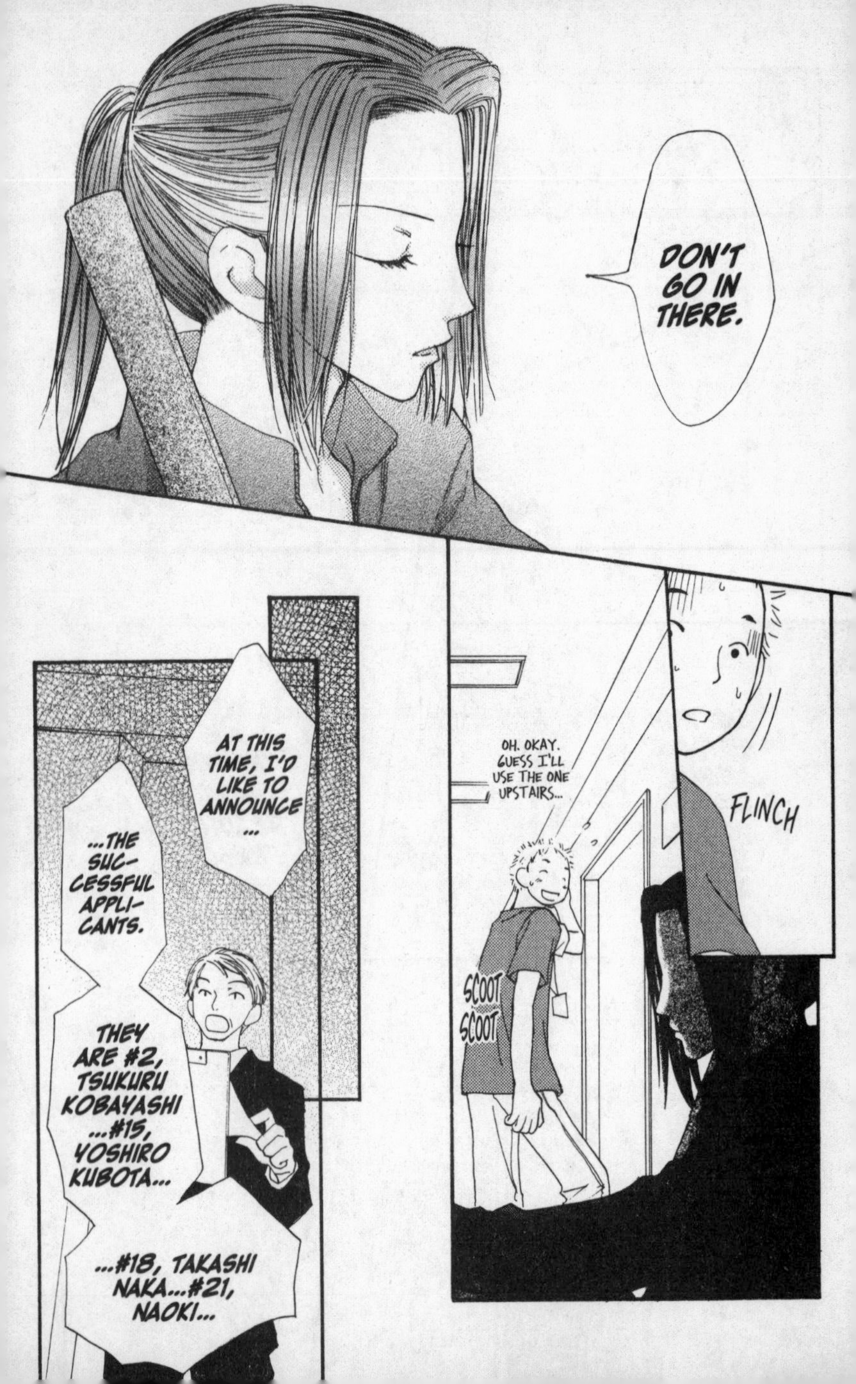
DON'T GO IN THERE.
FLINCH
OH. OKAY. GUESS I'LL USE THE ONE UPSTAIRS...
SCOOT SCOOT
AT THIS TIME, I'D LIKE TO ANNOUNCE ...
...THE SUC-CESSFUL APPLI-CANTS.
THEY ARE #2, TSUKURU KOBAYASHI ...#15, YOSHIRO KUBOTA...
...#18, TAKASHI NAKA...#21, NAOKI...

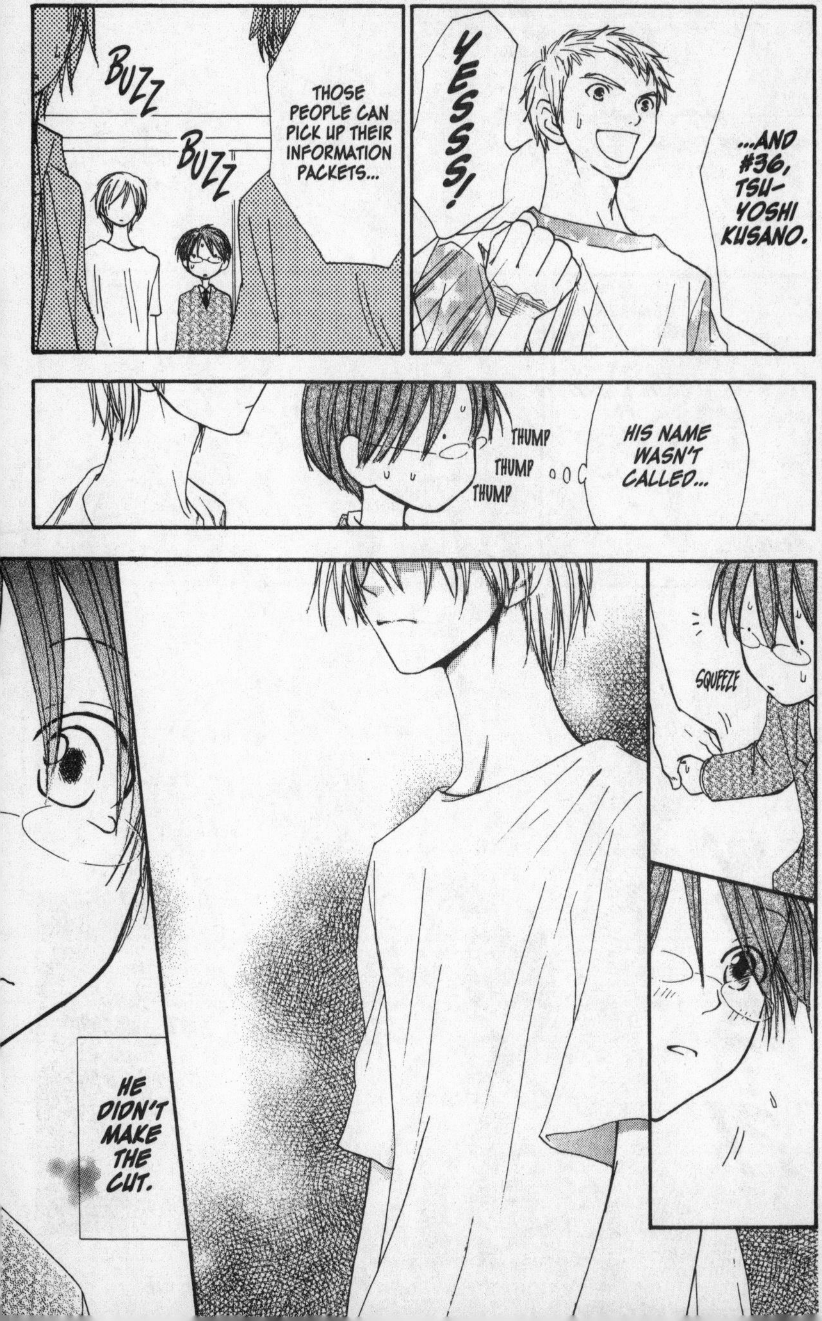
...AND #36, TSUYOSHI KUSANO.
YESSS!
THOSE PEOPLE CAN PICK UP THEIR INFORMATION PACKETS...
BUZZ
BUZZ
HIS NAME WASN'T CALLED...
THUMP
THUMP
THUMP
SQUEEZE
HE DIDN'T MAKE THE CUT.

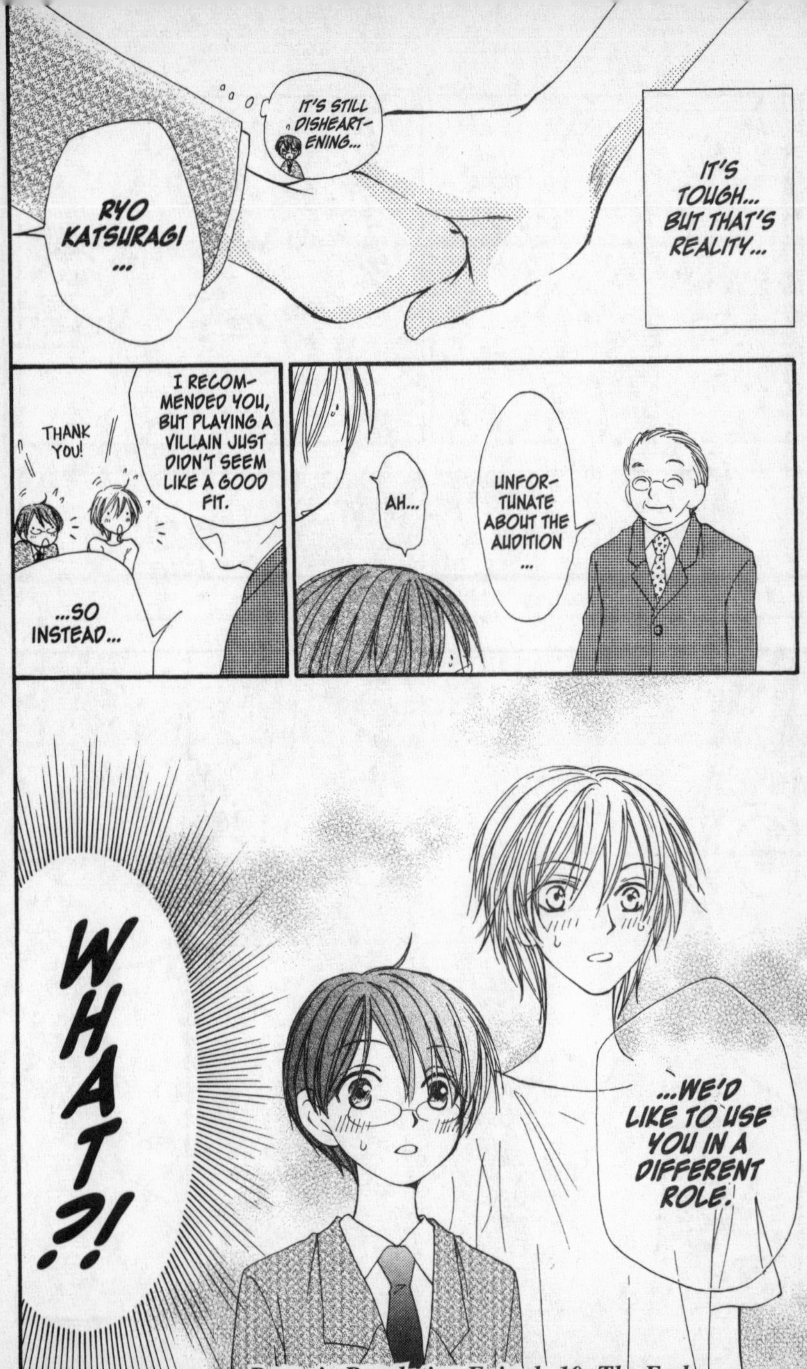
IT'S TOUGH... BUT THAT'S REALITY...
IT'S STILL DISHEARTENING...
RYO KATSURAGI ...
UNFORTUNATE ABOUT THE AUDITION ...
AH...
I RECOMMENDED YOU, BUT PLAYING A VILLAIN JUST DIDN'T SEEM LIKE A GOOD FIT.
THANK YOU!
...SO INSTEAD...
...WE'D LIKE TO USE YOU IN A DIFFERENT ROLE.
WHAT?!

Penguin Revolution Episode 10: The End

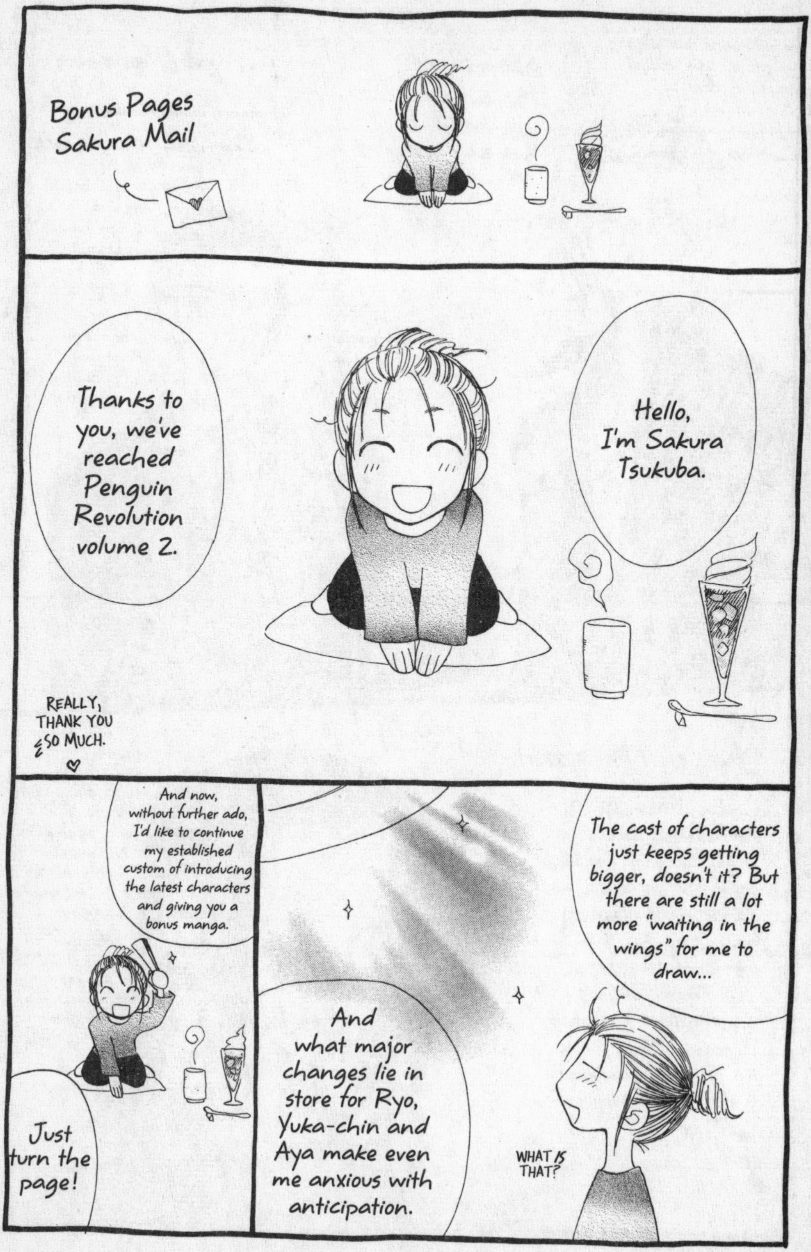
Bonus Pages
Sakura Mail
Hello, I'm Sakura Tsukuba.
Thanks to you, we've reached Penguin Revolution volume 2.
REALLY, THANK YOU SO MUCH.
The cast of characters just keeps getting bigger, doesn't it? But there are still a lot more "waiting in the wings" for me to draw...
And what major changes lie in store for Ryo, Yuka-chin and Aya make even me anxious with anticipation.
WHAT IS THAT?
And now, without further ado, I'd like to continue my established custom of introducing the latest characters and giving you a bonus manga.
Just turn the page!

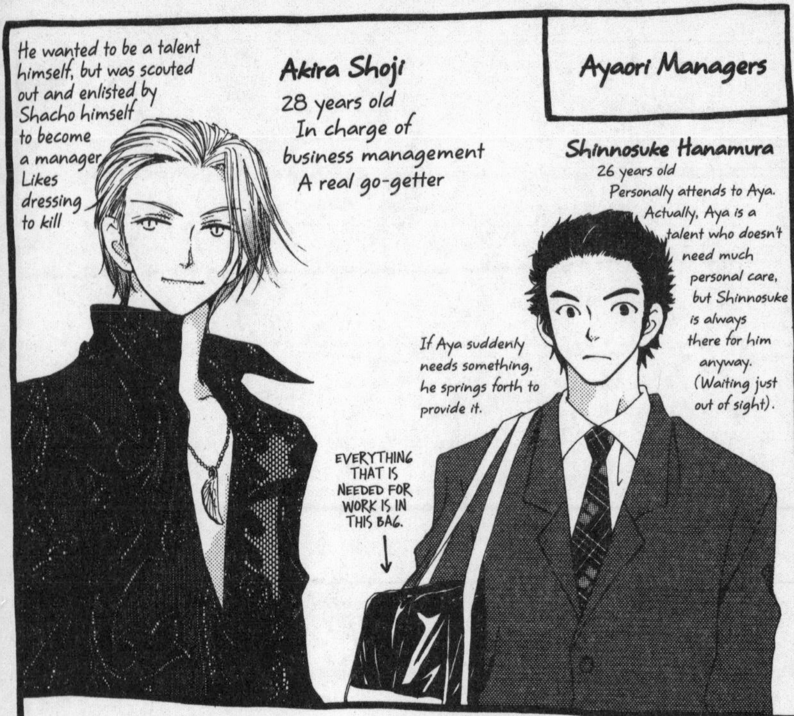
Ayaori Managers
Shinnosuke Hanamura
26 years old
Personally attends to Aya. Actually, Aya is a talent who doesn't need much personal care, but Shinnosuke is always there for him anyway. (Waiting just out of sight).
If Aya suddenly needs something, he springs forth to provide it.
EVERYTHING THAT IS NEEDED FOR WORK IS IN THIS BAG.
Akira Shoji
28 years old
In charge of business management
A real go-getter
He wanted to be a talent himself, but was scouted out and enlisted by Shacho himself to become a manager.
Likes dressing to kill

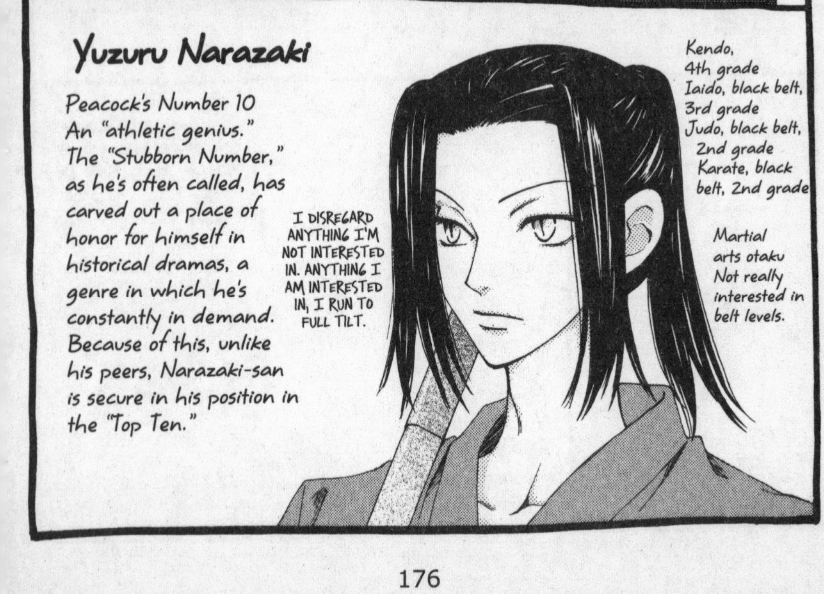
Kendo, 4th grade
Iaido, black belt, 3rd grade
Judo, black belt, 2nd grade
Karate, black belt, 2nd grade
Martial arts otaku
Not really interested in belt levels.
I DISREGARD ANYTHING I'M NOT INTERESTED IN. ANYTHING I AM INTERESTED IN, I RUN TO FULL TILT.
Yuzuru Narazaki
Peacock's Number 10
An "athletic genius."
The "Stubborn Number," as he's often called, has carved out a place of honor for himself in historical dramas, a genre in which he's constantly in demand. Because of this, unlike his peers, Narazaki-san is secure in his position in the "Top Ten."

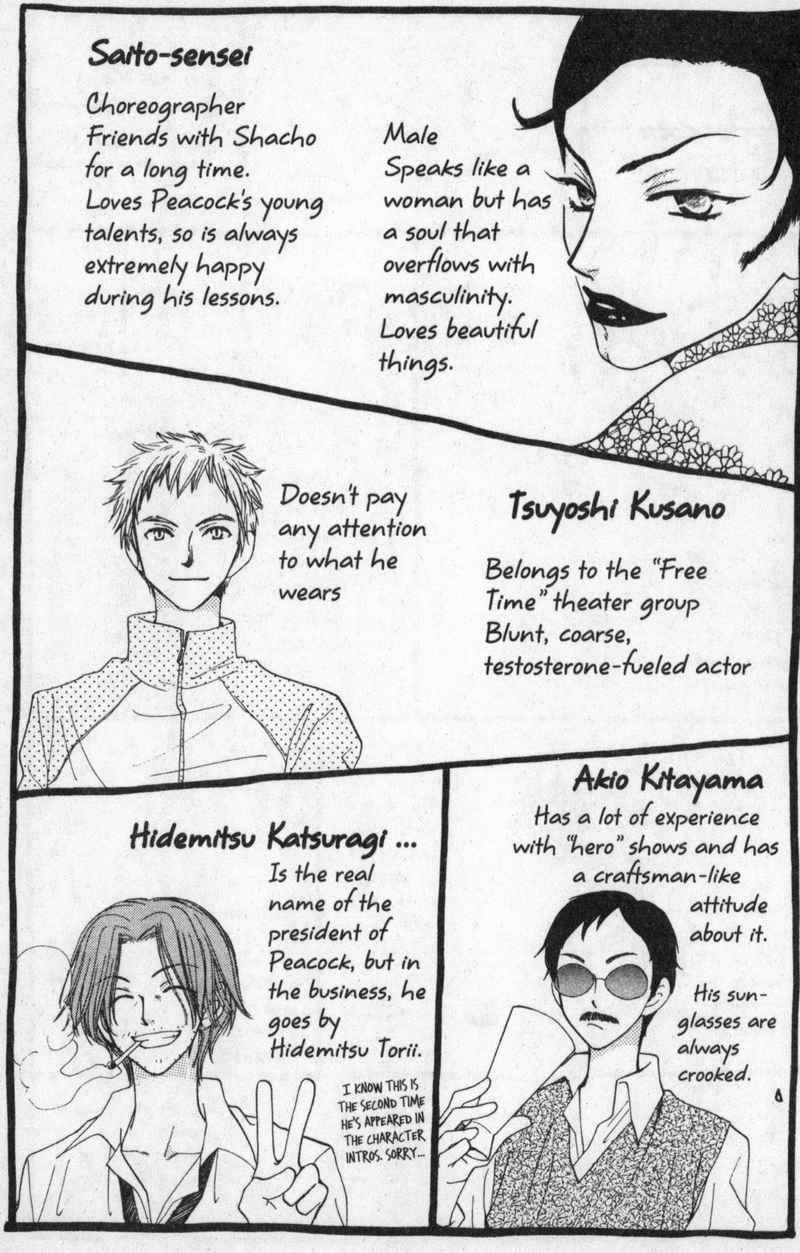
Saito-sensei
Choreographer
Friends with Shacho for a long time.
Loves Peacock's young talents, so is always extremely happy during his lessons.
Male
Speaks like a woman but has a soul that overflows with masculinity.
Loves beautiful things.
Tsuyoshi Kusano
Belongs to the "Free Time" theater group
Blunt, coarse, testosterone-fueled actor
Doesn't pay any attention to what he wears
Akio Kitayama
Has a lot of experience with "hero" shows and has a craftsman-like attitude about it.
His sun-glasses are always crooked.
Hidemitsu Katsuragi ...
Is the real name of the president of Peacock, but in the business, he goes by Hidemitsu Torii.
I KNOW THIS IS THE SECOND TIME HE'S APPEARED IN THE CHARACTER INTROS. SORRY...

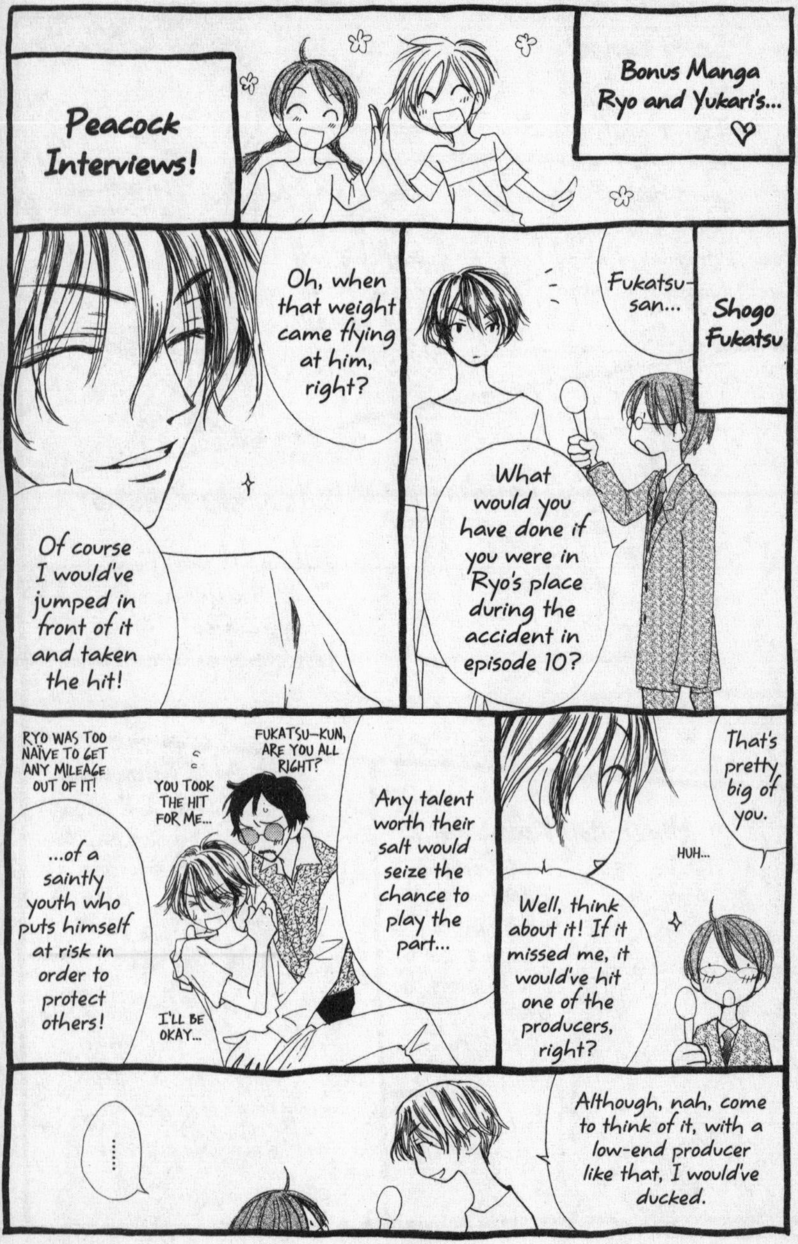

Bonus Manga Ryo and Yukari's... ♡
Peacock Interviews!
Shogo Fukatsu
Fukatsu-san...
What would you have done if you were in Ryo's place during the accident in episode 10?
Oh, when that weight came flying at him, right?
Of course I would've jumped in front of it and taken the hit!
That's pretty big of you.
HUH...
Well, think about it! If it missed me, it would've hit one of the producers, right?
Any talent worth their salt would seize the chance to play the part...
FUKATSU-KUN, ARE YOU ALL RIGHT?
YOU TOOK THE HIT FOR ME...
I'LL BE OKAY...
RYO WAS TOO NAÏVE TO GET ANY MILEAGE OUT OF IT!
...of a saintly youth who puts himself at risk in order to protect others!
Although, nah, come to think of it, with a low-end producer like that, I would've ducked.
......

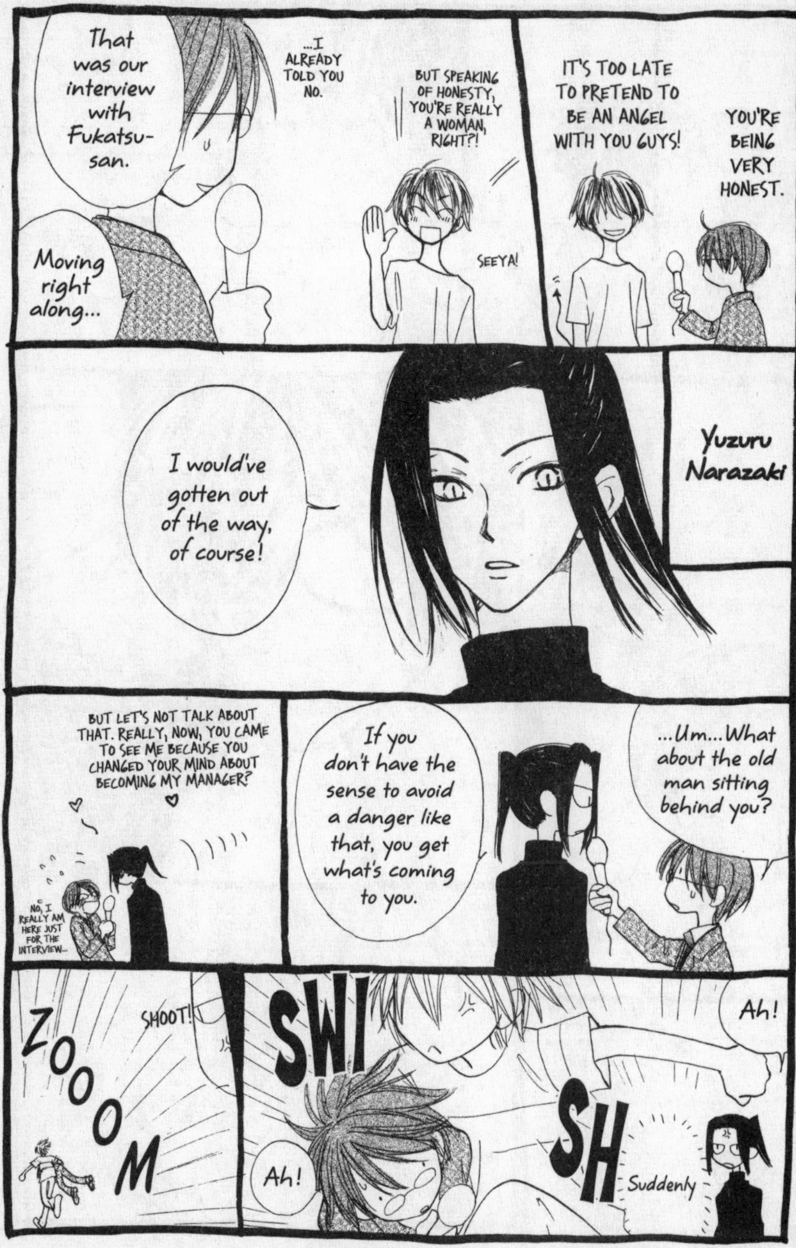
YOU'RE BEING VERY HONEST.
IT'S TOO LATE TO PRETEND TO BE AN ANGEL WITH YOU GUYS!
BUT SPEAKING OF HONESTY, YOU'RE REALLY A WOMAN, RIGHT?!
...I ALREADY TOLD YOU NO.
SEEYA!
That was our interview with Fukatsu-san.
Moving right along...
Yuzuru Narazaki
I would've gotten out of the way, of course!
...Um...What about the old man sitting behind you?
If you don't have the sense to avoid a danger like that, you get what's coming to you.
BUT LET'S NOT TALK ABOUT THAT. REALLY, NOW, YOU CAME TO SEE ME BECAUSE YOU CHANGED YOUR MIND ABOUT BECOMING MY MANAGER? ♡
NO, I REALLY AM HERE JUST FOR THE INTERVIEW...
Ah!
SWI
SH
Suddenly
Ah!
SHOOT!
ZOOOOM

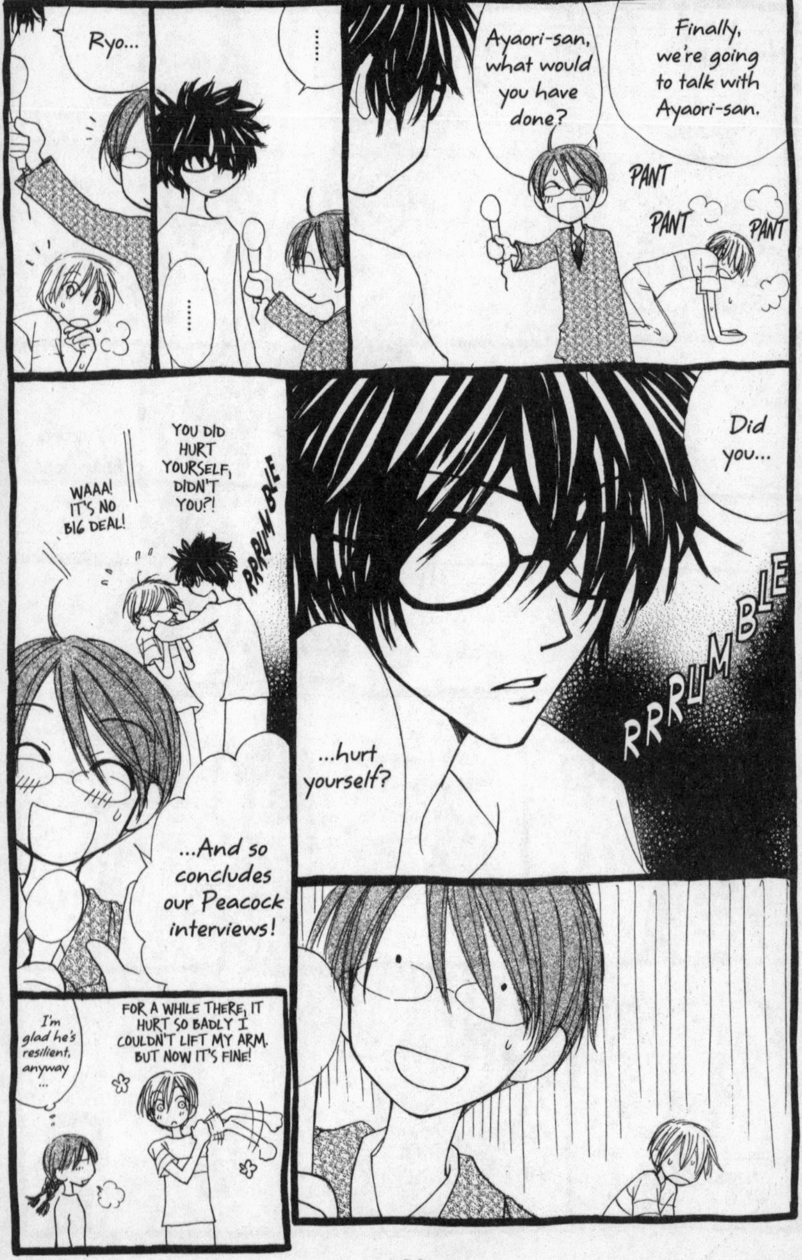

Finally, we're going to talk with Ayaori-san.
Ayaori-san, what would you have done?
PANT
PANT
PANT
......
......
Ryo...
Did you...
RRRUMBLE
...hurt yourself?
YOU DID HURT YOURSELF, DIDN'T YOU?!
RRRUMBLE
WAAA! IT'S NO BIG DEAL!
...And so concludes our Peacock interviews!
FOR A WHILE THERE, IT HURT SO BADLY I COULDN'T LIFT MY ARM. BUT NOW IT'S FINE!
I'm glad he's resilient, anyway ...

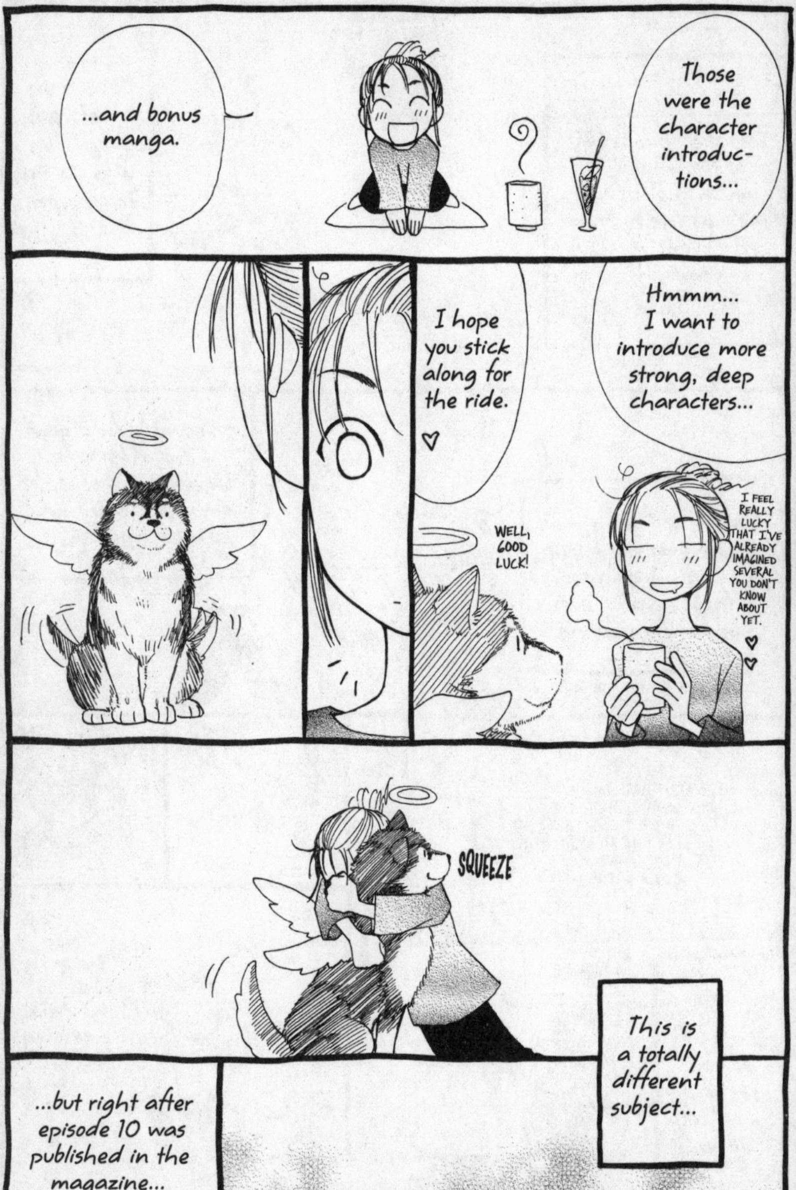
Those were the character introductions...
...and bonus manga.
Hmmm... I want to introduce more strong, deep characters...
I feel really lucky that I've already imagined several you don't know about yet.
I hope you stick along for the ride.
Well, good luck!
SQUEEZE
This is a totally different subject...
...but right after episode 10 was published in the magazine...

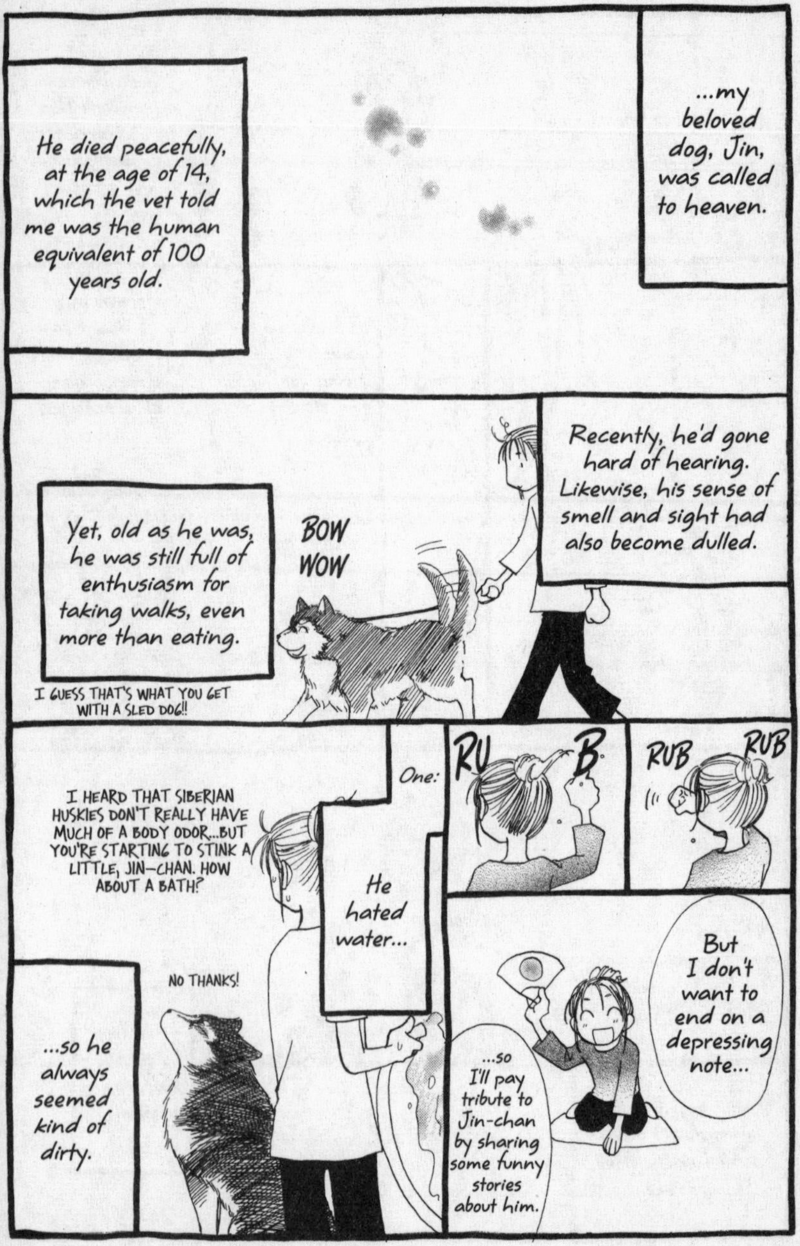
...my beloved dog, Jin, was called to heaven.
He died peacefully, at the age of 14, which the vet told me was the human equivalent of 100 years old.
Recently, he'd gone hard of hearing. Likewise, his sense of smell and sight had also become dulled.
BOW WOW
Yet, old as he was, he was still full of enthusiasm for taking walks, even more than eating.
I GUESS THAT'S WHAT YOU GET WITH A SLED DOG!!
RUB RUB
RU B.
But I don't want to end on a depressing note...
...so I'll pay tribute to Jin-chan by sharing some funny stories about him.
One:
I HEARD THAT SIBERIAN HUSKIES DON'T REALLY HAVE MUCH OF A BODY ODOR...BUT YOU'RE STARTING TO STINK A LITTLE, JIN-CHAN. HOW ABOUT A BATH?
He hated water...
NO THANKS!
...so he always seemed kind of dirty.

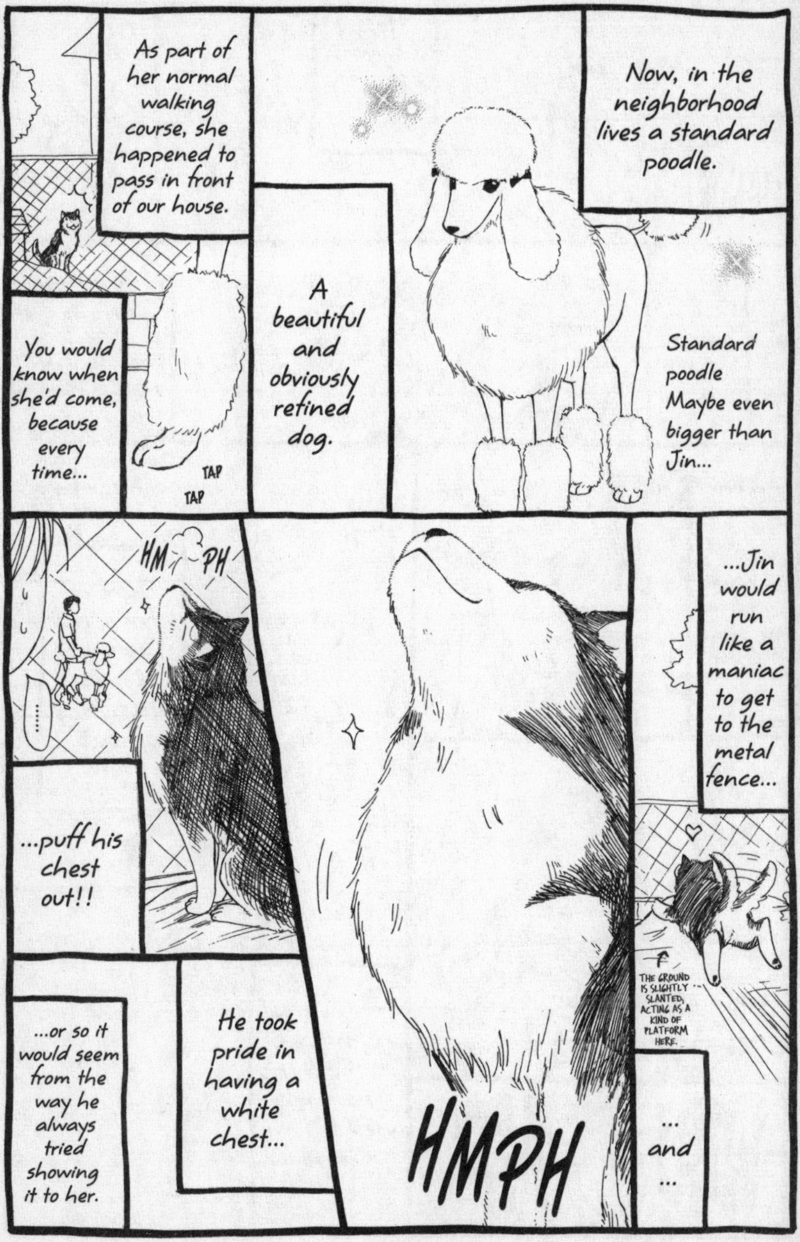
Now, in the neighborhood lives a standard poodle.
Standard poodle Maybe even bigger than Jin...
A beautiful and obviously refined dog.
As part of her normal walking course, she happened to pass in front of our house.
You would know when she'd come, because every time...
TAP
TAP
...Jin would run like a maniac to get to the metal fence...
THE GROUND IS SLIGHTLY SLANTED, ACTING AS A KIND OF PLATFORM HERE.
... and ...
HMPH
HM PH
......
...puff his chest out!!
He took pride in having a white chest...
...or so it would seem from the way he always tried showing it to her.

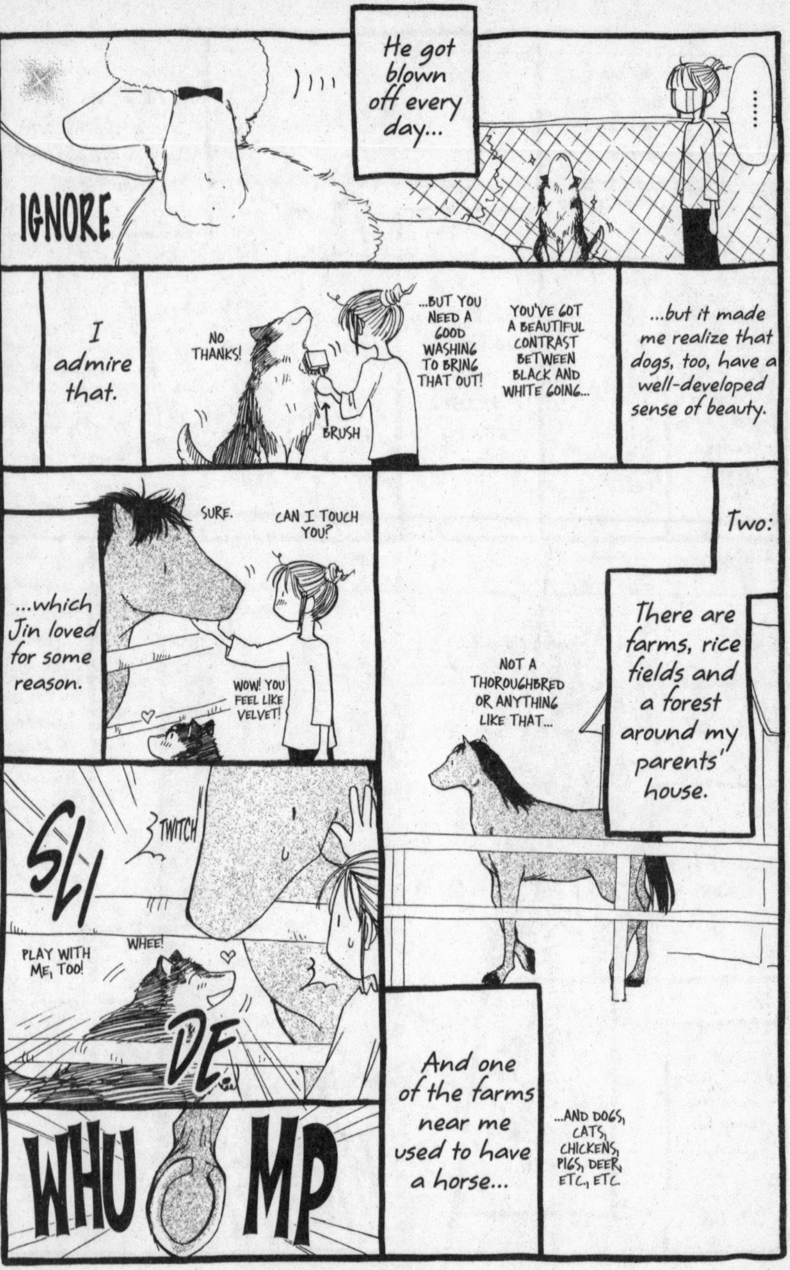
......
He got blown off every day...
IGNORE
...but it made me realize that dogs, too, have a well-developed sense of beauty.
YOU'VE GOT A BEAUTIFUL CONTRAST BETWEEN BLACK AND WHITE GOING...
...BUT YOU NEED A GOOD WASHING TO BRING THAT OUT!
NO THANKS!
BRUSH
I admire that.
Two:
There are farms, rice fields and a forest around my parents' house.
NOT A THOROUGHBRED OR ANYTHING LIKE THAT...
And one of the farms near me used to have a horse...
...AND DOGS, CATS, CHICKENS, PIGS, DEER, ETC., ETC.
CAN I TOUCH YOU?
SURE.
...which Jin loved for some reason.
WOW! YOU FEEL LIKE VELVET!
TWITCH
SLI
WHEE!
PLAY WITH ME, TOO!
DE
WHU
MP

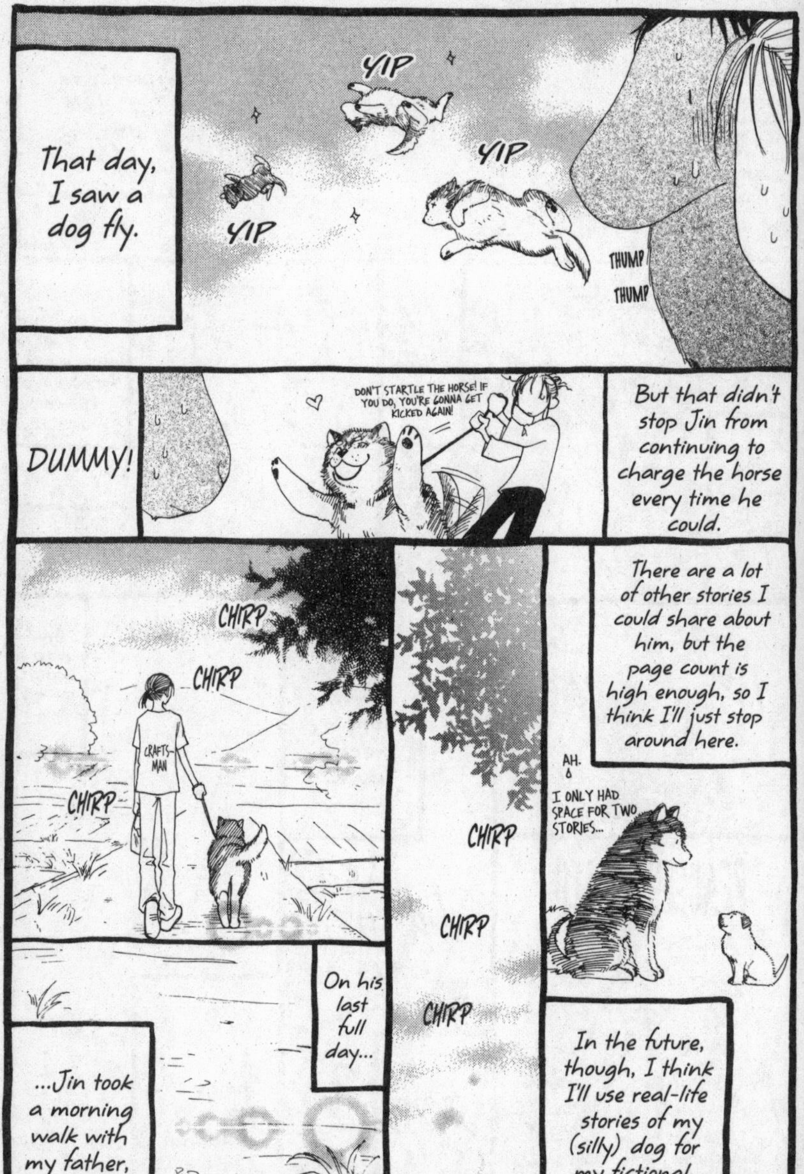
THUMP
THUMP
YIP
YIP
YIP
That day, I saw a dog fly.
But that didn't stop Jin from continuing to charge the horse every time he could.
DON'T STARTLE THE HORSE! IF YOU DO, YOU'RE GONNA GET KICKED AGAIN!
DUMMY!
There are a lot of other stories I could share about him, but the page count is high enough, so I think I'll just stop around here.
AH.
I ONLY HAD SPACE FOR TWO STORIES...
In the future, though, I think I'll use real-life stories of my (silly) dog for my fictional stories.
CHIRP
CHIRP
CHIRP
CHIRP
CHIRP
CRAFTS-MAN
CHIRP
On his last full day...
...Jin took a morning walk with my father, as always.

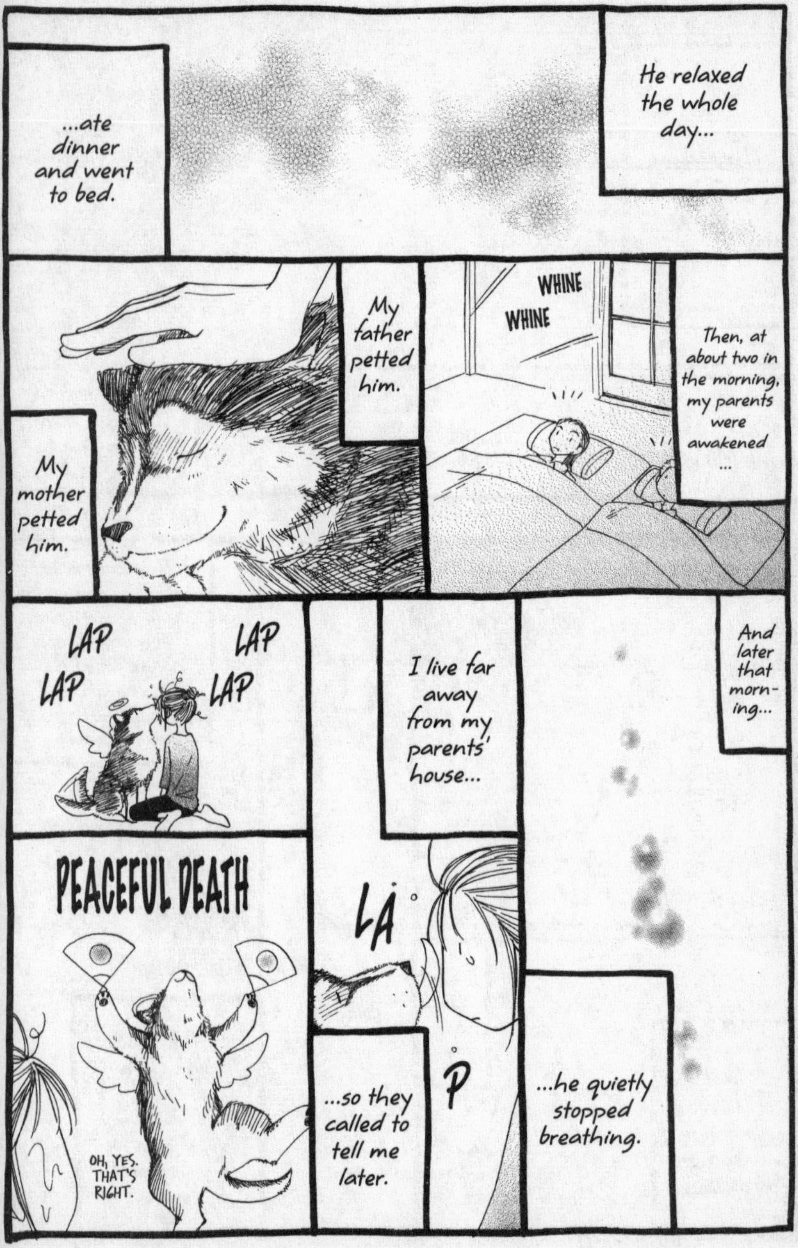
He relaxed the whole day...
...ate dinner and went to bed.
Then, at about two in the morning, my parents were awakened ...
WHINE
WHINE
My father petted him.
My mother petted him.
And later that morning...
...he quietly stopped breathing.
I live far away from my parents' house...
LA
P
...so they called to tell me later.
LAP
LAP
LAP
LAP
PEACEFUL DEATH
OH, YES. THAT'S RIGHT.

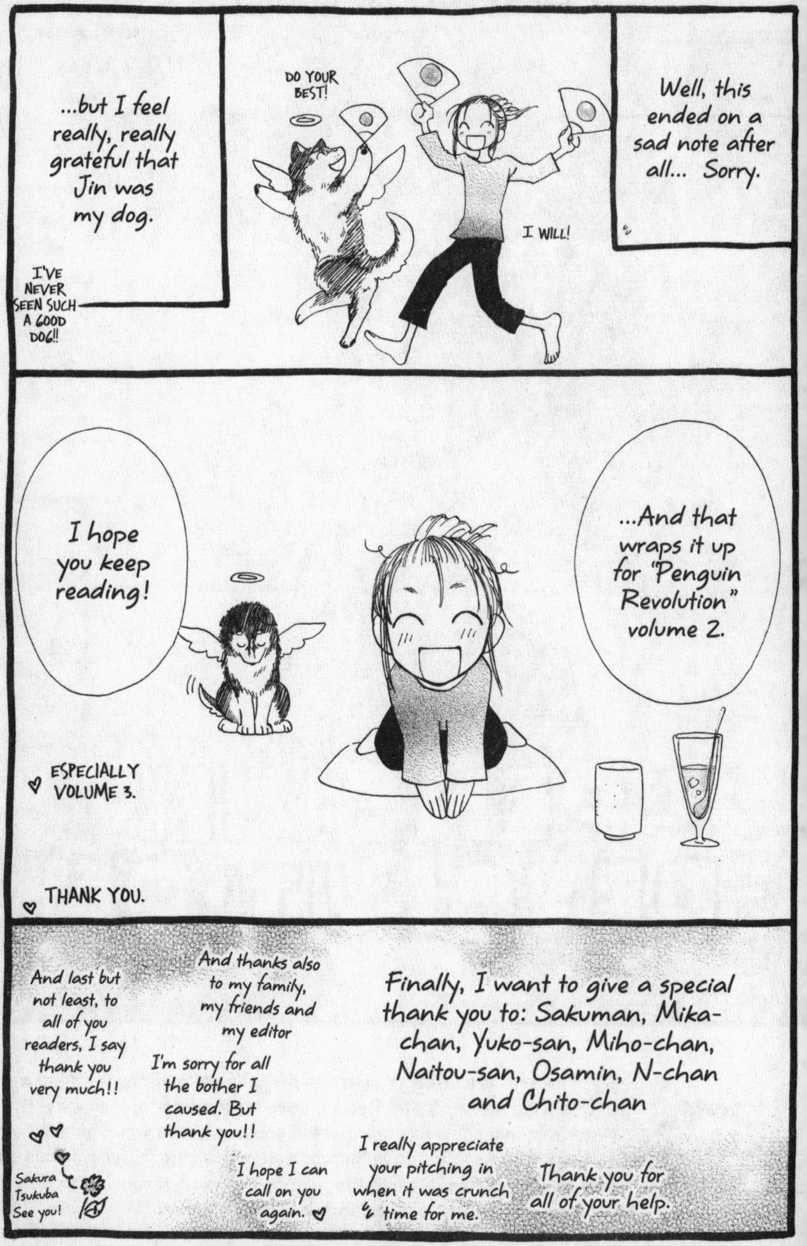

Well, this ended on a sad note after all... Sorry.
DO YOUR BEST!
I WILL!
...but I feel really, really grateful that Jin was my dog.
I'VE NEVER SEEN SUCH A GOOD DOG!!
...And that wraps it up for "Penguin Revolution" volume 2.
I hope you keep reading!
ESPECIALLY VOLUME 3.
THANK YOU.
Finally, I want to give a special thank you to: Sakuman, Mika-chan, Yuko-san, Miho-chan, Naitou-san, Osamin, N-chan and Chito-chan
Thank you for all of your help.
I really appreciate your pitching in when it was crunch time for me.
And thanks also to my family, my friends and my editor
I'm sorry for all the bother I caused. But thank you!!
I hope I can call on you again.
And last but not least, to all of you readers, I say thank you very much!!
Sakura Tsukuba See you!

Bonus Pages Sakura Mail: The End

WILL RYO GET A NEW MANAGER?
FIND OUT IN APRIL!

PENGUIN REVOLUTION
Volume 3

By Sakura Tsukuba. Yukari – in the guise of male agent Yutaka – is now managing her friend Ryo's career for the Peacock agency. Ryo's minor role in a show has unexpected consequences when an explosion on the set turns him into an improvisational wizard. Suddenly, his star may be on the rise, leading the agency's President to want to turn his career management over to someone else's care!

THE FINAL BATTLE
HAS BEGUN!

Kamikaze KAITO Jeanne

Volume 7

By Arina Tanemura. It all comes down to this! In the breathtaking finale, Maron goes to Heaven and meets God. She learns of the Devil, the Fall, and finally has the fate of the world placed on her shoulders when she squares off one last time against the Devil, only to come face to face with herself!

KAMIKAZE KAITO JEANNE © 1998 by Arina Tanemura/SHUEISHA Inc.

CHECK OUT THESE HOT SERIES!

PENGUIN KAKUMEI Volume 2 © 2005 Sakura Tsukuba. All
Rights Reserved. First published in Japan in 2005 by
HAKUSENSHA, INC., Tokyo.

PENGUIN REVOLUTION Volume 2, published by WildStorm
Productions, an imprint of DC Comics, 888 Prospect St.
#240, La Jolla, CA 92037. English Translation © 2007. All
Rights Reserved. English translation rights in U.S.A. and
Canada arranged by HAKUSENSHA, INC., through Tuttle-
Mori Agency Inc., Tokyo. The stories, characters, and inci-
dents mentioned in this magazine are entirely fictional.
Printed on recyclable paper. WildStorm does not read or
accept unsolicited submissions of ideas, stories or artwork.
Printed in Canada.

DC Comics, a Warner Bros. Entertainment Company.

Sheldon Drzka – Translation and Adaptation

AndWorld Design – Lettering

Larry Berry – Design

Jim Chadwick – Editor

ISBN:1-4012-1131-3
ISBN-13: 978-1-4012-1131-8

All the pages in this book were created—and are printed here—in Japanese RIGHT-to-LEFT format. No artwork has been reversed or altered, so you can read the stories the way the creators meant for them to be read.

RIGHT TO LEFT?!

Traditional Japanese manga starts at the upper right-hand corner, and moves right-to-left as it goes down the page. Follow this guide for an easy understanding.

For more information and sneak previews, visit cmxmanga.com. Call 1-800-COMIC BOOK for the nearest comics shop or head to your local book store.

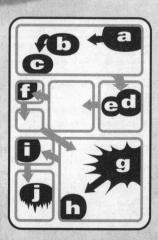